BIOGRAPHICAL ENCYCLOPEDIA of SCIENTISTS

BIOGRAPHICAL ENCYCLOPEDIA
of
SCIENTISTS

Volume 5
Schwarzschild – Zworykin
Index

Editor
RICHARD OLSON

Associate Editor
ROGER SMITH

Marshall Cavendish
New York • London • Toronto

FEB 1 9 1998

Project Editor: Tracy Irons-Georges
Research Supervisor: Jeffry Jensen
Acquisitions Editor: Mark Rehn
Photograph Editor: Karrie Hyatt
Production Editor: Cynthia Breslin Beres
Proofreading Supervisor: Yasmine A. Cordoba
Layout: James Hutson

Photograph Researcher: Susan Hormuth, Washington, D.C.

Published By
Marshall Cavendish Corporation
99 White Plains Road
Tarrytown, New York 10591-9001
United States of America

Library of Congress Cataloging-in-Publication Data

Biographical encyclopedia of scientists / editor Richard Olson, associate editor Roger Smith.
    p.   cm.
Complete in 5 v.
Includes bibliographical references and index.
    1. Scientists—Biography—Encyclopedias. 2. Science—Encyclopedias. 3. Science—Dictionaries. I. Olson, Richard, 1940-   . II. Smith, Roger, 1953 Apr. 19-   .
ISBN 0-7614-7064-6 (set)
ISBN 0-7614-7098-0 (vol. 5)
Q141.B532   1998
509'.2'2—dc21   97-23877
                                                                            CIP

First Printing

PRINTED IN THE UNITED STATES OF AMERICA

Contents

As an aid to users of the *Biographical Encyclopedia of Scientists*, guides to pronunciation for profiled scientists with foreign names have been provided with the first mention of the name in each entry. These guides are rendered in an easy-to-use phonetic manner. Stressed syllables are indicated by capital letters.

Letters of the English language, particularly vowels, are pronounced in different ways depending on the context. Below are letters and combinations of letters used in the phonetic guides to represent various sounds, along with examples of words in which those sounds appear and corresponding guides for their pronunciation.

Symbols	Pronounced As In	Spelled Phonetically
a	answer, laugh	AN-sihr, laf
ah	father, hospital	FAH-thur, HAHS-pih-tul
aw	awful, caught	AW-ful, kawt
ay	blaze, fade, waiter	blayz, fayd, WAYT-ur
ch	beach, chimp	beech, chihmp
eh	bed, head, said	behd, hehd, sehd
ee	believe, leader	bee-LEEV, LEED-ur
ew	boot, loose	bewt, lews
g	beg, disguise, get	behg, dihs-GIZ, geht
i	buy, height, surprise	bi, hit, sur-PRIZ
ih	bitter, pill	bih-TUR, pihl
j	digit, edge, jet	DIH-jiht, ehj, jeht
k	cat, kitten, hex	kat, KIH-tehn, hehks
o	cotton, hot	CO-tuhn, hot
oh	below, coat, note	bee-LOH, coht, noht
oo	good, look	good, look
ow	couch, how	kowch, how
oy	boy, coin	boy, koyn
s	cellar, save, scent	SEL-ur, sayv, sehnt
sh	issue, shop	IH-shew, shop
uh	about, enough	uh-BOWT, ee-NUHF
ur	earth, letter	urth, LEH-tur
y	useful, young	YEWS-ful, yuhng
z	business, zest	BIHZ-ness, zest
zh	vision	VI-zhuhn

BIOGRAPHICAL ENCYCLOPEDIA of SCIENTISTS

Karl Schwarzschild

Areas of Achievement: Astronomy and mathematics

Contribution: Schwarzschild is best known for the Schwarzschild radius, which calculates the theoretical point at which a collapsing star would emit no radiation, not even light, because of the intensity of gravitational pull.

Oct. 9, 1873	Born in Frankfurt am Main, Germany
1889	Publishes his first astronomical articles at the age of sixteen
1891	Enters the University of Strasbourg
1896	Receives a doctorate from the University of Munich
1901	Becomes a professor at the University of Göttingen and director of its observatory
1909	Assumes directorship of the Astrophysical Observatory in Potsdam
Oct. 22, 1909	Marries Else Rosenbach
1910	Publishes the first catalog of photographic magnitudes of stars
1910	Visits observatories in the United States
1914	Volunteers for service in World War I and is assigned to a weather station in Belgium
1916	Writes three papers on general relativity while serving in Russia
1916	Contracts a rare skin disease and returns to Potsdam
May 11, 1916	Dies in Potsdam, Germany

Early Life

Karl Schwarzschild (pronounced "SHVAWRT-shihlt") was born on October 9, 1873, as the son of a prominent Jewish businessman, Moses Martin Schwarzschild, and his wife, Henrietta Sabel. Karl grew up in his hometown of Frankfurt am Main, where he enjoyed the benefits of a highly cultured civic and family life. His early education was parochial, but he attended high school at the municipal preparatory school, or Gymnasium. There, he became actively interested in astronomy and was encouraged in his pursuits by his father, who knew a local mathematician with a private observatory.

By the age of sixteen, Schwarzschild had published two papers on the orbits of double stars. After the Gymnasium, he spent two years at the University of Strasbourg, then an important center for astronomy and related studies. In 1893, he entered the University of Munich, receiving his doctorate there in 1896.

Schwarzschild took a job as assistant in the Kuffner Observatory near Vienna that year and remained until the summer of 1899. He then began giving lectures on astronomy for general audiences, serving as a docent at Munich for two years. His first professorship was at the University of Göttingen, beginning in 1901.

Schwarzschild as a professor at the University of Göttingen. (AIP Niels Bohr Library)

Black Holes

Schwarzschild is best known for his mathematical speculations on the mechanics of a star in gravitational collapse.

The actual terminology of his 1916 paper dealt with a theoretical "fluid sphere" of constant density. Such a body collapsing below the limit proposed by Schwarzschild (hence, the Schwarzschild radius) would become so gravitationally dense that no radiation could escape outward. The star would in effect disappear.

Scientists in the English-speaking world have since come to refer to this phenomenon as a black hole, and the boundary beneath which no trace of the star can be detected as the event horizon. In other words, the last detectable "event" related to the star would occur just before it shrinks beneath that boundary. Theoretically, the star of Schwarzschild's calculations could collapse down to a singularity, or body of zero radius and infinite density. Any nearby or approaching matter would be consumed. The popular belief, however, that such a black hole would gather momentum and suck in surrounding bodies like a giant maelstrom is not founded in physics.

In the 1980's, circumstantial evidence from binary star systems and X-ray sources began to accumulate for the existence of black holes. In 1995, an unusual object was discovered in the elliptical galaxy M87 of the constellation Virgo. This previously "hidden" object, with a mass 3 billion times that of the sun, seemed to be the best observational candidate yet for satisfying Schwarzschild's predictions.

The actual equation for the Schwarzschild radius is "$R = 2\ Gm/c^2$," where R is the gravitational radius for an object with mass m, G is the universal gravitational constant, and c is the speed of light. Albert Einstein welcomed Schwarzschild's work on the geometry of space in the proximity of a point of mass—work which had been prompted by problems posed by Einstein's general gravitational equations in relativity theory.

Bibliography

Black Holes and Time Warps: Einstein's Outrageous Legacy. Kip S. Thorne. New York: W. W. Norton, 1994.

The Collapsing Universe. Isaac Asimov. New York: Walker, 1977.

Gravity's Fatal Attraction: Black Holes in the Universe. Mitchell C. Begelman. New York: Scientific American Library, 1995.

Space, Time, and Gravity: The Theory of the Big Bang and Black Holes. Robert M. Wald. Chicago: University of Chicago Press, 1992.

Unveiling the Edge of Time: Black Holes, White Holes, Wormholes. John Gribbin. New York: Harmony Books, 1992.

The Formation of a Black Hole

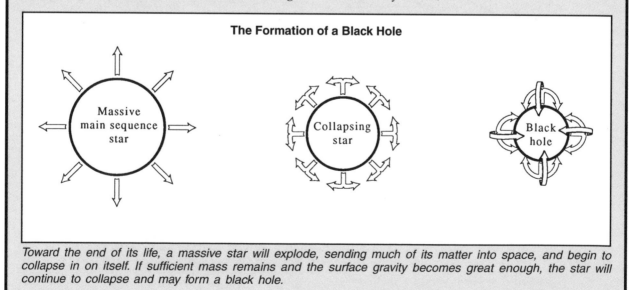

Toward the end of its life, a massive star will explode, sending much of its matter into space, and begin to collapse in on itself. If sufficient mass remains and the surface gravity becomes great enough, the star will continue to collapse and may form a black hole.

Celestial Mechanics

Schwarzschild never accepted the dichotomy between theory and practice; he produced practical astronomical instruments as well as sidereal-mathematical speculations.

His first major research effort, begun in Vienna, was to apply photographic methods to the measurement of radiant energy from stars, replacing the trained but subjective eye of the conventional astronomer. This work culminated in the publication of the first compendium of objectively measured magnitudes in 1910. The work appeared in a revised and supplemented version in 1912.

During this period, Schwarzschild was also working on the question of non-Euclidean geometry and curved space, an idea that was becoming more prominent and that forms an essential premise of general relativity.

Photometry, the Stars, and the Sun

Of the numerous advances in the study of light from stars, Schwarzschild is known for developing basic procedures for analyzing solar spectra during solar eclipses and for determining the exact relationship between spectral type and star color. He modernized photometry by introducing objective techniques for determining the magnitude of stars by photographic means. Of special interest to him were the processes of stellar radiation and the movement of heat within stellar atmospheres, for which he devised a hypothesis of stellar motion fundamental to modern astronomy.

Again from a more practical perspective, Schwarzschild studied data gathered on the solar eclipse of 1905, which he observed from Algeria, and on Halley's comet of 1910. He developed instruments to study solar spectra and speculated on the nature of energy transfer within and on the surface of the sun.

When Schwarzschild took over the observatory at Potsdam in 1909, he concentrated on stellar statistics and the related, burgeoning science of spectroscopy. World War I interrupted his work, but even at the front he continued to consider theoretical problems and to maintain contact with colleagues in the field, such as Albert Einstein, to whom he sent two articles that were subsequently published in the papers of the Prussian Academy of Sciences at Berlin in 1916. The second of these papers on general relativity contained the famous mathematical speculations on collapsing stars now referred to as black holes.

Schwarzschild's work was masterful in all areas: the practical as well as the theoretical, the macrocosmic as well as the microcosmic. At the level of electron orbits, for example, Schwarzschild's analysis of spectral lines from stellar light was early confirmation of Niels Bohr's theory of atomic spectra. He became ill with a rare and, at the time, untreatable skin disease known as pemphigus, from which he died on May 11, 1916.

Bibliography
By Schwarzschild
"Die Poincarésche Theorie des Gleichgewichts einer homogenen rotierenden Flüßigkeitsmasse" (Poincaré's theory of the stability of a unitary rotating fluid mass), *Neue Annalen der K. Sternwarte in München,* 1898

"Aktinometrie der Sterne der BD bis zur Grösse 7,5 in der Zone 0° bis + 20° Deklination: Teil A," *Abhandlungen der K. Gesellschaft der Wissenschaften zu Göttingen, Math.-Phys. Kl.,* 1910 (with Br. Meyermann, A. Kohlschütter, and O. Birck)

"Aktinometrie der Sterne der BD bis zur Grösse 7,5 in der Zone 0° bis + 20° Deklination: Teil B," *Abhandlungen der K. Gesellschaft der Wissenschaften zu Göttingen, Math.-Phys. Kl.,* 1912 (with Meyermann, Kohlschütter, Birck, and W. Dziewulski)

"Über das Gravitationsfeld einer Kugel aus inkompressibler Flüssigkeit nach der Einsteinschen Theorie" (concerning the gravitational field of a fluid sphere with constant density, according to Einstein's theory), *Siztungsberichte der Preussischen Akademie der Wissenschaften zu Berlin,* 1916

Über das System der Fixsterne, 1909 (concerning the system of fixed stars)

About Schwarzschild
"Karl Schwarzschild." In *Dictionary of Scientific Biography,* edited by Charles Coulston Gillispie. Vol. 11. New York: Charles Scribner's Sons, 1975.

(Mark R. McCulloh)

Julian Seymour Schwinger

Area of Achievement: Physics

Contribution: Schwinger made several fundamental contributions to quantum electrodynamic theory, including a form of the theory consistent with relativity and experimental measurements.

Feb. 12, 1918	Born in New York, New York
1936	Receives a B.S. from Columbia University
1939	Awarded a Ph.D. in physics from Columbia
1939	Hired as a research associate by J. Robert Oppenheimer
1941	Appointed as an instructor in physics at Purdue University
1942-1945	Conducts war-related radar research at the Massachusetts Institute of Technology's Radiation Laboratory
1946	Hired as an assistant professor of physics at Harvard
1947	Marries Clarice Carrol
1948	Presents a relativistic quantum field theory at the Pocono Conference
1948-1949	Publishes a three-paper series on quantum electrodynamics in *Physical Review*
1949	Given the Charles L. Mayer Nature of Light Award
1951	Develops a quantum action principle for quantum field theory
1965	Wins the Nobel Prize in Physics
July 16, 1994	Dies in Los Angeles, California

Early Life

Julian Seymour Schwinger was born in New York City in 1918. His father, a clothing designer, was a successful businessman, and Schwinger grew up in an upper-middle-class environment.

A true child prodigy, Schwinger was graduated from Townsend Harris High School, one of the premier academic preparatory schools in the country, at the age of sixteen. Following his graduation, he enrolled at the City College of New York, but he transferred to Columbia University after a year upon the suggestion I. I. Rabi, a noted physicist at Columbia who recognized Schwinger's unusual aptitude in theoretical physics.

As an undergraduate at City College, Schwinger had already written one research paper on quantum electrodynamics. He published several additional papers as an undergraduate and, in fact, completed his doctoral dissertation before receiving his bachelor of science degree in physics from Columbia in 1936. He continued at Columbia for a year, working with Rabi, before spending eighteen months at the University of Wisconsin.

In 1939, following his return to New York, Schwinger was awarded a Ph.D. in physics from Columbia University. He spent the next two years at the University of California, Berkeley, working with J. Robert Oppenheimer and other theoreticians. During this time, his research focused on the electromagnetic properties of deuterium and many particle systems. In 1941, Schwinger accepted an offer of an instructor position at Purdue University.

The War Years

In early 1942, following the entry of the United States into World War II, Schwinger accepted a staff position at the Radiation Laboratory at the Massachusetts Institute of Technology (MIT), where he worked on the development of radar systems. He soon became an expert on microwave propagation and wave guide theory, and he developed new mathematical techniques for solving problems in these areas.

Aside from a short period in the summer of 1943, when he worked on nuclear reactor design at the University of Chicago, Schwinger remained at MIT's Radiation Laboratory until

1945. While he focused on war-related research, Schwinger found time to work on problems related to synchrotron radiation in particle accelerators. Shortly before the end of the war, he gave a series of lectures summarizing his research in microwave propagation. The notes from these talks were published under the title *Discontinuities in Wave Guides* in 1965.

Quantum Electrodynamics

After the war ended in 1945, physicists were free again to work on fundamental research. A major problem that remained from the prewar years was reconciling quantum mechanics and relativity. While each theory appeared correct when taken separately, difficulties appeared when the theories were combined.

Quantum Electrodynamics

Quantum electrodynamics provides a unified description of the interaction of charged particles with electromagnetic fields. Calculations based on the theory have been confirmed experimentally to a high degree of accuracy.

Quantum electrodynamics refers to the theory governing electromagnetic fields and their interaction with charged particles. In its most general form, the theory combines the quantum description of particles and fields with the theory of relativity. Stringent tests of quantum electrodynamics have demonstrated remarkable agreement between predictions based on the theory and experimental measurements.

The initial development of quantum electrodynamics was based on work by several scientists, including Werner Heisenberg, Wolfgang Pauli, and Paul A. M. Dirac. Heisenberg and Pauli demonstrated that a quantized description of the electromagnetic field could account for the wave and particle properties of light. Dirac's contribution to the theory was to find a wave equation for the electron that incorporates both relativity and quantum mechanics, as well as to demonstrate that such an equation is consistent with the observed properties of electrons. One consequence of the Dirac equation is the prediction of the existence of positrons, or positively charged electrons, which were discovered shortly after his equation was calculated.

Despite the initial successes of quantum electrodynamics, technical problems in the application of the theory soon developed. When Dirac's theory of the electron was combined with the quantized description of the electromagnetic field, calculations diverged if carried out to a higher order. This divergence, demonstrated most clearly by a calculation performed by J.

Robert Oppenheimer in 1930, called into question the fundamental correctness of the theory.

The solution to the problems encountered in quantum field theory was the development of a process called renormalization. Renormalization makes use of a redefinition of electron mass and charge in terms of the values that these quantities would possess in the absence of photon absorption and emission. This redefinition cancels the infinities that appear in calculations so that only terms of finite size remain. Calculations by Schwinger (and, independently, Richard P. Feynman) showed that a relativistic renormalizable form of quantum electrodynamics correctly predicts the anomalous magnetic moment of the electron, as well as small shifts observed in the energies of low-lying states of the hydrogen atom.

In the early 1970's, quantum electrodynamics was used as a model for the development of a unified theory for electromagnetic and weak interactions. Later in the decade, quantum chromodynamics was developed to provide a unified description of electromagnetic interactions and both strong and weak nuclear forces. The successes in developing unified theories for describing the fundamental interactions occurring between particles encouraged researchers in their search for a "final theory" incorporating gravity with the other forces of nature.

Bibliography

Dreams of a Final Theory. Steven Weinberg. New York: Pantheon Books, 1992.

QED: The Strange Theory of Light and Matter. Richard P. Feynman. Princeton, N.J.: Princeton University Press, 1985.

Quantum Theory of Radiation. Edward R. Pike. New York: Oxford University Press, 1995.

In 1947, following a physics conference at Shelter Island, Hans Albrecht Bethe showed how one could account for an unexpected energy difference between low-lying states of the hydrogen atom using nonrelativistic quantum field theory. Schwinger was able to modify Bethe's results so that they were consistent with general relativity. Using the same approach, he was also able to account for the anomalous magnetic moment of the electron.

Schwinger presented the results of his calculations at a meeting of the American Physical Society in January, 1948. He presented a more detailed explanation at the Pocono Conference, held at the end of March of the same year, and in a series of three papers on quantum electrodynamics that appeared in 1948 and 1949. For this work, Schwinger shared the Nobel Prize in Physics for 1965 with Richard P. Feynman and Shin'ichiro Tomonoga.

(The Nobel Foundation)

Later Work

Following his initial success in relativistic quantum electrodynamics, Schwinger continued to develop the theory. In 1951, he published a series of papers on "source theory," based on the quantum action principle, which extended his previous results. He then attempted to use symmetry to understand the properties of the large number of new particles being discovered in subatomic physics experiments. While unsuccessful, his work was useful to other workers in particle physics.

During the 1960's, Schwinger carried out further work on source theory, which he saw as an alternative to the gauge field theories used by most other physicists. This work continued after he moved to the University of California, Los Angeles, in 1971. In the 1980's, Schwinger became interested in research outside the mainstream of conventional physics, such as cold fusion. He died in 1994 at the age of seventy-six.

Bibliography
By Schwinger

Discontinuities in Waveguides: Notes on Lectures, 1945

"On Quantum Electrodynamics and the Magnetic Moment of the Electron," *Physical Review*, 1948

"Quantum Electrodynamics I: A Covariant Formulation," *Physical Review*, 1948

"Quantum Electrodynamics II: Vacuum Polarization and Self-Energy," *Physical Review*, 1949

"Quantum Electrodynamics III: The Electromagnetic Properties of the Electron—Radiative Corrections to Scattering," *Physical Review*, 1949

Differential Equations of Quantum Field Theory, 1956

The Theory of the Fundamental Interactions, 1957

Selected Papers on Quantum Electrodynamics, 1958 (as editor)

Lectures on Quantum Field Theory, 1967

Particles and Sources, 1969

Particles, Sources, and Fields, 1970-1989 (3 vols.)

Quantum Kinematics and Dynamics, 1970

Selected Papers (1937-1976) of Julian Schwinger, 1979

Einstein's Legacy: The Unity of Space and Time, 1986

About Schwinger

Atomic Scientists: A Biographical History. Henry A. Boorse, Lloyd Motz, and Jefferson Hane Weaver. New York: John Wiley & Sons, 1989.

"Julian Schwinger: Prodigy, Problem Solver, Pioneering Physicist." Paul C. Martin and Sheldon L. Glashow. *Physics Today* (October, 1995).

"Julian Seymour Schwinger." In *The Nobel Prize Winners: Physics*, edited by Frank N. Magill. Pasadena, Calif.: Salem Press, 1989.

QED and the Men Who Made It: Dyson, Feynman, Schwinger, and Tomonaga. Silvan S. Schweber. Princeton, N.J.: Princeton University Press, 1994.

(Jeffrey A. Joens)

Glenn Theodore Seaborg

Areas of Achievement: Chemistry and science (general)

Contribution: Seaborg received the Nobel Prize in Chemistry for his discovery of "not less than four more transuranium elements." He also discovered, in collaboration with other chemists, all the elements from 94 to 102 on the periodic table.

Apr. 19, 1912	Born in Ishpeming, Michigan
1934	Earns a B.A. in chemistry from the University of California, Los Angeles (UCLA)
1937	Receives a Ph.D. in chemistry from the University of California, Berkeley (UCB)
1939-1982	Teaches chemistry at UCB
1942-1946	Takes wartime leave to work on the Manhattan Project
1948-1950	Serves on the Atomic Energy Commission's General Advisory Committee
1951	Awarded the Nobel Prize in Chemistry
1954	Named associate director of the Lawrence Radiation Laboratory
1958-1961	Acts as chancellor of UCB
1958	Given the Thomas Alva Edison Foundation Award for the best book in science for youth
1959	Receives the Enrico Fermi Award
1961-1971	Serves as chair of the Atomic Energy Commission
1976	Named a decorated officer by the French Legion of Honor
1982	Retires from UCB

Seaborg, as chair of the Atomic Energy Commission, speaks at the 1962 World's Fair in Seattle. (AP/Wide World Photos)

Although he knew early that he wanted to study chemistry, Seaborg's initial studies in that subject were unfocused. It was not until he was well along in graduate school that he began to concentrate on isotopes of the elements on the periodic table, the heavier elements of which at this point remained undiscovered, although scientific evidence suggested their existence.

Seaborg ultimately focused his research on these undiscovered transuranium elements. He spent two postdoctoral years at UCB as a research chemist, continuing his doctoral research on how isotopes of lead are altered by bombardments of fast neutrons. In time, he discovered a number of new isotopes.

Seaborg's work with Enrico Fermi, which began in 1934, led him toward the discovery of new elements in the periodic table, for which he would receive the Nobel Prize in Chemistry in 1951.

The Manhattan Project

When the United States entered World War II in 1941, the nation embarked on an accelerated program of scientific research that led to the eventual development of nuclear energy and to the building of the first atomic bombs. Seaborg, on leave from UCB, became a member of the blue-ribbon staff of the Manhattan Project.

It was there, where he focused on developing chemical means of separating plutonium from uranium in sufficient quantities to use in building weaponry, that his work on the transuranium elements moved toward its fullest development. By 1944, Seaborg's group achieved its aim of separating plutonium from uranium on a scale large enough to build the "superbomb" that a nation at war required.

Early Life

Glenn Theodore Seaborg began life in a small mining community on Michigan's upper peninsula, where he was born to Herman Theodore Seaborg, a machinist, and his wife, Selma, on April 19, 1912. The family moved to Southern California when Seaborg was ten. When he entered the University of California, Los Angeles (UCLA), in 1929, the Westwood campus consisted of four buildings.

Excelling in chemistry, Seaborg received a bachelor of arts degree in 1934. He continued his studies at the University of California, Berkeley (UCB), receiving a doctorate in chemistry from that institution in 1937.

By 1945, the group had produced enough plutonium to build the atomic bombs that the United States would use against Japan. It was the dropping of these bombs on the Japanese cities of Nagasaki and Hiroshima that ended World War II.

Public Scientific Service

From 1939 until he retired in 1982, Seaborg was a member of the UCB faculty, although he was given frequent extended leaves to fulfill a variety of public obligations, the most notable of which was serving as chair of the Atomic Energy Commission from 1961 until 1971.

Immediately before his appointment to this position, Seaborg, now a Nobel laureate, served as chancellor of the Berkeley campus of the University of California for three years. Never a detached scientist, Seaborg had a genuine commitment to serving humankind. His considerable administrative ability led to his being appointed to such positions as associate director of the famed Lawrence Radiation Laboratory at UCB.

In such books as *Education and the Atom* (1964), *Man and Atom: Shaping a New World Through Technology* (1971), and *Kennedy, Khrushchev, and the Test Ban* (1981), Seaborg examined the ethics of using atomic energy. After he officially retired, he joined UCB's Graduate School of Education, convinced that science education is of the utmost importance for

Discovering Transuranium Elements

Seaborg's most significant contribution to the field of chemistry was his discovery, with colleagues, of ten new elements and three new nuclear energy isotopes.

In the course of his distinguished career, Seaborg discovered a number of new isotopes—forms of the same element that have an identical number of protons but differ in the number of their neutrons—for many common elements on the periodic table.

By 1934, Enrico Fermi was convinced of the existence of elements heavier than uranium, at that time the heaviest element on the periodic table. Fermi, and other researchers working independently in Germany, added neutrons to the nuclei of uranium atoms, but this act did not produce heavier atoms. Rather, atoms of the uranium nuclei split, resulting in the release of incredible energy.

Knowledge of these experiments drew Seaborg into his extensive research on the transuranium elements, as the new elements were called. The result was a scientific exploration that led to the discovery by Seaborg and his colleagues of elements 94 through 102 on the periodic table, as well as element 106.

Some of Seaborg's colleagues at the University of California, Berkeley, observed that when neutrons are aimed at uranium atoms, some of the atomic nuclei that the neutrons hit do not split. Rather, they decay, emitting an electron that in-creases their atomic number by one, thereby creating a new element. Edwin Mattison McMillan, with whom Seaborg shared the Nobel Prize in 1951, named the resulting element "neptunium."

Seaborg and his fellow researchers found that as neptunium decays, it emits beta waves as electrons increase its atomic weight by one, resulting in another element that Seaborg named "plutonium." Before they were done, Seaborg and his colleagues had discovered ten new elements (plutonium, americium, curium, berkelium, californium, einsteinium, fermium, mendelevium, nobelium, and element 106), three new nuclear energy isotopes (plutonium 239, uranium 233, and neptunium 237), and such other isotopes as iodine 131, iron 59, tellurium 99m, and cobalt 60.

It is for this pioneering work that Seaborg and McMillan were awarded the Nobel Prize in Chemistry in 1951, a year short of Seaborg's fortieth birthday. These discoveries paved the way for the nuclear age, which began shortly before the end of World War II.

Bibliography

The Elements Beyond Uranium. Walter D. Loveland and Glenn Seaborg. New York: John Wiley & Sons, 1990.

The Transuranium Elements. Joseph J. Katz, Winston M. Manning, and Glenn Seaborg, eds. New York: McGraw-Hill, 1949.

American society. In these latter years of his professional life, he became a trainer of future science teachers.

Bibliography
By Seaborg
The Transuranium Elements, 1949 (as editor, with Joseph J. Katz and Winston M. Manning)

Production and Separation of U-233, 1951 (with Leonard I. Katzin)

Comprehensive Inorganic Chemistry, 1953 (with others)

The Actinide Elements, 1954 (with Katz)

The Chemistry of Actinide Elements, 1957

Elements of the Universe, 1958 (with E. G. Valens)

The Transuranium Elements, 1958

Science and Liberal Education in the Space Age, 1959

Man-Made Transuranium Elements, 1963

The Nuclear Properties of the Heavy Elements, 1964 (with Earl K. Hyde and Isadore Perlman)

Education and the Atom, 1964 (with Daniel M. Wilkes)

The International Atom: A New Appraisal, 1969

Oppenheimer, 1969 (with others)

Man and Atom: Shaping a New World Through Technology, 1971 (with W. R. Corliss)

Nuclear Milestones, 1972

Transuranium Elements: Products of Modern Alchemy, 1978 (as editor)

Primary Papers in Physical Chemistry and Chemical Physics, 1978

Kennedy, Khrushchev, and the Test Ban, 1981 (with Benjamin Loeb)

Stemming the Tide: Arms Control in the Johnson Years, 1987

The Elements Beyond Uranium, 1990 (with Walter D. Loveland)

About Seaborg
"Glenn Theodore Seaborg." In *The Nobel Prize Winners: Chemistry*, edited by Frank N. Magill. Pasadena, Calif.: Salem Press, 1990.

Great Swedish Heritage Awards Night. Nils William Olsson and Christopher Olssen, eds. Minneapolis: Swedish Council of America, 1984.

Nobel Prize Winners: An H. W. Wilson Biographical Dictionary. Tyler Wasson, ed. New York: H. W. Wilson, 1987.

Talks with Social Scientists. Charles F. Madden, ed. Carbondale: Southern Illinois University Press, 1968.

There Was a Light: An Autobiography of a University—Berkeley, 1868-1968. Irvin Stone, ed. Berkeley: University of California Press, 1970.

(R. Baird Shuman)

Emilio Gino Segrè

Areas of Achievement: Chemistry and physics

Contribution: A theoretical and experimental physicist, Segrè won the Nobel Prize in Physics, with colleague Owen Chamberlain, for his discovery of the antiproton, the subnuclear antiparticle of the proton.

Feb. 1, 1905	Born in Tivoli, Italy
1922	Graduated from the Liceo Mamiani in Rome
1925	Meets his mentor, Enrico Fermi
1928	Earns a Ph.D. in physics from the University of Rome
1936	Marries Elfriede Spiro
1936	Becomes a professor of physics at the University of Palermo
1937	Uses a cyclotron to discover a new chemical element, technetium
1938	Becomes a researcher at the University of California, Berkeley (UCB)
1938	Discovers astatine, another new chemical element
1941	Participates with Glenn Seaborg in the discovery of plutonium
1943-1946	Works on the Manhattan Project at Los Alamos, New Mexico
1944	Becomes a U.S. citizen
1955	Research at UCB leads to his discovery of the antiproton
1959	Awarded the Nobel Prize in Physics with his former student Owen Chamberlain
1970	Becomes a widower and marries his second wife, Rosa Mines
Apr. 22, 1989	Dies in Lafayette, California

Early Life

Emilio Gino Segrè (pronounced "suh-GRAY") was born in central Italy into a prosperous family led by his father, Giuseppe Segrè, an industrialist. As a youngster, Emilio loved mathematics, but he was also adventurous and particularly enjoyed outdoor sports and mountain climbing.

As an undergraduate studying engineering at the University of Rome, Segrè attended lectures by Enrico Fermi, the university's gifted physics professor. With Fermi, Segrè attended an international physics conference held in Italy in 1927, where he met some of the eminent physicists in the world. Soon afterward, Segrè switched from engineering to physics, and, in 1928, he was awarded a doctorate for his research on the spectroscopy of lithium.

Early Academic Career

Following a year of military service in 1929, Segrè returned to the University of Rome as an

(The Nobel Foundation)

Subnuclear Particles

The isolation of the antiproton bolstered the theory of complete particle-level symmetry, indicating the possibility of a parallel physical world composed of antimatter.

Segrè identified a new building block of matter, the antiproton, which is among the tiniest fragments of atoms. His work in this area began in the 1930's with experiments to bombard atoms with high-speed neutrons. This technique led to his codiscovery of new chemical elements, including technetium in 1937, astatine in 1938, and plutonium in 1941.

Segrè then focused on examining the physical properties of the particles emanating from his bombardment experiments. Using new machines in the early 1950's, he was able to propel protons at greater velocities than previously possible, creating high-speed atomic collisions. Using "time of flight" measurements and the detection of blue light flashes from particles traveling faster than the speed of light, Segrè observed a rare, negatively charged particle never before

identified, the antiproton.

Antiprotons are negative twins, or antiparticles, of the positive protons, which, along with negative electrons, make up most of the matter in the world. The behavior of this oppositely charged twin of the proton suggested to physicists that elsewhere in the universe, matter may be constructed differently than it is in this galaxy. Segrè's discovery supported this theory of antimatter and contributed to the development of modern astrophysics.

Bibliography

Introduction to Experimental Particle Physics. Richard Fernow. Cambridge, England: Cambridge University Press, 1986.
Nuclear and Particle Physics. W. E. Burcham. New York: John Wiley & Sons, 1995.
The Prediction of Antimatter. P. A. M. Dirac. Ann Arbor: University of Michigan Press, 1978.
A Tour of the Subatomic Zoo: A Guide to Particle Physics. Cindy Schwarz. New York: American Institute of Physics, 1992.

assistant in the physics laboratories. While continuing his work with Fermi, he also seized upon opportunities to travel and work with other physicists, notably in Germany and the Netherlands.

Segrè's growing international reputation led to his appointment as a professor at the University of Palermo in 1936. He soon visited the United States, establishing working relationships with physicists at the University of California, Berkeley (UCB), including Ernest O. Lawrence.

The Rise of Fascism in Italy

Political tensions were increasing in Italy, where Benito Mussolini's government controlled the universities. Mussolini had also introduced a series of laws that restricted the freedoms of Italy's Jewish population. Like other Italian physicists, Segrè was concerned about his freedom to continue his research in Italy.

In 1938, while he was again visiting UCB, his position at Palermo was jeopardized by new anti-Semitic laws. He decided not to return to Italy. Remaining at UCB, Segrè was given a job teaching in the physics department.

The Manhattan Project

As war spread in Europe and Asia, Segrè's research acquired military significance. He joined the top secret American initiative to develop atomic weapons, known as the Manhattan Project. In 1943, he moved to its secluded laboratories in Los Alamos, New Mexico, where he led a research group in experimental physics. His work helped the United States build the atomic weapons that were used to end World War II in 1945.

Postwar Research

After the war, Segrè returned to teaching. He conducted revolutionary new research utilizing special equipment available only at UCB. In 1955, he discovered a new particle of matter, the antiproton. For this accomplishment, Segrè and his student, Owen Chamberlain, shared the Nobel Prize in Physics in 1959.

Other Interests

The death of Fermi in 1954 profoundly affected Segrè. Although he continued teaching at UCB, he also began to write about the role of science in society. He authored a biography of Fermi and several historical works on classical and modern physics. He also wrote an autobiography.

At the end of his career, Segrè was recognized both as one of the world's leading physicists and as an important interpreter of the social impact of scientific research. He died in 1989.

Bibliography

By Segrè

Experimental Nuclear Physics, 1953-1959 (3 vols.)
"Antiprotons," *Nature*, 1956 (with C. Wiegand, T. Ypsilantis, and O. Chamberlain)
Nuclei and Particles: An Introduction to Nuclear and Subnuclear Physics, 1964
Great Men of Physics: The Humanistic Element in Scientific Work, 1969 (with others)
Enrico Fermi: Physicist, 1970
From X-Rays to Quarks: Modern Physicists and Their Discoveries, 1980
From Falling Bodies to Radio Waves: Classical Physicists and Their Discoveries, 1984
A Mind Always in Motion: The Autobiography of Emilio Segrè, 1993

About Segrè

Atoms, Bombs, and Eskimo Kisses: A Memoir of Father and Son. Claudio G. Segrè. New York: Viking Press, 1995.
Illustrious Immigrants: The Intellectual Migration from Europe, 1930-41. Laura Fermi. Chicago: University of Chicago Press, 1968.
Pioneers of Science: Nobel Prize Winners in Physics. Robert L. Weber. New York: American Institute of Physics, 1980.

(Laura M. Calkins)

Nikolai Semenov

Areas of Achievement: Chemistry and physics

Contribution: Semenov won the 1956 Nobel Prize in Chemistry for his work on branched chain chemical reactions in combustion processes. Understanding this type of reaction has been important in the development of internal combustion engines and plastic polymerization processes.

Apr. 15, 1896	Born in Saratov, Russia
1914-1917	Studies chemistry at Petrograd University
1917-1920	Lectures at Tomsk University
1920-1928	Serves as a lecturer at Petrograd Polytechnic Institute
1920	Appointed director of the Electron Phenomenon Laboratory of Petrograd Physical-Technical Institute
1924	Begins work on combustion processes
1924	Marries Natalia Burtseva
1928	Publishes a paper on a theory of combustion processes
1928	Appointed a full professor at Petrograd Polytechnic Institute
1932	Becomes a member of the Soviet Academy of Sciences
1934	Publishes *Tsepnye reaktsii* (*Chemical Kinetics and Chain Reactions*, 1935)
1939	Appointed director of the Institute of Chemical Physics of the Soviet Academy of Sciences
1956	Wins the Nobel Prize in Chemistry
Sept. 25, 1986	Dies in Moscow, Soviet Union

Early Life

Nikolai Nikolayevich Semenov (pronounced "sih-MYOH-nuhf") was born in Saratov, Russia, on April 15, 1896. He completed his secondary education there and then enrolled at Petrograd University, where he studied chemistry from 1914 to 1917, completing his degree on the eve of the Bolshevik Revolution.

Semenov taught chemistry in Tomsk, western Siberia, during the troubled civil war period and in 1920 returned to Petrograd (later St. Petersburg, then Leningrad, and then St. Petersburg again). He taught chemistry at the Petrograd Polytechnical Institute and conducted research at the Petrograd Physical-Technical Institute, where he was director of the Electron Phenomenon Laboratory. He married Natalia Burtseva in 1924; the couple had two children.

Scientific Career

In 1924, Semenov became involved in the research of Yuri Khariton and Z. Val'ta, who were investigating the oxidation of phosphorus vapor. This explosive reaction displayed a number of anomalous features that could not be explained by the simple kinetic model (Arrhenius' law) in use at the time. Semenov was able to formulate a model that explained these anomalous features by postulating that a chain reaction was involved. He published his results in 1928 in the landmark paper "K teorii protsessov goreniyaa, Soobsch. i" (toward a theory of combustion processes, part 1).

The chain reaction model proved to be useful in explaining many combustion processes and to have immense practical importance. Understanding that the burning of gasoline is a chemical chain reaction led directly to improvements in the efficiency of internal combustion engines.

Semenov became a member of the Soviet Academy of Sciences in 1932 and director of its Institute of Chemical Physics in 1939. In 1943, while Leningrad was being besieged by German troops, the institute was permanently

Chain Reactions and the Theory of Combustion

Combustion involves a collision between two molecules, breaking the chemical bonds between atoms and recombining them.

Some energy must be supplied to break the initial bonds between atoms. This may be in the form of heat, causing the molecules to move more rapidly and collide with greater force. If the reaction releases heat, then an increasing number of collisions will occur and combustion will increase in intensity until so many of the original molecules are used up that the frequency of collisions between them declines. This is the simple linear model of combustion.

In a branched chain reaction, the initial collision between reacting products creates not only the stable end product but also an unstable intermediary product capable of initiating a chemical reaction at a lower velocity.

Chemical chain reaction theory depends on the role of free radicals in chemical reactions. A free radical is an atom or fragment of a molecule that has an unpaired electron in its outer electron shell. Free radicals are more reactive than stable molecules, which have complete outer electron shells, so lower collision energies are required for reactions involving them. In the case that Semenov investigated initially, the explosive combination of oxygen and phosphorus vapor, each collision between a free radical and a molecule produces a stable end product plus three free radicals, and a chain reaction occurs.

Chemical chain reactions have many of the characteristics of atomic chain reactions: They require a high initiation energy, are violently explosive, and can be controlled by introducing a substance that removes free radicals. The octane in gasoline that removes free radicals from burning fuel mixtures is analogous to the graphite rods in a nuclear reactor, which efficiently absorb alpha particles.

Bibliography

Gas Phase Reactions: Kinetics and Mechanisms. V. N. Kondratev and E. E. Nikitin. New York: Springer-Verlag, 1981.

The Mathematical Theory of Combustion and Explosions. Ya. B. Zelkovich. New York: Consultant's Bureau, 1985.

moved to Moscow. Association with the Academy of Sciences is a high honor that brought Semenov a substantial increase in salary, preferential access to funding and publication, and the opportunity to travel abroad.

Awards and Honors

Semenov's accomplishments were honored in the Soviet Union and abroad well before he received the Nobel Prize. He received the Stalin Prize and held honorary doctorates from the Universities of Oxford and Brussels. He was also a foreign member of the Royal Society of London and of the U.S., Indian, German, and Hungarian academies of sciences.

Semenov shared the 1956 Nobel Prize in Chemistry with Sir Cyril Hinshelwood of Great Britain, who had also made discoveries in chemical kinetics. Semenov was the first citizen of the Soviet Union to receive a Nobel Prize in any field. He died in 1986.

(The Nobel Foundation)

Bibliography

By Semenov

"K teorii protsessov goreni-yaa, Soobsch. i," *Zhurnal fizicheskoy khimii*, 1928

Tsepnye reaktsii, 1934 (*Chemical Kinetics and Chain Reactions*, 1935)

"Kinetica slozhnykh reaktsiyakh," *Zhurnal fizicheskoy khimii*, 1943

O nekotorykh problemakh khimicheskoi kinetiki i reaktsionnoi sposobnosti, 1954 (*Some Problems in Chemical Kinetics and Reactivity*, 1958, 2 vols.)

Heterogeneous Catalysis in the Chemical Industry, 1955 (with V. V. Voevodskii)

"Some Problems Relating to Chain Reactions and to the Theory of Combustion" in *Chemistry*, 1964-1972 (4 vols.)

Nauka i obshchestvo, 1973

About Semenov

"Nikolai Nikolaevich Semenov, on His Seventieth Birthday." V. N. Kondrat'ev. *Soviet Physics Uspekhi* 9 (1966).

"The Road into Science." N. N. Semenov. *Soviet Physics Uspekhi* 29 (1986).

(Martha A. Sherwood)

Michael Servetus

Areas of Achievement: Medicine and physiology

Contribution: Servetus discovered the lesser (pulmonary) circulation of the blood. He also held elementary ideas on metabolism, believing that digestion produced heat in the body.

1511?	Born in Villanueva de Sixena, Spain
1526	Enters the service of churchman and statesman Juan de Quintana
1528	Leaves Spain to study law in Toulouse, France
1529	Returns to Quintana's service at the court of Emperor Charles V
1530	Moves to Basel, Switzerland
1531	Moves to Strasbourg and publishes *De trinitatis erroribus libri septem* against the doctrine of the Trinity
1532	Publishes *Dialogorum de trinitate libri duo, de justicia regni Christi capitual quatuor*
1533	Takes up residence in Paris and studies medicine
1535	Publishes *Ptolemaeus geographicae* at Lyons
1536	Publishes his first medical book, *In Leonardum Fuchsium apologia*
1537	Publishes *Syruporum universa ratio*
1538	Publishes *Apologetica disceptatio pro astrologia*
1553	Publishes his most important work, *Christianismi restitutio*
1553	Arrested and jailed for heresy in Vienne, France
Oct. 27, 1553	Burned at the stake in Geneva, Switzerland

Early Life

Michael Servetus (pronounced "suhr-VEET-uhs"), also known as Miguel Serveto, was probably born in Villanueva de Sixena, Spain, on September 29, 1511. The argumentative and abrasive son of nobles, he studied law in France in 1528 but soon returned to Spain. About this time, he denied that the Bible taught the doctrines of the Trinity—that the Godhead comprises the three coequal and unified spiritual beings of Father, Son, and Holy Spirit—and of infant baptism, opinions that made him infamous with both Protestants and Roman Catholics.

Because of his notoriety, Servetus left for Basel, Switzerland, in 1530 and thereby initiated a life of wandering made necessary by his unpopular religious convictions. He stayed for nearly a year in the home of the Protestant reformer John Oecolampadius. When his host decided to oppose his unorthodox theology, Servetus moved on to Strasbourg.

MICHAEL SERVETVS HISPANVS DE ARAGONIA.

(National Library of Medicine)

Pulmonary Circulation

Servetus argued that blood from the right ventricle of the heart moves into the pulmonary artery to the lungs and then returns to the left ventricle to be pumped to the rest of the body.

In the sixteenth century, most scholars followed the second century physician Galen in believing that blood moves in the heart from the right ventricle to the left by passing through invisible pores in the septum separating the ventricles. Although Servetus' work on circulation was hypothetical rather than experimental, and his motivation was primarily theological rather than scientific (to explain how the immaterial spirit of God entered and spread in the material body), his alternative explanation represented a major advance in anatomical thinking.

Servetus found the pulmonary artery inappropriately large solely to furnish blood to the lungs. Additionally, he was convinced that the septum was impermeable.

Servetus proposed that the pulmonary artery routes blood from the right ventricle to the lungs, where it is oxygenated and returned to the left ventricle, bypassing the septum. From the left ventricle, arteries disperse blood to the body, and veins return it to the heart.

Thus, Servetus not only described the lesser circulation with almost complete accuracy but also came near depicting the greater (systemic) circulation as well.

Bibliography

Blood: Pure and Eloquent. M. M. Winetrobe, ed. New York: McGraw-Hill, 1980.

Circulation of the Blood: Men and Ideas. A. P. Fishman and D. W. Richards, eds. New York: Oxford University Press, 1964.

The Pulmonary Circulation and Gas Exchange. Wiltz Wagner and Kenneth Weir, eds. Mount Kisco, N.Y.: Futura Press, 1994.

There, Servetus associated with Martin Bucer, another leading Protestant reformer, and enjoyed the city's toleration until he wrote *De trinitatis erroribus libri septem* (1531). No longer welcomed in Strasbourg, he returned to Basel, where he endured even harsher criticism for two more books against the Trinity.

Medical Studies and Career

In Paris in 1533, Servetus studied medicine and masqueraded as Michel de Villeneuve, so scandalous and dangerous had his true name become. In 1535, he moved to Lyons and published a successful book on geography and, in 1536 and 1537, two books on medicine.

Back in Paris and short of money, Servetus lectured on geography. When he also began to teach astrology and its alleged benefits for medicine, he provoked the anger of the medical faculty, who charged that he lacked teaching credentials and who considered astrology heretical. To counter their accusations, he published *Apologetica disceptatio pro astrologia* (1538).

Still posing as Michel de Villeneuve, Servetus happily practiced medicine near Lyons between 1538 and 1553. In Vienne, France, he was the physician to Archbishop Pierre Palmier and had a large private practice, including many charity patients. His last book, *Christianismi restitutio* (1553), combined his medical and religious interests and contained his most enduring scientific discovery: the pulmonary circulation of the blood.

Servetus' Death

Incautiously, Servetus opened a correspondence with John Calvin, the noted Protestant reformer in Geneva. Calvin despised Servetus, whom he considered a heretic, and unmasked his true identity to authorities at Vienne. To one of his colleagues, Calvin remarked that "if Servetus ever comes to Geneva, I will not suffer him to live." After three days in prison in April, 1553, Servetus escaped and fled to Italy by way of Geneva.

On August 13, Servetus was apprehended at a church service and, on Calvin's insistence, tried, convicted, and condemned, despite defending himself eloquently. His death at the stake was particularly brutal; the flames and smoke took half an hour to choke out his life.

Bibliography

By Servetus

De trinitatis erroribus libri septum, 1531 (on the errors of the Trinity)

Dialogorum de trinitate libri duo, de justicia regni Christi capitual quatuor, 1532 (commonly known as *De trinitate*; on the Trinity)

Ptolemaeus geographicae, 1535 (the geography of Ptolemy)

In Leonardum Fuchsium apologia, 1536 (in defense of Leonhard Fuchs)

Syruporum universa ratio, 1537

Apologetica disceptatio pro astrologia, 1538 (in defense of astrology)

Christianismi restitutio, 1553 (Christianity restored)

Michael Servetus: A Translation of His Geographical, Medical, and Astrological Writings, with Introduction and Notes, 1953 (Charles Donald O'Malley, ed.)

About Servetus

Hunted Heretic: The Life and Death of Michael Servetus. Roland Bainton. Boston: Beacon Press, 1953.

Michael Servetus: A Case Study in Total Heresy. Jerome Friedman. Geneva: Droz, 1978.

Michael Servetus: Humanist and Martyr. John F. Fulton. New York: Herbert Reichner, 1953.

(David Allen Duncan)

Harlow Shapley

Area of Achievement: Astronomy
Contribution: Shapley developed a means of determining distances within the solar system that enabled him to locate its center and to establish the earth's position within it.

Nov. 2, 1885	Born in Nashville, Missouri
1910	Receives an A.B. from the University of Missouri
1911	Receives an A.M. in astronomy from Missouri
1913	Receives a Ph.D. from Princeton
1914	Joins the staff at Mount Wilson Observatory in California
1918	Measures the Milky Way's dimensions and locates its center
1921	Becomes the director of Harvard Observatory
1926	Given the Draper Medal by the National Academy of Sciences
1927	Given an honorary LL.D. by the University of Missouri
1933	Granted honorary degrees form both Harvard and Princeton
1939	Made president of the American Academy of Arts and Sciences
1946	Helps found the United Nations Educational, Scientific, and Cultural Organization (UNESCO)
1947	Elected president of the American Association for the Advancement of Science
1956	Retires as director of Harvard Observatory
Oct. 20, 1972	Dies in Boulder, Colorado

Early Life

Harlow Shapley and his twin brother were born November 2, 1885, on the family hay farm in Missouri. Harlow had a pleasant childhood, but his early education was limited to a few years in a rural schoolhouse. At sixteen, he tried his luck as a crime reporter for a newspaper in Chanute, Kansas. While in Chanute, Shapley began to read history and poetry in the public library and decided to continue his education. He and a younger brother tried to enter high school but were not qualified to enroll.

Shapley did manage to attend a very small Presbyterian school and then to enroll at the University of Missouri. Because of his newspaper experience, he wanted to study journalism. A journalism major was not offered at the time, however, and he chose astronomy instead. One of his professors recommended him for a fellowship to attend graduate school at Princeton, and he enrolled there in 1911.

After receiving his Ph.D. in astronomy in 1914, Shapley was hired to work at the Mount Wilson Observatory in California. On his way to Mount Wilson, he stopped in Kansas City to marry Martha Betz, a college classmate whom he had met while at the University of Missouri.

(AP/Wide World Photos)

Finding the Size of the Milky Way

Shapley used the properties of Cepheid variable stars to establish a distance scale for the Milky Way.

Astronomers have long known that some stars change in brightness over fairly short periods of time. For some of these, called Cepheid variables, the longer it takes to brighten and then dim, the more luminous the star is. This characteristic was key to Shapley's discovery.

To an observer on Earth, a star's brightness depends on its luminosity and the distance to it. By measuring the time required for a Cepheid's brightening cycle, its luminosity can be determined using the relationship between period and luminosity. Then by comparing this luminosity to the observed brightness, the distance to the star can be computed. Shapley used this principle to locate globular clusters of stars within the Milky Way by determining the distance to Cepheids contained within them. Assuming these clusters to be uniformly distributed in the Galaxy, he was able to locate the center of the Milky Way and the position of Earth relative to it. The outcome established a distance scale for the Galaxy and showed that the sun is not near its center. The distances that he computed were far greater than previous estimates and forever changed the way that astronomers thought about the Milky Way.

Bibliography

Exploration of the Universe. George O. Abell, David Morrison, and Sidney C. Wolff. 5th ed. New York: Saunders College Publishing, 1987.

The Milky Way. Bart J. Bok and Priscilla F. Bok. 4th ed. Cambridge, Mass.: Harvard University Press, 1974.

Astronomical Research

At Mount Wilson, Shapley worked with Frederick Seares measuring the brightness and colors of stars and also made his own observations of stars whose brightness varied. He became interested in Cepheid variable stars and globular clusters.

This work formed the basis for his primary achievement: finding a way to determine the size of the Milky Way and the location of its center. He was also able to locate the sun within it. His estimates of distances within the Galaxy were distrusted at first by many astronomers but were eventually accepted.

Later Career

In 1921, Shapley was appointed director of the Harvard Observatory, where he presided over a dramatic growth in the programs that soon attracted large numbers of top students. He also participated in the establishment of the National Science Foundation and the United Nations Educational, Scientific, and Cultural Organization (UNESCO). Shapley wrote numerous articles and books, many of which helped stimulate popular interest in astronomy. He became widely known and was awarded a total of seventeen honorary degrees.

Throughout his life, he pursued a curious side interest: He was fascinated by ants. He studied their behavior, collected specimens all over the world, and occasionally wrote articles describing his observations. Shapley died on October 20, 1972.

Bibliography

By Shapley

"The Scale of the Universe, Part I," *Bulletin of the National Research Council*, 1921

Starlight, 1926

Star Clusters, 1930

Flights from Chaos: A Survey of Material Systems from Atoms to Galaxies, 1930

Of Stars and Men, 1958

Science Ponders Religion, 1960

The View from a Distant Star, 1963

Through Rugged Ways to the Stars, 1969

About Shapley

American Astronomers. Carole Ann Camp. Springfield, N.J.: Enslow, 1996.

"Dr. Harlow Shapley." *Nature* 240 (1972).

Through Rugged Ways to the Stars. Harlow Shapley. New York: Charles Scribner's Sons, 1969.

(Cecil O. Huey, Jr.)

Sir Charles Scott Sherrington

Areas of Achievement: Medicine and physiology

Contribution: Sherrington's work, recognized with the Nobel Prize in Physiology or Medicine, laid the foundation for the understanding of reflexes and the nervous system.

Nov. 27, 1857	Born in London, England
1884	Receives an MRCS from St. Thomas' Hospital, London
1887	Named a Fellow of Gonville and Caius College, Cambridge University
1891	Moves to London as a professor at Brown Animal Sanatory Institution
1893	Elected a Fellow of the Royal Society of London
1895	Promoted to the Holt Professorship of Physiology at the University of Liverpool
1904	Delivers the Silliman Lectures at Yale University
1913	Named to the Waynflete Chair of Physiology at Oxford University
1920-1925	Serves as president of the Royal Society of London
1924	Receives the Order of Merit
1932	Awarded the Nobel Prize in Physiology or Medicine
1935	Retires from Oxford
1937-1938	Delivers the Gifford Lectures at the University of Edinburgh
Mar. 4, 1952	Dies in Eastbourne, Sussex, England

Early Life

Charles Scott Sherrington was the son of James Norton and Anne Brookes Sherrington of Great Yarmouth, England. He went to Ipswich Grammar School, where he was deeply influenced by one of the masters, a poet. His father died when Sherrington was quite young, and the home of his stepfather in Ipswich was a gathering place for good conversationalists.

After an impressive academic and athletic career at school, Sherrington proceeded to Gonville and Caius College at Cambridge University. While there, he played rugby for his college and continued his academic success.

At Cambridge, Sherrington was singled out by the physiologist Sir Michael Foster to help with his research. His first publication was read to the Royal Society of London while he was still an undergraduate. He received a first-class degree on the natural science tripos (examination for honors) and subsequently received both bachelor's and doctor's degrees in medicine from Cambridge. After his graduation, he conducted studies in Germany and France, studying cholera at first hand in Spain and Italy.

Experimental Work

In 1887, Sherrington became a lecturer in systematic physiology at St. Thomas' Hospital in London. Over the next decade, he was affected in the direction of his research by the work of Santiago Ramón y Cajal, a Spanish anatomist who had refuted the theory that nerve fibers form a continuous network throughout the body. Sherrington worked on the nervous system his entire professional life and was able to explain, on a physical basis, previously puzzling interactions of the nerves.

Among his successes was the mapping of the regions of the cerebral cortex that apply to motion. A particularly useful observation was that the response to electric stimulation of parts of the brain can be affected by previous stimulation of the same region. Sherrington summarized much of his early work in the lectures that he delivered at Yale University in 1904, which were published two years later.

The Head of His Profession

In 1913, Sherrington took the Waynflete Chair of Physiology at Oxford University, signaling

(The Nobel Foundation)

his role as the most visible scholar in his field. During World War I, he took time to study industrial fatigue for the War Office, but most of his effort was given over to supervising the most productive research laboratory in the world. Sherrington received the Order of Merit from the British government, its highest honor, and the Nobel Prize in Physiology or Medicine, along with a host of honorary degrees.

In addition to his personal influence, Sherrington published writings that had a long-lasting effect on the study of the central nervous system. He always maintained a broad range of interests, and the terminology that he introduced has remained standard. In 1891, he married Ethel Mary Wright, who died in 1933; they had one child, a railway economist whose memoirs are a useful source of information about his father. Sherrington died of heart failure in 1952.

Bibliography
By Sherrington
The Integrative Action of the Nervous System, 1906
The Reflex Activity of the Spinal Cord, 1932
The Brain and Its Mechanism, 1933

Putting the Mind Back in the Body

The behavior of the body attributable to the nervous system can be understood on the basis of physicochemical changes inside the body.

Sherrington performed experiments on animals which had parts of their brains removed, allowing him to discover the complexity of reflexes determined by the spinal cord, as well as the control exerted over those reflexes by the parts of the brain. His study of synapses recognized the crucial importance of these connections between neurons (nerve cells).

Dualism is the view that there is a fundamental discontinuity between mental activity and physical processes. In the absence of any way to explain the complexity of mental behavior in physical terms, dualism was the prevailing philosophy for centuries, even among physiological researchers. Sherrington explained behavior patterns via a continuity between the anatomical and physiological elements on the one hand and overt (visible) behavior on the other.

Sherrington recognized that the central nervous system is a network of synapses. He noted the importance of the kind of receptor that could gather information about an animal's surroundings without requiring direct physical contact. If direct physical contact with a stimulus were required in order to produce a reaction, there would be little hope of escape when the source of the stimulus turned out to be dangerous.

Bibliography
Reflex Action. Franklin Fearing. Baltimore: The Johns Hopkins University Press, 1930.
Reflexes and Motor Integration. Judith P. Swazey. Cambridge, Mass.: Harvard University Press, 1969.
The Strategy of Life. Timothy Lenoir. Dordrecht, the Netherlands: Kluwer, 1982.

Man on His Nature, 1941
The Endeavour of Jean Fernel, 1946

About Sherrington
Charles Scott Sherrington: An Appraisal. Ragnar Granit. Garden City, N.Y.: Doubleday, 1967.
The Discovery of Reflexes. E. G. T. Liddell. Oxford, England: Oxford University Press, 1960.
Sherrington, His Life and Thought. Sir John Carew Eccles and William C. Gibson. New York: Springer, 1979.
Sherrington: Physiologist, Philosopher, and Poet. Lord Cohen of Birkenhead. Liverpool, England: University of Liverpool Press, 1958.

(Thomas Drucker)

Charles G. Sibley

Areas of Achievement: Biology and zoology

Contribution: Sibley, an ornithologist and educator, pioneered the use of biochemical methods to determine the phylogenetic relationships among groups of organisms, primarily birds.

Aug. 7, 1917	Born in Fresno, California
1940	Earns an A.B. in zoology from the University of California, Berkeley (UCB)
1941-1942	Works as a field biologist for the U.S. Public Health Service
1948	Awarded a Ph.D. in zoology from UCB
1948-1949	Appointed Instructor in Zoology and Curator of Birds, the University of Kansas
1949-1953	Named assistant professor of zoology, San Jose State College
1953-1965	Serves as associate and then full professor of zoology and as Curator of Birds, Cornell University
1965-1986	Serves as professor of biology, William Robertson Coe Professor of Ornithology, and Curator of Birds, Yale University
1970-1976	Directs the Peabody Museum of Natural History at Yale
1986	Retires from Yale as professor emeritus
1986-1992	Named Dean's Professor of Science and Professor of Biology, San Francisco State University
1986-1988	Elected president of the American Ornithologists' Union
1993	Invited to become adjunct professor of biology, Sonoma State University

Early Life

Charles Gald Sibley was born in Fresno, California, in 1917. His family moved to the San Francisco Bay Area at about the time that he entered school. His interest in natural history was encouraged by his Boy Scout scoutmaster and by naturalists on the Oakland Council and at a camp in the Oakland hills in the San Francisco Bay Area of Northern California. The books of Ernest Thompson Seton and the essays of John Burroughs added to Sibley's interest and expanded his knowledge. With two other students, and helped by his high-school science teacher, Sibley organized the Natural Science Club at University High School in Oakland.

Sibley received an A.B. from the University of California, Berkeley (UCB), in 1940 with a major in zoology. As an undergraduate, he learned that field identification includes behavioral aspects of the animal—its flight pattern, size, and probability of occurrence in a given habitat—as well as its physical characteristics.

From 1941 to 1942, Sibley worked as a field biologist with the Bubonic Plague Suppressive Measures division of the U.S. Public Health Service. On February 7, 1942, he married Frances Louise Kelly; they would have three daughters—Barbara Susanne, Dorothy Ellen, and Carol Nadine. During World War II, he served as a commissioned officer in the U.S. Navy in the Communications and Medical Service Corps.

After the war, Sibley returned to academia, earning a Ph.D. in zoology from UCB, with minors in paleontology and botany, in 1948. During his long career, he would teach at many universities, including the University of Kansas, San Jose State College, and Cornell, Yale, San Francisco State, and Sonoma State Universities.

The Study of Birds

Sibley gained a reputation as a scientific generalist who had not lost sight of the importance of field observations and the collection of specimens while he was involved in making

(Alburtus-Yale News Bureau)

the tens of thousands of deoxyribonucleic acid (DNA) comparisons that led to proposed relationships among the approximately ten thousand species of birds.

Sibley understood the importance of good field records and journals. One of his projects was the study of hybridization between different species of birds, including two species of red-eyed towhees in Mexico that hybridize in some places where they are in contact, but not in others. He described this complex situation in articles published in 1950, 1954, and 1964.

Previously, such studies had been based on comparisons of plumage color patterns and measurements of wings, tails, bills, and other physical characteristics. In 1957, Sibley began to use biochemical methods to compare proteins as evidence of genetic

The DNA-Based Classification of Birds

Sibley conducted hybridization experiments with deoxyribonucleic acid (DNA) in order to determine the evolutionary relationships among the major groups of birds.

Knowledge of the double helix structure of DNA, proposed by James D. Watson and Francis Crick in 1953, led to new methods in many areas of biology. Among them was the technique of DNA-DNA hybridization, which was developed during the 1960's. This method measures the degree of genetic similarity between the DNAs of different species.

Sibley began using DNA-DNA hybridization in 1974 to determine the degrees of evolutionary change among the major groups of birds. The methods and equipment that he used are described in his 1986 article in *Scientific American*. From 1974 to 1986, he employed DNA hybridization to compare the genetic material of 1,700 species of birds, representing all the orders and nearly all the families.

DNA hybridization produced evidence that some of the traditional ideas about the evolutionary history (phylogeny) of birds were wrong. The most interesting discoveries concerned the phenomenon of convergent evolution. A well-known example on convergence is the similarity between a shark and a dolphin—a fish and a mammal that are similar in structure because both are adapted to life in the sea.

Convergence among birds is more difficult to detect because all birds have feathers and most are able to fly. Thus, they share many similarities. Different groups isolated from one another on different continents, however, have adapted to similar habitats and become similar in structure, although they are derived from different ancestors.

For example, bird species that feed on flower nectar have evolved specialized tongues to take in liquid nectar, as in the honey-eaters of Australia and the sunbirds of Africa. These species look so much alike that they had always been assumed to be closely related. The DNA hybridization comparisons showed that the honey-eaters are more closely related to other Australian birds that are not nectar-feeders than they are to the African sunbirds.

The new classification system for bird species differs from that based on morphology and has produced controversy. The relationship between honey-eaters and sunbirds, and many other examples of convergent evolution, have been supported by independent studies, some of them using the technique of DNA sequencing.

Bibliography

Animal Tracks and Hunter Signs. Ernest Thompson Seton. Garden City, N.Y.: Doubleday, 1958.

The Double Helix: A Personal Account of the Discovery of the Structure of DNA. James D. Watson. New York: New American Library, 1968.

John Burroughs: Selections from the Writings of the Hudson River Naturalist. John Burroughs. New York: Devin-Adair, 1952.

"Reconstructing Bird Phylogeny by Comparing DNA's." Charles G. Sibley and J. E. Ahlquist. *Scientific American* 254 (1986).

relationships among birds. Blood and egg-white proteins were compared using the techniques of electrophoresis, which produces patterns in filter paper or agar gel. This method provided some information about the relationships among orders and families of organisms, but it was not sensitive to differences between closely related species. The patterns were compared by eye, not by independent measurements.

The technique of DNA hybridization was developed during the 1960's as a method to measure the degree of genetic similarity between the DNA of different species. It offered more precise information about the relationships among closely related species, particularly birds.

An Excursion into Anthropology

Sibley also used DNA hybridization to determine the relationships among primates, including the great apes and humans. The results showed that the chimpanzees are more closely related to humans than they are to gorillas. The gorilla lineage branched off about 10 million years ago, and the divergence between human and chimpanzee branches occurred about 6 to 7 million years ago. It had been traditionally thought that chimpanzees and gorillas were more closely related and that the human lineage branched much earlier. These results have been supported by an independent DNA hybridization study and by several DNA sequence studies.

Field Research
Sibley maintained his interest in field biology throughout his life. He participated in field expeditions in the late 1930's to collect mammal and bird specimens in Mexico, as well as during his service in the Navy in the South Pacific. He traveled and collected specimens in many countries around the world, often with his wife and daughters. He always maintained a relationship, however, with a museum and a university.

Sibley received many honors, including the Brewster Memorial Medal of the American Ornithologists' Union in 1971, membership in the National Academy of Sciences in 1986 and that academy's Daniel Giraud Elliot Medal in 1988, and the Alessandro Ghighi Medal of the National Institute of Wildlife Biology, Italy, in 1991. He served as president of the American Ornithologists' Union from 1986 to 1988 and as president of the Twentieth International Ornithological Congress, which met in New Zealand.

Bibliography
By Sibley
The following is a selected list of articles and books:
"Fossil Fringillids from Rancho La Brea," *Condor*, 1939
"Hybridization in the Red-Eyed Towhees of Mexico," *Evolution*, 1954
"Coloration in Animals" in *Encyclopedia Americana*, 1963
"Hybridization in the Red-Eyed Towhees of Mexico: The Populations of the Southeastern Plateau Region," *Auk*, 1964 (with F. C. Sibley)
"Proteins: History Books of Evolution," *Discovery*, 1967
"A Comparative Study of the Egg White Proteins of Passerine Birds," *Bulletin of the Peabody Museum of Natural History*, 1970
"A Comparative Study of the Egg White Proteins of Non-passerine Birds," *Bulletin of the Peabody Museum of Natural History*, 1972 (with J. E. Ahlquist)
"The Phylogeny and Classification of Birds Based on the Data of DNA-DNA Hybridization" (with Ahlquist) in *Current Ornithology*, 1983 (R. F. Johnston, ed.)
"The Phylogeny of the Hominoid Primates, as Indicated by DNA-DNA Hybridization," *Journal of Molecular Evolution*, 1984 (with Ahlquist)
"Reconstructing Bird Phylogeny by Comparing DNA's," *Scientific American*, 1986 (with Ahlquist)
"Avian Phylogeny Reconstructed from Comparisons of the Genetic Material, DNA" (with Ahlquist) in *Molecules and Morphology in Evolution: Conflict or Compromise*, 1987 (C. Patterson, ed.)
"DNA Hybridization Evidence of Hominoid Phylogeny: Results from an Expanded Data Set," *Journal of Molecular Evolution*, 1987 (with Ahlquist)
"A Classification of the Living Birds of the World, Based on DNA-DNA Hybridization Studies," *Auk*, 1988 (with Ahlquist and B. L. Monroe, Jr.)
"DNA Hybridization Evidence of Hominoid Phylogeny: A Reanalysis of the Data," *Journal of Molecular Evolution*, 1990 (with J. A. Comstock and Ahlquist)
Phylogeny and Classification of the Birds of the World: A Study in Molecular Evolution, 1990 (with Ahlquist)
Distribution and Taxonomy of the Birds of the World, 1990 (with Monroe)
A World Checklist of Birds, 1993 (with Monroe)
"Point-of-View: On the Phylogeny and Classification of Living Birds," *Journal of Avian Biology* (formerly *Ornis Scandinavica*), 1994
"Continental Breakup Ordinal Diversification of Birds and Mammals," *Nature*, 1996 (with S. B. Hedges, P. H. Parker, and S. Kumar)

About Sibley
"Charles G. Sibley." In *Who's Who in America 1997*. New Providence, N.J.: Marquis Who's Who, 1996.

Review of *Distribution and Taxonomy of the Birds of the World*, by Charles G. Sibley and B. L. Monroe, Jr. Jared M. Diamond. *Nature* 350 (April 11, 1991).

Review of *Phylogeny and Classification of the Birds of the World*, by Charles G. Sibley and J. E. Ahlquist. Frank B. Gill. *Science* 252 (May 17, 1991).

In addition, the World Wide Web page http://www.birding.com contains a biography of Sibley at sibbiog.htm, as well as other bird-related information.

(Martha J. Mitchell)

Vesto Melvin Slipher

Area of Achievement: Astronomy

Contribution: Slipher's discovery that spiral nebulas are receding into space at extremely high speeds helped convince astronomers that these nebulas are independent galaxies and that the universe is expanding.

Nov. 11, 1875	Born in Mulberry, Indiana
1902	Starts spectrographic work at Lowell Observatory
1903	Measures the rotational speed of Venus
1904	Marries Emma Rosalie Munger
1906	Begins to study the spectra of spiral nebulas
1908	Finds calcium gas in space
1909	Receives a doctorate at Indiana University
1912	Identifies the Pleiades nebula as dust reflecting local starlight
1912-1913	Discovers that the Andromeda nebula is rapidly moving toward the sun
1915	Becomes an assistant director of Lowell Observatory
1919	Receives the Lalande Prize of the Académie des Sciences
1922	Wins the National Academy of Sciences' Draper Gold Medal
1926	Becomes the director of Lowell Observatory
1930	Supervises Clyde Tombaugh's discovery of Pluto
1933	Wins the Gold Medal of the Royal Astronomical Society
Nov. 8, 1969	Dies in Flagstaff, Arizona

Early Life

An Indiana farm boy, Vesto Melvin Slipher (pronounced "SLI-fur") was one of eleven children.
He entered Indiana University at Bloomington,
where he received a degree in mechanics and
astronomy. After graduation, he found work at
Lowell Observatory in Flagstaff, Arizona.

At that time, the observatory was highly
controversial. Its director, Percival Lowell, in-
correctly believed that Mars was covered with
long, thin lines or "canals" built by Martians.
Lowell also thought that he saw similar puzzling features on the surface of Venus and, by
observing their motion, tried to time the
Venusian rotation speed. To support his timing
estimate, Lowell ordered Slipher to study Venus with a spectrograph—specifically, to measure its Doppler shift. In that way, Slipher
found that Venus rotates much more slowly
than generally thought.

Later, Slipher measured the rotation speeds
of the planets Jupiter, Saturn, Uranus, and
Mars. In 1908, while examining the spectrum
of a binary star, he noticed a puzzling spectral
line associated with calcium gas. He correctly
concluded that the space between planets and
stars is not empty. Rather, it contains vast
clouds of gas. He also detected dust clouds in
the Orion nebula.

Spiral Nebulas

In 1913, using the spectrograph, Slipher made
his greatest discovery. He observed that the
spiral-shaped Andromeda nebula is approaching the sun at hundreds of miles a second.
Over the next decade, he found that most spiral nebulas are receding from the sun, some at
much faster speeds. Astronomers later realized
that the universe is expanding and that spiral
nebulas are actually distant galaxies.

After Lowell's death, Slipher ran the observatory until 1952. Under his supervision, observatory staff member Clyde Tombaugh discovered the planet Pluto in 1930.

Although little known to the general public,
Slipher was highly esteemed by other astronomers. He received major international awards
and also held high posts in the International
Astronomical Union, the American Astronomical Society, and the American Association for
the Advancement of Science. A savvy investor

(Archive Photos/New York Times)

in local businesses and properties, he died a
rich man a few days before his ninety-fourth
birthday.

Bibliography

By Slipher
"A Spectrographic Investigation on the Rota-
    tional Velocity of Venus," *Lowell Observatory
    Bulletin*, 1903
"Peculiar Star Spectra Suggestive of Selective
    Absorption of Light in Space," *Lowell Obser-
    vatory Bulletin*, 1909
"The Radial Velocity of the Andromeda Neb-
    ula," *Lowell Observatory Bulletin*, 1913
"Spectrographic Observations of Nebulae,"
    Popular Astronomy, 1915

About Slipher
*The Explorers of Mars Hill: A Centennial History
    of Lowell Observatory, 1894-1994.* William
    Lowell Putnam et al. West Kennebunk,
    Maine: Phoenix, 1994.
Lowell and Mars. William Graves Hoyt. Tucson:
    University of Arizona Press, 1976.
"V. M. Slipher's Trailblazing Career." J. S. Hall.
    Sky and Telescope 39 (February, 1970).

(Keay Davidson)

The Doppler Shift of the Andromeda Nebula

A large Doppler shift in its spectrum indicates that the Andromeda nebula is moving at 300 kilometers per second.

With a spectrograph attached to a telescope, an astronomer can measure the chemical composition and velocity of a star as it moves through space. The spectrograph breaks light from the star into a rainbowlike spectrum, which contains thin lines that represent chemicals in the stellar atmosphere. If the star is moving, then the lines shift position—the bigger the shift, the faster the star.

In the early twentieth century, many astronomers believed that spiral nebulas were clouds of dust and gas within the only known galaxy, the Milky Way. Perhaps the spiral nebulas were condensing into new planetary systems, they thought.

In late 1912 and early 1913, however, Slipher showed that the spiral nebula Andromeda had a remarkably high Doppler shift of 300 kilometers (about 190 miles) per second. It was moving in the general direction of the earth's solar system. Later, he found other spiral nebulas moving faster than 1,000 kilometers per second. Unlike Andromeda, however, most spiral nebulas are moving away from the sun, as if fleeing into the outer universe.

Astronomers interpreted their high speeds to mean that spiral nebulas are, in fact, separate galaxies far from the Milky Way. As a typical galaxy contains billions of stars and is millions or billions of light years away, the cosmos had to be far larger than previously thought.

In the 1920's, Edwin Hubble relied heavily on Slipher's work to show that the fastest spiral nebulas are also the most distant. This observation is best explained by assuming that the universe as a whole is expanding, like an inflating balloon. By the 1970's, most cosmologists attributed the expansion to the "big bang," a primordial explosion that spawned space, time, and matter billions of years ago.

Bibliography

Cosmology and Controversy: The Historical Development of Two Theories of the Universe. Helge Kragh. Princeton, N.J.: Princeton University Press, 1996.

The Realm of the Nebulae. Edwin Hubble. Reprint. New Haven, Conn.: Yale University Press, 1982.

The Red Limit: The Search for the Edge of the Universe. Timothy Ferris. New York: William Morrow, 1977.

Wrinkles in Time. George Smoot and Keay Davidson. New York: William Morrow, 1993.

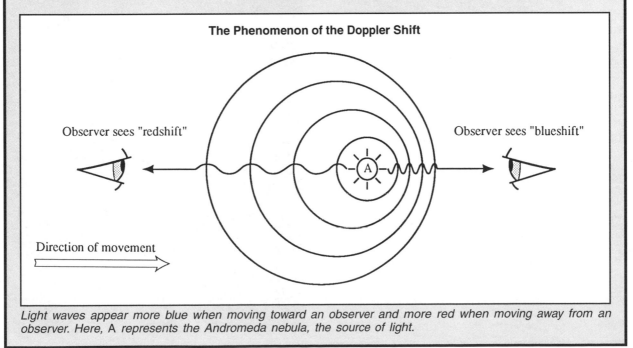

The Phenomenon of the Doppler Shift

Observer sees "redshift"

Observer sees "blueshift"

Direction of movement

Light waves appear more blue when moving toward an observer and more red when moving away from an observer. Here, A represents the Andromeda nebula, the source of light.

Richard E. Smalley

Area of Achievement: Chemistry

Contribution: With Robert F. Curl, Jr., and Sir Harold W. Kroto, Smalley won the Nobel Prize in Chemistry for the discovery of fullerenes, a family of highly symmetrical carbon cage molecules.

June 6, 1943	Born in Akron, Ohio
1961-1963	Attends Hope College in Holland, Michigan
1965	Earns a B.S. in chemistry from the University of Michigan
1965-1969	Works as a research chemist for Shell Oil Company
1969-1973	Earns an M.A. and a Ph.D. from Princeton University
1973-1976	Works as a graduate research assistant at the James Franck Institute at the University of Chicago
1976-1982	Promoted from assistant to associate to full professor of chemistry at Rice University
1978-1980	Named an Alfred P. Sloan Fellow
1982	Named Gene & Norman Hackerman Professor of Chemistry
1986-1996	Serves as chair of the Rice Quantum Institute
1990	Elected to the National Academy of Sciences
1990	Appointed a professor of physics at Rice
1992	Wins the Robert A. Welch Award in Chemistry
1996	Awarded the Franklin Medal
1996	Named director of the Center for Nanoscale Science and Technology
1996	Wins the Nobel Prize in Chemistry

Early Life

Richard Errett Smalley grew up in an upper-middle-class neighborhood in Kansas City, Missouri. A quiet child, he spent most of his time in his father's basement workshop, where he achieved one of his first successes: He kept the family collie out of the rose garden by rigging it so that any intruder would set off fireworks.

An erratic student, Smalley did not become interested in chemistry until he took the subject in his junior year in high school, the first time that he did well academically. After an engineer-scientist spoke at his school, Smalley was motivated to pursue those fields.

Undergraduate and Postgraduate Studies

On the recommendation of his aunt, a professor of organic chemistry, Smalley attended Hope College in Holland, Michigan. After his favorite professor died and the chair of the organic chemistry department retired, he

(Reuters/Adrees A. Latif/Archive Photos)

transferred to the University of Michigan, where, distracted by a difficult relationship with a woman at Hope, he received only mediocre grades.

After earning his B.S. in chemistry, he worked for four years as a research chemist with the Shell Oil Company, receiving an industrial deferment that kept him out of the

Fullerenes, a New Form of Carbon

The fullerenes, a family of highly symmetrical carbon cage molecules whose atoms are arranged in the shape of a soccer ball, opened up a new branch of chemistry with numerous possible applications.

Several widely diverse scientific areas coincided in the serendipitous discovery of the fullerenes, a third allotropic form of carbon (the first two being graphite and diamond).

During the 1980's, Sir Harold W. Kroto, a professor of chemistry at the University of Sussex in England, used microwave spectroscopy to analyze gas in space and found that the spectral lines in the atmospheres of carbon-rich giant stars could be attributed to cyanopolyenes (long-chain molecules composed of carbon and nitrogen). Desiring to study the formation of these substances more closely, he contacted an acquaintance, Robert F. Curl, Jr., a professor of chemistry at Rice University and an authority on microwave and infrared spectroscopy.

Smalley, an authority on a branch of chemical physics called cluster chemistry, had designed and built a laser supersonic cluster beam apparatus capable of vaporizing almost any known material into a plasma of atoms. When atoms in a gas phase condense into clusters (aggregates of atoms or molecules between microscopic and macroscopic particles in size), they form a series in which the size of the clusters varies from a few to hundreds of atoms.

Often, certain cluster sizes may predominate. The number of atoms in these clusters is called a "magic number," a term borrowed from nuclear physics. These dominant cluster sizes are assumed to possess high stability or high symmetry.

Through Curl, Kroto arranged to use Smalley's apparatus to study the vaporization and cluster formation of carbon, which might provide evidence that cyanopolyenes could have been formed in hot regions of stellar atmospheres. The crucial experiments, carried out in September,

1985, by Curl, Kroto, and Smalley with graduate students James R. Heath and Sean C. O'Brien, detected the formation of clusters of sixty and seventy atoms, especially the former.

Abandoning the idea of long chains, they proposed that C_{60} could have the highly symmetrical structure of a truncated (cut off) icosahedral cage, the shape of a soccer ball or American architect R. Buckminster Fuller's geodesic dome. Therefore, they named the substance buckminsterfullerene (or fullerene or buckyball).

Their article on this unique structure in the November 14, 1985, issue of *Nature* aroused wide interest and a mixed reception—both criticism and enthusiastic acceptance. The discovery remained of primarily theoretical significance, however, until 1990, with the work of physicists Wolfgang Krätschmer of the Max Planck Institute for Nuclear Physics in Heidelberg, Germany, and Donald R. Huffman of the University of Arizona, Tucson. They developed a method for preparing fullerenes in macroscopic amounts, leading to a tremendous amount of research on this new family of molecules, with the potential for numerous practical applications.

Bibliography

An Atlas of Fullerenes. P. W. Fowler and D. E. Manolopoulos. New York: Oxford University Press, 1995.

Buckminsterfullerenes. W. Edward Billups and Marco A. Ciufolini, eds. New York: VCH, 1993.

The Fullerenes: New Horizons for the Chemistry, Physics, and Astrophysics of Carbon. Harold W. Kroto and D. R. M. Walton, eds. New York: Cambridge University Press, 1993.

The Most Beautiful Molecule: The Discovery of the Buckyball. Hugh Aldersey-Williams. New York: John Wiley & Sons, 1995.

Perfect Symmetry: The Accidental Discovery of Buckminsterfullerene. Jim Baggott. New York: Oxford University Press, 1995.

Smalley holds a model of a "buckyball," the nickname for buckminsterfullerene. (Reuters/Adrees A. Latif/Archive Photos)

Vietnam War and developed his scientific skills.

In 1969, Smalley entered Princeton University to become a quantum chemist. He studied condensed-matter spectroscopy under Elliot R. Bernstein and earned an M.A. in 1971 and a Ph.D. in 1973. At the University of Chicago, under Lennard Wharton and Donald H. Levy, he pioneered supersonic beam laser spectroscopy, which has become one of the most powerful techniques in chemical physics.

Rice University

In 1976, Smalley joined the faculty of Rice University, rising rapidly through the ranks to become Gene & Norman Hackerman Professor of Chemistry in 1982, as well as professor of physics in 1990, chair of the Rice Quantum Institute from 1986 to 1996, and director of the Center for Nanoscale Science and Technology in 1996.

He made pioneering advances in developing many new techniques—such as supercold pulsed beams, ultrasensitive laser detection, and laser-driven sources of free radicals, triplets, metals, and both metal and semiconductor cluster beams—and applied them to a wide range of problems in chemical physics. He discovered and characterized buckminsterfullerene (C_{60}), a soccer ball-shaped molecule. He was the first to prepare fullerenes with metals trapped inside, and he produced continuous carbon fibers, which are essentially giant single-fullerene molecules.

Awards and Honors

The recipient of honorary degrees and an editorial board member of several journals, Smalley received numerous awards and honors, including the Langmuir Prize in Chemical Physics in 1991, the American Physical Society International Prize for New Materials in 1992, the Ernest O. Lawrence Memorial Award in 1992, the William H. Nichols Medal in 1993, the Harrison Howe Award in 1994, and the Madison Marshall Award in 1995.

For his work with fullerenes, Smalley shared the 1996 Nobel Prize in Chemistry with Robert F. Curl, Jr., and Sir Harold W. Kroto.

Bibliography
By Smalley
"C$_{60}$: Buckminsterfullerene," *Nature*, 1985 (with Harold W. Kroto, James R. Heath, Sean C. O'Brien, and Robert F. Curl, Jr.)
"Photophysics of Buckminsterfullerene and Other Carbon Cluster Ions," *Journal of Chemical Physics*, 1988 (with O'Brien, Heath, and Curl)
"Probing C$_{60}$," *Science*, 1988 (with Curl)
"Great Balls of Carbon: The Story of Buckminsterfullerene," *Sciences*, 1991
"Fullerenes," *Scientific American*, 1991 (with Curl)
"Self-Assembly of the Fullerenes," *Accounts of Chemical Research*, 1992

About Smalley
"The All-Star of Buckyball." Philip Yam. *Scientific American* 269, no. 3 (September, 1993).
"Fullerenes Gain Nobel Stature." Rudy Baum. *Chemical & Engineering News* 75, no. 1 (January 6, 1997).

(George B. Kauffman)

William Smith

Area of Achievement: Earth science
Contribution: Smith is best known for being the first to recognize that fossils occur in a definite, consistent, vertical order, referred to as the principle of fossil succession. He also produced the first geologic map of an entire country.

Mar. 23, 1769	Born in Churchill, Oxfordshire, England
1787	Becomes a surveyor's assistant
1793	Begins to survey for the construction of a canal proposed to transport coal
Jan., 1796	Discovers that beds of the same rock type can be distinguished by the types of fossils found in them
1799	Ends his work for the canal company and dictates a list of rock layers and their fossils
1802-1812	Prepares a series of geological maps of England and Wales
1816	Publishes the first two parts of his book *Strata Identified by Organized Fossils*
1817	Publishes *Stratigraphical System of Organized Fossils*
1831	Awarded the first Wollaston Medal by the Geological Society of London
Aug. 28, 1839	Dies in Northampton, Northamptonshire, England

Early Life
William Smith was born in Churchill, Oxfordshire, England, the eldest of five children. His father, John, a blacksmith, died when William was seven. The young boy attended the village school but had no other formal education.

Work as a Surveyor

At eighteen, Smith became an assistant to a surveyor named Edward Webb in Stow-on-the-Wold, Gloucestershire. In 1791, Smith was sent to survey an estate near Bath. He stayed at a farmhouse that he later called "the birthplace of English Geology," for it was here that he began thinking about rock layering. Smith sketched and mapped underground coal mines, which stimulated his interest in rock layers.

In 1793, Smith began surveying for a canal to transport coal from the mines. He determined that the dip of the rock layers was regular, and not random as miners had maintained. Smith was able to distinguish a definite sequence of rock layers. While in London in 1794, Smith looked for books on geology to find out if his discovery about the regularity of rock layers was already known, but he was unsuccessful.

The Discovery of Fossil Succession

Smith worked for the Canal Company from 1794 to 1799 as an engineer and surveyor. During this time, he became familiar with the rocks through which the canal passed, from red Triassic marlstone to Jurassic oolite. He collected fossils and began to color maps to show where different beds of rock cropped out.

On January 5, 1796, Smith wrote that he had made the significant finding that beds of the same rock type can be distinguished from one another by the types of fossils found in them. This concept was not previously recognized by geologists of the time, and it forms one of the basic principles of geology, now known as the principle of fossil succession.

The First Geological Map of England

Smith traveled after leaving the canal company and worked as a land drainer, mineral surveyor, and civil engineer from 1800 to 1820. In 1802, he proposed the preparation of a geological map of England and Wales to Sir Joseph Banks, the president of the Royal Society of London. Publication of his series of geological maps covering England and Wales began in

The Principle of Fossil Succession

Stratigraphy is the study of layered rocks, their fossils, and the time periods that they represent. Smith is called the founder of stratigraphy because of his recognition that fossils are arranged in a definite, consistent, vertical order.

The principle of fossil succession states that the sequence of fossils is so regular that it can be used to identify rocks formed during a particular interval of geologic time. Rocks of the same age have similar fossil assemblages. This principle has also been referred to as the principle of biologic succession, the law of faunal succession, and the law of biotal succession.

At about the same time that Smith published his discovery of fossil succession in England, Georges Cuvier and Alexandre Brongniart were coming to the same conclusion in France. The discovery of the time value of fossils paved the way for the development of the geologic time chart. Geologic time began to be subdivided into eras, periods, epochs, and smaller units based on differences in fossil assemblages. In the forty years after Smith's discovery of fossil succession, most of the main divisions of the geologic time chart were named, defined, and placed in sequence.

Smith observed the regularity of the vertical sequence of fossils in the geologic record more than fifty years before Charles Darwin published his theory of evolution. Today, fossil succession is interpreted to reflect the natural appearance and disappearance of species through time as a result of evolutionary and ecological changes.

Bibliography

The Earth Through Time. Harold L. Levin. 5th ed. Fort Worth, Tex.: Saunders College Publishing, 1996.

Evolutionary Biology. Eli C. Minkoff. Reading, Mass.: Addison-Wesley, 1984.

Historical Geology: The Science of a Dynamic Earth. Leigh W. Mintz. Columbus, Ohio: Charles E. Merrill, 1972.

Oasis in Space. Preston Cloud. New York: W. W. Norton, 1988.

Stratigraphy and Earth History. Marshall Kay and Edwin H. Colbert. New York: John Wiley & Sons, 1965.

1812, and the completed map, *A Delineation of the Strata of England and Wales, with Part of Scotland*, was exhibited in London in 1815. For his map, which was the first mineralogical map of England and Wales, Smith received an award of fifty guineas. Approximately four hundred copies of the map were produced and sold; fewer than one hundred are known to exist.

In 1816, Smith published *Strata Identified by Organized Fossils*, and he published *Stratigraphical System of Organized Fossils* in 1817. About this time, he fell into financial difficulties and sold his fossil collection to the British Museum; about two thousand of his fossils are still in the collections there. Smith produced geologic maps until 1824, and he lectured on geology despite his rheumatism and increasing deafness.

In 1831, Smith was awarded the first Wollaston Medal by the Geological Society of London "in consideration of his being a great original discoverer in English Geology; and especially for his having been the first, in this country, to discover and teach the identification of strata, and to determine their succession by means of their imbedded fossils."

Smith died suddenly from a chill on his way to a meeting in Birmingham, England, on August 28, 1839.

Bibliography

By Smith
Order of the Strata, and Their Imbedded Organic Remains, in the Neighbourhood of Bath: Examined and Proved Prior to 1799, 1799
A Delineation of the Strata of England and Wales, with Part of Scotland, 1815
Strata Identified by Organized Fossils, 1816-1819 (4 parts)
Stratigraphical System of Organized Fossils, Part I, 1817

(Library of Congress)

Memoirs of William Smith, LL.D., 1844 (John Phillips, ed.)

About Smith
"New Light on William Smith and His Work." L. R. Cox. *Proceedings of the Yorkshire Geological Society* 25 (1942).
"William Smith (1769-1838): A Bibliography of His Published Writings, Maps, and Geological Sections, Printed and Lithographed." Joan M. Eyles. *Journal of the Society for the Bibliography of Natural History* 5 (1969).
"William Smith: Some Aspects of His Life and Work." Joan M. Eyles. In *Toward a History of Geology*. Cambridge, Mass.: MIT Press, 1969.

(Pamela J. W. Gore)

George D. Snell

Areas of Achievement: Biology, genetics, and immunology

Contribution: A pioneer in immunogenetic research, Snell discovered the major histocompatibility complex, a genetic group responsible for controlling tissue graft rejection in mice.

Dec. 19, 1903	Born in Bradford, Massachusetts
1926	Earns a B.S. in biology from Dartmouth College
1930	Earns a Sc.D. in genetics from Harvard University
1935	Takes a position at the Jackson Laboratory in Bar Harbor, Maine
1952	Elected to the American Academy of Arts and Sciences
1962	Receives the Bertner Foundation Award
1967	Given an honorary M.D. by Charles University in Prague
1967	Awarded the Gregor Mendel Medal of the Czechoslovak Academy of Sciences
1970	Elected to the National Academy of Sciences
1974	Awarded an honorary Sc.D. by Dartmouth
1976	Receives the Gairdner Foundation Award
1978	Elected a member of the French Académie des Sciences
1978	Wins the Wolf Foundation Prize in Medicine
1980	Awarded the Nobel Prize in Physiology or Medicine
June 6, 1996	Dies in Bar Harbor, Maine

(AP/Wide World Photos)

Early Life

George Davis Snell, the son of an inventor and manufacturer of ignition systems for internal combustion engines, grew up in Brookline, Massachusetts. As a boy, he was interested in mathematics, physics, and astronomy, but his interests were not exclusively scientific. While growing up, he also enjoyed neighborhood games of football and baseball, and, in high school, he became a member of the Brookline band.

In 1926, Snell earned his B.S. in biology from Dartmouth College, where he was an excellent clarinet player and Dartmouth band member. He went on to Harvard University for a doctorate in science. There, he worked with Ernest Castle, a research biologist studying Mendelian principles of genetic inheritance.

While finishing his doctoral degree, Snell became an instructor at Dartmouth College. After earning his Sc.D. in genetics from Harvard in 1930, he taught for a year at Brown University. In 1931, he was awarded a National Research Council Fellowship and went to the University of Texas, Austin, to research the effects of X rays on mice. Snell's research was the first to show that X rays cause mutations in the structure of mammalian chromosomes.

The Jackson Laboratory
Snell took a research position in 1935 at the Roscoe B. Jackson Memorial Laboratory in Bar

---

The Major Histocompatibility Complex

In his studies of mice, Snell discovered the major histocompatibility complex (MHC), a group of closely linked genes that determines the rejection of grafted tissue.

The first step in the discovery of the MHC was Snell's correlation of physical signs on mice, which are known as markers, to tissue graft rejection. For example, in one specially crossed strain of mice, a kinked tail was found to be a marker of subsequent tissue graft rejection.

Snell developed what are called congenic mice in order to study the function of transplantation-related genes separately. Congenic mice are identical to one another except for the specific genetic locus that is to be investigated. This method of scientific investigation, which Snell invented, allowed him to track the effects of particular genes.

Snell identified a set of approximately ten genetic loci or sites that control the antigens responsible for graft acceptance at the cellular level. An antigen is a complex molecule that initiates and mediates antibody action in the immune system. In Snell's group of sites, one locus was found to play a dominant role in controlling antigens and subsequently producing immune resistance to tissue grafts.

Peter Gorer, of Guy's Hospital in London, had also been working on graft rejections in specially bred strains of mice. Through his research in serology, a blood-based rather than a genetic investigation, Gorer had also discovered antigens on cell surfaces that, depending on the particular strain of mice, determined the rejection of grafted tissue. He designated these particular antigens "Antigen II." When Gorer came to work with Snell for a year at the Jackson Laboratory, they found that the genetic coding of Gorer's serology-based Antigen II was located in the identical genetic loci that Snell had isolated.

Snell's concept of histocompatibility—a term he coined in 1948—refers to the genetically programmed antigens on the cell surface that are responsible for the rejection of foreign tissue. Snell and Gorer designated the site that controlled these antigens "H-2," a combination of Snell's histocompatibility and Gorer's Antigen II. Histocompatibility antigens determine the compatibility of tissues from two different bodies. Tissues that are compatible possess similar histocompatibility antigens on the surface of their cells. Tissues that are not compatible possess different histocompatibility antigens on cellular surfaces. Matching these antigens when transplanting tissue from one body to another is necessary if the tissue is not to be attacked and, therefore, rejected by the recipient's immune system.

Snell had thought that the H-2 locus was a single gene that controlled the action of histocompatibility antigens. Further research determined that the site was a complex set of interrelated genes and was designated the major histocompatibility complex. The MHC is located in mice on chromosome number 17.

Snell's discovery of the MHC group of genes helped make possible not only human organ transplants but also research into the human immune system itself. His research laid the foundation for the study of infectious diseases and for subsequent cancer and acquired immunodeficiency syndrome (AIDS) research. Because of the far-reaching impact of Snell's pioneering work, he is considered the founder of modern immunogenetics.

Bibliography
Biology of the Mouse Histocompatibility-2 Complex: Principles of Immunogenetics Applied to a Single System. Jan Klein. Berlin: Springer-Verlag, 1975.
The Natural History of the Major Histocompatibility Complex. Jan Klein. New York: John Wiley & Sons, 1986.

Harbor, Maine, where he remained for the rest of his career. In his early work at the Jackson Laboratory, he continued his research on X rays and genetic mutation in mice. Snell wanted to broaden his genetic inquiry, however, and began to conduct research into the genetic factors underlying organ and tissue transplantation. He wanted to isolate and identify the genetic loci responsible for the acceptance or rejection of grafted tissue.

In 1948, Snell and the English geneticist Peter A. Gorer, who was responsible for serologically based antigen research, reported their discovery of the H-2 locus ("H" for "histocompatibility" and "2" for "Antigen II"). This genetic site is responsible for cellular reactions that determine transplant rejection.

Further research showed that the H-2 group of linked genes is not formed at one genetic location but is made up of several different loci. Subsequently, the H-2 locus came to be known as the major histocompatibility complex (MHC). The MHC in mice controls cellular responses to grafted tissues recognized as foreign and determines successful transplantation.

Snell's research directly informed Jean Dausset's discovery of the genetically controlled histocompatibility system in humans in 1958, which led surgeons to begin performing tissue typing for organ transplants. Snell and Dausset, along with Stanley Nathenson, wrote a book called *Histocompatibility* (1976).

Snell's discovery of the MHC system in mice gave the study of cancer and tumor immunology a great boost in the 1950's. The relationship between immunology and the MHC generated significant research into how immune responses might be strengthened to fight infectious diseases and cancer. Along with J. R. Tennant, Snell conducted research that linked the success of viral leukemia in certain strains of mice to the function of the histocompatibility complex.

Scientific Career and Recognition

In 1947, Snell founded the scholarly journal *Immunogenetics*, and he remained its editor until 1980. From 1957 to 1968, he was the senior staff scientist at the Jackson Laboratory. He became emeritus senior staff scientist in 1968, officially retiring in 1973.

Snell's long list of awards, prizes, and honors includes the Hektoen Silver Medal of the American Medical Association and the Career Award of the National Cancer Institute. For discovering the genetic factors that laid the groundwork for the successful transplantation of tissues and organs in humans, Snell won the 1980 Nobel Prize in Physiology or Medicine. He shared the prize with American immunologist Baruj Benacerraf and French immunogeneticist Dausset.

Late in life, Snell expanded his area of inquiry once more, this time to include philosophy and ethics, publishing a book entitled *Search for a Rational Ethic* (1988). This book investigated social problems from the point of view of genetics and evolutionary theory, and it also looked at the impact of science and ethics on modern society. In recognition of a lifetime of scientific achievement, Maine's governor Angus King signed a proclamation declaring March 14-21, 1996, as "Dr. George D. Snell Week." Snell died on June 6, 1996.

Bibliography

By Snell

Biology of the Laboratory Mouse, 1941 (as editor)
Cell Surface Antigens: Studies in Mammals Other than Man, 1973 (with others)
Genetic and Biological Aspects of Histocompatibility Antigens, 1973 (with others)
Histocompatibility, 1976 (with Jean Dausset and Stanley Nathenson)
Search for a Rational Ethic, 1988

About Snell

Current Biography Yearbook 1986. Charles Moritz, ed. New York: H. W. Wilson, 1986.
"1980 Nobel Prize in Physiology or Medicine." Jean L. Marx. *Science* 210 (November 7, 1980).
"A Nobel Piece of Research." Matt Clark. *Newsweek* (October 20, 1980).
"We Have a Donor": The Bold New World of Organ Transplants. Mark Dowie. New York: St. Martin's Press, 1988.

(Mark Gray Henderson)

Frederick Soddy

Area of Achievement: Chemistry

Contribution: In collaboration with Ernest Rutherford, Soddy developed the disintegration theory of radioactive transformation. He also explored other concepts crucial to the subsequent understanding of radioactivity.

Sept. 2, 1877	Born in Eastbourne, Sussex, England
1898	Graduated from Oxford University
1900	Travels to Canada, where he collaborates with Ernest Rutherford at McGill University in Montreal
1903	Returns to England to work with Sir William Ramsay at University College in London
1903	Shows that helium is produced in the disintegration of radium
1904	Lectures about physical chemistry and radioactivity at Glasgow University
1910	Elected a Fellow of the Royal Society of London
1913	Awarded the Cannizzaro Prize in Rome
1913	Proposes the term "isotope"
1914	Teaches physical chemistry at the University of Aberdeen
1919	Appointed Lee Professor of Chemistry at Oxford
1921	Wins the Nobel Prize in Chemistry
1934	Given an honorary LL.D. degree by Glasgow University
1936	Retires from Oxford
Sept. 22, 1956	Dies in Brighton, Sussex, England

Early Life

Frederick Soddy was the last of seven children born to Benjamin Soddy, a successful London corn merchant, and Hannah (Green) Soddy. Frederick's mother died less than two years after his birth, and he was reared by an older sister. The family held strong Calvinist beliefs that, even though rejected by Soddy as an adult, seem to have shaped his attitudes about getting at the truth.

Soddy showed no interest in science until he came under the influence of the science master at Eastbourne College. Together with his mentor, Soddy published his first scientific paper at the age of seventeen. He entered Merton College at Oxford University in 1896 and was graduated with first-class honors in chemistry two years later.

Research into Radioactivity

After two more years of study at Oxford, Soddy applied for the post of professor of

(The Nobel Foundation)

chemistry at the University of Toronto in Canada and, without waiting for a response, traveled there to further his application in person. When he found no chance of success, he set out for home but stopped on the way at McGill University in Montreal.

There, in May, 1900, he accepted the position of junior demonstrator in chemistry. By September, he had met Ernest Rutherford, a professor of physics at McGill. With their combined knowledge of chemistry and physics, they embarked on a joint study of thorium and other recently discovered radioactive elements.

After this successful collaboration, Soddy returned to London in 1903 to work with Sir William Ramsay. They showed that helium is produced in the radioactive disintegration of radium. The following year, Soddy accepted a position as a lecturer in physical chemistry at Glasgow University.

Before taking his post, however, he went on a speaking tour through western Australia. In addition to delivering his lectures, he visited Australian mining towns, New Zealand, Ceylon, Honolulu, the Grand Canyon, and the 1904 St. Louis Exposition.

At Glasgow, Soddy continued his research into radioactivity. His major accomplishments included the development of the concept of isotopes, two or more forms of the same chemical element with different masses, and the displacement law, which traces the products of radioactive disintegration through their positions in the periodic table as a result of the emission of either alpha particles (helium nuclei) or beta particles (electrons).

Other Interests

In 1914, Soddy became a professor of chemistry at the University of Aberdeen. The outbreak of World War I interrupted his research into radioactivity, and he undertook technical work in chemistry for the war effort. The war also caused him to become more concerned about the connections of science with society at large, and he wondered "why so far the progress of science has proved as much a curse as a blessing to humanity."

When the war ended in 1918, Soddy became Lee Professor of Chemistry at Oxford University, but he did little further scientific work, turning instead to problems of economics and

The Disintegration Theory

In collaboration with Ernest Rutherford, Soddy proposed the idea that radioactive transformation occurs through the spontaneous disintegration of one radioactive element with the simultaneous production of another element, which may or may not be radioactive itself. This theory led to a radical change in scientific thinking about the stability of matter.

The element thorium was known to give off a radioactive gas, or emanation, which quickly loses its radioactivity. Rutherford and Soddy found that when thorium is precipitated out of a solution, it does not initially produce any emanation, while the material remaining in solution—termed thorium-X—does. After a month, the thorium regains its previous ability to produce the emanation, but the thorium-X loses its ability. Thus, Rutherford and Soddy demonstrated that the radioactive gas is given off by thorium-X rather than by thorium itself.

Their disintegration theory proposed that the transformation of thorium occurs through the spontaneous disintegration of some of its atoms to produce thorium-X, which in turn undergoes the disintegration of some of its atoms with the simultaneous production of the emanation, which is now known to be radon gas. Rutherford and Soddy also found that the rate of this radioactive disintegration follows a well-known law: The number of atoms that disintegrate at a particular time is directly proportional to the total number of such atoms present.

Bibliography

General Chemistry. P. W. Atkins and J. A. Beran. 2d ed. New York: Scientific American Books, 1992.
Radiochemistry and the Discovery of Isotopes. Alfred Romer, ed. New York: Dover, 1970.
"Some Recent Advances in Radioactivity." Frederick Soddy. *Contemporary Review* 83 (1903).
Understanding Radioactivity. Lorus J. Milne and Margery Milne. New York: Atheneum, 1989.

monetary policy. When his wife of twenty-eight years, Winifred Moller Beilby, died suddenly in 1936, he retired from teaching and spent the rest of his life writing on economic questions, trying to solve social problems, and traveling to out-of-the-way places. He died in Brighton in 1956 at the age of seventy-nine.

Bibliography
By Soddy
"Some Recent Advances in Radioactivity," *Contemporary Review*, 1903
Radio-Activity: An Elementary Treatise from the Standpoint of the Disintegration Theory, 1904
The Interpretation of Radium, 1909
The Chemistry of the Radio-Elements, 1911
Matter and Energy, 1912
Science and Life, 1920
"The Origins of the Conception of Isotopes," *Nature*, 1923
The Inversion of Science and a Scheme of Scientific Reformation, 1924
Wealth, Virtual Wealth, and Debt, 1926
Money Versus Man, 1931
The Interpretation of the Atom, 1932
The Role of Money, 1934
The Story of Atomic Energy, 1949

About Soddy
Atomic Transformation: The Greatest Discovery Ever Made, from Memoirs of Frederick Soddy. Muriel Howorth, ed. London: New World, 1953.
"Frederick Soddy." Alexander Fleck. *Biographical Memoirs of Fellows of the Royal Society* 3 (1957).
Pioneer Research on the Atom. Muriel Howorth. London: New World, 1958.
The Self-Splitting Atom: The History of the Rutherford-Soddy Collaboration. Thaddeus J. Trenn. London: Taylor & Francis, 1977.

(Richard E. Rice)

Arnold Sommerfeld

Area of Achievement: Physics
Contribution: Sommerfeld modified the circular electron orbits in Niels Bohr's model of the atom by proposing elliptical orbits for particular electrons. He increased the explanatory power of his model by using Albert Einstein's relativity theory to account for the fine structure of lines observed in atomic spectra.

Dec. 5, 1868	Born in Königsberg, Prussia (now Kaliningrad, Russia)
1891	Receives a doctorate from the University of Königsberg
1893-1894	Becomes an assistant in the Mineralogical Institute at the University of Göttingen
1894-1896	Serves as Felix Klein's assistant in mathematical physics
1895	Becomes a privatdozent (unpaid lecturer) in mathematics at Göttingen
1897-1910	Collaborates with Klein on a four-volume treatise on gyroscopes
1897	Becomes a professor of mathematics at the Mining Academy in Clausthal
1900	Named full professor of technical mechanics at the Technische Hochschule of Aachen
1906	Accepts the chair of theoretical physics at the University of Munich
1935-1940	Nazi scientists try to force him from his chair at the Institute for Theoretical Physics
1940	Retires from the institute
1943-1948	Publishes his course on theoretical physics in six volumes
Apr. 26, 1951	Dies in Munich, Germany

Early Life

Arnold Johannes Wilhelm Sommerfeld (pronounced "ZAWM-ur-fehlt") was born in Königsberg, East Prussia, in 1868. His father was a physician and a dedicated naturalist. Arnold attended the Altstädtisches Gymnasium, an academic high school where, in his words, he was "almost more interested in literature and history than in the exact sciences." After passing his *Abitur* (a qualifying examination for admission to a university) in 1886, he entered the University of Königsberg.

Initially, he continued his interests in philosophy and other humanistic subjects, but he eventually settled on mathematics, which then developed into a fascination with mathematical physics. David Hilbert, an outstanding mathematician who also published on mathematical physics, was one of his teachers, as was Franz Neumann, a mineralogist who had recently published an introduction to theoretical physics.

In his dissertation, Sommerfeld studied the mathematical basis of the harmonic analyzer, a mechanical instrument that meteorologists used to reduce observed temperature curves to

(California Institute of Technology)

trigonometric series. Sommerfeld's study established a pattern for his career—the use of advanced mathematics to solve complex physical problems.

After receiving his doctorate in 1891 from Königsberg, he spent the following academic year preparing to qualify as a Gymnasium teacher of mathematics and physics. In the fall of 1892, he began a year of obligatory military service. For the next decade, he periodically participated in military exercises, ultimately rising to the rank of lieutenant.

In 1893, attracted to the University of Göttingen as a place of "mathematical high culture," Sommerfeld obtained an assistantship in the Mineralogical Institute before becoming Felix Klein's assistant in the Mathematical Institute. Klein became his model in mathematical physics.

Advancing up the rungs of the academic ladder, Sommerfeld was appointed privatdozent (licensed university lecturer) in 1895, and in the next year he solved a diffraction problem for his *Habilitationsschrift* (inaugural dissertation). He lectured on advanced mathematics and physics for five terms at Göttingen before accepting a professorship in mathematics at the Mining Academy in Clausthal in 1897.

Although the courses that he taught were not as advanced as those at Göttingen, his salary was sufficient for him to marry Johanna Höpfner, the daughter of a Göttingen trustee who was a strong advocate of Klein's projects. Since Clausthal was close to Göttingen, Sommerfeld was able to continue his collaboration with Klein on a thousand-page study of gyroscopes.

In 1900, as a result of Klein's influence, Sommerfeld accepted the chair of applied mechanics with the rank of full professor at the Technische Hochschule of Aachen, where, through his investigations of turbulence in viscous fluids and of how certain fluids lubricate machine parts, he was able to demonstrate the great value of mathematics in solving traditional engineering problems.

The Institute for Theoretical Physics

In the summer of 1906, Sommerfeld received an invitation to occupy the chair of theoretical physics at the University of Munich that had

Sommerfeld's Quantum Theory of the Atom

Sommerfeld enhanced Niels Bohr's theory of the atom by using elliptical electron orbits and a relativistic treatment of the electron's speed to explain the detailed structure of spectral lines.

When scientists use powerful spectroscopes to study the light coming from atoms, they find a detailed but regular splitting of spectral lines. Bohr's theory of the atom, based on the assumptions that atoms can exist only in certain quantized energy states and that radiation emitted from the atom is caused by electron transitions between these states, was unable to account for the fine structure of spectral lines. Sommerfeld discovered two ideas that allowed him to do what Bohr could not.

Sommerfeld's first idea was to replace Bohr's circular orbits for electrons in atoms with elliptical orbits. In working out the mathematics of these elliptical orbits, Sommerfeld found that he needed two quantum numbers, which he called inner and outer, instead of Bohr's one. Sommerfeld presented his preliminary theory of the hydrogen atom in 1915 to the Bavarian Academy of Sciences, although he realized that the atom might be even more complicated than his proposal.

Sommerfeld's second idea was to use Albert Einstein's theory of relativity in his extension of Bohr's model. According to relativity, the faster an electron moves, the heavier it becomes. Starting with the equation of motion of an electron in an electric field of a stationary nucleus, Sommer-feld used the relativistic correction to devise a formula that quantitatively explained the fine structure of hydrogen's spectral lines. He published his theory of the relativistic one-electron atom in 1916.

When considered retrospectively, Sommerfeld's achievement was the climax of the old quantum theory. Bohr's theory as generalized by Sommerfeld would never be as powerful as it was in 1916, because Sommerfeld and Bohr based their treatment of the atom on an odd mix of quantum and traditional physics. What Sommerfeld called the musical language of spectroscopy, however, with its harmonious chords of integral relationships, would soon require a new interpretation—quantum mechanics—that would explain more satisfactorily than the old quantum theory the deep mysteries of the atom.

Bibliography

The Conceptual Development of Quantum Mechanics. Max Jammer. New York: McGraw-Hill, 1966.

Men Who Made a New Physics: Physicists and the Quantum Theory. Barbara Lovett Cline. Chicago: University of Chicago Press, 1987.

The Quantum Theory of Planck, Einstein, Bohr and Sommerfeld: Its Foundation and the Rise of Its Difficulties, 1900-1925. Jagdish Mehra and Helmut Rechenberg. Vol. 1, part 1 of *The Historical Development of Quantum Theory.* New York: Springer-Verlag, 1982.

The Strange Story of the Quantum. Banesh Hoffmann. 2d ed. New York: Dover, 1959.

remained vacant since 1899, when Ludwig Boltzmann left for Vienna. Sommerfeld agreed to accept the position if the university provided his Institute for Theoretical Physics with facilities for experimental research.

Although a laboratory might appear out of place in a theoretical institute, Sommerfeld's experimental facilities proved their worth in the spring of 1912 when Walter Friedrich, his new experimental assistant, and Paul Knipping demonstrated Max von Laue's prediction that a crystal will diffract X rays, one of the greatest discoveries of the twentieth century.

Sommerfeld's early work in Munich cen-tered on the quantum theory. This theory, initiated by Max Planck in 1900, used the idea that energy at the atomic level exhibits clumplike or "quantum" behavior. Sommerfeld became as convinced as Albert Einstein, however, that Planck unduly restricted the quantum idea to the interactions between radiation and atoms, whereas Sommerfeld believed that the quantum had much to tell physicists about the actions of electrons in atoms.

The Bohr-Sommerfeld Theory of the Atom

In the summer of 1913, Niels Bohr, the noted Danish physicist, published his first paper on the structure of atoms. Sommerfeld read it and began corresponding with Bohr, informing him that he would like to use Bohr's ideas to explain the changes in light emitted from atoms located in the field of powerful magnets (the Zeeman effect). Bohr concurred, and, by the winter semester of 1914-1915, Sommerfeld was lecturing to his students about his new theory of the fine structure of the spectral lines of hydrogen.

In the developed theory, which he published in 1916, Sommerfeld showed how Johannes Kepler's idea of elliptic planetary orbits and Einstein's idea of the relativistic increase of mass with velocity could be used to explain the motion of electrons in atoms. The formula that Sommerfeld derived quantitatively accounted for the splitting of lines observes in the Zeeman effect.

Sommerfeld's extension of Bohr's theory contributed to its widespread acceptance. In 1919, Sommerfeld showed how powerful this Bohr-Sommerfeld atomic theory was in his comprehensive exposition of the entire field, *Atombau und Spektrallinien* (*Atomic Structure and Spectral Lines*), 1923, the first edition becoming the bible of atomic physicists and the successive editions chronicling the progress of the field up to the birth of quantum mechanics.

Quantum Mechanics
Although he was not among the physicists who overthrew the old quantum theory that he and Bohr had done so much to establish, Sommerfeld was an enthusiastic supporter of the new quantum mechanics, particularly in Erwin Schrödinger's formulation, which was based on treating the electron as a wave. In 1929, Sommerfeld published one of the first textbooks on wave mechanics, and, in the late 1920's and early 1930's, he applied wave mechanics to the behavior of electrons in metals.

Throughout his career in Munich, Sommerfeld was an inspiring teacher of theoretical physics. Students from all over the world came to learn the old quantum theory and the new quantum mechanics from him, and many of them went on to have very distinguished careers, including Peter J. W. Debye and Laue

(from the early period), Wolfgang Pauli and Werner Heisenberg (from the early to the mid-1920's), and Linus Pauling and Hans Bethe (from the mid- to late 1920's). All these scientists went on to win Nobel Prizes.

The Years of Crisis
As anti-Semitism intensified in Germany, Sommerfeld courageously came to the defense of Einstein and other Jewish scientists. After the Nazis came to power in the 1930's, those wanting to extirpate what they called the "Jewish spirit" in German physics accused Sommerfeld and others of being "white Jews of science" and "agents of Judaism in German intellectual life." Sommerfeld managed to hold on to his post until 1940, when he was forced to retire. He was then forbidden from entering the Institute for Theoretical Physics.

During World War II, he devoted his time to preparing for publication his six-semester cycle of lectures on theoretical physics. At war's end, he resumed the directorship of the institute for several years. Early in April, 1951, while walking with his grandchildren, Sommerfeld stepped into the street and was struck by an automobile. A few weeks later, he died of the injuries that he suffered.

Bibliography
By Sommerfeld
Theorie des Kreisels, 1897-1910 (with Felix Klein)
Atombau und Spektrallinien, 1919 (*Atomic Structure and Spectral Lines*, 1923)
Three Lectures on Atomic Physics, 1926
Vorlesungen Über theoretische Physik, 1943-1952 (*Lectures on Theoretical Physics*, 1949-1956)

About Sommerfeld
"Arnold Johannes Wilhelm Sommerfeld." Max Born. *Obituary Notices of Fellows of the Royal Society of London* 8 (1952).
Physics of One- and Two-Electron Atoms: Proceedings of the Sommerfeld Centennial Memorial Meeting. Fritz Bopp and Hans Kleinpoppen, eds. Amsterdam: North Holland, 1969.

(*Robert J. Paradowski*)

Lazzaro Spallanzani

Areas of Achievement: Bacteriology, biology, earth science, and physiology

Contribution: A brilliant, meticulous experimenter, Spallanzani helped discredit spontaneous generation, demonstrated the importance of semen in fertilization, and showed digestion to be primarily a process of chemical dissolution.

Jan. 12, 1729	Born in Modena, Duchy of Modena (now Italy)
1744	Attends a Jesuit seminary in Reggio Emilia
1754	Earns a Ph.D. from the University of Bologna
1755	Takes a teaching post at the College of Reggio Emilia
1757	Appointed a lecturer at the University of Reggio Emilia
1757	Ordained a priest
1763	Accepts a teaching position at Modena University
1768	Elected a Fellow of the Royal Society of London
1769	Becomes a professor of natural history at the University of Pavia and director of Pavia's Museum of Natural History
1776	Elected to the Berlin Academy of Sciences
1783	Founds a marine zoological laboratory at Portovenere
1784	Turns down the chair of natural history at the University of Padua
1786	Receives a medal from Emperor Joseph II in Vienna
1788	Studies Mounts Etna and Vesuvius
Feb. 11, 1799	Dies in Pavia, Cisalpine Republic (now Italy)

(Library of Congress)

Early Life

Lazzaro Spallanzani (pronounced "spahl-lahn-TSAH-nee") was born in a small town in northern Modena (now Italy). At the age of fifteen, he enrolled in a Jesuit seminary in nearby Reggio Emilia, where he excelled academically.

In 1749, Spallanzani began taking courses at the University of Bologna, with the intention of becoming a lawyer like his father. After three years, however, he abandoned the study of law in order to pursue other interests, such as natural philosophy and theology. In 1757, he was ordained a priest. From that point on, he was known as "the Abbé Spallanzani."

Reggio Emilia and Modena

After earning a Ph.D. in 1754, Spallanzani held teaching positions, first at Reggio Emilia and then at Modena University. While at Modena, Spallanzani published *Saggio di osservazioni microscopiche relative al sistema della generazione dei Signori Needham e Buffon* (1765), in which he discredited the theory of spontaneous generation, which held that living organisms could arise from lifeless matter. Three years later, he published *Prodromo di un' opera da imprimersi*

Discrediting the Theory of Spontaneous Generation

Spallanzani showed that microorganisms will grow in broth only when it has been contaminated by contact with air.

In the late seventeenth century, the Italian physician Francesco Redi performed a number of experiments proving that flies are not generated spontaneously from rotting meat. In 1748, however, at the urging of the Comte de Buffon (Georges Louis Leclerc), the microscopist John Needham published experiments on boiled meat and vegetable juices that seemed to indicate that microorganisms, such as bacteria, do indeed arise by spontaneous generation.

Spallanzani refuted Needham's findings by using glass flasks with very slender necks that could be quickly sealed with a flame. He discovered that if broth is heated vigorously for one hour and then hermetically sealed in a glass container, it will remain sterile indefinitely. If the seal is broken, however, so that the broth is exposed to air, microorganisms soon proliferate in great numbers. Spallanzani's experiments not only discredited the theory of spontaneous generation but also would prove of practical importance to the canning industry.

Despite Spallanzani's efforts, many scientists continued to believe in spontaneous generation until Louis Pasteur finally put the issue to rest nearly a century later. Pasteur was so inspired by Spallanzani's example that he hung a portrait of his scientific hero in his apartment.

Bibliography

The History of Bacteriology. William Bulloch. London: Oxford University Press, 1960.

Microbe Hunters. Paul de Kruif. New York: Blue Ribbon Books, 1926.

Science and the Enlightenment. Thomas L. Hankins. Cambridge, England: Cambridge University Press, 1985.

---

sopra le riproduzioni animali (1768; *An Essay upon Animal Reproductions*, 1769), which described his experiments on tissue regeneration.

Pavia

In 1769, Spallanzani accepted a post at the University of Pavia. At that time, the city of Pavia was part of Austria. The Austrian government not only made Spallanzani a professor of natural history but also appointed him director of Pavia's Museum of Natural History. Thanks to Spallanzani's tireless efforts, the museum became one of the jewels of the Austrian Empire.

Not long after arriving at Pavia, Spallanzani performed a number of experiments in which he observed for the first time the minute vascular connections between arteries and veins in warm-blooded animals. In 1776, he published a book on the nature of animals and vegetables that contained more experimental evidence against spontaneous generation. That same year, he was elected to the Berlin Academy of Sciences by arrangement of Frederick the Great, king of Prussia.

Spallanzani turned his attention to gastric digestion. In a series of fascinating experiments, some of which were performed on himself, he demonstrated that digestion is a process of chemical dissolution, rather than one of grinding, fermentation, or putrefaction.

His findings on digestion were published in *Dissertazioni di fisica animale e vegetabile* (1780; *Dissertations Relative to the Natural History of Animals and Vegetables*, 1784). This treatise also contains an important section on the role of semen in the process of fertilization.

Final Years

In 1784, Spallanzani received an offer to move to the prestigious University of Padua. In order to retain him at Pavia, Emperor Joseph II increased Spallanzani's salary and allowed him to take an extended leave of absence so that he could travel to Constantinople. Spallanzani used this opportunity to accumulate new specimens for his museum of natural history.

With apparently little concern for the inherent dangers, Spallanzani journeyed to Sicily and southern Italy in 1788 in order to study the volcanoes Mount Etna and Mount Vesuvius at close range. His findings and courageous adventures are described in *Viaggi alle due Sicilie e in alcune parti dell'Appennino* (1792-1797; *Travels in the Two Sicilies, and Some Parts of the Apennines*, 1798).

Spallanzani died on February 11, 1799. Characteristically, his mind was on science until the end. In the posthumously published *Mémoires sur la respiration* (1803), he describes experiments, carried out in the 1790's, demonstrating that living tissues consume oxygen and release carbon dioxide.

Bibliography

By Spallanzani

Saggio di osservazioni microscopiche relative al sistema della generazione dei Signori Needham e Buffon, 1765

Prodromo di un' opera da imprimersi sopra le riproduzioni animali, 1768 (*An Essay upon Animal Reproductions*, 1769)

De' fenomeni della circolazione, 1773 (*Experiments upon the Circulation of the Blood Throughout the Vascular System*, 1801)

Opusculi di fisica animale e vegetabile, 1776 (*Tracts on the Nature of Animals and Vegetables*, 1799)

Dissertazioni di fisica animale e vegetabile, 1780 (*Dissertations Relative to the Natural History of Animals and Vegetables*, 1784)

Viaggi alle due Sicilie e in alcune parti dell'Appennino, 1792-1797 (*Travels in the Two Sicilies, and Some Parts of the Apennines*, 1798)

Mémoires sur la respiration, 1803

About Spallanzani

"Lazzaro Spallanzani." Aldo Massaglia. *Medical Life* 32 (May, 1925).

Lectures on the History of Physiology During the Sixteenth, Seventeenth, and Eighteenth Centuries. Michael Foster. 1901. Reprint. New York: Dover, 1970.

(William Tammone)

Wendell Meredith Stanley

Areas of Achievement: Cell biology and chemistry

Contribution: Stanley was the first person to isolate and characterize a virus, proving that it was a macromolecule.

Aug. 16, 1904	Born in Ridgeville, Indiana
1926	Graduated from Earlham College
1929	Earns a Ph.D. in chemistry from the University of Illinois
1930	Receives a National Research Council fellowship
1931	Joins the Rockefeller Institute for Medical Research
1935	Announces the isolation of tobacco mosaic virus (TMV)
1936	Disputes the discovery of nucleic acid in TMV
1941	Elected to the National Academy of Sciences
1943	Develops the first effective influenza vaccine
1946	Awarded the Nobel Prize in Chemistry
1948	Becomes director of the Virus Laboratory at the University of California
1959	Writes a public television series on viruses
1960	Obtains the complete amino acid sequence of TMV protein
1961	Publishes *Viruses and the Nature of Life*
June 15, 1971	Dies in Salamanca, Spain

Early Life

Wendell Meredith Stanley grew up in a small Indiana town, serving as delivery boy, reporter, and typesetter for his parents' newspaper. In 1922, he entered Earlham College. He excelled in athletics, making the all-Indiana football team in his senior year.

After receiving a B.S. in chemistry, Stanley traveled to the University of Illinois to visit the athletic department, planning to become a football coach. He also visited the chemistry department and was so impressed that he registered for its graduate program instead.

Stanley received a Ph.D. in 1929. In the same year, he married another chemistry graduate, Marion Staples Jay.

Research to 1932

By 1929, Stanley had thirteen published papers. His investigations focused on the synthesis and structure of the constituents of chaulmoogric oil, then the most promising chemical agents for treating leprosy.

(The Nobel Foundation)

After a postdoctoral year in Germany, he joined the Rockefeller Institute in New York. His superiors found him so outstanding in research that they invited him in 1932 to become the research chemist at the institute's new department of plant pathology in Princeton, New Jersey.

The Princeton Years

For the rest of his career, Stanley investigated the chemistry of plant viruses. In 1932, the nature of viruses was unknown. Scientists debated whether they were minute organisms or chemical molecules. In 1935, Stanley disclosed that the tobacco mosaic virus was a giant protein molecule. He then elaborated its physical and chemical properties and received the 1946 Nobel Prize in Chemistry for his accomplishments.

World War II diverted his research to the development of an influenza (flu) vaccine under government contract. He produced a multistrain, inactive virus vaccine. First used in a 1943 type A epidemic, it greatly reduced the incidence of influenza and became the first flu vaccine to be tested and proven effective.

The University of California

In 1948, Stanley became the director of the new Virus Laboratory at the University of California, Berkeley. He shaped it into the largest research center of its kind.

During the 1950's anticommunist crusade, the state of California imposed a loyalty oath to the United States on university faculty. Stanley led the resistance to the requirement, strongly defending those who refused to sign the oath and bringing the legal issues to the courts, where the oath was declared unconstitutional.

Stanley also became concerned about the communication of science to the public. He wrote a public television series on viruses in 1959 and a popular book, *Viruses and the Nature of Life* (1961).

In the 1960's, he devoted himself to the relationship of viruses to cancer and helped win passage of the 1971 National Cancer Act, a program to combat cancer through research and education. His death in 1971 followed a heart attack while he was attending an international conference on viruses in Spain.

The Nature of Viruses

Viruses are nucleoproteins with nucleic acid as their active agent.

In 1935, Stanley isolated and crystallized the tobacco mosaic virus (TMV) by chemically treating extracts of diseased plant juices. His tests indicated that the virus was a protein. In 1936, British scientists found his work inaccurate, because 6 percent of the virus was ribonucleic acid (RNA). Stanley argued that the RNA was not an integral part of the virus molecule, the protein alone being the viral agent.

The debate over the nature of the virus continued into the 1940's. Discoveries made in Stanley's Virus Laboratory vindicated the British scientists. A Stanley appointee, Heinz Fraenkel-Conrat, separated TMV into its protein and RNA parts in 1955. Examined with the electron microscope, the protein consisted of hollow cylinders and RNA in long, thin strands. Only the RNA displayed viral activity. In the intact nucleoprotein virus, the RNA was tucked inside the protein cylinders. The protein thus served as a protective shield for the fragile RNA strands.

Stanley demonstrated that a virus was a chemical molecule capable of being isolated and characterized by chemical methods. His achievement, modified with the recognition that nucleic acids played the central role in the virus molecule, opened and shaped research into the 1950's in the field of molecular biology.

Bibliography

"The Genetic Code of a Virus." Heinz Fraenkel-Conrat. *Scientific American* 211 (October, 1964).

The Thread of Life. John S. Kendrew. Cambridge, Mass.: Harvard University Press, 1968.

Virology. Heinz Fraenkel-Conrat, Paul Kimball, and Jay Levy. New York: Academic Press, 1988.

Bibliography

By Stanley

"Chemical Studies on the Virus of Tobacco Mosaic: VI. The Isolation from Diseased Turkish Tobacco Plants of a Crystalline Protein Possessing the Properties of Tobacco-Mosaic Virus," *Phytopathology*, 1936

"The Reproduction of Virus Proteins," *The American Naturalist*, 1938

"Chemical Properties of Viruses," *Scientific Monthly*, 1941

Problems and Trends in Virus Research, 1947 (with Thomas Rivers and Wilbur A. Sawyer)

"The Isolation and Properties of Crystalline Tobacco Mosaic Virus" in *Les Prix Nobel en 1947*, 1949

The Viruses: Biochemical, Biological, and Biophysical Properties, 1959 (as editor, with F. M. Burnet)

About Stanley

"Wendell Meredith Stanley." John T. Edsall. In *American Philosophical Society Yearbook 1971*. Philadelphia: American Philosophical Society, 1972.

Virus Hunters. Greer Williams. New York: Alfred A. Knopf, 1959.

"W. M. Stanley's Crystallization of the Tobacco Mosaic Virus." Lily E. Kay. *Isis* 77 (1986).

(Albert B. Costa)

Johannes Stark

Area of Achievement: Physics
Contribution: A master of experimental techniques, Stark won the Nobel Prize in Physics for his discovery of the splitting of spectral lines in an electric field.

Apr. 15, 1874	Born in Schickenhof, Bavaria, Germany
1897	Earns a doctorate in physics from the University of Munich
1900	Appointed a privatdozent at the University of Göttingen
1904	Founds the journal *Jahrbuch der Radioaktivität und Elektronik*
1906	Becomes a dozent at Technical College in Hannover
1909	Appointed a full professor at Technical College in Aachen
1913	Observes the effect named for him
1914	Awarded the Vahlbruch Prize by the Göttingen Academy of Sciences
1919	Receives the Nobel Prize in Physics
1920	Succeeds Wilhelm Wien at the University of Würzburg
1922	Resigns from Würzburg
1930	Joins the Nazi Party
1933	Appointed president of Physico-technical Reichsanstalt
June 21, 1957	Dies in Traunstein, Bavaria, West Germany

(The Nobel Foundation)

Early Life

Little is known of the early life of Johannes Stark (pronounced "shtahrk"), the son of a farmer. He attended local schools in Bayreuth and Regensburg, Germany, and entered the University of Munich in 1894, receiving his doctoral degree in physics in 1897. After pass-ing a couple of examinations required for teaching mathematics, he began work in 1897 at Munich. Three years later, he became an assistant to Eduard Riecke at the University of Göttingen.

Even at this early stage of his career, Stark's strengths and weaknesses were already visible. His colleagues observed that his experimental skills were remarkable but that he was lacking in the area of translating physical situations into mathematical models. Stark's first book, on the electric conduction of gases, appeared in 1902.

Successes and Disagreements

By the first few years of the twentieth century, Stark was one of the researchers most familiar with the details of particle physics. One of the initial successes of his career was the discovery of an optical equivalent of the Doppler effect (a shift in frequency dependent on the motion of the source) in canal rays, a beam of positive particles. Even while he was achieving this distinction, however, Stark was liable to errors of interpretation and frequently lost theoretical arguments in physics journals.

He left the Technical College in Hanover as a result of disagreements with his supervisor and came to the Technical College of Aachen in 1909. There, he had his greatest success in 1913 with the discovery of the splitting of spectral lines in an electric field. This result had been thought plausible because of the Zeeman effect, splitting in a magnetic field. Stark succeeded where many others had failed, which was the major contribution to his Nobel Prize in Physics in 1919.

From Academia to Politics

In 1920, Stark was able to parlay his Nobel Prize into a position at the University of Würzburg, succeeding the distinguished physicist Wilhelm Wien. Within two years, however, Stark had resigned. He never took another academic position and instead returned to the region of his birth to help promote the porcelain industry. From that time forward, his connec-

tions with the scientific community were via politics rather than research.

Stark joined with the physicist Philipp Lenard in a campaign against what he saw as the "Jewish" and "dogmatic" elements in physics. Stark joined the Nazi Party in 1930 and sought to become the leader of the physics community in Germany after it was purged of its Jewish members following Adolf Hitler's rise to power in 1933. In fact, Stark was appointed president of two national scientific research institutions in 1933 and 1934.

Stark's success was short-lived, however, as his inability to work with others prevented him from profiting from political alliances. Before World War II, he retired to the country and lived in obscurity until his death in 1957.

Bibliography

By Stark
Die Elektrizität in Gasen, 1902
Die Prinzipien der Atomdynamik, 1910-1915 (3 vols.)
Die Gegenwärtige Krisis in der Deutschen Physik, 1922
Die Axialität der Lichtemission und Atomstruktur, 1927

Splitting Spectral Lines

The characteristic spectra of chemical elements are altered by the presence of an electric field.

Stark discovered what is now known as the Stark effect, a crucial experimental result that helped to lead to the acceptance of quantum mechanics. It had been known that chemical elements emitted light in certain characteristic frequencies that could be used to identify the elements. For example, helium was identified thanks to its frequencies of emitted light, called its spectrum. Even under ordinary circumstances, light is emitted at more than one frequency.

When the element is in the presence of a magnetic field, however, there is a further multiplication of these spectral lines. This effect had been discovered by Pieter Zeeman, and, in view of the similarity of behavior exhibited in the presence of magnetic and electric fields, it was expected

that the same sort of multiplication would take place for electric fields. Stark successfully identified this splitting for hydrogen, the simplest atom and therefore the most studied.

The Stark effect furnished an example of a phenomenon that could be more readily explained by the new theory of quantum mechanics than by classical physics. It remains a useful example ordinarily included in introductions to quantum mechanics.

Bibliography

Molecular Beams. N. F. Ramsey. Oxford, England: Oxford University Press, 1969.
Physics of the Atom. M. R. Wehr, J. A. Richards, and T. W. Adair. 4th ed. Palo Alto, Calif.: Addison-Wesley, 1985.
The Theory of Atomic Spectra. E. V. Condon and G. H. Shortley. Cambridge, England: Cambridge University Press, 1970.

Atomstruktur und Atombindung, 1928
Adolf Hitler und die Deutsche Forschung, 1935
Jüdische und Deutsche Physik, 1941

About Stark

"Johannes Stark." In *The Nobel Prize Winners: Physics*, edited by Frank N. Magill. Pasadena, Calif.: Salem Press, 1989.

Scientists Under Hitler. Alan D. Beyerchen. New Haven, Conn.: Yale University Press, 1977.

(Thomas Drucker)

Ernest Henry Starling

Areas of Achievement: Medicine and physiology

Contribution: Starling determined that pressure and protein concentrations regulate the distribution of water and dissolved substances between blood and tissues. He also studied the mechanisms that allow the heart to adjust the strength of each contraction to match demand.

Apr. 17, 1866	Born in London, England
1887	Appointed demonstrator in physiology at Guy's Hospital Medical School
1889	Receives a bachelor of medicine degree
1890	At University College, works with physiologist William Bayliss
1892	Works with Rudolf Heidenhain in Germany
1896	Describes the regulation of fluid exchange in tissues
1899	Appointed to the Jodrell Professorship at University College
1899	Elected to the Royal Society of London
1905	Introduces the term "hormone"
1909	Delivers a Harvey Lecture in New York
1914	Publishes an article on the factors determining heart output
1914-1918	During World War I, serves in the British army working on chemical warfare and food problems
1922	Accepts the Royal Society's Foulerton Research Professorship
May 2, 1927	Dies on a cruise ship and is buried in Kingston, Jamaica

Early Life

Ernest Henry Starling was born in London, England, as the son of a barrister of fundamentalist convictions who served most of his career in India, returning to England to his family every three years or so. Starling and his siblings were brought up by their mother.

Although his family had only limited resources, Starling had an excellent education and was admitted in 1882, at the age of sixteen, to Guy's Hospital Medical School. He had a brilliant academic record and received his bachelor of medicine degree in 1889, at the age of twenty-two.

Starling had spent a summer in Heidelberg, Germany, where he began to focus on physiology, probably because it offered the basis of a more scientific and less empirical approach to clinical medicine.

Work with Bayliss

Starling was inventive in his research, with tendencies to speculate. These tendencies were moderated by renowned physiologist William Bayliss, who was more cautious and methodical. Their collaboration led to the discovery of secretin, a hormone (a term coined by Starling) of the gastrointestinal tract. Their later collaboration centered on the heart and the circulation.

Focus on Capillaries

A brief return to work with Rudolf Heidenhain alerted Starling to problems related to the small vessels, the capillaries, and their permeability properties. He also studied lymph production and the effects of hydrostatic pressures and protein concentrations on water and small solute transfers across the capillaries.

Much of Starling's research activities focused on these matters. The results of his studies and his interpretations of them were generally accepted and utilized, even more than a hundred years after they were first reported in 1896. They are referred to as Starling's hypothesis.

Jodrell Professor at University College

From 1899 on, Starling had the benefit of collaborating with Bayliss. He changed his emphasis once again, this time from the capillaries

(Library of Congress)

to the motor of the circulation, the heart. His studies involved both the factors controlling heart action and the responses of the heart to increasing loads, as in exercise.

His experiments were highly ingenious in design and quite innovative in concept. He was able to keep isolated organs such as the heart and kidneys functioning outside the body for prolonged periods. In this manner, he eliminated factors that would otherwise have made interpretations of results more difficult, if not questionable.

Service in World War I

Starling was made director of research at the college of the Royal Army Medical Corps, where he worked on the means of protection against war gases such as chlorine. He also played a role in food and nutrition as a delegate to the Inter-Allied Food Commission. It

Fluid Distribution and the Action of the Heart

A necessary complement to Starling's studies of fluid distribution in tissues was to determine how the heart action provides the hydrostatic pressure in the capillaries.

Starling demonstrated unequivocally that the factors determining the distribution of water and small solutes, such as ions, between blood and tissues are the hydrostatic and colloid (protein) osmotic pressures in the two compartments.

An increase of hydrostatic pressure in the blood moves fluid (water plus small solutes) from blood to tissues, as does a decrease of colloid osmotic pressure. Conversely, an increase of colloid osmotic pressure in the blood moves fluid from tissues to blood. At equilibrium, the difference of the osmotic and hydrostatic pressures in blood is equal to that difference in tissue fluid. If protein leaks across the capillaries, the effect of the protein concentrations is diminished.

Hydrostatic pressure is created by the action of the heart. In isolated hearts, Starling found that the energy set free on the passage from the resting (diastolic) to the contracted (systolic) phase of the heart depends on the length of the muscle fibers. Thus, a heart receiving more blood per unit time is stretched and responds by ejecting more forcibly the blood that it contains. This response to work load accounts for the heart's ability to pump more blood during exercise. With too high a load (too much stretching), the ability to pump blood drops from its peak and heart failure may follow.

The fluid distribution relationship is known as Starling's hypothesis and the heart action as Starling's law of the heart.

Bibliography

Edema. Norman C. Staub and Aubrey E. Taylor, eds. New York: Raven Press, 1984.

"One Hundred Years of Starling's Hypothesis." C. C. Michel. *News in Physiological Sciences* 11 (1996).

Textbook of Physiology. Arthur C. Guyton. 8th ed. Philadelphia: W. B. Saunders, 1991.

---

was a difficult time for Starling, however, who had to accommodate military bureaucratic stodginess. He finally resigned his commission as an officer.

Later Years

After his military experiences, Starling's scientific activities declined. He was concerned that education in Britain was neglected in comparison to the emphasis placed on it in other countries. He called for education reform—or "even revolution." He was not successful in achieving that goal, but he was able to bring about a much more scientific approach to clinical medicine. In this effort, his studies in physiology complemented the clinical approaches of Sir William Osler.

Bibliography

By Starling
"On the Absorption of Fluid from Connective Tissue Space," *Journal of Physiology, London*, 1896

"The Arris and Gale Lectures on Some Points in the Pathology of Heart Disease: I. On the Compensatory Mechanism of the Heart"; "II. The Effects of Heart Failure on the Circulation"; "III. On the Causation of Dropsy in Heart Disease," *Lancet*, 1897

"The Mechanism of Pancreatic Secretion," *Journal of Physiology*, 1902 (with William Bayliss)

The Fluids of the Body, 1909

"On the Mechanical Factors Which Determine the Output of the Ventricles," *Journal of Physiology*, 1914 (with S. W. Patterson)

Linacre Lecture on the Law of the Heart, 1918

About Starling
"Ernest Starling: His Contribution to Medicine." Ralph Colp, Jr. *Journal of the History of Medicine* 7 (1952).

"Obituary: Ernest Henry Starling, C.M.G., M.D., F.R.S." C. J. Martin. *British Medical Journal*, May 14, 1927.

(Francis P. Chinard)

Jack Steinberger

Area of Achievement: Physics
Contribution: Steinberger won the Nobel Prize in Physics for creating the first laboratory-made beam of neutrinos and discovering a new type of neutrino, which contributed to the development of the "Standard Model" classification of matter.

May 25, 1921	Born in Bad Kissingen, Germany
1934	Immigrates to the United States
1942	Earns a B.S. at the University of Chicago
1948	Receives a Ph.D. in physics at Chicago
1948-1949	Serves as a member of the Institute for Advanced Study at Princeton University
1949-1950	Works as a research assistant at the University of California, Berkeley
1950-1971	Appointed Higgins Professor of Physics at Columbia University
1962	Conducts experiments on neutrinos at Brookhaven National Laboratory
1968	Serves as a senior experimentalist at the Conseil Européen pour la Recherche Nucléaire (CERN) in Geneva, Switzerland
1986	Retires
1988	Presented with the National Medal of Science
1988	Awarded the Nobel Prize in Physics jointly with Leon Max Lederman and Melvin Schwartz

Early Life

Jack Steinberger was born in Germany in 1921. He and his brother, the sons of a Jewish community leader and cantor, fled to the United States in 1934 after the Nazis took power in Germany. They lived in Chicago, where the rest of their family would later join them with the help of their host, Barnard Faroll, a grain broker.

Steinberger studied chemical engineering at the Illinois Institute of Technology and then earned a B.S. in physics from the University of Chicago. After the United States entered World War II, he enlisted in the Army and was assigned to the Radiation Laboratory at the Massachusetts Institute of Technology (MIT), where he worked on radar bombsights and studied physics. Steinberger subsequently returned to the University of Chicago to pursue his interest in muons (semistable electrical particles), neutrinos, and the weak nuclear force, subsequently earning his doctorate in physics in 1948.

(The Nobel Foundation)

After one year as a physics professor at the University of California, Berkeley, Steinberger moved on to Columbia University, where, as Higgins Professor of Physics, he would eventually conduct the work on neutrinos that would lead to the Nobel Prize in Physics.

High-Energy Neutrino Experiments

The roots of Steinberger's Nobel Prize lay in a coffee-break conversation at Columbia. Steinberger, his former student Melvin Schwartz, and Leon Max Lederman were all hoping to examine the effect of weak nuclear forces at

The First Laboratory-Made Neutrino Beam

In order to study the weak nuclear force, Steinberger and two colleagues created a beam of high-energy subatomic particles called neutrinos.

The history of the first laboratory-made neutrino beam began with the problem of missing energy from beta decays—a riddle that called into question the law of the conservation of energy. In 1931, Austrian physicist Wolfgang Pauli proposed the existence of a new particle to account for the missing energy. Enrico Fermi developed the idea further and, in 1932, named the particle the neutrino, an Italian word meaning "small neutral particle." Although it remained undetected because of its lack of electrical charge and its extremely small mass, the neutrino became an essential element in the theoretical explanation of weak forces and some of the decay processes attributed to them.

Physicists considered neutrinos to be potentially valuable tools for studying this weak nuclear force—one of the fundamental forces in elementary particles. They were thwarted, however, by their inability to detect neutrinos in controlled situations. In 1956, however, two physicists detected a neutrino in a laboratory experiment, thus opening up new research possibilities.

Interested in studying the weak nuclear force, Steinberger and two of his colleagues at Columbia University, Leon Max Lederman and Melvin Schwartz, devised an experiment to produce and detect high-energy neutrino beams of a magnitude sufficient to penetrate an atomic nucleus.

Using the accelerator at the Brookhaven National Laboratory, the three physicists fired beams of protons at 15 billion electronvolts toward a target of beryllium metal. The resulting collision split the beryllium nuclei into their constituent protons and neutrons and created other forms of matter, known as pions, which immedi-

ately decay into muons and high-energy neutrinos. To filter out everything except the neutrinos from the spray of subatomic particles, they had erected a barrier of steel 40 feet thick, most of which came from the scrapped battleship USS *Missouri*.

The strong and electromagnetic forces trapped the protons, neutrons, and other material within the steel. Lacking an electrical charge or detectable mass, however, the neutrinos passed through the steel, striking a detector consisting of aluminum plating weighing 10 tons. The detector revealed traces of the rare collisions of neutrinos and aluminum atoms, thus confirming the creation of a high-energy, high-density neutrino beam.

In conducting this experiment, Steinberger, Lederman, and Schwartz also made a discovery that would contribute to the creation of a new theory regarding the structure of matter. Previously, the only known neutrino was produced by the kind of radioactive decay that also produced an electron. Most of the neutrinos arising from their experiment, however, were accompanied by a completely different kind of particle dubbed the mu-meson, or muon. Theorists used this and other evidence to develop the Standard Model theory according to which matter is categorized into three "generations" of different kinds of components, the second generation of which was brought to light by the collaborative work of Steinberger, Lederman, and Schwartz.

Twenty-six years later, the three scientists were recognized with the Nobel Prize in Physics for their work, which charted new paths in particle physics research and theory.

Bibliography
Twentieth Century Physics. L. M. Brown, A. Pais, and B. Pippard, eds. Vol. 2. New York: AIP Press, 1995.

high energies. They were also concerned with the elusive, recently detected neutrino.

A generally felt theoretical crisis existed at the time because of the great proliferation of subatomic particles being discovered. Many physicists thought that a key piece of the puzzle was missing, one that would help to introduce some order in the collection of more than a hundred pions, muons, kaons, and other particles.

Schwartz suggested to his colleagues the idea of a laboratory-made beam of neutrinos for use in high-energy particle research. The three physicists subsequently conducted their experiments at the Brookhaven National Laboratory during the years from 1960 to 1962. They succeeded in their attempt to create a beam of neutrinos usable for research, and they also discovered a new type of neutrino. For these results, they shared the Nobel Prize in 1988.

Steinberger was awarded the National Medal of Science the same year.

Work With CERN
In 1968, Steinberger left to take a post at the Conseil Européen pour la Recherche Nucléaire (CERN), or European Organization for Nuclear Research, in Geneva, Switzerland, where he continued to conduct research in high-energy physics. He participated in experiments on the properties of kaons, the interactions of

neutrinos at high energies, the quark structure of nucleons, and the spin and parity of mesons, pions, and some strange particles.

Steinberger, described by his colleagues as one of the most gifted experimentalists in high-energy physics, officially retired in 1986, but he continued to conduct experiments in elementary particles.

Bibliography
By Steinberger
"Observation of High-Energy Neutrino Reactions and the Existence of Two Kinds of Neutrinos," *Physical Review Letters*, 1962 (with others)

"A Nuclear-Weapon-Free World: Is It Desirable? Is It Necessary?" (with Essam Galal and Mikhail Milstein) in *A Nuclear-Weapon-Free World: Desirable? Feasible?*, 1993 (Steinberger, Joseph Rotblat, and Bhalchandra Udgaonkar, eds.)

About Steinberger
"Jack Steinberger." In *The Nobel Prize Winners: Physics*, edited by Frank N. Magill. Pasadena, Calif.: Salem Press, 1989.

"Three American Physicists Get Nobel for Landmark Work." *The New York Times*, October 20, 1988.

(Rosa Alvarez Ulloa)

Otto Stern

Area of Achievement: Physics
Contribution: Stern developed molecular beam methods that he used to verify the wave nature of particles, to show that the orbital angular momentum of atomic electrons is quantized, and to measure the magnetic moments of the proton and the deuteron.

Feb. 17, 1888	Born in Sohrau, Upper Silesia, Germany (now Zory, Poland)
1912	Earns a Ph.D. in physical chemistry from the University of Breslau
1912-1913	Studies under Albert Einstein
1914-1918	Serves in the German army in a technical capacity during World War I
1921-1924	Publishes a series of papers describing the results of the Stern-Gerlach experiments
1921	Named associate professor of theoretical physics at the University of Rostock
1923	Appointed professor of physical chemistry and laboratory director at the University of Hamburg
1933	Resigns in protest against the Nazi persecution of Jews and emigrates to the United States
1933	Appointed a research professor of physics at the Carnegie Institute of Technology
1943	Awarded the Nobel Prize in Physics
1946	Elected to the National Academy of Sciences
Aug. 17, 1969	Dies in Berkeley, California

Early Life

Otto Stern (in German, pronounced "shtehrn") was born in 1888, the first of five children who would be born to Oskar Stern and Eugenie Rosenthal. Oskar came from a prosperous Jewish family of grain merchants and flour millers. As a college student, the family prosperity allowed Otto to wander among the universities of Germany, pursuing whatever interested him.

Stern attended lectures on theoretical physics by Arnold Sommerfeld, a premier physicist of the day. He was fascinated by Ludwig Boltzmann's works on molecular theory and statistical mechanics and by the works on thermodynamics of Rudolf J. E. Clausius and Walther Hermann Nernst. Eventually, Stern returned to the University of Breslau to pursue his interests in thermodynamics and to earn a doctorate in physical chemistry.

Stern the Theoretician

From 1912 to 1919, Stern's scientific activity was as a theorist. For the first two years, he worked as a postdoctoral assistant to Albert Einstein, who became a lifelong friend. Although Einstein was a theorist, perhaps the most important lessons that Stern learned from Einstein were which questions to ask and what experiments to attempt in order to find the answers. Stern and Einstein coauthored a paper showing that molecular motion need not cease at a temperature of absolute zero. Stern also published a paper in which he calculated the absolute entropy (disorder) of a monatomic gas.

During World War I, Stern served in the German army, from 1914 to 1918. As a meteorologist in Poland, his primary duty was to record instrument readings twice a day. To occupy his time, he prepared a paper on the energy of a system of coupled point masses. During the last part of the war, Stern was transferred to the University Berlin to do military research under Nernst. While there, he met two first-rate experimentalists, James Frank and Max Volmer. They became lifelong friends and probably influenced Stern's decision to become an experimentalist.

Stern the Experimentalist

From 1919 until his retirement in 1945, Stern worked primarily as an experimentalist. Following the war, Stern moved to the Institute for

Experimental Physics in Frankfurt and, while there, did a beautiful experiment that measured the velocity distribution of gas atoms. Next, Stern joined colleague Walter Gerlach in a series of experiments proving that the electrons which orbit the nucleus of an atom can do so only in certain fixed directions in space. Later, at the University of Hamburg, he used molecular beams to demonstrate the wave nature of matter and to measure the magnetic moments of the proton and the deuteron.

Stern, a Jew himself, resigned his position at Hamburg in 1933 to protest the Nazi persecution of his Jewish colleagues. He emigrated to the United States and accepted a position at the Carnegie Institute of Technology. While there, he continued to refine his previous experiments, but he was hampered by the lack of sufficient funding.

Stern was elected to the National Academy

Molecular Beam Methods

Stern showed that molecular beams can be used to measure several fundamental properties of matter.

Molecular beam experiments are important because their results are easy to interpret. In the ideal beam, the molecules are uncharged and are far enough apart so that they do not interact with one another.

A typical molecular beam apparatus consists of three parts: a beam source, an experiment region, and a detector. The beam source may be an electrically heated crucible inside a vacuum chamber. Source material such as silver is placed in the crucible and heated to produce silver vapor. A tiny hole allows a stream of silver vapor to escape from the oven into the surrounding vacuum chamber. The stream then passes through collimating slits into the experiment region.

In one experiment, Stern placed two rotating toothed wheels in the beam path. Only atoms with a certain speed (which could be calculated) could pass through the gaps between the teeth of both wheels. Placing a detector beyond the second wheel allowed Stern to measure how many silver atoms had a particular speed. In this fashion, he confirmed the stunning prediction of James Clerk Maxwell, who had used a simple model of gas atoms as bouncing balls to calculate the fraction of gas atoms that should have a particular speed.

An early model of the atom had pictured electrons orbiting the atomic nucleus as planets orbit the sun. By 1920, scientists realized that such a picture was vastly oversimplified. They learned that both the energy of an electron and its angular momentum could take on only certain values, or quantities. (This is the origin of the term "quantum.") Theory also suggested that the orbital plane of an electron could make only a few specific angles with the equator of the atom; this is called space quantization.

Stern and his colleague Walter Gerlach placed a magnet in the experiment region of their molecular beam apparatus. One pole of the magnet had a V-shaped cross section, and the other had a groove cut into it in order to produce a nonuniform field.

As the silver atoms passed between the poles, they were expected to align themselves with the magnetic field just as compass needles do. In the absence of space quantization, the atoms should orient themselves uniformly over a range of angles and form a single broad spot on the detector. With space quantization, the beam should be split into two distinct parts.

Photographic film was used as a detector, since it would be "exposed" by the silver atoms just as if light had struck it. When the film was developed, it did show a split beam. Molecular beam experiments proved so useful that they are still used to make sensitive measurements.

Bibliography

From X-Rays to Quarks. Emilio Segrè. San Francisco: W. H. Freeman, 1980.

"Otto Stern: The Wave Aspect of Matter and the Third Quantum Number." Rom Harré. In *Great Scientific Experiments*. Oxford, England: Phaidon Press, 1981.

"Space Quantization: Otto Stern and Walter Gerlach." In *The World of the Atom*, edited by Henry A. Boorse and Lloyd Motz. Vol. 2. New York: Basic Books, 1966.

(The Nobel Foundation)

of Sciences in 1945 and retired to Berkeley, California, that same year. Awarded the 1943 Nobel Prize in Physics, he did not deliver his acceptance speech until 1946, after World War II had ended. He died on August 17, 1969, at the age of eighty-one.

Bibliography
By Stern
"Zur kinetishchen Theorie des Dampfdrucks einatomiger fester Stoffe und über die Entropiekonstante einatomiger Gase," *Physikalische Zeitschrift*, 1913

"Eine direkte Messung der thermischen Molekulargeschwindigkeit," *Zeitschrift für Physik*, 1920

"Ein Weg zur experimentellen Prüfung der Richtungsquantelung im Magnetfeld," *Zeitschrift für Physik*, 1921

"Der experimentelle Nachweis des magnetischen Moments des Silberatoms," *Zeitschrift für Physik*, 1921 (with W. Gerlach)

"Der experimentelle Nachweis der Richtungsquantelung im Magnetfeld," *Zeitschrift für Physik*, 1922 (with Gerlach)

"Das magnetische Moment des Silberatoms," *Zeitschrift für Physik*, 1922 (with Gerlach)

"Über die Richtungsquantelung im Magnetfeld," *Annalen der Physik*, 1924 (with Gerlach)

"The Method of Molecular Rays" in *Nobel Lectures, 1942-1962*, 1964

About Stern
Dictionary of Scientific Biography. Charles Coulston Gillispie, ed. Vol. 13. New York: Charles Scribner's Sons, 1976.

"Otto Stern." In *The Nobel Prize Winners: Physics*, edited by Frank N. Magill. Pasadena, Calif.: Salem Press, 1989.

"Otto Stern: A Biographical Memoir." Emilio Segrè. In *Biographical Memoirs*. Vol. 43. Washington. D.C.: National Academy of Sciences of the United States, 1973.

(Charles W. Rogers)

Nettie Maria Stevens

Areas of Achievement: Biology, cell biology, and genetics

Contribution: Stevens demonstrated that sex is determined by a particular chromosome. She was the first person to establish that chromosomes exist as paired structures in body cells and the first to ascertain that certain insects have supernumerary chromosomes.

July 7, 1861	Born in Cavendish, Vermont
1880	Graduated from Westford Academy
1883-1896	Works as a schoolteacher and a librarian
1892	Enters the Normal School in Westfield, Massachusetts
1899	Earns a B.A. from Stanford University
1900	Earns an M.A. from Stanford
1901-1902	Receives a fellowship to study abroad
1903	Earns a Ph.D. from Bryn Mawr College
1904	Named a Reader in Experimental Morphology
1905	Publishes a monograph that identifies the X and Y chromosomes
1905	Awarded the Ellen Richards Research Prize of $1,000 by the association maintaining the American Women's Table at the Naples Zoological Station
1905-1912	Awarded the rank of Associate in Experimental Morphology
1908-1909	Studies at the University of Würzburg with Theodor Boveri
May 4, 1912	Dies in Baltimore, Maryland

Early Life

Nettie Maria Stevens was the second of three children born to Ephraim and Julia Stevens. Aside from the fact that her father was a carpenter and sawyer, little is known of her family background and the first three decades of her life. She worked as a schoolteacher and a librarian for many years before continuing her education.

In September, 1892, at the age of thirty-one, Stevens entered the Normal School in Westfield, Massachusetts; she transferred as an undergraduate to Stanford University four years later. Majoring in physiology, she received her B.A. and M.A. from Stanford in 1899 and 1900, respectively.

Further Education

As an undergraduate, Stevens spent three summers at the Hopkins Seaside Laboratory in Pacific Grove, California. Her research began on the life cycle of *Boveria*, a protozoan parasite of sea cucumbers. Her findings were published in the *Proceedings of the California Academy of Sciences* in 1901.

(Science Photo Library)

The Chromosomal Determination of Sex

Stevens' most important research dealt with chromosomes and their relation to heredity.

When Stevens began her work, Gregor Johann Mendel's laws on the transmission of hereditary factors had been rediscovered in 1900, and the studies of Theodor Boveri and Walter S. Sutton on chromosome behavior had suggested that Mendel's factor might actually be associated with chromosomes. It is not known exactly when Stevens became interested in the problem of chromosomes and sex determination. In 1903, however, she described one of her research interests as the "histological side of the problems of heredity connected with Mendel's Principles of Heredity."

Stevens and Edmund Beecher Wilson worked independently to demonstrate that the sex of an organism is determined by a particular chromosome. During the period of Stevens' research, investigators were exploring the relationship between chromosomes and heredity. Although the behavior of the chromosomes had been experimentally confirmed, no trait had been traced from the chromosomes of the parent to those of the offspring, nor had a specific chromosome been linked with a specific characteristic.

Working with the mealworm (*Tenebrio molitor*) using Mendel's laws of inheritance, Stevens confirmed that males produce two kinds of sperm, one carrying a large X chromosome and the other carrying a small Y chromosome. The unfertilized eggs, however, were all alike in possessing two X chromosomes. Stevens suggested that eggs fertilized by sperm carrying X chromosomes produce females and those eggs fertilized by sperm carrying Y chromosomes produce males. Although, Stevens' hypothesis was not universally accepted by biologists at the time, the theory of sex determination has now been proven and this discovery is considered to be of profound importance.

Bibliography

The Cell in Development and Heredity. Edmund B. Wilson. 3d ed. New York: Macmillan, 1937.

A History of Cytology. Arthur Hughes. London: Abelard-Schuman, 1959.

"Nettie M. Stevens and the Discovery of Sex Determination by Chromosomes." Stephen G. Brush. *Isis* 69 (1978).

"The Scientific Work of Miss N. M. Stevens." Thomas Hunt Morgan. *Science* 36 (1912).

A Short History of Genetics: The Development of Some of the Main Lines of Thought, 1864-1939. L. C. Dunn. New York: McGraw-Hill, 1965.

In 1900, Stevens entered Bryn Mawr College as a graduate student in biology. In her second year, a fellowship enabled her to study at the Zoological Station in Naples, Italy, and at the University of Würzburg, Germany, under Theodor Boveri.

In 1903, she received a Ph.D. from Bryn Mawr with a thesis on ciliate protozoa. Stevens continued at Bryn Mawr as a research fellow in biology and an associate in experimental morphology. In 1905, the association that maintained the American Women's Table at the Naples station awarded Stevens the Ellen Richards Research Prize of $1,000, given to promote scientific research by women.

Research Interests

Stevens carried out research in three major areas of biology. Her earliest work was concerned with the morphology (physical characteristics) and taxonomy (classification) of ciliate protozoan. Later, she became interested in cytology, particularly the histology (tissue study) of regenerative processes in hydroids and planarians. In 1904, with the geneticist Thomas Hunt Morgan, she published a paper on the regenerative processes in the hydroid *Tubularia*.

Stevens' research was characterized by precise observations and cautious interpretations. She published thirty-eight papers in eleven years.

Stevens died of breast cancer on May 4, 1912, before she could accept the research professorship created for her by the Bryn Mawr trustees.

Bibliography

By Stevens
Studies in Spermatogenesis with Especial Reference to the "Accessory Chromosome," 1905

"A Study of the Germ Cells of *Aphis rosae* and *Aphis oenotherae*," *Journal of Experimental Zoology*, 1905

Studies in Spermatogenesis: A Comparative Study of the Heterochromosomes in Certain Species of Coleoptera, Hemiptera, and Lepidoptera, with Especial Reference to Sex Determination, 1906

Studies on the Germ Cells of Aphids, 1906

"Further Studies on Heterochromosomes in Mosquitoes," *Biological Bulletin of the Marine Biological Laboratory*, 1911

About Stevens

American Women in Science. A Biographical Dictionary. Martha J. Bailey. Santa Barbara, Calif.: ABC-CLIO, 1994.

Mothers of Invention: From the Bra to the Bomb: Forgotten Women and Their Unforgettable Ideas. Ethlie Ann Vare and Greg Ptacek. New York: William Morrow, 1988.

"Nettie Maria Stevens (1861-1912): Her Life and Contributions to Cytogenetics." Marilyn Bailey Ogilvie and Clifford J. Choquette. *Proceedings of the American Philosophical Society* 125 (1981).

Notable Twentieth-Century Scientists. Emily J. McMurray, ed. Detroit: Gale Research, 1987.

Women in Science: Antiquity Through the Nineteenth Century. Marilyn Bailey Ogilvie. Cambridge, Mass.: MIT Press, 1986.

(Margaret H. Major)

Alfred H. Sturtevant

Areas of Achievement: Biology, genetics, and zoology

Contribution: A pioneer in classical genetics, Sturtevant discovered the principles of gene mapping, the first reparable gene defect, and the phenomenon of position effect.

Nov. 21, 1891	Born in Jacksonville, Illinois
1908	Enters Columbia University
1910	Joins the "fly room" of Thomas Hunt Morgan at Columbia University
1914	Earns a doctorate from Columbia University
1914	Remains at Columbia as a research investigator for the Carnegie Institution of Washington
1920	Discovers the first reparable gene defect, the vermillion eye color mutation in fruit flies
1925	Presents the concepts of position effect and of unequal crossing-over at meiosis
1928	Appointed a professor of genetics at the California Institute of Technology
1932	Travels to England and Germany as visiting professor of the Carnegie Endowment for International Peace
1951	Completes the genetic map of *Drosophila*
1968	Awarded the National Medal of Science
Apr. 5, 1970	Dies in Pasadena, California

Early Life

Alfred Henry Sturtevant, the youngest of six children, spent his early education in a one-room schoolhouse in Alabama. As a boy, one of Sturtevant's hobbies was to draw the genetic pedigrees of his father's horses and of his own family. In 1908, he entered Columbia University and with the encouragement of his brother, a teacher at nearby Barnard College, began reading books on heredity, thereby stimulating his interest in genetics.

Sturtevant submitted his findings on coat color inheritance patterns in horses to noted Columbia University geneticist Thomas Hunt Morgan. Morgan encouraged Sturtevant to publish his findings, which appeared in the *Biological Bulletin* in 1910, and invited him to join his research group.

The "Fly Room"

Morgan's cramped laboratory in which as many as eight scientists worked at one time was called the "fly room." In this rarified atmosphere of excited exchange and debate of scientific ideas, Sturtevant worked with Morgan, H. J. Muller, and C. B. Bridges, among others. While still an undergraduate student, Sturtevant developed the first chromosome map of *Drosophila melanogaster*, the fruit fly, and introduced the concept of using the frequency of crossing-over of linked genes as a means to construct such a genetic map.

Sturtevant's doctoral work was completed in 1914, and he remained at Columbia in the "fly

(California Institute of Technology)

Gene Mapping in Chromosomes

The relative distance between genes linked to the same chromosome can be determined by the frequency of crossing-over between genes.

Sturtevant observed that on occasion the offspring of a genetic cross exhibit combinations of traits unlike those of either parent. He mated fruit flies with two or more particular traits known to be located on the same chromosome—one homozygous recessive for both traits and the other heterozygous for both—and counted the percentage of progeny exhibiting new combinations of traits, called recombinants.

Sturtevant determined that the exchange of chromosome pieces between a homologous pair of chromosomes of a heterozygote during the process of meiosis, or crossing-over, resulted in the recombination of traits. For example, if one parent fly was purple-eyed and short-winged and the other parent was red-eyed and long-winged, all progeny should have resembled one of the parents. A small percentage of offspring, however, were always purple-eyed and long-winged, or red-eyed and short-winged, because

of crossing-over in the heterozygous parent.

In addition, Sturtevant discovered that the farther apart the two genes are on a chromosome, the more frequently they will cross-over, resulting in more recombinant offspring. Armed with this information and performing many genetic crosses, he was able to elucidate linear maps of the chromosomal location of genes and to infer the distances between them.

Sturtevant's research led to the production of genetic maps for a variety of organisms and was a major advance in the understanding of how the genetic material is organized in all organisms, including humans.

Bibliography

The Cartoon Guide to Genetics. Larry Gronick and Mark Wheelis. New York: Harper and Row, 1994.

An Introduction to Genetic Analysis. David Suzuki, Anthony Griffiths, Jeffrey Miller, and Richard Lewontin. New York: W. H. Freeman, 1989.

The Logic of Life: A History of Heredity. François Jacob. New York: Pantheon Books, 1974.

room" conducting research until 1928. During this time, Sturtevant published works that significantly advanced the field of genetics, including a 1925 paper entitled "The Effects of Unequal Crossing Over at the Bar Locus in *Drosophila*," which detailed the phenomena of unequal crossing-over of chromosomes during meiosis and of position effect in the expression of genes. Additional publications described the maternal inheritance pattern of some genetic traits, including shell coiling in snails.

The California Institute of Technology

In 1928, Sturtevant became professor of genetics in the new division of biology established by Morgan at the California Institute of Technology (Caltech) in Pasadena. Sturtevant maintained an active laboratory in the style of the "fly room." In addition, he collaborated extensively with his colleagues in genetics and taught courses in genetics, general biology, and entomology.

Sturtevant combined his expertise as a naturalist with his skills as a geneticist to pursue evolutionary studies of several *Drosophila* species, and, in 1935, he published a series of three "Essays on Evolution" in the *Quarterly Review of Biology*. He also was able to complete the difficult task of elucidating a genetic map of the last, tiny fourth chromosome of *Drosophila*.

After 1951, Sturtevant also published articles on the genetic effects of high-energy radiation on humans and the social implications of human genetics. In his 1954 presidential address to the Pacific Division of the American Association for the Advancement of Science, Sturtevant warned of the genetic hazards of fallout from the testing of atomic bombs.

Sturtevant remained at Caltech pursuing an active research program until his death in 1970. His last published work, *A History of Genetics* (1965) was an outgrowth of his lectures at many universities and a lifelong interest in the history of science.

Bibliography

By Sturtevant

The Mechanism of Mendelian Heredity, 1915 (with T. H. Morgan, H. J. Muller, and C. B. Bridges)

The North American Species of Drosophila, 1921

An Introduction to Genetics, 1939 (with G. W. Beadle)

Genetics and Evolution, Selected Papers of A. H. Sturtevant, 1961 (E. B. Lewis, ed.)

A History of Genetics, 1965

About Sturtevant

"A. H. Sturtevant." In *Notable Twentieth-Century Scientists*, edited by Emily J. McMurray. Detroit: Gale Research, 1995.

"Alfred Henry Sturtevant." Sterling Emerson. *Annual Review of Genetics* 5 (1971).

"Sturtevant Produces the First Chromosome Map." James H. Anderson. In *Great Events from History II: Science and Technology Series*, edited by Frank N. Magill. Pasadena, Calif.: Salem Press, 1991.

(Karen E. Kalumuck)

Thomas Sydenham

Area of Achievement: Medicine

Contribution: Sydenham was the foremost clinical physician of his time. By studying epidemics rather than individual patients, he drew up a new classification of diseases as distinct entities with unique sets of symptoms. He also invented liquid laudanum and prescribed cinchona, or quinine, for malaria.

Sept. 10, 1624	Baptized in Wynford Eagle, Dorset, England
1643	Fights in the English Civil War on the parliamentary side
1648	Receives a bachelor of medicine degree from Oxford University
1651	Fights with Oliver Cromwell's army in Scotland
1655	Establishes a private practice in London and begins to study epidemics
1663	Becomes a licentiate of the Royal College of Physicians in London
1666	Publishes *Methodus curandi febres* (methods of curing fevers)
1676	Receives an M.D. from Pembroke College, Cambridge
1676	Publishes *Observationes medicae* (medical observations)
1683	Publishes *Tractatus de podagra et hydrope* (treatise on gout and dropsy)
Dec. 29, 1689	Dies in London, England
1693	*Processus integri in morbis fere omnibus curandis* (*The Compleat Method of Curing Almost All Diseases*, 1694) is published posthumously

Early Life

Thomas Sydenham was born into a country gentry family of devout Puritans. At seventeen, he entered Magdalen College, Oxford University, but left after only two months to join his father and brothers fighting in the parliamentary army against King Charles I. Two of his brothers and his mother were killed during the English Civil War (1642-1649).

Sydenham returned to Oxford in 1647 and received the bachelor of medicine degree the next year. In 1651, however, he again left Oxford for the army and, as a Captain of Horse, fought for Oliver Cromwell against the Scots. Returning to Oxford University, he became friends with Robert Boyle, who did much to further Sydenham's career as a doctor.

A London Physician

At thirty-one, Sydenham married Mary Gee and settled in London. With encouragement from Boyle, he began his clinical study of London epidemics shortly after Charles II was restored as king in 1660. Two years later, he regularized his status as a doctor practicing in London by becoming a licentiate of the Royal College of Physicians.

In 1665, when the plague broke out, Sydenham, his wife, and their three sons fled the city. In the countryside, he was able to finish and publish his five-year study of the London epidemics, dedicating it to Boyle. Among Sydenham's medical pupils were John Locke, the noted political theorist, and Hans Sloane, whose collections later became the basis for the British Museum.

Sydenham was renowned for his squabbles with other leading physicians of the day, such as Thomas Willis, over their treatments of various diseases. Some of his ill temper may have been attributable to the fact that he suffered from the painful disease of gout from the age of thirty. In 1683, he vividly described the onset, pain, and progress of his own gout in a book

"The English Hippocrates"

Sydenham's approach to medicine was guided by the Puritan principle that increasing useful knowledge was a religious duty and the belief that experience was the best teacher. He attempted to classify diseases, like plants, in a scientific manner.

As a follower of Hippocrates and Francis Bacon, Sydenham made general histories of the diseases that he encountered while taking care of the sick poor in London hospitals, with the intention of classifying their illnesses like plants. Unlike many of his contemporaries, he believed that diseases were real entities or collections of symptoms that could be sorted into groups. His close clinical observations led to his fame as "the English Hippocrates."

Sydenham stressed the value of observation at the bedside. He integrated his personal observations of patients with seasonal and atmospheric variations in order to draw up a taxonomy (classification) of fevers. Previously, fevers such as smallpox, measles, and typhus had been vaguely classified as "continued," "intermittent," or "eruptive." Sydenham, however, used case histories to build disease histories and, for fourteen years, carefully observed the prevailing maladies of each season in London. From his data, he concluded that it was the differing epidemic constitutions of the atmosphere that caused certain outbreaks of fever.

Sydenham's "ontogenic" concept of disease was very influential. Because of his publications, later physicians began to distinguish between different diseases with similar symptoms such as smallpox, measles, and scarlet fever—all of which had been previously labeled as "eruptive fevers."

Bibliography

"The Global Eradication of Smallpox." World Health Organization. In *Final Report of the Global Commission for the Certification of Smallpox Eradication.* Geneva, Switzerland: Geneva WHO, 1979.

History of AIDS: Emergence and Origins of a Modern Pandemic. Mirko D. Grmek. Translated by R. C. Maulitz and J. Duffin. Princeton, N.J.: Princeton University Press, 1990.

Unnatural Causes: The Three Leading Killer Diseases in America. Russell C. Maulitz. New Brunswick, N.J.: Rutgers University Press, 1988.

(Library of Congress)

entitled *Tractatus de podagra et hydrope*, describing the many remedies with which he had experimented. Sydenham died at home in London from the complications of gout in 1689.

Bibliography
By Sydenham
Methodus curandi febres, 1666; *Observationes medicae*, 1676; and *Tractatus de podagra et hydrope*, 1683 (English trans. in *The Works of Thomas Sydenham, M.D.*, 1848, 2 vols.)
Processus integri in morbis fere omnibus curandis, 1693 (*The Compleat Method of Curing Almost All Diseases*, 1694)
De arte medica, 1669 ("De Arte Medica" in *Dr. Thomas Sydenham (1624-1689)*, 1966, Kenneth Dewhurst, ed.)
Anatomia 1668 ("Anatomie" in *Dr. Thomas Sydenham (1624-1689)*, 1966, Kenneth Dewhurst, ed.)

About Sydenham
Dr. Thomas Sydenham (1624-1689): His Life and Original Writings. Kenneth Dewhurst. Berkeley: University of California Press, 1966.
Patient's Progress: Sickness, Health, and Medical Care in England, 1650-1850. Dorothy and Roy Porter. Berkeley: University of California Press, 1988.
"Thomas Sydenham: Epidemics, Experiment, and the 'Good Old Caus'." Andrew Cunningham. In *The Medical Revolution of the Seventeenth Century*, edited by Roger French and Andrew Wear. Cambridge, England: Cambridge University Press, 1989.

(Lynda Stephenson Payne)

Albert Szent-Györgyi

Areas of Achievement: Cell biology, chemistry, and physiology

Contribution: During his career as a researcher, Szent-Györgyi isolated vitamin C, discovered vitamin P, and studied the molecular structure of muscles and the physiology of muscle contraction.

Sept. 16, 1893	Born in Budapest, Austro-Hungarian Empire (now Hungary)
1917	Receives a medical degree from the University of Budapest
1917-1918	Serves in the Austro-Hungarian army during World War I
1927	Earns a Ph.D. in chemistry and physiology from Cambridge University
1932	Becomes chair of medical chemistry at the University of Szeged
1937	Awarded the Nobel Prize in Physiology or Medicine for his work on vitamin C and food oxidation in the body
1947	Establishes the Institute for Muscle Research at the Marine Biological Laboratory in Woods Hole, Massachusetts
1948-1949	Discovers vitamin P
1954	Receives the Albert Lasker Award of the American Heart Association for his work on cardiovascular diseases
1956	Elected to the National Academy of Sciences
1957	Elected to the American Academy of Arts and Sciences
Oct. 22, 1986	Dies in Woods Hole, Massachusetts

Early Life

Albert Szent-Györgyi (pronounced "saynt JAHR-jee"), in full Albert Imre Szent-Györgyi von Nagyrapolt, was born in Budapest on September 16, 1893. At the age of eighteen, he entered medical school at the University of Budapest and began scientific research in his freshman year. Following family tradition, his early research dealt with anatomical topics, and, before he received his medical degree in 1917, he had already published several scientific papers.

World War I caused Szent-Györgyi to leave medical school to serve in the Austro-Hungarian army on both the Russian and Italian fronts. He was wounded and decorated for bravery.

Maturing as a Researcher

After the war, Szent-Györgyi had a large number of professional positions at several European universities and the Mayo Clinic in the United States. Those experiences put him in contact with many scientists whose interests

(The Nobel Foundation)

were the chemical processes inside the cells of living creatures. As a result, he obtained another degree, a Ph.D. in chemistry and physiology from Cambridge University.

With a primary interest in research, a medical background, the ability to ask the right questions, a charismatic demeanor, and a background in several scientific disciplines, Szent-Györgyi entered the field of cell biology at a time when major discoveries were being made. He contributed to these discoveries with the isolation of vitamin C.

In 1932, he became the chair of the department of medical chemistry at the University of Szeged, Hungary. In 1937, he was awarded the Nobel Prize in Physiology or Medicine for "discoveries in connection with the biological combustion processes, with special reference to Vitamin C and the catalysis of fumaric acid."

Another war affected Szent-Györgyi's career just as he had begun research on muscle physiology. During World War II, he avoided the Nazis by living in neutral countries, foreign legations, and finally the Underground—all this time continuing his research.

Early in the war years, he isolated the proteins that cause muscle contractions and was able, with the addition of adenosine triphosphate (ATP), to cause them to contract outside of a muscle cell. In 1966, he reflected on this event: "To see these little artificial muscles jump for the first time was perhaps the most

Vitamin C

Szent-Györgyi determined the molecular structure of vitamin C and studied some of its functions in human metabolism.

Early in his career, Szent-Györgyi worked on adrenal glands and extracted minute quantities of a substance that he called hexuronic acid. He wondered if browning of the skin, a symptom of Addison's disease, was related to the browning of some fruits and the lack of it in others, notably citrus fruits.

This substance, vitamin C, had been discovered in 1907. Because quantities found were so small, however, its chemical structure had not been determined. Szent-Györgyi realized that paprika, Hungarian red pepper spice, was a rich source of hexuronic acid. With the help of another scientist, he isolated approximately 1 kilogram of the pure white acid crystals. He was then able to determine its molecular structure and some of its functions in metabolism.

One important function is the prevention of scurvy. Some scientists hypothesized that an impurity was the effective agent in these fruits, while others proposed that it was vitamin C. Szent-Györgyi proved that hexuronic acid is the antiscurvy agent and suggested changing its name to antiscorbutic acid; vitamin C is now called ascorbic acid. Many scientists, such as Linus Pauling, firmly believe that vitamins, especially vitamin C, can cure and prevent diseases such as cancer and the common cold.

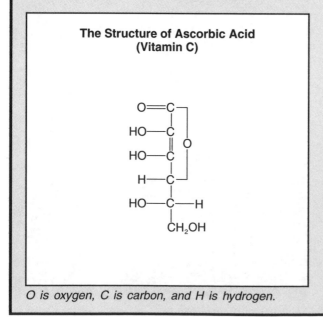

The Structure of Ascorbic Acid (Vitamin C)

O is oxygen, C is carbon, and H is hydrogen.

Bibliography

How Did We Find Out About Vitamins? Isaac Asimov. New York: Walker, 1974.

The Role of Citrus Fruits in Health and Disease. Willard A. Krehl. Gainesville: University Presses of Florida, 1976.

Vitamin C Against Cancer. Herbert L. Newbold. New York: Stein & Day, 1979.

Vitamin C, the Common Cold, and the Flu. Linus Pauling. San Francisco: W. H. Freeman, 1976.

exciting experience of my scientific life." After the war, he worked for a short time at the University of Budapest and was elected to the Hungarian parliament.

Woods Hole
Leaving Hungary in 1947, Szent-Györgyi established the Institute for Muscle Research at the Marine Biological Laboratory in Woods Hole, Massachusetts, with the original group of researchers from Szeged. He continued making discoveries, including vitamin P and its use in treating radiation damage. His interest in muscles and how they work led to publications relating the principles of muscle physiology to heart disease.

Much of Szent-Györgyi's research on vitamins was motivated by a desire to find the cause of and cure for cancer. He added significantly to the understanding of the physiology of living things, as explained by his philosophy, "To see what everyone has seen and think what no one has thought." He died in Woods Hole in 1986 at the age of ninety-three.

Bibliography
By Szent-Györgyi
On Oxidation, Fermentation, Vitamins, Health, and Disease, 1939
Chemistry of Muscular Contraction, 1947
The Nature of Life, 1948
Chemical Physiology of Contraction in Body and Heart Muscle, 1953
Bioenergetics, 1957
Science, Ethic, and Politics, 1963
"Fifty Years of Poaching in Science," The Graduate Faculties Newsletter, 1966
Bioelectronics: A Study in Cellular Regulations, Defense, and Cancer, 1968
The Crazy Ape: Written by a Biologist for the Young, 1970
What Next?!, 1971
The Living State: With Observations on Cancer, 1972
Electronic Biology and Cancer: A New Theory of Cancer, 1976
The Living State and Cancer, 1978

About Szent-Györgyi
"Albert Szent-Györgyi Dead; Research Isolated Vitamin C." The New York Times, October 25, 1986.
Free Radical: Albert Szent-Györgyi and the Battle over Vitamin C. Ralph W. Moss. New York: Paragon House, 1988.
"A Genius for Discovery." George Weber. Saturday Evening Post 256 (May/June, 1984).

(Leonard J. Garigliano)

Igor Yevgenyevich Tamm

Area of Achievement: Physics
Contribution: Tamm, working with Ilya Frank, developed the physical theory to explain Cherenkov radiation, the light emitted by a particle moving through a medium faster than the local speed of light.

July 8, 1895	Born in Vladivostok, Siberia
1918	Earns a bachelor of science degree in physics from Moscow State University
1919-1921	Teaches at the Crimean University
1930	Named the head of the physics department at Moscow State University
1933	Awarded a Ph.D. in physics from Moscow State University
1934	Named director of Technical Studies at the P. N. Lebedev Physical Institute
1934	Predicts that the neutron, although uncharged, would have a magnetic moment
1937-1939	Develops a theory to explain Cherenkov radiation
1953	Elected as an active member of the Academy of Sciences of the Soviet Union
1958	Awarded the Nobel Prize in Physics with Ilya Frank and Pavel Cherenkov
Apr. 12, 1971	Dies in Moscow, Soviet Union

Early Life

Igor Yevgenyevich Tamm was born on July 8, 1895, to Evgenii Tamm and Olga Davydova in Vladivostok, Siberia. His father was a civil engineer. In 1901, the family moved to the Ukraine, where Tamm was educated. After his graduation from the Elizavetgrad Gymnasium in 1913, he spent a year at the University of Edinburgh, Scotland. He returned to Russia at the outbreak of World War I and enrolled at Moscow State University, where he studied physics and mathematics.

Tamm received his bachelor's degree in 1918 and taught at the Crimean University from 1919 to 1921. He returned to Moscow in 1922, teaching first at the J. M. Sverdlov Communist University and later at Moscow State University, where he became head of the physics department in 1930. He was awarded a Ph.D. in physics in 1933. Tamm was named director of Technical Studies at the P. N. Lebedev Physical Institute in Moscow in 1934.

Research in Quantum Mechanics

Tamm's interest was theoretical physics, and, during the 1920's and 1930's, he set about to apply the newly developing ideas of quantum mechanics to the understanding of solids. His calculations showed that electrons at the surface of a crystalline solid are bonded differently than those in the interior. His discovery of these so-called Tamm surface levels had important implications in the understanding of semiconductors, which are used in computers.

Tamm also applied quantum mechanics to modeling the properties of the nuclei of atoms. In 1934, he predicted that the neutron, although it has no electric charge, has a magnetic moment (the torque exerted on a magnetic system when it is placed in a magnetic field).

Cherenkov Radiation

While in the Crimea, Tamm met Leonid Mandelshtam, an expert in crystal optics, and became interested in the interaction of light with crystals. In 1932, Pavel Cherenkov, a research student at the Lebedev Institute, began studying the light emitted by transparent substances placed near radioactive sources. Tamm, along with Ilya Frank, developed the theory explaining how this radiation was produced. For this work, Cherenkov, Frank, and Tamm were awarded the Nobel Prize in Physics in 1958.

Nuclear Weapons and Arms Control

In the 1950's, Tamm was named leader of a group working on the theory of gas discharge in strong magnetic fields. This research was important in the understanding of thermonuclear reactions. Andrei Sakharov, a member of Tamm's group, made the breakthrough needed for the demonstration of the Soviet hydrogen bomb. Tamm later became active in the Pugwash movement, a worldwide group of scientists opposed to the use of nuclear weapons.

Tamm died in Moscow on April 12, 1971.

Bibliography

By Tamm

"Nuclear Magnetic Moments and the Properties of the Neutron," *Nature*, 1934

"Svechenie chistykh zhidkostey pod deystviem bystrykh elektronov" *Izvestiya Akademii nauk*, 1938 (with Ilya Frank and Pavel Cherenkov; luminescence of pure liquids under the influence of fast electrons)

"The Transmutations of the Cosmic-Ray Electrons and the Nuclear Forces," *Physical Review*, 1938

"Radiation Emitted by Uniformly Moving Electrons," *Journal of Physics of the USSR*, 1939 (with Frank and Cherenkov)

"The Energy Spectrum of Cascade Electrons," *Physical Review*, 1946 (with S. Z. Belenky)

(The Nobel Foundation)

Cherenkov Radiation

The detection of Cherenkov radiation has become an important measuring tool in the fields of particle physics and cosmic-ray physics.

In 1932, Pavel Cherenkov observed the light emitted when high-energy gamma rays (and later high-energy electrons) passed through transparent liquids and solids. Although Cherenkov measured the properties of this radiation, he could not explain how it was produced.

In 1937, Tamm, working with Ilya Frank, developed the theory to explain how an electron moving through matter at a speed greater than the speed of light in the medium emits a conical wave front of light. The emission is similar to the conical "sonic boom," or shock wave, produced when an aircraft travels through the air at a speed greater than the speed of sound in air. Frank and Tamm showed how the angle of this emission depends on the speed of the electron and the speed of light in the medium.

Cherenkov was able to test their theory by measuring this emission angle, confirming that Frank and Tamm had developed an explanation of the radiation that Cherenkov had observed.

Bibliography

Cherenkov Radiation. J. V. Jelley. New York: Pergamon Press, 1958.

"Radiation Emitted by Uniformly Moving Electrons." Ilya M. Frank, Igor Tamm, and Pavel Cherenkov. *Journal of Physics of the USSR* (1939).

"General Characteristics of Vavilov-Cherenkov Radiation," *Science*, 1960
Sobranie nauchnykh trudov, 1975
Vospominaniya, 1981
Selected Papers of Igor E. Tamm, 1991

About Tamm
"A Lively Interest in Science History." Sergei Leskov. *The Bulletin of the Atomic Scientists* (May, 1993).
Reminiscences About I. L. Tamm. E. L. Feinberg, ed. Moscow: Nauka, 1987.
Review of *Selected Papers of Igor E. Tamm.* John M. Charap. *Nature* (July 16, 1992).

(George J. Flynn)

Edward Lawrie Tatum

Areas of Achievement: Bacteriology and cell biology
Contribution: With George Wells Beadle, Tatum pioneered the study of gene function through the use of biochemical mutations.

Dec. 14, 1909	Born in Boulder, Colorado
1931	Earns a B.A. in chemistry at the University of Wisconsin
1932	Receives an M.S. in microbiology from Wisconsin
1934	Earns a Ph.D. in biochemistry at Wisconsin
1936	Awarded a General Education Board Fellowship to study in Utrecht, the Netherlands
1937-1945	Travels to Stanford University and works with George Wells Beadle
1944	Joins the staff of the Office of Scientific Research and Development to produce penicillin
1946	Serves as a professor of microbiology at Yale University
1946	Collaborates with Joshua Lederberg
1948-1956	Returns to Stanford as a professor of biology
1953	Receives the Remsen Award of the American Chemical Society
1956	Promoted to chair of biochemistry at Stanford
1957-1975	Serves as a professor at the Rockefeller Institute (later Rockefeller University) in New York City
1958	Awarded the Nobel Prize in Physiology or Medicine
Nov. 5, 1975	Dies in New York, New York

One Gene, One Enzyme

Enzymes are the primary products of genes and the means by which genes control cellular processes.

Working with George Wells Beadle, Tatum investigated the mechanisms of gene action through mutated forms of the bread mold *Neurospora*. By exposing the mold colonies to X rays, they increased dramatically the number of mutant forms.

Growing these mutants on different kinds of culture media, Tatum and Beadle were able to determine which gene had mutated. Thus, on a culture to which vitamin B_6 had been added, they found that a mutant mold colony grew normally, although it grew poorly or died on other kinds of growth media. This result suggested that the gene responsible for making vitamin B_6 had been affected by the mutation. It also suggested that a single gene controls a single enzyme.

They proved that this induced mutation behaved exactly like a natural mutation and that genes have a direct role in the production of enzymes and thus the control of cellular biochemistry.

The methods that Tatum and Beadle developed to analyze developmental and physiological processes are central to studies of cell development, physiology, and genetics and are of great importance to biotechnology.

Bibliography

Biochemistry: A Functional Approach. Robert W. McGilvery, ed. Philadelphia: W. B. Saunders, 1983.

A Biologist's Guide to Principles and Techniques of Practical Biochemistry. Bryan L. Williams and Keith Wilson, eds. New York: American Elsevier, 1975.

Principles and Techniques of Practical Biochemistry. Keith Wilson and John M. Walker, eds. 4th ed. Cambridge, England: Cambridge University Press, 1994.

Early Life

Edward Lawrie Tatum was the first surviving son of Arthur L. Tatum, a physician who also held doctorates in pharmacology and physiology, and Mabel Webb. Edward's twin brother, Elwood, died shortly after birth. The family moved often but settled in Madison, Wisconsin, in 1925, where Edward's father was a professor of pharmacology at the University of Wisconsin.

Edward Tatum, benefiting from the intellectual climate of his family and the city in which he lived, earned his B.A. in chemistry in 1931. In quick succession, he earned an M.S. in microbiology in 1932 and a doctorate in biochemistry in 1934, both at the University of Wisconsin.

Tatum won a fellowship in 1936 that took his family to Utrecht in the Netherlands. Although Tatum thought that his research there lacked focus, he was exposed to methods and theories of microbial culture and nutrition.

The *Neurospora* Work

From 1937 to 1945, Tatum worked at Stanford University on problems relating to the nutri-

(The Nobel Foundation)

tional requirements and cellular biochemistry of microorganisms. As a reflection of his life-long interest in teaching, he also developed a biochemistry graduate curriculum, which was unprecedented at the time.

In the early 1940's, Tatum collaborated with George Wells Beadle on the research that would later earn them the Nobel Prize in Physiology or Medicine. They determined the chemical processes involved in the genetic inheritance patterns of a species of bread mold of the genus *Neurospora*.

Sexual Reproduction in Bacteria
After a semester at Washington University in St. Louis, Tatum accepted a tenured position in the botany department of Yale University in 1945. At Yale, Tatum worked with a student named Joshua Lederberg. Through a series of experiments, Tatum and Lederberg determined that bacteria, like animals and plants, reproduce sexually. This discovery was important in demonstrating the continuity of life from microorganisms to higher plants and animals.

In 1958, Tatum shared one half of the Nobel Prize in Physiology or Medicine with Beadle for their work on *Neurospora*, which demonstrated that genes act by regulating chemical events within cells. The other half of the award went to Lederberg.

Ups and Downs
While Tatum's scientific career seemed to move from one important discovery to another, his personal life was characterized by ups and downs.

Tatum married a fellow student, June Alton, in 1934. They had two daughters and divorced in 1956. Within a year, Tatum married Viola Kantor, an employee of the March of Dimes, for which he served as a scientific adviser. They remained together until Viola's death in 1974.

Tatum himself suffered from ill health during his final years, and he died at his home in New York City in 1975.

Bibliography
By Tatum
"Experimental Control of Development and Differentiation," *American Naturalist*, 1941 (with George Wells Beadle)

"Genetic Control of Biochemical Reactions in *Neurospora*," *Proceedings of the National Academy of Sciences of the United States of America*, 1942 (with Beadle)

"The Genetic Control of Biochemical Reactions in *Neurospora*: A Mutant Strain Requiring Isoleucine and Valine," *Archives of Biochemistry*, 1943 (with David Bonner and Beadle)

"X-Ray Induced Growth Factor Requirements in Bacteria," *Proceedings of the National Academy of Sciences of the United States of America*, 1944 (with C. H. Gray)

"Novel Genotypes in Mixed Cultures of Biochemical Mutants of Bacteria," *Cold Spring Harbor Symposium on Quantitative Biology*, 1946 (with Joshua Lederberg)

"Gene Recombination in *Escherichia coli*," *Nature*, 1946 (with Lederberg)

About Tatum
"Edward Lawrie Tatum." Joshua Lederberg. *Biographical Memoirs of the National Academy of Sciences of the United States of America* 59 (1990).

"Tatum, Edward L." In *Nobel Prize Winners: An H. W. Wilson Biographical Dictionary*, edited by Tyler Wasson. New York: H. W. Wilson, 1987.

(Christopher S. W. Koehler)

Henry Taube

Area of Achievement: Chemistry
Contribution: Universally recognized as the founder of the modern study of inorganic mechanisms, Taube won the Nobel Prize in Chemistry for his work on electron transfer reactions.

Nov. 30, 1915	Born in Neudorf, Saskatchewan, Canada
1935	Earns a B.S. in chemistry from the University of Saskatchewan
1937	Receives an M.S. in chemistry from Saskatchewan
1940-1941	Earns a Ph.D. in chemistry from the University of California, Berkeley, and works as an instructor there
1941-1946	Serves as an instructor and assistant professor of chemistry at Cornell University
1942	Becomes a naturalized U.S. citizen
1946-1962	Promoted from assistant professor to professor of chemistry at the University of Chicago
1956-1959	Serves as chair of the chemistry department at Chicago
1962-1976	Professor of Chemistry, Stanford University
1976-1986	Named Marguerite Blake Wilbur Professor of Chemistry at Stanford
1977	Wins the National Medal of Science
1983	Awarded the Nobel Prize in Chemistry
1985	Given the Priestley Medal by the American Chemical Society
1986	Named emeritus professor at Stanford and becomes a consultant for Catalytica Associates

(The Nobel Foundation)

Early Life

Henry Taube was the youngest of four brothers whose parents were German peasant immigrants from Ukraine; his first language was German. He spent his first two years in a rented sod hut. His father was a farm hand, and his mother cleaned houses. When he was four, his father rented a farm, and the family moved to a two-room shack. Taube attended a one-room school until the age of thirteen, when he left home to study for the ministry at Luther College in the provincial capital of Regina.

Because his father lost the little that he had saved in the stock market crash of 1929, Taube helped in the school chemistry laboratory to pay for his stay. Although he planned to major in English literature, hoping to become a writer, he registered at the University of Saskatchewan for a chemistry course because all the other courses had long registration lines.

After earning B.S. and M.S. degrees in chemistry, he pursued graduate work at the University of California, Berkeley (UCB), where he finally became deeply interested in chemistry, earning a Ph.D. with a study of the oxidation-reduction (redox) reactions of oxygen- and halogen-containing oxidizing agents. Teaching jobs were scarce during the Great Depression, so he remained at UCB as an instructor and became a U.S. citizen while he sought a permanent position.

Mechanistic Coordination Chemistry

Taube continued to work on the subject of his Ph.D. research during his years at Cornell University, from 1941 to 1946. He used isotopic labeling techniques to study the mechanisms (how the atoms or molecules actually react) of the redox reactions of oxychlorine species and related molecules in aqueous solutions. This work brought him the American Chemical Society (ACS) Award for Nuclear Applications in Chemistry in 1955.

It was only as an assistant professor at the University of Chicago, when he taught a course in coordination chemistry, that he began to work in this field. Although much was known about the composition, structure, and reactivity of inorganic coordination compounds (complexes) by 1950, little was known about the actual mechanisms involved.

Taube explained reactivity as a unified concept based on the configuration of the electrons of the central metal ion and on the influence of the ligands (groups bonded around the central ion) of the coordination compound. He originated the valuable concept of inner (inert) and outer (labile) spheres to correlate the rates of ligand substitution reactions of complexes.

One of the leading pioneers in modern inorganic chemistry, Taube established the basis for various conceptual advances and investigated many aspects of chemical reactivity using new techniques. His research on electron transfer in metal complexes not only forms the basis for modern inorganic chemistry but also has led to a fuller understanding of the biochemical reactions that maintain life.

Later Work

Taube's more than three hundred articles include work on mixed valence ions in a series of iron, ruthenium, and osmium complexes; intramolecular electron transfer between metal ions applied to biological systems; molecular nitrogen complexes; and transition metal organometallic compounds. Despite his retire-

The Mechanism of an Electron Transfer Reaction

Taube's study of one electron transfer reaction exemplifies his new way of looking at such processes.

In the reaction between the inert pentaamminechlorocobalt(III) ion and the labile hexaaquachromium(II) ion the products are the pentaaquachlorochromium(III) ion and the pentaammineaquacobalt(II) ion. The electron transfer is thus connected with a chloride ion transfer from cobalt to chromium. Before Taube's work, however, no knowledge existed of how the reaction takes place.

According to Taube, the chloride ligand in the inert cobalt(III) reactant neither could have left the cobalt coordination sphere before electron transfer nor could have entered the coordination sphere of the inert chromium(III) product after electron transfer.

Taube proved experimentally with a radioactively labeled chloride ion that the chloride ion was part of both the cobalt and the chromium coordination spheres at the moment of electron transfer. He found that, in forming, the chromium(III) product picks up almost no radioactivity, demonstrating that the transfer is direct; the chloride ion bridges the two metal centers before the chromium(II) reactant is oxidized.

Thus, Taube demonstrated that formation of ligand bridges between two interacting complexes is one of the fundamental mechanisms of electron transfer in such complexes.

Bibliography

"The 1983 Nobel Prize in Chemistry." Harry B. Gray and James P. Collman. *Science* 222 (1983).
"Understanding the Electron." Lionel Milgrom and Ian Anderson. *New Scientist* 100 (October, 1983).

ment in 1986, he continued to be active in research.

He enjoys gardening, sour mash bourbon whiskey, and listening to 78 rpm vocal records from his vast collection.

Bibliography

By Taube

"The Exchange of Water Between Aqueous Chromic Ion and Solvent," *Journal of Chemical Physics*, 1950 (with John P. Hunt)

"Rates and Mechanisms of Substitution in Inorganic Complexes in Solution," *Chemical Reviews*, 1952

"Observations on the Mechanism of Electron Transfer in Solution," *Journal of the American Chemical Society*, 1953 (with Howard Myers and Ronald L. Rich)

"Nuclear Magnetic Resonance Studies on Hydration of Cations," *Journal of Chemical Physics*, 1960 (with Jasper A. Jackson and Joe Fred Lemons)

"Oxygen-17 NMR Shifts in Aqueous Solutions of Rare-Earth Ions," *Journal of Chemical Physics*, 1962 (with W. Burton Lewis, Jackson, and Lemons)

"A Direct Approach to Measuring the Franck-Condon Barrier to Electron Transfer Between Metal Ions," *Journal of the American Chemical Society*, 1969 (with Carol Creutz)

Electron Transfer Reactions of Complex Ions in Solution, 1970

"Rates of Intramolecular Electron Transfer," *Journal of the American Chemical Society*, 1973 (with Stephan S. Isied)

"Electron Transfer Between Metal Complexes: Retrospective," *Science*, 1984

About Taube

"Henry Taube." Jerry Walsh. In *Nobel Laureates in Chemistry, 1901-1992*, edited by Laylin K. James. Washington, D.C.: American Chemical Society, 1993.

"Interview: Henry Taube." István Hargittai. *The Chemical Intelligencer* 3 (1997).

(George B. Kauffman)

Helen Brooke Taussig

Areas of Achievement: Medicine and physiology

Contribution: Taussig developed a surgical procedure to treat blue baby syndrome and was instrumental in preventing thalidomide, a drug that causes severe birth defects, from being used in the United States.

May 24, 1898	Born in Cambridge, Massachusetts
1917-1919	Attends Radcliffe College
1921	Earns a bachelor's degree from the University of California, Berkeley
1921	Attends Harvard University
1922-1924	Attends Boston University
1927	Earns an M.D. from The Johns Hopkins Medical School
1927	Receives a fellowship to the cardiac station at Johns Hopkins
1928-1930	Serves an internship in pediatrics at Johns Hopkins
1930-1946	Works as an instructor at Johns Hopkins
1930-1963	Directs the Children's Heart Clinic at Johns Hopkins
1946	Promoted to associate professor
1959	Appointed a full professor at Johns Hopkins
1963	Promoted to professor emeritus
1964	Awarded the Medal of Freedom
1965-1966	Serves as president of the American Heart Association
1977	Awarded the National Medal of Science
May 20, 1986	Dies in Kennett Square, Pennsylvania

Early Life

Helen Brooke Taussig was born on May 24, 1898, in Cambridge, Massachusetts. Her father, Frank William Taussig, was a renowned economist at Harvard University. Her mother, Edith Guild Taussig, was one of the first students at Radcliffe College and had a strong interest in natural science.

Helen Taussig attended several colleges and universities, mostly in her native New England. She spent two years at Radcliffe beginning in 1917 and then traveled across the United States to the University of California, Berkeley, where she earned a bachelor's degree in 1921. After studying briefly at Harvard in 1921, she transferred to Boston University, where she specialized in diseases of the heart.

In 1924, Taussig began her long association with The Johns Hopkins Medical School in Baltimore, Maryland. She earned her M.D. in 1927, spent a year studying heart disease under a fellowship, and then served an internship in pediatrics. In 1930, she was appointed physician-in-charge of the Children's Heart Clinic, a position that she would hold until 1963.

The Blalock-Taussig Shunt

Throughout the 1930's and early 1940's, Taussig worked on the problem of blue baby syndrome, a disease in which children are born with heart defects that prevent enough oxygen

The Flow of Blood in a Normal Heart

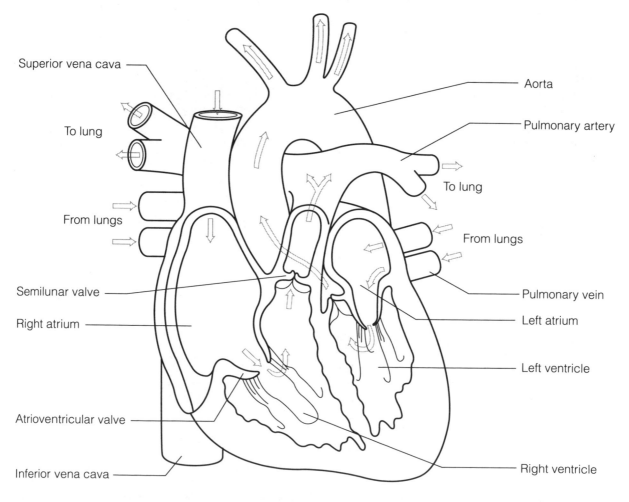

Superior vena cava

To lung

From lungs

Semilunar valve

Right atrium

Atrioventricular valve

Inferior vena cava

Aorta

Pulmonary artery

To lung

From lungs

Pulmonary vein

Left atrium

Left ventricle

Right ventricle

(Hans & Cassady, Inc.)

from reaching their blood. These patients develop bluish-gray skin and almost always died at an early age.

Taussig became an expert at using the newly developed X-ray fluoroscope, a device that projects an image of the body's organs onto a glowing screen. She also became adept with an electrocardiograph, which records the electrical activity of the heart. Using these machines, along with her skill at physical examination, Taussig was able to determine the exact heart defects of her patients.

Armed with this knowledge, Taussig worked with surgeon Alfred Blalock and his assistant Vivian Thomas to develop a surgical method to treat blue baby syndrome. Thomas performed experimental surgery on two hundred dogs until the new technique was perfected. A surgical team led by Blalock performed the surgery on a human patient for the first time on November 29, 1944, saving the life of eleven-month-old Eileen Saxon. The technique, known as the Blalock-Taussig shunt, has been performed successfully on thousands of children.

The Correction of Blue Baby Syndrome

Taussig developed an effective treatment for blue baby syndrome, a birth defect involving major heart abnormalities.

The heart is divided into four chambers; the upper two are the left and right atria, and the lower two are the left and right ventricles. A wall called the septum separates the left and right sides of the heart. Each atrium is connected to its corresponding ventricle by a valve that controls the flow of blood.

Blood full of oxygen is pumped from the left ventricle through a large artery called the aorta and is transported throughout the body by smaller arteries. The oxygen is supplied to body tissues through microscopic blood vessels called capillaries. The deoxygenated blood then travels through small veins to two larger veins called the superior vena cava and the inferior vena cava.

These large veins carry the blood into the right atrium, from which it flows into the right ventricle. The right ventricle pumps the blood through the pulmonary artery to the lungs, where it picks up oxygen. The newly oxygenated blood flows through the pulmonary veins to the left atrium, from which it flows into the left ventricle, beginning the cycle again.

Children born with blue baby syndrome usually have four heart abnormalities known as the tetralogy of Fallot, named after French pathologist Étienne-Louis-Arthur Fallot. These four abnormalities are an opening in the septum between the ventricles, a narrowing of the pulmonary artery, a thickening of the muscle of the right ventricle, and an aorta displaced to the right so that blood

enters it from both ventricles. The overall effect of these abnormalities is that less blood reaches the lungs to be oxygenated, resulting in bluish-gray skin, shortness of breath, and early death.

Taussig realized that the primary problem in blue baby syndrome was that not enough blood was being carried to the lungs through the pulmonary artery. She reasoned that the best way to treat this problem was to use another blood vessel to carry blood to the lungs.

The first time that a patient with blue baby syndrome underwent this kind of surgery, Taussig devised a technique in which one of the child's two subclavian arteries (large blood vessels that carry blood to the arms) was surgically attached to the pulmonary artery. In later operations, another large artery near the heart known as the innominate artery was sometimes used. In either case, the result was the same: The lungs received more blood through the pulmonary artery, and the decreased flow of blood through the surgically manipulated artery did not cause any serious problems.

Taussig's pioneering surgical procedure saved thousands of lives and paved the way for later, more technologically advanced procedures.

Bibliography

Essentials of Pediatric Cardiology. James H. Moller. Philadelphia: F. A. Davis, 1978.
Heart Disease in Infancy and Childhood. John D. Keith, Richard Desmond Rowe, and Peter Vlad. New York: Macmillan, 1978.
Pediatric Cardiology. Alexander S. Nadas. Philadelphia: W. B. Saunders, 1972.

(AP/Wide World Photos)

The Thalidomide Problem

In 1946, Taussig was promoted from instructor to associate professor at Johns Hopkins. During the late 1940's and 1950's, she received numerous awards and served on many national and international committees. In 1959, she became the first woman to be named a full professor in the history of The Johns Hopkins Medical School.

In January, 1962, Taussig was visited by a former student from Germany who told her about a possible problem with a drug called thalidomide. It had been used in Europe as a sedative and to prevent nausea during pregnancy since the late 1950's. A connection seemed to exist between use of the drug during pregnancy and a formerly rare birth defect called phocomelia, in which a child is born with arms and legs that resemble flippers rather than normal limbs.

Taussig traveled to Germany in February, 1962, to investigate the situation. She noted that phocomelia did not occur among the chil-

dren of U.S. soldiers stationed in Germany, except for the child of one mother who had purchased the drug away from the military base, where thalidomide was prohibited. This was strong evidence that thalidomide was responsible for phocomelia. Taussig's testimony helped to prevent the drug from being approved for use in the United States, saving thousands of children from being born with a severe birth defect.

An Active Retirement

In 1963, Taussig was promoted to professor emeritus. In 1964, she was awarded the Medal of Freedom from President Lyndon B. Johnson. Although she was officially retired, she continued her research. From 1965 to 1966, she served as the first female president of the American Heart Association.

In a series of articles published in the 1970's, Taussig studied the long-term effects of the Blalock-Taussig shunt. She discovered that the majority of the patients who had undergone surgery as children had become healthy adults. In 1977, Taussig was awarded the National Medal of Science from President Jimmy Carter. She died in an automobile accident on May 20, 1986.

Bibliography

By Taussig
"The Surgical Treatment of Malformations of the Heart in Which There Is Pulmonary Stenosis or Pulmonary Atresia," *The Journal of the American Medical Association*, 1945 (with Alfred Blalock)
Congenital Malformations of the Heart, 1947
"The Thalidomide Syndrome," *Scientific American*, 1962

About Taussig
Adventures in Medical Research: A Century of Discovery at Johns Hopkins. A. McGhee Harvey. Baltimore: The Johns Hopkins University Press, 1976.
Doctors: The Biography of Medicine. Sherwin B. Nuland. New York: Alfred A. Knopf, 1988.
To Heal the Heart of a Child: Helen Taussig, M.D. Joyce Baldwin. New York: Walker, 1992.

(Rose Secrest)

Moddie Daniel Taylor

Area of Achievement: Chemistry

Contribution: During World War II, Taylor worked on the Manhattan Project, the U.S. program to build an atomic bomb. His contributions to science education in the postwar years included writing a textbook for college-level chemistry courses.

Mar. 3, 1912	Born in Nymph, Alabama
1935	Graduated from Lincoln University in Jefferson City, Missouri, as valedictorian
1935-1939	Works as an instructor at Lincoln
1939-1941	Promoted to full professor at Lincoln
1939	Earns a master's degree from the University of Chicago
1943	Awarded a Ph.D. in chemistry from the University of Chicago
1943-1945	Serves as an associate chemist on the Manhattan Project
1948	Hired as an associate professor at Howard University in Washington, D.C.
1959	Promoted to full professor at Howard
1960	Publishes *First Principles of Chemistry*, a college-level chemistry textbook
1965	Appointed by President Lyndon B. Johnson to serve on the Assay Commission
1969-1976	Serves as head of the chemistry department at Howard University
Sept. 15, 1976	Dies in Washington, D.C.

Early Life

Moddie Daniel Taylor was born on March 3, 1912, to an African American family in Nymph, Alabama, and grew up in St. Louis, where his father worked as a postal clerk. After his graduation from Charles H. Sumner High School in 1931, Taylor attended Lincoln University in Jefferson City, Missouri, where he was graduated summa cum laude as the class valedictorian in 1935.

A College Professor

That same year, Taylor began teaching at Lincoln University, first as an instructor and then, from 1939 to 1941, as a full professor. Meanwhile, he had enrolled in the University of Chicago's graduate chemistry program. He received his master's degree in 1939 and was awarded a Ph.D. degree in 1943.

The Manhattan Project

From 1943 until 1945, Taylor worked as an associate chemist on the Manhattan Project, the U.S. government's secret program to build an atomic bomb. At the University of Chicago, he joined a team that helped to develop the process of separating plutonium from uranium 238.

The process was perfected, and plutonium was used in the first atomic explosive device tested at Jornada del Muerto, New Mexico, as well as the bomb that was dropped on Nagasaki, Japan. For his work on the Manhattan Project, Taylor would be awarded a Certificate of Merit from Secretary of War Henry Stimson.

Return to Teaching

After the war, Taylor returned to Lincoln University. In 1948, he was hired as an associate professor of chemistry at Howard University in Washington, D.C. He became a full professor in 1959 and headed the chemistry department from 1969 until 1976.

During the 1950's and 1960's, Taylor was involved in numerous activities in addition to his teaching and research duties at Howard. He lectured at high schools and colleges around the country.

In 1960, he published *First Principles of Chemistry*, a college-level chemistry textbook. That same year, he received the Manufacturing Chemists Association award as one of six outstanding college chemistry teachers in the United States.

In addition to teaching, Taylor served on a

Separating Plutonium from Uranium

While working for the Manhattan Project, Taylor was part of a team that developed a chemical method for separating plutonium from irradiated uranium 238.

Uranium naturally occurs in two isotopes. Uranium 235 is fissionable, which means that the nucleus will split when hit by neutrons. Uranium 238, which is 140 times more common, will absorb neutrons but will not split. When uranium 238 absorbs neutrons, however, it eventually becomes plutonium, which is fissionable—and therefore good atomic bomb fuel.

It was discovered that plutonium could be produced inside atomic "piles" within nuclear reactors. When a chain reaction began, uranium 238 within the pile absorbed neutrons produced by the fission process and eventually turned into plutonium. After several days, a considerable amount of plutonium could be produced.

Scientists had to cope with the problem of how to separate the plutonium from the uranium, which is highly toxic. It was eventually found that bismuth phosphate could serve as a carrier—a catalytic agent used to transfer one element to another—for plutonium.

A plutonium separation plant was set up in Hanford, Washington, that used techniques developed by the University of Chicago research team that included Taylor. Uranium from the reactor containing plutonium was immersed in water, which absorbed the toxic radiation, and was dragged through canals to the plant. There, the plutonium was separated from the uranium using the bismuth phosphate process.

Bibliography

"Forgotten Pioneers of the Atomic Age." Monroe Little, Jr. *The Indianapolis Star*, February 26, 1996, p. AO 5.

The Manhattan Project. Stephane Groueff. New York: Bantam Books, 1967.

The Story of Atomic Energy. Laura Fermi. New York: Random House, 1962.

---

number of boards and commissions. He served on the examinations committee for the college board's chemistry achievement test during the 1960's. In 1965, President Lyndon B. Johnson appointed him to serve on the Assay Commission.

Taylor retired from Howard University as a professor emeritus on April 1, 1976. On September 15 of that year, he died in Washington, D.C., of cancer.

Bibliography
By Taylor
First Principles of Chemistry, 1960

About Taylor
Blacks in Science and Medicine. Vivian Sommers Overton. New York: Hemisphere, 1990.

Holders of Doctorates Among American Negroes. Henry Washington Greene. Newton, Mass.: Crofton, 1974.

"Moddie Taylor, 64, Dies." *The Washington Post*, September 18, 1976, p. D6.

Notable Twentieth-Century Scientists. Emily J. McMurray, ed. Vol. 4. Detroit: Gale Research, 1995.

(Lawrence K. Orr)

Edward Teller

Areas of Achievement: Physics and technology

Contribution: Teller worked on the Manhattan Project, which resulted in the development of the atomic bomb. He is known as the creator of the hydrogen bomb, the high-powered successor to the atomic bomb.

Jan. 15, 1908	Born in Budapest, Hungary
1930	Earns a Ph.D. from the University of Leipzig in Germany
1933	Leaves Germany to escape the Nazis
1935	Appointed a professor of physics at George Washington University in Washington, D.C.
1941	Becomes a United States citizen
1942-1946	Works on the Manhattan Project to build the atomic bomb
1954	Testifies against J. Robert Oppenheimer, whose security clearance is revoked
1954-1975	Serves as the associate director of the Lawrence Livermore National Laboratory in California
1956	Appointed a professor of physics at the University of California, Berkeley
1960's	Advocates the development of an antiballistic missile system
1962	Receives the Fermi Award
1980's	Lobbies for implementation of the Strategic Defense Initiative (SDI)

Early Life

Edward Teller was born to prosperous Jewish parents in Budapest, Hungary, on January 15, 1908. He was educated at the Institute of Tech-nology in Budapest and then in Germany. In 1930, Teller was awarded a Ph.D. from the University of Leipzig, in Germany. He left Germany in 1933, when Adolf Hitler came to power, because of the rising anti-Semitism in the country.

Teller went first to Denmark, then to England. In 1935, he finally settled in the United States and was appointed a professor of physics at George Washington University in Washington, D.C. He became a United States citizen in 1941.

Work on the Atomic Bomb

In 1941, Teller was recruited to work at the Los Alamos Laboratory on the Manhattan Project, which was developing the first atomic bomb. He was interested in the problem of containing the fissionable material—heavy atomic nuclei that release energy if they are separated into two lighter nuclei, usually accompanied by the

(Lawrence Radiation Laboratory, courtesy of AIP Niels Bohr Library)

release of neutrons—long enough for an explosion to take place.

If a large enough mass of fissionable material, such as plutonium, is brought together, the neutrons emitted from one fission event induce other nearby atoms to undergo fission, which produces more neutrons and more fission in a cascading process called a chain reaction. The heat released in the reaction, however, usually causes the fissionable material to expand and come apart before a large amount of energy can be released.

Teller became aware of Seth Neddermeyer's solution to this problem. Neddermeyer proposed surrounding the fissionable material with a sphere of high explosives that, when detonated, would implode, sending a shock wave inward to compress the fissionable material.

Teller witnessed the first testing of an atomic bomb, conducted in New Mexico on July 15, 1945, from an observation area about 20 miles from the explosion.

The Hydrogen Bomb

Even before the first atomic bomb had been tested, Teller set his sights on a more powerful weapon, referred to as the superbomb. This device consisted of an atomic bomb surrounding a container of light elements. Teller and others proposed the use of the atomic explosion to compress and heat these light elements, causing their nuclei to combine into heavier nuclei, a process that is accompanied by the release of energy.

J. Robert Oppenheimer, the physicist who directed the development of the atomic bomb, was the chair of the General Advisory Committee of the Atomic Energy Commission, and he opposed the development of the superbomb. Teller later testified against Oppenhe-

The Hydrogen Bomb

Teller is widely credited with developing the idea of how to use an atomic bomb to trigger the fusion process in the hydrogen bomb. While his specific design remains classified, he is believed to have suggested using the X rays from the atomic bomb to ignite the fusion core.

Stars generate their enormous heat by nuclear fusion, a process whereby two light nuclei come together to form a heavier nucleus and energy is released. Fusion takes place at high temperatures and high pressures, which are found near the center of stars. The development of the atomic bomb provided an opportunity to reach those temperatures and pressures on Earth, since the explosion of an atomic bomb generates an enormous amount of heat and a high-pressure shock wave.

Even before the first successful test of the atomic bomb, in 1945, Teller and other scientists working on the Manhattan Project realized that the atomic bomb could provide a trigger for the hydrogen bomb. Enrico Fermi suggested the basic idea that a container of fusible nuclei, such as of deuterium, could be surrounded by an atomic bomb. When the atomic bomb exploded, the heat released would cause the deuterium to fuse.

The key problem was to devise a way to allow enough deuterium to fuse before the entire apparatus was dispersed by the explosion. In January, 1950, when President Harry S Truman ordered the Atomic Energy Commission to develop a hydrogen bomb, scientists and engineers at the Los Alamos Laboratory had a plan to accomplish this feat. Polish-born mathematician Stanislaw Ulam showed, however, that what was thought to be the most promising design would not work.

The solution to the problem was developed by Ulam and Teller. Ulam proposed using the shock wave from the atomic bomb to compress the deuterium as well as heating it, allowing it to stay together long enough to fuse. Teller suggested a variation on this plan, in which the X rays generated by the atomic explosion would initiate the deuterium reaction. The details of Ulam's and Teller's designs remain secret, but Teller is widely regarded as the creator of the hydrogen bomb.

Bibliography

The Firecracker Boys. Dan O'Neill. New York: St. Martin's Press, 1994.
Men Who Play God: The Story of the Hydrogen Bomb. Norman Moss. London: Victor Gollancz, 1968.

imer, whose security clearance was revoked in 1954 under a cloud of suspicion that he had communist sympathies.

Teller lobbied within the scientific and the political communities to bring about the development of the superbomb. It was not until the Soviet Union tested its first atomic bomb, in August, 1949, that Teller's proposal met with serious interest.

On January 29, 1950, President Harry S Truman directed that development proceed. Teller was appointed assistant director of Weapons Development at Los Alamos with responsibility for the hydrogen bomb project. The superbomb was tested successfully at Eniwetok Atoll in the Pacific Ocean in November, 1952.

An Advocate of High-Tech Weapons

Following the success of the hydrogen bomb, Teller devoted much of his career to the promotion of high-tech weapons systems. He advised policymakers, including President Ronald Reagan, and sought out opportunities to act as a spokesperson for advanced weapons systems.

In the 1960's, Teller advocated the development and construction of the antiballistic missile (ABM) system, which would have fired nuclear-tipped rockets to intercept and destroy incoming ballistic missiles. The U.S. ABM system was abandoned in 1972, but the Soviet Union deployed a limited ABM system around Moscow.

In the 1980's, Teller was one of several scientists who influenced Reagan's decision to proceed with the Strategic Defense Initiative (SDI), a program to shield the United States from nuclear attack. Teller advocated orbiting an array of satellites containing X-ray lasers, which would destroy incoming ballistic missiles. With the decline of international tensions in the 1990's, Teller suggested continued development of SDI technology for use as a shield against incoming asteroids or comets, which might do serious damage to the planet.

Bibliography

By Teller
The Structure of Matter, 1949 (with F. O. Rice)
Our Nuclear Future: Facts, Dangers, and Opportunities, 1958 (with A. L. Latter)
The Future of Nuclear Tests, 1961 (with Hans A. Bethe)
The Legacy of Hiroshima, 1962 (with Allen Brown)
The Reluctant Revolutionary, 1964
Better a Sword than a Shield: Perspectives on Defense and Technology, 1987

About Teller
The Advisors, Oppenheimer, Teller, and the Superbomb. Herbert F. York. San Francisco: W. H. Freeman, 1976.
The Firecracker Boys. Dan O'Neill. New York: St. Martin's Press, 1994.
Men Who Play God: The Story of the Hydrogen Bomb. Norman Moss. London: Victor Gollancz, 1968.
Teller's War: The Top Secret Story Behind the Star Wars Deception. William Broad. New York: Simon & Schuster, 1992.

(George J. Flynn)

Nikola Tesla

Areas of Achievement: Invention, physics, and technology

Contribution: Tesla was an eccentric, brilliant inventor and electrical engineer who laid the groundwork for much of the technology that is now taken for granted.

July 9, 1856	Born in Smiljan, Croatia
1875	Enters the Austrian Polytechnic School in Graz
1881	Works in the telegraph office in Budapest
1882	Takes a job with the Continental Edison Company in Paris
1885	Becomes an assistant to Thomas Alva Edison, but resigns
1886	Offered his own company, for which he develops an improved arc lamp, but again resigns
1887	Forms the Tesla Electric Company and files alternating current patents
1888	Offered a contract by George Westinghouse
1893	His system provides power for the Chicago World's Fair
1893	Niagara Falls Commission awards a contract for three generators to Westinghouse
1898	Builds a laboratory in Colorado Springs to develop a worldwide broadcasting system
1906	Designs a turbine to drive an ocean liner across the Atlantic in three days
1917	Awarded the Edison Medal of the American Institute of Electrical Engineers
Jan. 7, 1943	Dies in New York, New York

Early Life

Nikola Tesla was born on July 9, 1856, in Smiljan, Croatia. His father, Milutin, was a clergyman, but it was his mother, Djuka, who had the more profound influence on his life. Although she was illiterate, Tesla's mother was a clever inventor. Tesla excelled at science and mathematics and showed an aptitude for mechanical problems. Even as a boy, he exhibited the rigid self-discipline and unshakable confidence that would lead him to success.

In 1875, Tesla attended the Austrian Polytechnic School. He was a voracious student, sometimes studying twenty hours a day. Financial problems, however, forced Tesla to move to Prague, where he studied at the university but never formally enrolled.

With the death of his father in 1881, Tesla moved to Budapest to work for the central telegraph office. While walking one evening, reciting a passage from Johann Wolfgang von Goethe's epic poem *Faust*, Tesla had a flash of intuition. He saw the principle of the rotating magnetic field upon which all polyphase induction motors are based. He would not be able to act on this inspiration for several years.

(Smithsonian Institution)

Motors, Dynamos, and Transformers

Tesla developed dynamos, transformers, and motors that allowed the large-scale production and distribution of electricity.

A current is a flow of charge. Current is produced in two types: direct current and alternating current. The electrical power provided to a device is the product of the current and voltage. When a current passes through a wire, however, some of this power is lost to heat. The power lost is proportional to the square of the current. Thus, the most efficient way to transmit electrical power over long distances is at low currents and high voltages.

Current-carrying wires experience a force when they pass through an external magnetic field. Similarly, a changing magnetic field will induce a current in a coil. These effects are used together to produce several devices.

Motors and dynamos consist of a coil of wire placed between the poles of a magnet. In a motor, when a current runs through the coil, the magnetic field will twist the coil, making it rotate. In a dynamo, if the coil is rotated mechanically, the resultant changing magnetic field will induce a current in the coil. This is the basic principle behind electric power plants, which use water flow or steam to rotate the coil.

In a transformer, two independent coils are wrapped around an iron core. When an alternating current runs through one of the coils, it produces an alternating magnetic field in the core, which then induces an alternating current in the second coil. The voltages in the coils depend on the number of turns in the coils, allowing the voltage to be stepped up or down. An alternating current can be transmitted at very high voltages with little power loss and then stepped down to safe levels at its destination.

Bibliography

Conceptual Physics. Paul G. Hewitt. New York: HarperCollins College Publishing, 1993.

The Feynman Lectures on Physics. Richard P. Feynman, R. B. Leighton, and M. Sands. Reading, Mass.: Addison-Wesley, 1963.

The Physics of Everyday Phenomena: A Conceptual Introduction to Physics. W. Thomas Griffith. Dubuque, Iowa: Wm. C. Brown, 1992.

The Radio Amateur's Handbook. Doug DeMaw, ed. Newington, Conn.: American Radio Relay League, 1971.

University Physics. Hugh D. Young and Roger Freedman. Reading, Mass.: Addison-Wesley, 1996.

Coming to America

In 1884, Tesla decided to try his luck in the United States. In New York, he became Thomas Alva Edison's assistant. Edison was committed to the use of direct current electricity, while Tesla was sure that alternating current was the future, a dispute that became the "battle of the currents." Tesla eventually quit because of a disagreement over money. In 1886, a group of investors gave Tesla the money to start his own electric company, but again he quit the company. He was forced to work as a common laborer and to develop his ideas in his spare time.

In 1887, Tesla formed the Tesla Electric Company, with the help of A. K. Brown of the Western Union Telegraph Company, and his luck began to change. He was finally able to perfect his polyphase motor, which allowed strong currents to be transmitted over long distances. His inventions began to attract attention. George Westinghouse bought one of Tesla's patents and hired him. Tesla became famous and lectured widely throughout the United States and Europe. He built the first hydroelectric generating plant at Niagara Falls, putting an end to Edison's direct current.

Tesla turned his attention to the idea that radio waves could carry electrical energy and demonstrated the idea of wireless communication. In 1898, he moved to Colorado Springs, where he continued this research on a large scale. Although Tesla's research in radio waves produced no immediate practical results, it was acknowledged as the basis for Pyotr Kapitsa's research in magnetism that won for him the 1978 Nobel Prize in Physics.

In 1900, Tesla closed his laboratory in Colorado Springs and returned to New York. The next year, with backing from financier J. P. Morgan, he began work on a transmitter for a worldwide broadcasting system at Wardenclyffe, Long Island. The project failed, however, because of labor troubles and the withdrawal of Morgan's support. Tesla's career lagged. In 1906, he designed a new turbine to drive an ocean liner across the Atlantic in three days, but he could not find the funds to build it.

Contributions and Ambitions
Tesla did have successes. He made alternating current transmission feasible and designed dynamos, transformers, and motors that made possible large-scale production and transmission of electrical power. He built the Tesla coil, discovered the healing possibilities of high-frequency currents applied to the human body, and invented the carbon button lamp, the shadowgraph, and a new reciprocating dynamo, the predecessor of the electric clock.

He also described the principle of radio broadcasting before Guglielmo Marconi and demonstrated the first radio-controlled model boat. He developed the basic principles of radar and wanted to create artificial lightning to control the weather.

Later Years
Although Tesla's research led to many indispensable developments, at the time its applications were unappreciated. He received some royalties from his patents but realized only a small fraction of the fortune produced by alternating current power production, leaving him almost destitute.

For the remainder of his life, he lived as a recluse in a hotel in New York City. He continued to conduct research, but he became increasingly eccentric, troubled by phobias, and his ideas became more outlandish. At his death on January 7, 1943, he was finally accorded the recognition that he had missed while living. Political figures and leading scientists praised him as a visionary, and Yugoslavia made him a national hero.

Bibliography
By Tesla
Nikola Tesla: Lectures, Patents, Articles. 1956 (Vojin Popovic, Radoslav Horvat, and Nikola Nikolic, eds.)

About Tesla
Lightning in His Hand: The Life Story of Nikola Tesla. Inez Hunt and Wanetta W. Draper. Denver: Sage Books, 1964.
"Tesla: A Scientific Saint, Wizard, or Carnival Sideman?" Stephen H. Hall. *Smithsonian* 17 (June, 1986).
Tesla: Man Out of Time. Margaret Cheney. Englewood Cliffs, N.J.: Prentice Hall, 1981.

(Linda L. McDonald)

Thales of Miletus

Area of Achievement: Science (general)
Contribution: Thales is considered by many to be the founder of Greek science. He is also credited, probably without basis, for having predicted eclipses and developed a system of navigation.

c. 625 B.C.E.	Born, probably in Miletus, Ionia, Asia Minor (now Turkey)
c. 585 B.C.E.	Said to predict a solar eclipse, which perhaps occurred on May 28
c. 547 B.C.E.	Dies, probably in Miletus, Ionia, Asia Minor

Early Life

Details of the life of Thales (pronounced "THAY-leez") of Miletus are largely unknown, as there are neither contemporary accounts of his activities nor any autobiographical information. Even his birth and death dates are matters of conjecture. It is known that he lived, and was probably born, in the city of Miletus, which was located on the coast of what is now Turkey. He is said to have been the son of Examyes and Cleobuline, possibly Milesian aristocrats.

(Library of Congress)

Practical Accomplishments

Tradition views Thales as a man who combined ability in philosophical investigation with shrewdness in practical affairs. He is described as an entrepreneur, politician, mathematician, and engineer. For example, it was recounted that he invented a system of government for the city of Teos and carried out projects that might now be called civil engineering, such as diverting a river for military reasons.

Anecdotes

Aristotle tells a story about him that is probably untrue but that gives an idea of Thales' reputation for coupling mathematical brilliance with practical shrewdness. Thales is said to have employed astronomical calculations to predict a bumper olive crop and then to have used the information to make considerable money by buying up all available olive presses.

Plato tells a rather different tale: Thales was said to have fallen into a well because he was so busy looking at the heavens. Thus, he became an object of ridicule by a servant girl, who remarked that he foolishly tried to understand the heavens while being quite unaware of what was happening at his own feet.

The contrast between these two entirely unreliable anecdotes probably says more about the two writers than about Thales himself. One should also keep in mind that Plato and Aristotle were hardly contemporaries of Thales, Plato having been born about two hundred years after Thales and Aristotle having been born about fifty years after Plato.

Thales enjoyed a great reputation in classical times, Aristotle referring to him as the founder of natural philosophy, now known as science. A central ingredient in this fame was the story, recounted in Herodotus' *History*, that Thales had successfully predicted the solar eclipse of 585 B.C.E.

This is almost undoubtedly untrue: There is no evidence that anyone in the classical era, or even hundreds of years later, possessed astronomical knowledge sufficient for such a prediction. The eighteenth century British astronomer Edmond Halley, namesake of the famous comet, suggested that Thales might have known about a Babylonian eclipse pre-

The Search for a Primary Substance

An important element in Greek natural philosophy (that is, science) for more than several hundred years was the idea that one, or a few, primary substances formed the physical basis for the entire universe.

Thales of Miletus was probably the initiator of this effort to identify this underlying substance (Greek, *Archei*), lending credence to Aristotle's identification of him as the first natural philosopher. Indeed, it should be said that all that is known about Thales' efforts in this direction is from a few passages in Aristotle's *Metaphysica* (c. 335-323 B.C.E.; *Metaphysics*, 1801). There, one learns that Thales believed that water is the fundamental constituent of all things. Not only was water the fundamental building block of matter, but the entire Earth floated on it. Earthquakes were to be explained by the earth sloshing about in its bath. Solids came from water by condensation; gases arose through its evaporation.

Thales apparently saw that all life requires water and that fluids such as blood and semen are fundamental to life processes. Arguing by analogy, he envisioned the earth as a sort of organism, dependent on water in all respects: physically supported by it, imbibing it as rain, and containing it as the basis of all material substance. Finally, as movement or change appeared to be a fundamental feature of life and of the physical world, the obvious ability of water to flow from place to place enhanced its appeal as the primary substance.

That this "water theory" entitles Thales to be considered the founder of Greek natural philosophy can be supported by two factors. First, the theory initiated a series of efforts to identify the primary substance (or substances) of the universe. After Thales and his specification of water as primary, Anaximenes of Miletus proposed air, Heraclitus suggested fire, and Democritus saw matter as composed of tiny atoms. Empedocles, about a century after Thales, introduced the idea that four elements—earth, air, fire, and water—together formed matter. This influential view persisted throughout the classical period and well beyond.

A second and perhaps greater reason to honor Thales (and his theory) is that he was a pioneer for believing that an underlying substance could explain the properties of physical reality. Before him, the search for causes in nature resorted only to myth. Thus, the gods caused things to happen: Zeus was the author of thunderstorms and the hurler of lightning, and Poseidon, the "earth shaker," was responsible for earthquakes. Thales was the first Greek to seek natural, material causes. In this, he was a true revolutionary and the rightful ancestor of all scientists who, through subsequent ages, have tried to understand the universe.

Bibliography
Before Philosophy. H. Frankfort. London: Penguin Books, 1949.
The Beginnings of Western Science. David C. Lindberg. Chicago: University of Chicago Press, 1992.
Metaphysics. Aristotle. H. G. Apostle, trans. Grinell, Iowa: Peripatetic Press, 1979.

diction method entailing a 223-lunar month cycle, but such a method did not exist. A great reputation, it seems, can have an extremely thin basis.

Bibliography
By Thales
None of his writings survive.

About Thales
The Exact Sciences in Antiquity. O. Neugebauer. Reprint. Mineola, N.Y.: Dover, 1957.
History. Herodotus. A. D. Godley, trans. Vol. 1. Cambridge, Mass.: Harvard University Press, 1920.
A History of Greek Philosophy. W. K. C. Guthrie. Vol. 1. Cambridge, England: Cambridge University Press, 1962.
The Presocratic Philosophers. G. S. Kirk and J. E. Raven. Cambridge, England: Cambridge University Press, 1957.

(John L. Howland)

Hubert Mach Thaxton

Areas of Achievement: Mathematics, physics, and technology

Contribution: Thaxton, a noted African American physicist, was a pioneer in the theoretical analysis of proton-proton scattering.

Dec. 28, 1912	Born in Lynchburg, Virginia
1939	Earns a Ph.D. in physics from Wisconsin University
1939-1944	Serves as chair and professor of physics at North Carolina Agricultural and Technology College
1944	Named chair and professor of mathematics at Delaware State College
1949-1950	Works on radar and television antenna systems for Sperry Gyroscope
1950	Named chief engineer of research and development of color television at Sylvania Electric
1952-1956	Serves as a chief engineer at Balco Research
1956-1960	Named chief engineer of semiconductors and devices at Astron
1960-1961	Works as a project engineer for the design of special-purpose jet aircraft at Curtis-Wright
1961	Named a chief engineer at Engelhard-Hanovia
1963	Named director of the digital computer facility at Kollsman Instrument Company
1971-1973	Teaches mathematics at the City College of New York
Jan. 3, 1974	Dies in New York, New York

Early Life

Hubert Mach Thaxton was born in Lynchburg, Virginia, in 1912. His parents were poor but hardworking people who valued education and encouraged their son always to perform at a high level of achievement. Thaxton showed an early interest in science and mathematics. After his graduation from high school, he attended Howard University. There, he majored in both mathematics and physics and received two degrees, a B.S. in 1931 and an M.S. in 1933.

Thaxton continued his graduate work at Wisconsin University, where he obtained an M.A. in mathematics in 1936. Remaining at the university, he also received a Ph.D. in theoretical physics in 1939. His research topic was the scattering of protons by protons.

Nuclear Physics

From 1939 to 1942, Thaxton continued his theoretical studies on proton-proton scattering. Four of his five publications during this period had coauthors who either were or would soon become internationally known scientists in nuclear physics.

Thaxton's papers presented some of the first detailed studies of one of the most basic nuclear processes; namely, proton-proton scattering. This work was also of direct relevance in the effort to construct the atomic bomb in the early 1940's.

Career in Education

Thaxton enjoyed working with students and, throughout his scientific career, always found ways to teach. Immediately after receiving his Ph.D. in physics, he accepted the position of chair and professor of physics at North Carolina Agricultural and Technology College. He would assume similar positions at Delaware State College and Walter Hervey Junior College in New York.

He joined the City College of New York's evening faculty in 1946 and became a full-time member of the mathematics department there in 1971. His application for tenure was denied, however, and an extended legal battle ensued between Thaxton and the college involving charges of racial discrimination. He died before this issue could be resolved.

Industrial Employment

From 1947 to 1971, Thaxton held positions at a number of high-technology companies. Each change of employment led to greater levels of scientific leadership and managerial responsibility.

The projects under his direction involved what was then cutting-edge technology. He helped to advance scientific principles in the following areas: the theory, design, and operation of radar and television systems; the analysis of the effects of nuclear radiation on electrical components and other materials; the application of ultrasonics to problems relating to sound propagation, production, and detection in materials; and the application of the digital computer to the solutions of problems of interest to industry.

Thaxton was heavily involved in classified government contract work at several of the companies at which he was employed. Most of the projects centered on atomic processes and long-range radar.

Recognition

While Thaxton's contributions to science and technology are not widely known in the scientific community, the general significance of his research can be judged in part by the distinguished persons with whom he collaborated. Included among these names are four Nobel Prize winners: He worked with Sir Arthur Eddington on proton-proton scattering related to a theory of stellar structure, Ernest Orlando Lawrence on the cyclotron, Eugene P. Wigner on quantum statistics, and Don Kerst on the betatron.

In his lifetime, Thaxton had more than two hundred publications. Most of them, however, are classified technical reports.

Bibliography

By Thaxton

"Analysis of Experiments on the Scattering of Protons by Protons," *Physical Review*, 1939 (with G. Breit and L. Eisenbud)

"Phase Shift Calculations for Proton-Proton Scattering at High Energies," *Physical Review*, 1939 (with L. E. Hoisington)

"Proton Scattering," with A. S. Eddington, in *Physica*, Vol. 7, pps. 122-124 (1940)

"Note on *p*-Wave Anomalies in Proton-Proton Scattering," *Physical Review*, 1940 (with Breit and C. Kittel)

"Note on the Low-Energy Scattering of Protons by Protons," *Indian Journal of Physics*, 1942

Proton-Proton Scattering

Proton-proton scattering provides information on the nuclear force.

Matter is made of various arrangements of atoms. Atoms have a massive nucleus in the center surrounded by electrons. The nucleus is composed of positively charged protons and neutrons having no charge. Except for properties related to charge, protons and neutrons are the same. The simplest nucleus is that of the element hydrogen. It consists of a single proton.

A technique for determining the structure of an object is to collide two of them together and examine what happens. This is called a scattering experiment. Thaxton, using experimental data from proton-proton scattering experiments, determined certain properties of the nuclear force acting between protons. His analysis was based on the use of various mathematical techniques and principles of quantum physics.

A knowledge of this force is necessary to the understanding of general nuclear processes and their applications to the construction of nuclear power reactors, atomic bombs, and the energy-generating mechanism of stars.

Bibliography

The Atom and Its Nucleus. George Gamow. Englewood Cliffs, N.J.: Prentice Hall, 1961.

The Discovery of Subatomic Particles. Steven Weinberg. New York: W. H. Freeman, 1983.

Foundations of Modern Physical Science. Gerald Holton and Duane Roller. Reading, Mass.: Addison-Wesley, 1958.

Introduction to Atomic and Nuclear Physics. Henry Semat. New York: Holt, Rinehart and Winston, 1962.

"Minimum and Maximum Velocity of Lamb Waves in Quartz Plates," *Journal of Applied Physics*, 1962

"Interesting Anomaly in the Propagation of 5Mc Pulses Through Tantalum Rod," *Journal of the Acoustical Society of America*, 1962 (with J. P. Kearney)

"Exact Solutions of the Equations for Optical Maser Models," *Illuminating Engineering*, 1962 (with O. L. Galligher and Kearney)

About Thaxton

American Men of Science. 7th ed. New York: R. R. Bowker, 1944.

Blacks in Science and Medicine. Vivian O. Sammons. New York: Hemisphere, 1990.

Blacks in Science: Astrophysicist to Zoologist. Hattie Carwell. Hicksville, N.Y.: Exposition Press, 1977.

(Ronald E. Mickens)

Theophrastus

Area of Achievement: Botany

Contribution: Theophrastus, an ancient Greek philosopher and successor of Aristotle at the Lyceum in Athens, taught and wrote in many areas relating to philosophy and the natural sciences, but he is most renowned for his work with plants. Indeed, he can be viewed as the founder of the modern field of botany.

c. 372 B.C.E.	Born in Eresus, Lesbos
347 B.C.E.	The death of Plato, with whom Theophrastus may have studied
347-342 B.C.E.	Meets Aristotle, either in Asia Minor or on Lesbos
342-335 B.C.E.	Travels with Aristotle to Macedonia
335-323 B.C.E.	Teaches in the Lyceum
323 B.C.E.	Takes over research and teaching at the Lyceum after Aristotle is forced to retire
322 B.C.E.	The death of Aristotle
323-287 B.C.E.	Leads teaching and research at the Lyceum
317-307 B.C.E.	His pupil Demetrius Phalereus becomes ruler of Athens
c. 287 B.C.E.	Dies, perhaps in Athens, Greece

Early Life

Theophrastus (pronounced "thee-oh-FRAHS-tus") lived and worked in Greece in the fourth century B.C.E. His original name was Tyrtamos, and he was born in or around the year 372 B.C.E. in Eresus on the island of Lesbos in the Aegean Sea. His father was a fuller—a person who cleans, shrinks, and thickens cloth with moisture, heat, and pressure.

Theophrastus probably met Aristotle in Asia Minor or on Lesbos, traveled with him, and then taught for several years with Aristotle in the Lyceum, a public garden in Athens fre-

The frontispiece of this seventeenth century herbal portrays Theophrastus standing by the pillar on the left. (Library of Congress)

quented by teachers. This school came to be known also as the Peripatetic School because of Aristotle's method of teaching, which included walking about the grounds while engaging in discussions.

Upon Aristotle's death in 322 B.C.E., Theophrastus took over research and teaching at the Lyceum. Over the next thirty-five years, he had approximately two thousand students, including the physician Erasistratus, the philosopher Arcesilaus, and the comic poet Menander.

A Scientist and Philosopher

Many, perhaps most, of Theophrastus' works have been lost or destroyed, and several exist only in fragmentary form. In some cases, there is even uncertainty as to whether Theophrastus actually wrote them. To put the surviving

The First Botanist

Theophrastus' botanical writings constituted the first comprehensive scientific study of plants—and the only one for more than fifteen hundred years.

Theophrastus' *Historia plantarum* accomplished for plants what Aristotle's *Historia animalium* achieved for animals. In its nine books, Theophrastus describes, classifies, and analyzes the various known species of plants. He distinguishes between permanent and annual plant growth and classifies plant life by size and form into trees, shrubs, and herbs. He discusses domestic versus wild species, as well as plants particular to certain regions. He describes different types of wood and their uses, plant juices, and medicinal herbs.

Theophrastus includes approximately 550 species and varieties reported from throughout the known world. In building his ambitious account, he draws on many sources, from technical writings and oral reports to poetic works, as well as on the beliefs and practices of farmers and physicians.

The six books of Theophrastus' *De causis plantarum*, which was written after the *Historia plantarum* and which is comparable to Aristotle's *De partibus animalium*, are concerned with the causes, origins, and cycles of plant life. Theophrastus covers the generation (from seeds, as opposed to spontaneous generation) and propagation of plants, discussing cultivation and environmental factors. He devotes one book to seeds, one to the aging and death of plant species, and one to plant juices.

His physiological theory corresponds essentially to that of Aristotle: that living things have a life that depends on "innate heat" and moisture and on the proper relationship between the plants and their environments. Aristotle viewed plants as the lowest members in a hierarchy of life forms culminating in human beings. Theophrastus, however, concentrating on his observational work with plants, refrained from such generalization. Rather, his focus was on the senses and the human ability to use observation to describe the world of plants.

Categorizing plants is especially problematic because they are so diverse: Plants are recognized as having an essential nature, and yet they do not all have roots, stems, branches, leaves, flowers, fruit, or bark. Theophrastus' meticulous and impartial data collection, his careful systematization and characterization of plant species, his caution in speculating beyond what the facts at hand permit—all of these laid the groundwork for modern botany and continue to inform the methodology of much work in the natural sciences.

Theophrastus himself asserted that many aspects of his work needed further investigation. Much of what he wrote was not based on first-hand observation, and much is erroneous, tentative, or incomplete. By his own admission, his studies were to be understood as work in progress—as research, not as a completed textbook. Nevertheless, his writings and what is known of his work show that he was a brilliant and prolific teacher and natural scientist.

Bibliography

Ancient Science Through the Golden Age of Greece. George Sarton. New York: Dover, 1952.
The Beginnings of Western Science. David C. Lindberg. Chicago: University of Chicago Press, 1992.
Greek Science in Antiquity. Marshall Clagett. New York: Collier, 1955.

works in perspective, the two botanical works *De causis plantarum* (or *Peri phyton aition*; *De Causis Plantarum*, 1976-1990) and *Historia plantarum* (or *Peri phyton historias*; "Enquiry into Plants," 1916) put together are about double the size of his other surviving works combined.

Theophrastus' most important contribution to science was his work with plants. The smaller works and fragments attributed to him that have survived are mostly in subject areas relating to nature and natural phenomena, but they also include such subjects as metaphysics and history.

Theophrastus embraced and elaborated on all of Aristotle's research and philosophy, including the areas of metaphysics, physics, physiology, zoology, botany, ethics, politics, and history. He is credited with building on and strengthening the systematic unity of Aristotle's work. In his text *Ton meta ta physika* (*The Metaphysics*, 1929), Theophrastus is in basic agreement with Aristotle about fundamental reality. Relevant to his own philosophy of science, however, he suggests dealing with natural phenomena by starting from observations of the particular before moving to broader conclusions and higher principles.

The ancient understanding of matter proposed by Empedocles and subsequently adopted by Plato and Aristotle was that all things are made in different ways from four basic elements—earth, water, air, and fire. In *Peri pyros* (*De Igne*, 1971), Theophrastus concerns himself primarily with the generation, preservation, and extinction of elemental fire; he questions the validity of counting fire as one of the basic elements.

Peri ton lithon or *De lapidibus* (*Theophrastus's History of Stones*, 1746) represents his investigation into the inanimate compounds of the elements, based on the classifications of Plato and Aristotle that metals are composed of water and that stones and mineral earths are composed of elemental earth. This work, a systematic discussion of stones and mineral earths found in the Mediterranean region, contains the earliest Greek descriptive references to mineral oil and pearls, as well as accounts of the preparation of pigments and the uses of earths dug from pits. His was the first systematic study of minerals, and it was not equaled until the work of Georgius Agricola in the sixteenth century.

Theophrastus' book *Charakteres* (*The Characters*, 1616) consists of thirty brief descriptions of moral "types"—such as "The Shamelessly Greedy Man," "The Superstitious Man," and "The Coward"—developed from studies carried out by his mentor Aristotle for ethical and rhetorical purposes. His text *Physikon doxai* gathers the opinions and critiques of earlier Greek natural philosophers and, as such, provided the groundwork for much subsequent history of ancient philosophy.

A Leader and Benefactor

Theophrastus seems to have been a good leader as well as a good teacher. Under him, the enrollment of the Lyceum is said to have risen to its highest point. He was well regarded by the Athenian people: An attempt to prosecute him for "impiety" failed and caused a restrictive law against him and other philosophers to be repealed. One of Theophrastus' pupils, Demetrius Pharlereus, ruled during the years from 317 to 310 B.C.E., during which time Theophrastus was able to acquire additional property for the Lyceum. Upon his death, Theophrastus left the school's property, including the library compiled by Aristotle and himself, jointly to a number of relatives and associates to allow the continued study of philosophy and literature.

Bibliography

By Theophrastus

Charakteres (*The Characters*, 1616)

Peri phyton aition (also known as *De causis plantarum*; English trans. as *De Causis Plantarum*, 3 vols., 1976-1990)

Peri phyton historias (also known as *Historia plantarum*; "Enquiry into Plants" in *Enquiry into Plants and Minor Works on Odours and Weather Signs*, 1916)

Ton meta ta physika (*The Metaphysics*, 1929)

Peri pyros (also known as *De igne*; English trans. as *De Igne: A Post-Aristotelian View of the Nature of Fire*, 1971)

Peri osmon (*Concerning Odours*, 1916)

Peri ton lithon (also known as *De lapidibus*; *Theophrastus's History of Stones*, 1746)

Physikon doxai ("Opinions of Natural Philosophers" in *Doxographi Graeci*, 1879)

About Theophrastus
Theophrastus: His Psychological, Doxographical, and Scientific Writings. William W. Fortenbaugh and Dimitri Gutas, eds. New Brunswick, N.J.: Transaction Books, 1992.
Theophrastus of Eresus: On His Life and Work. William W. Fortenbaugh, Pamela M. Huby, and Anthony A. Long, eds. New Brunswick, N.J.: Transaction Books, 1985.
Theophrastus of Eresus: Sources for His Life, Writings, Thought, and Influence. W. Fortenbaugh, P. Huby, R. Sharples, and D. Gutas, eds. 2 vols. Leiden, the Netherlands: E. J. Brill, 1992.

(David E. Connolly)

E. Donnall Thomas

Areas of Achievement: Biology and medicine

Contribution: Thomas developed techniques that allowed the transplantation of bone marrow, a procedure that resulted in a means to treat blood diseases.

Mar. 15, 1920	Born in Mart, Texas
1946	Receives a medical degree from Harvard Medical School
1946-1947	Serves an internship in medicine at Peter Bent Brigham Hospital in Boston
1947-1948	Made a research fellow in hematology at Brigham Hospital
1948-1950	Serves in the U.S. Army, with assignments in internal medicine
1950-1951	Made a postdoctoral fellow in biology at the Massachusetts Institute of Technology (MIT)
1951-1953	Named chief medical resident at Brigham Hospital
1953-1955	Works as an instructor in medicine at Harvard Medical School and a hematologist at Brigham Hospital
1955-1963	Named physician in chief at Mary Imogene Bassett Hospital and associate clinical professor of medicine at Columbia University's College of Physicians and Surgeons
1963-1990	Serves as professor of medicine at the University of Washington School of Medicine
1974	Joins the Fred Hutchinson Cancer Research Center in Seattle and named director emeritus of clinical research
1990	Awarded the Nobel Prize in Physiology or Medicine

(The Nobel Foundation)

Early Life

Edward Donnall Thomas was born in 1920 in the small Texas town of Mart. His father was the local doctor, and his mother was a school-teacher. Thomas entered the University of Texas in 1937 as a chemistry major, living in a rooming house where his mother also served as cook. He also lettered in swimming.

Following his graduation in 1941, Thomas continued with his education at the university, earning a master's degree in 1943. In 1942, he married Dorothy Martin. Martin would contribute significantly to Thomas' work and would later be referred to as the "mother of bone marrow transplants."

In 1943, Thomas entered medical school in Galveston, but he soon transferred to Harvard Medical School, being graduated in 1946. He carried out his internship and residency at Peter Bent Brigham Hospital in Boston. Among his colleagues was Joseph Murray, who would later share the Nobel Prize in Physiology or Medicine with Thomas.

In 1948, Thomas entered the U.S. Army, where he served as a physician for two years.

Bone Marrow Transplantation

Returning to civilian life in 1950, Thomas was awarded a fellowship at the Massachusetts Institute of Technology (MIT), where he began his research on leukemia and transplantation. In 1955, he was appointed physician in chief at the Mary Imogene Bassett Hospital in Cooperstown, New York. In collaboration with Joseph Ferrebee, he carried out his first experiments on transplants between outbred species. Shortly afterward, Thomas also became associate clinical professor of medicine at Columbia University's College of Physicians and Surgeons, where he continued his research into bone marrow transplantation.

During the mid-1950's, the first successful organ transplantations between individuals had taken place. Thomas thought that similar procedures could be used in the treatment of blood diseases such as aplastic anemia and leukemia. In 1956, he performed the first bone marrow transplantation, transferring marrow to a leukemia patient from an identical twin. Although the procedure proved unsuccessful, Thomas continued his research.

In 1963, Thomas was appointed professor of medicine at the University of Washington School of Medicine in Seattle. He began to utilize new techniques of tissue matching and the use of immunosuppressive drugs. In 1969, his team successfully transplanted tissue to a leukemia patient from a matched donor.

Awards and Recognition

Thomas became the recipient of numerous awards and honors. In addition to the 1990 Nobel Prize in Physiology or Medicine, he received the Landsteiner Memorial Award in 1987, the Terry Fox Award in 1990, the Gairdner Foundation International Award in 1990, the North American Medical Association of Hong Kong Prize in 1990, and the National Science Medal in 1990. He also served on the editorial board for numerous scientific journals.

As an indication of his generosity and in recognition of the roles played by others in his work, Thomas donated his share of the Nobel award ($350,000) to the Hutchinson Cancer Research Center.

Bibliography
By Thomas
"Intravenous Infusion of Bone Marrow in Patients Receiving Radiation and Chemotherapy," *The New England Journal of Medicine,* 1957 (with H. L. Lochte, Jr., W. C. Lu, et al.)

"Supralethal Whole Body Irradiation and Isologous Marrow Transplantation in Man," *Journal of Clinical Investigation,* 1959 (with Lochte, J. H. Cannon, O. D. Sahler, and J. W. Ferrebee)

"Irradiation and Marrow Infusion in Leukemia: Observations in Five Patients with

---

Bone Marrow Transplantation

Thomas pioneered the techniques used in successful bone marrow transplantation.

In the mid-1950's, Joseph Murray developed techniques for successful organ transplantation. Thomas thought that similar procedures could be used in the transplantation of bone marrow. The techniques could then be applied in the treatment of diseases like leukemia. Difficulties following bone marrow transplantations had centered on two problems: host rejection and graft-versus-host disease (in which the transplanted cells, in effect, reject the host).

Thomas and his surgical team overcame the first problem through the use of whole-body radiation; irradiation could be used to destroy the host's immune system, preventing rejection. The procedure also served to destroy leukemic cells in the patient. Cells could then be successfully transplanted between identical twins.

By 1957, Thomas and Joseph Ferrebee had developed procedures to store large quantities of marrow. What remained to be found was the means to infuse these cells successfully into siblings other than twins or between unrelated individuals.

By the early 1960's, the advent of tissue typing had allowed for pairing of matched donors and recipients. Thomas also found that proper use of antimetabolites such as methotrexate could limit the extent of graft-versus-host reactions. In 1969, Thomas and his team performed the first successful bone marrow infusion using matched siblings rather than identical twins.

Bibliography
A Gift of Life: Observations on Organ Transplantation. Roy Calne. New York: Basic Books, 1970.

The Transplant Age. Ralph Porzio. New York: Vantage Press, 1969.

Transplant: The Give and Take of Tissue Transplantation. Francis Moore. New York: Simon & Schuster, 1972.

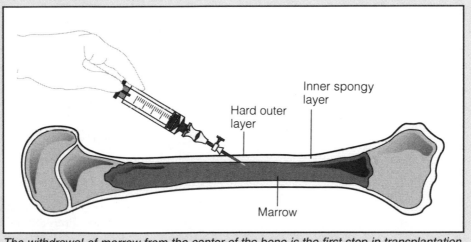

The withdrawal of marrow from the center of the bone is the first step in transplantation. (Hans & Cassady, Inc.)

Acute Leukemia Treated by Whole-Body Exposures of 1,400 to 2,000 Roentgens and Infusions of Marrow," *Archives of Internal Medicine*, 1961 (with E. C. Herman, Jr., Cannon, Sahler, Ferrebee, H. E. Kay, and M. Constantoulakis)

"Transplantation of Marrow and Whole Organs: Experiences and Comments," *Canadian Medical Association Journal*, 1962 (with Ferrebee)

"Methotrexate Regimens for Control of Graft-vs.-Host Disease in Dogs with Allogeneic Marrow Grafts," *Transplantation*, 1970 (with R. Storb, R. B. Epstein, and T. C. Graham)

"Studies of Immunological Reactivity Following Syngeneic or Allogeneic Grafts in Man," *Transplantation*, 1973 (with L. Fass and H. D. Ochs)

"Allogeneic Bone-Marrow Transplantation," *Immunological Reviews*, 1983 (with Storb)

Bone Marrow Transplantation, 1994 (as editor, with Stephen J. Forman and Karl G. Blume)

About Thomas

The Nobel Prize Winners: Physiology or Medicine. Frank N. Magill, ed., Pasadena, Calif.: Salem Press, 1991.

Notable Twentieth-Century Scientists. Emily J. McMurray, ed., Detroit: Gale Research, 1995.

"Overcoming Rejection to Win a Nobel Prize." Joe Palca. *Science* 250 (1990).

(Richard Adler)

Sir Joseph John Thomson

Area of Achievement: Physics
Contribution: Thomson was a pioneer of modern physics. His major contribution was the discovery that cathode rays consist of a stream of negatively charged particles now called electrons.

Dec. 18, 1856	Born in Cheetham Hill, near Manchester, England
1871-1876	Studies engineering, then physics, at Owens College in Manchester
1876	Receives an entrance scholarship to Trinity College, Cambridge University
1882	Wins the Adams Prize at Cambridge for his treatise on atoms in a gas
1884	Elected to head the Cavendish Laboratory
1897	Publishes his work on cathode rays in *Philosophical Magazine*
1903	Publishes *Conduction of Electricity Through Gases*
1905	Appointed a professor at the Royal Institution
1906	Awarded the Nobel Prize in Physics
1908	Receives a knighthood
1913	Publishes *Rays of Positive Electricity and Their Application to Chemical Analyses*
1915	Elected president of the Royal Society of London
1918	Named master of Trinity College
1923	Awarded the Franklin Institute's Scott and Franklin medals
Aug. 30, 1940	Dies in Cambridge, England

Early Life

Joseph John Thomson—who would be known throughout his life by family, friends, and colleagues as "J. J."—was born the son of a publisher and bookseller in a suburb of Manchester, England. It was intended that the young Thomson become an engineer and be apprenticed to a maker of steam-driven locomotives, but the waiting list was so long that his father took the advice of a friend and instead sent the fourteen-year-old student to a local college.

At Owens College, which in 1880 became Manchester University, Thomson studied mathematics, engineering, and physics under challenging teachers. The early death of his father, however, forced him to reconsider a projected career in engineering, since the cost of the required apprenticeship was beyond his family's means. He therefore studied for an entrance scholarship at Trinity College, at Cambridge University, where he was admitted. Thomson would spend the rest of his life at Trinity.

The Cavendish Laboratory

Thomson completed his undergraduate work in 1880 when he took his examinations for the

(AIP Emilio Segrè Visual Archives, W. F. Meggers Collection)

mathematical tripos over nine bleak January days. Among the examiners was the theoretical physicist James Clerk Maxwell, who is best known for his contributions to electromagnetic field theory. Following the successful completion of these examinations, Thomson wrote a dissertation about energy that resulted in two papers published in the *Philosophical Transactions of the Royal Society*.

Thomson's thesis won for him a fellowship at the university, where he began teaching and initiating a line of research in electrical theory that would point him in the direction of his most important work. It was at this time that he began his association with the recently founded Cavendish Laboratory at Cambridge. The laboratory was virtually unique in its day for providing both equipment and space for teaching and research in physics. In the following decades, it became a world-renowned facility that would nurture many future Nobel Prize winners, including Thomson himself. Under the guidance of the laboratory's director, Lord Rayleigh (John William Strutt), Thomson began his first experimental research. Following Rayleigh's death in 1884, Thomson was appointed to succeed him. He was only twenty-eight years old.

The Electron

The experimental study of the flow of electricity in gases at low pressures, and the consequent discharge of colored lights, was a relatively old subfield of physics. Thomson, who characterized himself as "very clumsy with my fingers," was fortunate to join forces at that time with a colleague, Richard Threlfall, whose talents lay in the right direction to get Thomson started on experimental work.

By 1897, Thomson had discovered that the molecules of a gas might be split not simply into ions (electrically charged fragments of atomic masses) but that under the influence of the recently discovered X rays, even the atoms of a monatomic gas seemed to acquire charge and could be made to conduct electricity. The lightest charge carrier—the negatively charged component, or electron—had some years earlier been postulated as a fundamental constituent of matter, although it had never been identified in the physical world.

The study of the conduction of electricity through gases and of so-called cathode rays would occupy Thomson for the greater part of his life. Cathode rays are emitted in gas-

A German cathode ray tube from the World War II era. (California Institute of Technology)

discharge tubes when very high voltages are applied at extremely low gas pressures. In the experiments performed by German physicist Heinrich Hertz, Thomson's contemporary, these cathode rays did not seem to be affected at all by electrical influences. Therefore, Hertz believed that they must be electromagnetic waves of some kind, as light itself was known to be, rather than charged particles.

Thomson's research would lead to the inevitable conclusion that the electron is indeed a charged particle. His experiments also led to the value of its charge-to-mass ratio, which turned out to be enormous when compared with any other known ion.

The Nobel Prize

Thomson was awarded the Nobel Prize in Physics in 1906 for his work on the electron. Appropriately, his acceptance speech was entitled "Carriers of Negative Electricity."

Thomson was not only a world-renowned experimentalist but also an individual whose sense of humor and insights concerning human behavior won for him many friends and admirers throughout the world. He received a knighthood in 1908. Thomson died in 1940 and was buried in Westminster Abbey in London.

It is an interesting fact in the history of science that Thomson's son, Sir George Paget Thomson, would himself win a Nobel Prize in

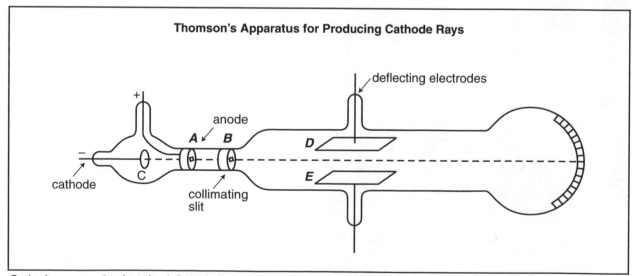

Thomson's Apparatus for Producing Cathode Rays

Cathode rays emitted at the left end of the tube pass through a defining slit in the anode and an adjacent metal plate. Charged plates further down the tube cause the cathode rays to be deflected up or down. (after Thomson, from Arnold Arons' *Development of Concepts of Physics*, 1965)

Physics in 1937 for research on the electron. The younger Thomson's experiments on the diffraction of electrons clearly demonstrated their diametrically opposite characteristics—their wave rather than particle behaviors.

Bibliography
By Thomson
A Treatise on the Motion of Vortex Rings, 1883

Notes on Recent Researches on Electricity and Magnetism, 1893

Elements of the Mathematical Theory of Electricity and Magnetism, 1895

"A Theory of the Connection Between Cathode and Röntgen Rays" in Röntgen Rays: Memoirs by Röntgen, Stokes, and J. J. Thompson, 1898 (George F. Barker, ed.)

Conduction of Electricity Through Gases, 1903; rev. ed., 1928-1933 (2 vols.; with George Paget Thomson)

Electricity and Matter, 1904

A Textbook of Physics, 1906-1928 (4 vols.; with J. Poynting)

The Corpuscular Theory of Matter, 1907

Cathode Rays

Thomson designed an experiment to determine whether cathode rays were electromagnetic waves or they consisted of a stream of negatively charged particles.

Cathode rays can be produced by applying a very high voltage between a pair of metal plates that are enclosed within a glass tube from which most of the air has been removed. The positively charged plate is called the anode, the negative the cathode. At very low pressures, the walls of the tube opposite the cathode will glow, or fluoresce, with a greenish light, and a metal object placed inside the tube will cast a distinct, sharp shadow on the tube wall.

In Thomson's apparatus, the rays generated at the cathode by the application of a high voltage between the cathode and anode proceed down the tube and strike the layer of fluorescent material on the far righthand wall. A tiny focused spot of light is seen at the point of impact. If a high electric voltage is then applied across the two deflecting plates—the upper plate is positive, the lower is negative—the spot is deflected upward by the electric field between them. A reversal of the polarity of the plates reverses the electric field's direction and causes a downward deflection. The size of the shift from the spot's original, undeflected position can then be measured.

Since electromagnetic waves are not affected by an electric field, Thomson believed that the cathode rays constituted a stream of negatively charged particles. In passing between the plates, these particles were pushed away from the negative one, since like charges repel, and attracted toward the positive one.

The actual path followed by the cathode rays is like that of a baseball thrown horizontally, in which the earth's gravitational field produces a downward deflection. Knowledge of the speed at which the baseball left one's hand, the horizontal distance that it traveled, and its vertical drop allows one to calculate the magnitude of the gravitational force that acted on the ball.

By analogy, Thomson was able to measure these corresponding quantities in his experiment and so could determine precisely the size of the electrical force that acted on the moving charges. Since that force depends on both the deflecting voltage as well as the charge and mass of the particle, he was able to find the value for the ratio of its electrical charge to its mass. His value, in modern units, is 1.76×10^{11} coulombs per kilogram.

Subsequent experiments would demonstrate the validity of Thomson's conclusion, and the particle was identified as the electron. In 1911, American physicist Robert A. Millikan devised an experiment to measure the electron's charge. Together with Thomson's value of the charge-to-mass ratio, this finding led to a determination of the electron's mass, the smallest of any particle known at that time.

Bibliography
Development of Concepts of Physics. Arnold Arons. Reading, Mass.: Addison-Wesley, 1965.

The Discovery of Subatomic Particles. Steven Weinberg. New York: W. H. Freeman, 1990.

Recollections and Reflections. J. J. Thomson. New York: Macmillan, 1937.

Rays of Positive Electricity and Their Application to Chemical Analyses, 1913

From Newton to Einstein: Changing Conceptions of the Universe, 1920 (with others; Benjamin Harrow, ed.)

The Electron in Chemistry, 1923

James Clerk Maxwell: A Commemorative Volume, 1831-1931, 1931 (with Max Planck, Albert Einstein, et al.)

Recollections and Reflections, 1936

About Thomson

J. J. Thomson: Discoverer of the Electron. G. P. Thomson. New York: Doubleday, 1965.

The Life of Sir J. J. Thomson, O.M. R. J. S. Rayleigh. Cambridge, England: Cambridge University Press, 1927.

Twenty-four Portraits. William Rothenstein. London: Allen and Unwin, 1920.

(David G. Fenton)

Samuel C. C. Ting

Area of Achievement: Physics

Contribution: Ting led the team of experimental physicists that detected the J particle, whose existence verified the theoretical prediction of a charmed quark.

Jan. 27, 1936	Born in Ann Arbor, Michigan
1959	Earns a bachelor's degree in physics and mathematics from the University of Michigan
1962	Earns a doctorate in physics from Michigan
1963	Receives a Ford Foundation Fellowship to the Conseil Européen pour la Recherche Nucléaire (CERN) in Switzerland
1964	Hired as an instructor at Columbia University
1965	Promoted to assistant professor at Columbia
1966	Leads experiments as a guest researcher at the Deutches Electronen Synchrotronen (DESY) in Hamburg, Germany
1967	Named an associate professor at the Massachusettes Institute of Technology (MIT)
1969	Promoted to full professor at MIT
1974	Heads a team at the Brookhaven National Laboratory that discovers the J particle
1976	Awarded the Nobel Prize in Physics
1976	Receives the Ernest Orlando Lawrence Award
1977	Named Thomas Dudley Cabot Institute Professor at MIT
1988	Given the DeGasperi Award from the government of Italy

Early Life

When Samuel Chao Chung Ting was born in January, 1936, his parents were at the University of Michigan at Ann Arbor. Two months later, the family returned to China, where his father, Kuan Hai Ting, was an engineering professor, and his mother, Tsun-Ying Wang, was a psychology professor. Because of the turmoil of World War II, Samuel Ting was unable to attend school until his family moved to Taiwan after the war.

In 1956, Ting returned to the United States alone and entered the University of Michigan. Despite knowing little English and having less money, he earned bachelor's degrees in physics and mathematics in only three years. The brilliance and discipline that made this feat possible would characterize his entire career.

Quantum Electrodynamics

In 1960, Ting married Kay Louise Kune, an architect, while studying for a doctorate in

The J/Ψ Particle and Charmed Quarks

The detection of the J/Ψ particle ranks among the most important experimental discoveries in late twentieth century physics because it provided evidence that two of the four fundamental forces of nature are related.

At the Brookhaven National Laboratory, the team of experimenters led by Ting used the gigantic particle accelerator to boost protons to high speeds and then slam the beam into a target of beryllium, a lightweight metal. Ting designed a pair of finely tuned sensors to detect pairs of electrons and positrons (positive electrons) spraying from a tiny fraction of the collisions between the protons and the nuclei of the beryllium atoms. The electron-positron pairs do not themselves result directly from the collisions; Ting suspected that the pairs should decay from a single particle that is the immediate product of the collision but exists so fleetingly (10^{-20} seconds) that it cannot be observed directly.

To find the telltale remnants of this particle, the experiment's particle detectors were tuned to sense electron-positron pairs in a narrow energy range—2,000 to 4,000 million electronvolts. Since Albert Einstein's formula $E = mc^2$ calculates the relation of energy and mass, pairs displaying a specific energy reveal the mass of the particle from which they decayed.

Theoretical physicists had already proposed that a new heavy particle might show up somewhere in the energy range that Ting's team was scanning. After months of repeating the experiment and analyzing the results with a computer, in 1974 the team found evidence of electron-positron pairs near 3,100 million electronvolts, an energy so specific that it could only have come from a new particle.

This J/Ψ particle deeply interested Sheldon L. Glashow, a theoretical physicist, because he suspected that it contained a new type of quark. Quarks are fundamental building blocks of some types of matter, and, before 1974, only three types (or "flavors") had been discovered—the up, down, and strange quarks. A theory created by Glashow and others proposed that quarks with greater mass than these three should exist. Analysis of the J/Ψ particle suggested that it was indeed made up of heavier quarks, which Glashow called charmed (or charm) quarks.

Experimenters soon found other particles composed of a charmed quark and an "anticharmed" quark, a type of matter they called charmonium. The existence of charmed quarks, as well as later discoveries of the bottom and top quarks, supports the theory that two fundamental forces of nature, electromagnetism and the weak interactions, are really aspects of the same "electroweak" force, which itself may reflect even deeper unity among the known types of matter and forces in the universe.

Bibliography
From Atoms to Quarks: An Introduction to the Strange World of Particle Physics. James Trefil. New York: Doubleday, 1994.
The God Particle: If the Universe Is the Answer, What Is the Question? Leon M. Lederman. New York: Houghton Mifflin, 1993.
Quarks: The Stuff of Matter. Harald Fritzsch. New York: Basic Books, 1983.

(The Nobel Foundation)

Germany. Ting's team employed an improved particle detector and, after painstaking analysis, showed that the Harvard experiment had been faulty.

High-Energy Physics

The experiment earned for Ting a reputation as an emerging talent in designing and administering a large project in high-energy physics. In 1971, Ting, now a full professor at the Massachusetts Institute of Technology (MIT), launched a large-scale investigation using the Brookhaven National Laboratory particle accelerator, this time hunting for new particles.

In 1974, his team detected a unknown heavy particle, which Ting dubbed the J particle. Almost simultaneously, a Stanford University experiment, led by Burton Richter, detected the same particle, which Richter called the Ψ (psi) particle. It has since been known as the J/Ψ particle, and Ting and Richter shared the 1976 Nobel Prize in Physics for the discovery.

That same year, Ting received the Ernest Orlando Lawrence Award. He was elected to the National Academy of Sciences, as well as to academies in Europe, Asia, and Russia. In the 1980's and 1990's, Ting led teams experimenting with antimatter at CERN and on a satellite.

Bibliography

By Ting
"Timelike Momenta in Quantum Electrodynamics," *Physical Review*, 1966 (with Stanley J. Brodsky)
"Leptonic Decays of Vector Mesons," *United States Atomic Energy Commission CONF-670923*, 1967
"Electrodynamics at Small Distances, Leptonic Decays of Vector Mesons, and Photoproduction of Vector Mesons," *Proceedings of the International Conference on High Energy Physics*, 1968
"Particle Discovery at Brookhaven," *Science*, 1975
The Search for Charm, Beauty, and Truth at High Energies, 1984 (as editor, with Gianpaolo Bellini)

About Ting
The Hunting of the Quark. Michael Riordan. New York: Simon & Schuster, 1987.

physics at the University of Michigan, which he received in 1962. The next year, he won a Ford Foundation Fellowship to conduct research at the Conseil Européen pour la Recherche Nucléaire (CERN), or European Organization for Nuclear Research, near Geneva, Switzerland. He worked with a proton accelerator, gaining experience in team work and with high-energy physics technology.

Returning to the United States, Ting joined the physics faculty of Columbia University in 1964. The previous year, a Harvard University experiment had questioned the validity of quantum electrodynamics (QED) theory, which describes the interactions between matter and electromagnetism.

Skeptical of these results, Ting led a group repeating the experiment at the Deutches Electronen Synchrotronen (DESY) in Hamburg,

"Samuel C. C. Ting." In *The Nobel Prize Winners: Physics*, edited by Frank N. Magill. Pasadena, Calif.: Salem Press, 1989.

The Second Creation: Makers of the Revolution in Twentieth-Century Physics. Robert P. Crease and Charles C. Mann. New York: Macmillan, 1986.

(Roger Smith)

Shin'ichiro Tomonaga

Area of Achievement: Physics
Contribution: For contributing to the development of quantum electrodynamics, simultaneously and concurrently with Julian Schwinger and Richard P. Feynman, Tomonaga shared the 1965 Nobel Prize in Physics with his American colleagues.

Mar. 31, 1906	Born in Tokyo, Japan
1929	Graduated from Kyoto Imperial University and stays as an unpaid research assistant
1932	Joins the Scientific Research Institute in Tokyo
1937	Travels to Leipzig, Germany, to study with Werner Heisenberg
1939	Awarded a doctorate from Tokyo Imperial University for his work in Leipzig
1941	Joins Tokyo Bunrika University
1943	Publishes a theoretical paper on quantum electrodynamics in the Japanese journal *Rikon Iho*
1946	An English-language version of his paper receives attention among U.S. physicists
1948	Receives the Japan Academy Prize
1949	Invited by J. Robert Oppenheimer to spend a year at the Institute for Advanced Study in Princeton
1964	Receives the Lomonosov Medal of the USSR Presidium of the Academy of Sciences
1965	Wins the Nobel Prize in Physics
1963-1969	Serves as director of the Institute for Optical Research and president of the Science Council of Japan
July 8, 1979	Dies in Tokyo, Japan

Early Life

Sanjuro Tomonaga was an eminent philosopher in Japan. His son, Shin'ichiro Tomonaga (pronounced "toh-muh-NAH-guh") was born in Tokyo. When Sanjuro Tomonaga joined the faculty of Kyoto Imperial University, he moved his family to Kyoto. Thus, Shin'ichiro came to be educated in Kyoto. During his high school days, the young Tomonaga found an ideal friend and companion with whom to study science in Hideki Yukawa, the first Nobel laureate in physics from Japan.

Tomonaga and Yukawa entered Kyoto University together. After his graduation in 1929, Tomonaga apprenticed in the laboratory of Kajuro Tamaki as an unpaid research assistant for three years. The year 1931 was a turning point for him: He met Yoshio Nishina, who had returned to Japan after working with Niels Bohr in Copenhagen. Nishina became his mentor,

(The Nobel Foundation)

and Tomonaga moved to Tokyo to work with him at the Institute of Physical and Chemical Research.

Influence of Nishina and Heisenberg

Tomonaga was enchanted by a paper published by Paul A. M. Dirac in 1932 in the *Proceedings of the Royal Society, London*. In this paper, Dirac had discussed the formulation of relativistic quantum mechanics, especially the situation in which electrons interact with an electromagnetic field. Tomonaga was attracted by the novelty of this paper's philosophy and the beauty of its form. His mentor Nishina had suggested that Tomonaga investigate the possibility of predicting some new phenomena by this theory.

Tomonaga then spent two years (1937-1938) with Werner Karl Heisenberg in Leipzig. This interaction with Heisenberg also played a significant role in Tomonaga's intellectual development. Reminiscing on Heisenberg's contribution to his research thinking, Tomonaga noted in his 1965 Nobel award lecture,

> Heisenberg, in his paper published in 1939, emphasized that the field reaction would be crucial in meson-nucleon scattering. Just at that time I was studying at Leipzig, and I still remember vividly how Heisenberg enthusiastically explained this idea to me and handed me galley proofs of his forthcoming paper. Influenced by Heisenberg, I came to believe that the problem of field reactions, far from being meaningless, was one which required a frontal attack.

Theory on Quantum Electrodynamics

After returning to Japan from Leipzig, Tomonaga became engaged in formulating a covariant field theory. As he mentioned in his Nobel award lecture, "What I wanted to know was what kind of relationship exists between the infinity associated with the scattering process and that associated with the mass." Tomonaga formulated the idea of intermediate coupling.

According to this idea, interactions between two particles could take place through the exchange of a third (virtual) particle, similar to the interactions between two ships, with one affecting the path of another by firing a missile. Along these lines, Tomonaga began in 1941 to formulate a quantum field theory of an elec-

The Development of Quantum Electrodynamics

Tomonaga showed that quantum theory could provide meaningful predictions.

The problem faced by Tomonaga in the early 1940's was the absence of a quantum theory applicable to subatomic particles with very high energies. The theory labeled by Paul A. M. Dirac as "many-time theory" in a 1932 paper explained how the state of a dynamical system changes with time. To describe how the probability amplitude changes with time (t) in quantum mechanics terms, Dirac had considered different time variables for each particle, so that the probability amplitude could be expressed as a function of $r_1t_1, r_2t_2, \ldots r_Nt_N$, in a system composed of N particles, where the coordinates of each particle is $r_1, r_2, \ldots r_N$ and time is $t_1, t_2, \ldots t_N$.

Tomonaga has observed that Dirac's theory satisfied the requirement of the principle of relativity that time and space be treated with complete equality. This theory was called the many-time theory because N distinct time variables were used in this way. Dirac treated electrons as particles in his many-time theory.

In quantum theory, however, any particle, including electrons, could be considered waves as well. This provided the impetus for Tomonaga to propose in 1942 his formulation of how two particles may interact. Thus, according to his Nobel award lecture, he set out, "to define a relativistically meaningful probability amplitude which would be manifestly relativistically covariant, without being forced to give up the causal way of thinking. In having this exception I was recalling Dirac's many-time theory which had enchanted me ten years before."

In the words of Freeman J. Dyson, who in 1949 provided the analysis that the theories of Tomonaga, Julian Schwinger, and Richard P. Feynman arrived at the same solution to the vexing problem of so-called divergence difficulties in quantum dynamics, the theory of quantum electrodynamics (QED) "is not an easy one to describe in nontechnical language" and "it must be placed in the context of some earlier history."

Dyson has given the following steps to understand the significance of Tomonaga's theory.

First, the physical basis for QED provided by Dirac, Werner Karl Heisenberg, Wolfgang Pauli, and Enrico Fermi in the late 1920's consisted of direct application of the methods of quantum mechanics to the Maxwell equations describing the electromagnetic field. Second, this approach failed to give exact predictions, although qualitatively providing a correct account of radiation processes. Thus, physicists were puzzled and searching for radical changes in the theory. In the colorful description of Dyson, "from 1935 to 1945, there was a succession of fruitless attempts to cure the divergence disease of quantum electrodynamics by methods of radical surgery."

In the words of Dyson, what Tomonaga (as well as Schwinger and Feynman) did was to resurrect the theory by keeping "the physical basis of the theory precisely as it had been laid down by Dirac," but by polishing and refining the "mathematical superstructure."

The significance of the theory of quantum electrodynamics lies in the fact that although making no claim to finality, it brought harmony and order to the laws of atomic structure, radiation, the creation and annihilation of particles, solid-state physics, plasma physics, maser and laser technology, optical and microwave spectroscopy, electronics, and chemistry. While Tomonaga focused on the rigor of basic physical principles, Schwinger constructed a complete mathematical formation. Feynman derived simple rules for the direct calculation of physically observable quantities. Thus, Tomonaga is considered as one of the three formulators of this theory.

Bibliography

Genius: The Life and Science of Richard Feynman. James Gleick. New York: Pantheon Books, 1992.

"The Radiation Theories of Tomonaga, Schwinger, and Feynman." Freeman J. Dyson. *Physical Review* 75 (1949).

Selected Papers on Quantum Electrodynamics. Julian Schwinger, ed. New York: Dover, 1958.

"Tomonaga, Schwinger, and Feynman Awarded Nobel Prize for Physics." Freeman J. Dyson. *Science* 150 (October 29, 1965).

tron interacting with a photon that was consistent with the theory of special relativity.

He published his paper in Japanese in the journal *Riko Iho* in 1943. Because of disruptions in scientific exchange during World War II, however, physicists in the United States did not have a chance to hear about Tomonaga's theory. Meanwhile, Richard P. Feynman and Julian Schwinger independently and concurrently developed their formulations of quantum electrodynamics (QED).

Tomonaga's theory of QED came to the attention of fellow physicists in the United States in 1946, when an English-language version was published in the *Progress of Theoretical Physics*. Freeman Dyson showed subsequently that Tomonaga, Schwinger, and Feynman had provided independent solutions to the same problem. For his significant contribution in the development of the theory of QED, Tomonaga shared the 1965 Nobel Prize in Physics with Schwinger and Feynman.

During the last twenty-five years of his life, Tomonaga spent his energy in scientific policy-making in Japan by serving in numerous capacities—as the director of research institutes, as the president of the Tokyo University of Education (formerly Tokyo Bunrika University), and as the president of the Science Council of Japan. He also authored an authoritative textbook, *Quantum Mechanics*, in 1962. He died in 1979.

Bibliography
By Tomonaga
"On the Creation of Electrons and Positrons by Heavy Charged Particles," *Scientific Papers of the Institute of Physical and Chemical Research,* 1935 (with Y. Nishina and M. Kobayasi)

"A Note on the Interaction of Neutron and Proton," *Scientific Papers of Institute of Physics and Chemistry Research,* 1936 (with Nishina and H. Tamaki)

"On the Collision of a High Energy Neutrino with a Neutron," *Scientific Papers of Institute of Physics and Chemistry Research,* 1937 (with Tamaki)

"Scattering and Splitting of Photons on the Non-Linear Field Theory of Born and Infeld," *Scientific Papers of Institute of Physics and Chemistry Research,* 1938 (with M. Kobayasi)

"On a Relativistically Invariant Formulation of the Quantum Theory of Wave Fields," *Progress of Theoretical Physics,* 1946

"On Infinite Field Reactions in Quantum Field Theory," *Physical Review,* 1948

Ryoshi-rikigaku, 1949-1953 (*Quantum Mechanics,* 1962-1968)

"Development of Quantum Electrodynamics: Personal Recollections," *Science,* 1966

Scientific Papers of Tomonaga, 1971-1976

About Tomonaga
QED and the Men Who Made It: Dyson, Feynman, Schwinger, and Tomonaga. S. S. Schweber. Princeton, N.J.: Princeton University Press, 1994.

Sin-itiro Tomonaga: Life of a Japanese Physicist. Cheryl Fujimoto and Takako Sano. Translated by M. Matsui. Tokyo: MYU, 1995.

"Sin-itiro Tomonaga, 1906-1979." K. Nishijima. *Nature* 282 (November 1, 1979).

(Sachi Sri Kantha)

Stanislaw Ulam

Areas of Achievement: Mathematics and physics

Contribution: A brilliant and imaginative mathematician, Ulam helped develop the Monte Carlo method of data analysis that found wide use in many scientific fields. He was also one of the designers of the first hydrogen bomb.

Apr. 3, 1909	Born in Lwów, Poland, Austrian Empire (now Lvov, Ukraine)
1933	Receives a doctorate from the Lwów Polytechnic Institute
1936	Joins the Institute for Advanced Study in Princeton, New Jersey
1936-1940	Teaches mathematics at Harvard University
1939	Meets his future wife, Françoise, at Harvard
1941	Becomes a U.S. citizen
1941-1943	Teaches at the University of Wisconsin
1944	Joins the atomic bomb project in Los Alamos, New Mexico
1946	Suffers from an attack of encephalitis and, while recovering, conceives of Monte Carlo analysis
1950	Determines that the original hydrogen bomb design is flawed
1951	Proposes, with Edward Teller, a new bomb design
1955	Suggests propelling spaceships with nuclear bombs
1965	Joins the teaching staff at the University of Colorado
1966	Elected to the National Academy of Sciences
May 13, 1984	Dies in Santa Fe, New Mexico

Early Life

The son of a lawyer, Stanislaw Marcin Ulam (pronounced "EW-lahm") was born in 1909 in the town of Lwów (or Lemberg), Poland, which at that time was in the Austrian Empire. He was fascinated by mathematics and by Albert Einstein's relativity theories. At the age of twenty, he published his first mathematical paper. He attended the Polytechnic Institute in Lwów and obtained his doctorate in 1933.

In 1936, the famed mathematician John von Neumann invited Ulam to join the Institute for Advanced Study in Princeton, New Jersey. In 1941, Ulam became a U.S. citizen.

The Atomic Bomb Project

In February, 1944, as World War II raged overseas, von Neumann brought Ulam to the heart of the top-secret Manhattan Project in Los Alamos, New Mexico. Its aim was to invent an atomic bomb. Meanwhile, working under physicist Edward Teller, Ulam investigated the feasibility of building an even more powerful

(Los Alamos National Laboratory)

hydrogen bomb. The first atomic bomb was exploded in July, 1945.

To develop nuclear weapons, scientists made extremely complex calculations based on high-speed interactions of numerous subatomic particles. They used an early, slow generation of electronic computers.

In 1946, Ulam thought of a way to hasten the calculations. While recovering from the illness encephalitis and playing the card game solitaire, he realized that he could better anticipate the outcome of his game by making intelligent bets based on a few cards, rather than on his entire hand. Likewise, he could simplify and speed nuclear calculations by basing them on the behavior, or "life histories," of a small sample of typical particles.

With von Neumann, Ulam developed this technique, later called the Monte Carlo method after the casino resort. After the war, researchers around the world applied Monte Carlo techniques in a wide range of subjects, from weapons design to economics and cosmology.

The Hydrogen Bomb Project

In the early 1950's, the United States raced to beat the Soviet Union to the development of the first hydrogen bomb. Ulam demonstrated that Teller's original plan for the bomb would not work. Ulam and Teller then jointly designed a new, workable bomb. The first hydrogen bomb developed in the United States was successfully tested on a Pacific atoll in 1952.

In later years, thanks to his restless imagination, Ulam explored subjects as diverse as nuclear-powered rockets, the human brain, the mapping of genetic codes, and the development of artificial intelligence for computers. He died in Santa Fe, New Mexico, on May 13, 1984.

Bibliography
By Ulam
"Thermonuclear Devices" in *Perspectives in Modern Physics: Essays in Honor of Hans A. Bethe*, 1966 (R. Marshak, ed.)

"Some Ideas and Prospects in Biomathematics," *Annual Review of Biophysics and Bioengineering*, 1972

The Hydrogen Bomb

A hydrogen bomb explosion is triggered by radiation from an atomic bomb blast.

An atomic bomb blast involves the splitting (fission) of extremely heavy elements, typically uranium or plutonium. In contrast, a hydrogen bomb blast requires the merging (fusion) of isotopes of the lightest element, hydrogen.

The nuclear fusion of hydrogen is what makes the sun burn. A fusion bomb, however, uses the two hydrogen isotopes deuterium and tritium. Ordinary hydrogen consists of a proton and an electron. Deuterium and tritium have both of these and, in addition, one and two neutrons, respectively.

Ulam's calculations showed that Edward Teller's original hydrogen bomb design would not work: Energy from the atomic blast would escape too fast to ignite a self-sustaining fusion reaction. Also, while deuterium was an abundant isotope, Teller's design would require impractical amounts of the rare tritium.

Together, Ulam and Teller developed a new bomb design. Specific details of the design remain a military secret, but the basic principle is that the bomb contains two main elements: an atomic bomb and a fusion component that includes a container of deuterium and tritium. The atomic bomb explodes, releasing intense radiation down a short, wide pipe. The radiation compresses the isotopes to an extremely high temperature and pressure, high enough for their atomic nuclei to overcome their normal repulsion. Thus, the isotopic nuclei merge, releasing fusion energy.

Bibliography
The Advisors: Oppenheimer, Teller, and the Superbomb. Herbert F. York. Stanford, Calif.: Stanford University Press, 1976.

Atomic Shield: A History of the United States Atomic Energy Commission. Richard G. Hewlett and Francis Duncan. Vol. 2. Berkeley: University of California Press, 1990.

The Legacy of Hiroshima. Edward Teller with Allen Brown. New York: Doubleday, 1962.

Adventures of a Mathematician, 1976
Science, Computers, and People: From the Tree of Mathematics, 1986 (Mark C. Reynolds and Gian-Carlo Rota, eds.)
Analogies Between Analogies: The Mathematical Reports of S. M. Ulam and His Los Alamos Collaborators, 1990 (A. R. Bednarek and Françoise Ulam, eds.)

About Ulam
Dark Sun: The Making of the Hydrogen Bomb. Richard Rhodes. New York: Simon & Schuster, 1995.
From Cardinals to Chaos: Reflections on the Life and Legacy of Stanislaw Ulam. N. G. Cooper, ed. New York: Cambridge University Press, 1989.

(Keay Davidson)

Harold Clayton Urey

Areas of Achievement: Astronomy, biology, chemistry, and physics
Contribution: Urey was awarded the 1934 Nobel Prize in Chemistry for his work that led to the discovery of deuterium (heavy hydrogen). His later scientific interests included astronomy and the origin of life.

Apr. 29, 1893	Born in Walkerton, Indiana
1911-1914	Teaches in rural schools in Indiana and Montana
1914-1917	Studies at Montana State University
1923	Earns a doctorate from the University of California, Berkeley
1924	Works with Niels Bohr in Copenhagen, Denmark
1925-1929	Serves as an associate in chemistry at The Johns Hopkins University
1930	Named associate professor of chemistry at Columbia University
1932	Discovers deuterium
1934	Wins the Nobel Prize in Chemistry
1940	Becomes a member of the Manhattan Project to build the atomic bomb
1945-1958	Conducts nuclear studies at the University of Chicago
1951	The Urey-Miller experiment produces amino acids
1952	Named Martin A. Ryerson Distinguished Service Professor
1971	Receives the Kepler Medal from the American Association for the Advancement of Science
1973	Receives the Priestley Medal from the American Chemical Society
Jan. 5, 1981	Dies in La Jolla, California

Early Life

Harold Clayton Urey was born in the small rural community of Walkerton, Indiana, on April 29, 1893. Perhaps his future interest in teaching and science came from his father, Samuel Clayton Urey, a schoolteacher and a lay minister in the Church of the Brethren. Unfortunately, his father died when Harold was only six years old. His mother, Cora Reinoehl Urey, later remarried. Harold had a sister, Martha, and a brother, Clarence. Two half sisters, Florence and Ina, were from his mother's second marriage. His stepfather was also a Brethren minister, and Harold grew up with a sincere respect for learning, education, and good values.

The Discovery of Deuterium and Its Implications

Deuterium (heavy hydrogen) is a relatively rare isotope; there are five thousand atoms of ordinary hydrogen for every one of deuterium.

The discovery of the fact that isotopes of various elements exist was first made by the British chemist Frederick Soddy in 1913. Finding isotopes of heavier elements was difficult enough, but isolating an isotope of a light element such as hydrogen was thought to be nearly impossible. Urey developed an experiment that would produce the desired result if heavy hydrogen actually existed.

The technique developed by Urey to identify heavy hydrogen required the vaporization of liquid hydrogen. His hypothesis suggested that the lighter form of hydrogen would evaporate first, leaving behind the heavier isotope.

In Urey's experiment, he began with 4 liters of liquid hydrogen that were allowed to evaporate very slowly. In the end, only 1 milliliter of liquid hydrogen was left. When he examined the product with a spectroscope, he found the exact predicted absorption lines for heavy hydrogen. The result was the discovery of deuterium.

Following the discovery of deuterium came the identification of several other isotopes, among them oxygen, nitrogen, carbon, and sulfur. It is the combination of deuterium and heavy oxygen that produces so-called heavy water, which was critical to the manufacture of the atomic bomb. Its principal use is to slow down the chain reaction rate in a nuclear fission reaction.

An additional discovery to result from Urey's work was the fact that isotopes tend to differ chemically from each other, if only in small ways. It was the belief that since the isotopes of a given element have a similar electronic configuration, they should have identical chemical properties.

Urey found a small difference in the reaction rates of isotopes because they have a characteristic difference in mass.

Urey's experience with isotopes became extremely important during World War II. Two German scientists, Otto Hahn and Fritz Strassman, discovered the principle of nuclear fission in 1939. Once this was known, the potential for creating a bomb became obvious. In 1940, Urey was invited to join the Uranium Committee for the Manhattan Project, the U.S. program to build an atomic bomb. His role was to separate uranium 235 from its heavier form, uranium 238. His success led to the development of the atomic bomb. After the war, Urey continued his work and extracted another isotope of hydrogen, called tritium, that was used to develop the hydrogen bomb.

Although Urey's discoveries concerning the isotopes of hydrogen led to weapons of mass destruction, they had other uses as well. After World War II he turned his attention to the relationship of oxygen isotopes to past climates.

Urey noted that in warmer climatic periods, organisms consume more of the lighter oxygen isotope and less of the heavier form. During cooler periods, the difference between the two isotopes is much less. From this fact, Urey was able to develop an "oxygen thermometer" based on oxygen isotope ratios found in the shells of sea creatures. This process is widely used today for the prediction of climatic changes, both past and present.

Bibliography

Chemical Evolution. Melvin Calvin. New York: Oxford University Press, 1969.

The Search for Life in the Universe. Donald Goldsmith and Tobias Owen. Menlo Park, Calif.: Benjamin/Cummings, 1980.

Urey was very fortunate to be able to complete high school, and he looked forward to attending college. Most people at that time did not have the opportunity to further their education much beyond elementary school. Times were hard, and they had to either work on the farm or go find a job in the city. Urey did not have the money to go directly to college, so he took a job teaching in country schools from 1911 to 1914 in order to pay for his education.

Beginning an Academic Life

At the age of twenty-one, Urey was able to enroll at Montana State University. At this early stage of his life, he chose biology as his course of study. His first original research work dealt with microorganisms found in the Missoula River. After three years of study, he was awarded a bachelor of science degree in zoology in 1917.

That year, the United States entered World War I. Because of his religious beliefs, Urey did not serve in the military. He did his part for the war effort by working in a chemical plant that developed high explosives, putting his scientific training to good use.

After World War I ended, Urey returned to Montana State University and taught chemistry there until 1921. His desire for additional knowledge took him to the University of California, Berkeley, where he enrolled into a doctorate program in physical chemistry. He received his degree in 1923. His research dealt with the calculations of heat capacities and entropies of various gases through the use of a spectroscope.

After receiving his doctorate, Urey traveled to Copenhagen, Denmark, to work and study with the famous physicist Niels Bohr. Bohr was working on the basic structure of the atom, and this research greatly excited Urey. It was this experience that developed Urey's interest in several atoms and their related isotopes.

A Promising Career

The year 1925 saw Urey accept an important position within the chemistry department at The Johns Hopkins University in Baltimore, Maryland. This would be the beginning of an exceptional career. It was also during this time that he married Frieda Daum, who was a scien-

(The Nobel Foundation)

tist and the daughter of an educator. It seemed to be the perfect match. They were married on June 12, 1926, in Lawrence, Kansas, and would have four children: Gertrude Elizabeth, Frieda Rebecca, Mary Alice, and John Clayton.

The turning point in Urey's professional life came in 1929 when he left Johns Hopkins to become an associate professor of chemistry at Columbia University in New York City. One year later, Urey and a colleague, Arthur E. Ruark, wrote a book entitled *Atoms, Molecules, and Quanta*, which was hailed as the first comprehensive English-language textbook on atomic structure. It was also significant in linking the new field of quantum physics to chemistry.

International Acclaim

The highpoint in Urey's career came in 1932, with the discovery of the isotope deuterium. Along with his coworkers Ferdinand Brickwedde and George M. Murphy, they were able to separate the deuterium isotope from the more common form of hydrogen. This discovery opened the door for a better understanding of isotopes in general and led to the discovery of many more for other elements.

For his work in the discovery of deuterium, Urey was awarded the 1934 Nobel Prize in Chemistry. Columbia University also recognized his accomplishment by appointing him Ernest Kempler Adams Fellow and later promoting him to professor of chemistry. In addition to these honors, Urey became the first editor of the prestigious publication *Journal of Chemical Physics*.

All these accomplishments were more than most scientists achieve in a lifetime, but there was much more in the future for Urey. The coming of World War II would place him at the center of the development of the atomic bomb. His research would be critical to the separation of the two isotopes of uranium that was required.

After the war, Urey's research interests varied. He would seek answers for the origin of the solar system and even of life itself. Urey died in 1981 at the age of eighty-seven.

Bibliography
By Urey
Atoms, Molecules, and Quanta, 1930 (with Arthur E. Ruark)
"On the Relative Abundances of Isotopes," *Physical Review*, 1931 (with C. A. Bradley, Jr.)
"A Hypothesis Regarding the Origin of the Movement of the Earth's Crust," *Science*, 1949
The Planets: Their Origins and Development, 1952
"The Origin of the Earth" in *Nuclear Geology: A Symposium on Nuclear Phenomena in the Earth Sciences*, 1954

About Urey
"Harold Urey and the Discovery of Deuterium." Ferdinand G. Brickwedde. *Physics Today* (September, 1982).
Harold Urey: The Man Who Explored from Earth to Moon. Alvin and Virginia Silverstein. New York: J. Day, 1970.
"Nickel for Your Thoughts: Urey and the Origin of the Moon." Stephen G. Brush. *Science* 217 (1982).
"Obituary: Harold Clayton Urey, 1893-1981." Carl Sagan. *Icarus* 48 (1981).

(Paul P. Sipiera)

James Van Allen

Area of Achievement: Physics
Contribution: During World War II, Van Allen developed the proximity fuse and experimented with captured German V-2 rockets. Analyzing information from early satellites, he discovered a region around the earth possessing a high density of fast-moving charged particles, now called the Van Allen belts.

Sept. 7, 1914	Born in Mount Pleasant, Iowa
1939	Earns a Ph.D. in physics from the State University of Iowa
1939-1942	Given a research fellowship in the Carnegie Institution's Department of Terrestrial Magnetism
1942	Takes a position at the Applied Physics Laboratory of The Johns Hopkins University
1942-1946	Accepts a commission in the U.S. Navy and develops a radio proximity fuse
1946	Becomes an administrator of V-2 rocket research for the Army
1951	Appointed a professor of physics and head of physics and astronomy at Iowa
1958	Discovers high-altitude radiation belts using satellites launched during the International Geophysical Year
1958	Wins the Space Flight Award of the American Astronautical Society
1977	Given the William Bowie Medal of the American Geophysical Union
1990	Wins the Royal Swedish Academy of Sciences Crafoord Prize
1994	Receives a lifetime achievement award from NASA

Early Life

James Alfred Van Allen was born in Mount Pleasant, Iowa, on September 7, 1914, as the second of four sons of Alfred Van Allen, a lawyer, and Alma Van Allen. James was interested in science from an early age. When he was twelve, he and one of his brothers built an electrostatic generator that produced bolts of artificial lightening. In high school, physics became his passion, and at times teachers would have to eject him forcibly from laboratories at the end of the school day.

Van Allen was graduated with a bachelor of science degree from Iowa Wesleyan College in 1935. He earned his master of science degree in 1936 and his Ph.D. in 1939 from the State University of Iowa, in Iowa City.

Military Research

In 1942, Van Allen took a position with the Applied Physics Laboratory at The Johns Hopkins University and accepted a commission in the U.S. Navy to conduct weapons research.

His first important scientific accomplishment came as a result of his war research: the radio proximity fuse. The fuse was a tiny radio transmitter and receiver attached to an explosive ordnance. Signals sent out and received by the fuse indicated when the weapon was close to the target, allowing it to explode before impact. Missile efficiency was greatly increased because it was no longer necessary to score a direct hit in order to knock out a target.

At the close of World War II, American scientists were permitted to experiment with some one hundred V-2 rockets captured from the German forces. These were far more advanced than anything then produced by the Allies and

Van Allen speaks at a press conference for the launching of the first U.S. satellite in 1958. (Library of Congress)

Van Allen Radiation

The Van Allen radiation belts consist of two doughnut-shaped regions within the earth's magnetic field, at the upper levels of atmosphere, in which charged atomic particles are trapped.

Van Allen analyzed the observations made by Explorer 1, the first satellite successfully launched by the United States, on January 31, 1958. A Geiger counter, which formed an important part of the satellite's 18-pound instrument package, registered anomalously high radiation in two altitude belts.

The earth's magnetic field gives rise to these regions, now known as the Van Allen radiation belts. These belts protect the earth and its inhabitants from the lethal, charged particles that are constantly streaming from the surface of the sun. Without a magnetic field to deflect the charged particles, these deadly particles would directly strike the earth's surface. It is likely that none of the familiar life forms on Earth, with the possible exception of viruses and some bacteria, could endure such a bombardment of radioactivity.

The earth's magnetic field, or magnetosphere, extends outward into space, similar to the fields of a bar magnet. The earth also has magnetic poles, which resemble the north and south poles of a magnet. The charged particles in the Van Allen radiation belts (mostly protons and electrons) are acted on by electromagnetic forces that cause the particles to spiral around the lines of the magnetic field and to oscillate back and forth between the poles. Because the molecules are scarce at high altitudes, collisions that could de-

flect the particles are rare, and the particles are trapped in the belts.

Van Allen radiation has been found to be so intense that satellites cannot be orbited within it for fear of damage to delicate electronic equipment. It is also hazardous for astronauts, who must wear protective outer suits when traversing the belts and who generally spend as little time as possible within these regions.

At the earth's magnetic poles, the Van Allen radiation belts curve downward as the charged particles follow the lines of the magnetic field. Thus, particles within the belts attain their lowest altitude over the poles, where they occasionally collide with and excite atoms in the earth's upper atmosphere. An electron orbiting a thus-excited atom must give up its excess energy, which is accomplished by emitting a proton of light. This "deexcitation" radiation constitutes the spectacular auroral displays in the night skies of regions of the earth close to the poles. The aurora borealis (northern lights) and the aurora australis (southern lights) appear as curtains of colored light draped across the evening sky. On rare occasions, the northern lights are seen as far south as Great Britain and the Great Lakes.

Bibliography

Astronomy: The Structure of the Universe. W. J. Kaufmann. New York: Macmillan, 1977.
Encyclopedia of Science and Technology. New York: McGraw-Hill, 1987.
Illustrated Science and Technology Encyclopedia. Westport, Conn.: McGraw-Hill, 1987.

promised to be valuable to scientists studying the earth's atmosphere. In 1946, the U.S. Army appointed Van Allen as administrator and coordinator of the V-2 research program at the White Sands Proving Grounds in New Mexico. In this position, he designed payloads to be sent into the atmosphere, selected projects for rocket research, and eventually designed an acceptable substitute rocket, the Aerobee.

University Research

Van Allen returned to his native Iowa in 1951 as professor of physics and head of the depart-

ment of physics and astronomy at the State University of Iowa; he held these positions until 1985, when he became a professor emeritus. As part of the International Geophysical Year (1957-1958), the U.S. government launched the Explorer series of satellites, the first one in January, 1958. Van Allen observed that the satellites recorded levels of cosmic radiation in the upper atmosphere that were much higher than anticipated.

In May, 1958, Van Allen hypothesized the existence of two belts of radiation, one at an altitude of 600 to 3,000 miles, the other at an

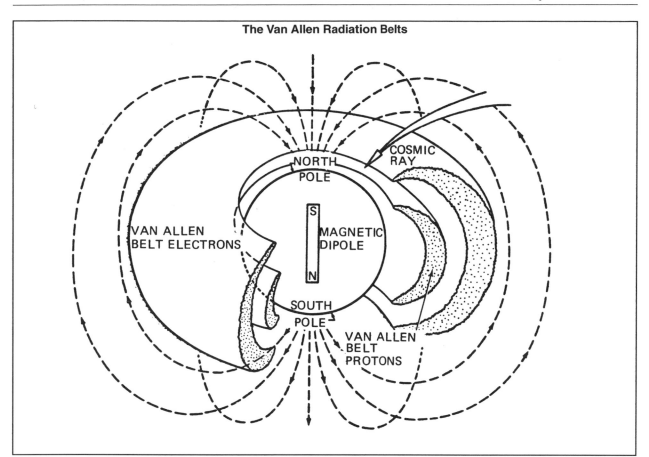

The Van Allen Radiation Belts

The Van Allen belts are formed when electrons and protons in cosmic rays from the sun become trapped in Earth's magnetic field. (National Aeronautics and Space Administration)

altitude of 9,000 to 15,000 miles. Later research confirmed this hypothesis and proved that the belts consist of high-velocity protons and electrons spiraling around the earth's magnetic lines of force. These are now known as the Van Allen radiation belts.

Bibliography
By Van Allen
Scientific Uses of Earth Satellites, 1956
Pioneer: First to Jupiter, Saturn, and Beyond, 1980 (with Richard O. Fimmel and Eric Burgess)
Origins of Magnetospheric Physics, 1983

About Van Allen
Modern Men of Science. J. E. Greene, ed. New York: McGraw-Hill, 1966.
Notable Twentieth-Century Scientists. Emily J. McMurray, ed. New York: Gale Research, 1995.
They Gave Their Names to Science. D. S. Halacy, Jr. New York: Putnam, 1967.

(Charles E. Herdendorf)

John H. Van Vleck

Area of Achievement: Physics

Contribution: Van Vleck's work in theoretical physics spanned both the old quantum theory and the subsequent quantum mechanics. In the latter, he focused on its application to magnetism, the theory of solids, and chemical physics.

Mar. 13, 1899	Born in Middletown, Connecticut
1922	Earns a Ph.D. at Harvard University
1922-1923	Works as a physics instructor at Harvard
1923-1928	Promoted from assistant to full professor at the University of Minnesota
1928-1934	Teaches physics at the University of Wisconsin
1934-1969	Teaches mathematical physics at Harvard
1942-1945	Serves as Director of Theory Group at the Radio Research Laboratory
1945	Appointed chair of the Harvard physics department
1951	Named dean of engineering and applied physics at Harvard
1952-1953	Serves as president of the American Physical Society
1960-1962	Teaches at the Universities of Leiden and Oxford
1974	Awarded the Lorentz Medal by the Royal Netherlands Academy of Arts and Sciences
1977	Shares the Nobel Prize in Physics with Philip W. Anderson and Sir Nevill Mott
Oct. 27, 1980	Dies in Cambridge, Massachusetts

Early Life

John Hasbrouck Van Vleck was born in Middletown, Connecticut, where his paternal grandfather, John, was professor of astronomy and his father, Edward, was a professor of mathematics at Wesleyan University. In 1906, Edward Van Vleck accepted a professorship at the University of Wisconsin.

Thus, young John grew up in Madison, Wisconsin, attending public schools and the University of Wisconsin until 1920, when his father became a visiting professor at Harvard University in Cambridge, Massachusetts.

Van Vleck had majored in physics at the University of Wisconsin, and he began graduate study at Harvard with Edwin C. Kemble, earning his Ph.D. in physics in 1922. His thesis on the helium atom was the first American theo-

(The Nobel Foundation)

retical dissertation to employ the quantum theory being developed in Europe.

Work in the "Old" Quantum Theory

Van Vleck's thesis did not successfully explain the helium atom because the quantum theory in use at that time was incapable of doing so. A newer quantum theory, known as quantum mechanics, was not developed until 1925. Van Vleck continued to work in the older idiom until 1926 and became recognized as one of the few American theoretical physicists capable of teaching and doing research in quantum theory.

Van Vleck was asked by the National Research Council to prepare a report entitled *Quantum Principles and Line Spectra* (1926). This masterful presentation of the soon-to-be "old" quantum theory was nevertheless valued by the physics community in the United States. Some 1,300 copies were sold, and the book consolidated Van Vleck's position in the emerging American theoretical physics community.

Electric and Magnetic Susceptibilities

From 1923 until 1928, Van Vleck was a member of the faculty of the University of Minnesota, teaching graduate courses and supervising the dissertations of three students. After moving to the University of Wisconsin in 1928, he continued his own research applying the methods of quantum mechanics to specific atoms and molecules. His book *The Theory of Electric and Magnetic Susceptibilities*, published in 1932, remained a classic work for decades. It provided a complete treatment of the topic from the classical, the old quantum theoretical, and the newer quantum mechanical points of view.

In addition to supervising the doctoral dissertations of nine graduate students and the work of several postdoctoral associates at the University of Wisconsin, Van Vleck wrote papers that contributed to the quantum mechanical theory of valence needed by chemists for their understanding of molecular structure. He also developed a theory of crystal structure known as ligand field theory.

Returning to Harvard University

In 1934, Van Vleck returned to Harvard as professor of mathematical physics, a post that he retained until his retirement in 1969. During those years, he continued his own research and

From Quantum Mechanics to Chemical Physics

Using the quantum mechanics introduced by physicists, chemists were able to apply its principles and methods to their analyses of atoms and molecules, thereby gaining insight into all states of matter—gaseous, liquid, and solid.

The theory of the atomic structure of hydrogen introduced by Niels Bohr in 1913 combined new quantum principles with older mechanical and electromagnetic concepts. It worked well in explaining spectroscopic observations but, despite the efforts of Bohr and Arnold Sommerfeld, was inadequate when extended to more complicated atoms with many electrons. These electrons were visualized as moving in well-defined orbits with specific energies and having the ability to undergo transition from one possible orbit to another.

The quantum mechanics introduced in matrix form by Werner Heisenberg and in wave form by Erwin Schrödinger abandoned the idea of localized electronic orbits but retained the concept of energy states. Both versions of quantum mechanics required advanced mathematical techniques. They were, however, successfully applied by both physicists and chemists to atoms and molecules more complicated than simple hydrogen.

All the elements in the periodic table were studied, yielding a scheme of energy states for the electrons involved. This scheme allowed chemists to understand valence properties of atoms and the structure of compound molecules. The same analytical techniques were successfully used by Van Vleck to explain the magnetic properties of substances and the formation of crystal structure.

Bibliography

Quantum Physics in America: The Years Through 1935. Katherine R. Sopka. New York: American Institute of Physics Press, 1988.

supervised the doctoral theses of more than thirty graduate students. One of these, Philip W. Anderson, would share the Nobel Prize in Physics with Van Vleck in 1977.

World War II

Van Vleck served on a national committee of physicists considering the feasibility of building an atomic bomb, but his main work during World War II was devoted to antiradar research. At the end of the war, he became chair of the physics department at Harvard, assuming the difficult task of revitalizing the department. Between 1951 and 1957, he was dean of the Division of Engineering and Applied Physics, a newly established entity at Harvard.

International Recognition and Honors

Van Vleck was a member of a group of young American physicists who entered the field at a crucial time in the history of the discipline. Their work and contributions to quantum theory helped establish theoretical physics as a profession and brought international recognition, resulting in the coming-of-age of physics in the United States.

Van Vleck's own work gained international repute before 1930. He was the only American invited to participate in the Solvay Congress on Magnetism held in Brussels in 1930. Within the United States, he was frequently a guest lecturer at universities and professional meetings. He was president of the American Physical Society from 1952 to 1953. In 1974, he was awarded the Lorentz Medal by the Royal Netherlands Academy of Arts and Sciences, an especially gratifying honor for Van Vleck, whose Dutch ancestors had come to America in the seventeenth century.

In 1977, he shared the Nobel Prize in Physics with Anderson and Sir Nevill Mott; all three were cited for "their fundamental theoretical investigations of the electronic structure of magnetic and disordered systems." Van Vleck, the eldest of the three recipients, has been called the founder of modern magnetism. He died in 1980 at the age of eighty-one.

Bibliography

By Van Vleck
Quantum Principles and Line Spectra, 1926
"The New Quantum Mechanics," *Chemical Reviews*, 1928
The Theory of Electric and Magnetic Susceptibilities, 1932
"The Theory of Antiferromagnetism," *Journal of Chemical Physics*, 1941

About Van Vleck
"John H. Van Vleck." In *The Nobel Prize Winners: Physics*, edited by Frank N. Magill. Pasadena, Calif.: Salem Press, 1989.
"Van Vleck, John Hasbrouck." Frederick Fellows. In *Dictionary of Scientific Biography*, edited by Charles Coulston Gillispie. Vol. 18. New York: Charles Scribner's Sons, 1984.

(Katherine R. Sopka)

Jacobus Henricus van't Hoff

Areas of Achievement: Chemistry and physics

Contribution: An early worker in the field of theoretical chemistry, van't Hoff won the Nobel Prize in Chemistry for his work on chemical dynamics and osmotic pressure in solutions.

Aug. 30, 1852	Born in Rotterdam, the Netherlands
1871	Receives a degree in engineering from the University of Delft
1874	Receives a doctorate, summa cum laude, from the University of Utrecht
1875	Publishes *La Chimie dans l'espace* (*Chemistry in Space*, 1891)
1875	Teaches at the Royal Veterinary School in Utrecht
1877	Appointed to the faculty of the University of Amsterdam
1887	Founds and edits, with Wilhelm Ostwald, the journal *Zeitschrift für physikalische Chemie*
1893	Wins the Davy Medal of the Royal Society of London
1894	Appointed Chevalier of the Legion of Honor
1896	Named a professor of experimental physics at the University of Berlin
1901	Elected president of the German Chemical Society
1901	Awarded the first Nobel Prize in Chemistry
1908	Directs his work toward the study of enzymes
Mar. 1, 1911	Dies in Steglitz (now Berlin), Germany

Early Life

Jacobus Henricus van't Hoff (pronounced "vahnt hawf"), following the usual Dutch education through the secondary level, entered the Polytechnic School at Delft at his parents' urging. Although he had already demonstrated an interest in pure science, his father believed that better career opportunities existed in the field of technology. Van't Hoff earned a technology diploma in 1871 with the highest score on the final examination.

A Career Is Chosen

A short stint working as a technologist in a sugar factory, however, convinced him that such a life would be dreary and unchallenging. Thus, van't Hoff's own decision to follow a career in pure science was made. He studied mathematics for a year at Leyden and then went to Bonn, where he studied chemistry for a time with Friedrich August Kekule von Stradonitz.

From there, van't Hoff moved to Paris to broaden his chemical studies with Charles-

(Library of Congress)

Adolphe Wurtz and returned to the Netherlands to receive a doctorate, summa cum laude, under Ernst Mulder at the University of Utrecht in 1874. From that point, van't Hoff continued with an academic career.

A Reputation Is Established

Van't Hoff stayed in Utrecht for three years and, in 1877, received an appointment as lecturer (later professor) at the University of Amsterdam, where he remained for eighteen years. He completed his career at the University of Berlin, continuing there as a research professor until his death.

Van't Hoff's doctoral dissertation was judged to be routine and uninspired; it was most likely offered as the safest course to the degree because he was already at work on a much more important and controversial work. His publication of a little pamphlet concerning the three-dimensional nature of molecules had the scientific community in a buzz. This pamphlet was expanded into his first publication, *La Chimie dans l'espace* (1875; *Chemistry in Space*, 1891).

It was on the strength of the gradual acceptance of this stereochemical work that van't Hoff received his appointment at Amsterdam. While holding this position, he did most of his groundbreaking research on chemical dynamics and equilibrium. This work and van't Hoff's writings at the time form one of the pillars supporting the new field of physical chemistry.

The Mature Scientist

His shift to the University of Berlin in 1896 signaled a change in van't Hoff's work as well. He spent much time traveling, lecturing, and enjoying the fame that he had earned. In 1901, he was awarded the first Nobel Prize in Chemistry. In his research, he dropped theoretical work and instead developed a systematic, me-

The Structure and Movement of Molecules

Many of the outwardly measurable chemical and physical properties of a substance can be explained by considering the structure and movement of the molecules of which the substance is made.

Prior to van't Hoff's work, molecules were thought of as static, two-dimensional objects. Van't Hoff pursued their three-dimensional character and their dynamics, which provided explanations in several areas of chemistry.

His findings ushered in the field of stereochemistry, the study of spatial relationships of atoms within molecules. Differing stereochemical arrangements of atoms accounted for the variety of properties found for molecules all having the same chemical formula. In particular, this concept explained the property of optical isomerism, in which molecules with identical formulas exhibit different responses to polarized light. These isomers differ from one another as do right and left hands.

Van't Hoff used his mathematical insight to describe the motion of molecules and their collisions with one another in order to lay the foundation for the branch of chemistry called kinetics. Further theorizing led him to the explanation of chemical equilibrium, the point at which no net change in the concentrations of chemicals in a reacting system occurs. He showed that this occurrence could be explained by both forward and reverse reactions taking place at equal rates.

His idea of molecules in motion also provided an explanation of osmotic pressure. Osmotic pressure arises when solutions of differing concentrations are separated by a semipermeable membrane, an effect that is very important in understanding biological cell function.

Bibliography

The Architecture of Molecules. Linus Pauling and Roger Hayward. San Francisco: W. H. Freeman, 1964.

Chemical Equilibrium. Allen J. Bard. New York: Harper & Row, 1966.

Chemical Kinetics: The Study of Reaction Rates in Solution. Kenneth A. Connors. New York: VCH, 1990.

Physical Chemistry: Principles and Applications in Biological Sciences. Ignacio Tinoco, Jr., Kenneth Sauer, and James C. Wang. Englewood Cliffs, N.J.: Prentice Hall, 1995.

Stereochemistry of Carbon Compounds. Ernest L. Eliel. New York: McGraw-Hill, 1962.

thodical approach applying chemistry to geological problems, resulting in the publication of more than fifty papers.

In 1908, a revitalized van't Hoff returned to theoretical chemistry and directed his efforts at understanding the action of enzymes as biological catalysts. Although few publications resulted from this work, those that exist show important insights. Van't Hoff died in 1911.

Bibliography

By van't Hoff

La Chimie dans l'espace, 1875 (*Chemistry in Space*, 1891)

Ansichten über die organische Chemie, 1878-1881

Études de dynamique chimique, 1884

"Lois de l'équilibre chimique dans l'état dilue, gazeux, ou dissous," *Kungliga svenska veteaskapakademiens handlingar*, 1886

Dix années dans l'histoire d'une théorie, 1887 (enlarged ed. of *La Chimie dans l'espace*)

Vorlesungen über Bildung und spaltung von Doppelsalzen, 1897

Vorlesungen über theoretische und physikalische Chemie, 1898-1900 (3 vols.; *Lectures on Theoretical and Physical Chemistry*, 1899-1900, 3 vols.)

Über die Theorie der losungen, 1900

Acht Vorträge über physikalische Chemie, 1902 (*Physical Chemistry in the Service of the Sciences*, 1903)

Zur Bildung der ozeanischen Salzablagerungen, 1905-1909 (2 vols.)

Gedachtnisrede auf Hans Heinrich Landolt, 1910

Die chemischen Grundlehren nach Menge, Mass, und Zeit, 1912

Untersuchungen über die Bildungsverhältnisse der ozeanischen Salzablagerungen insbesondere des Stassfurter salzlagers, 1912

About van't Hoff

"The Basic Work of Fischer and van't Hoff in Carbohydrate Chemistry." Claude S. Hudson. *The Journal of Chemical Education* 30 (1953).

"The Meeting of Ostwald, Arrhenius, and van't Hoff." Benjamin Harrow. *The Journal of Chemical Education* 7 (1930).

"My Reminiscences of van't Hoff." A. F. Holleman. *The Journal of Chemical Education* 29 (1952).

(*Kenneth H. Brown*)

Harold E. Varmus

Areas of Achievement: Cell biology and virology

Contribution: Varmus won the Nobel Prize in Physiology or Medicine for discovering the genes that give rise to cancer.

Dec. 18, 1939	Born in Oceanside, Long Island, New York
1961	Earns a B.A. in English literature from Amherst College
1962	Receives an M.A. in literature from Harvard University
1966	Earns an M.D. from Columbia University Medical School
1966-1968	Serves as resident physician at Columbia-Presbyterian Hospital
1968	Joins Ira Pastan's laboratory at the National Institutes of Health (NIH)
1970	Joins J. Michael Bishop at the University of California, San Francisco (UCSF)
1970-1979	Ascends to the rank of professor
1982	Wins the Lasker Foundation Award
1984	Becomes American Cancer Society Research Professor of Molecular Virology at UCSF
1984	Elected to the National Academy of Sciences
1988	Elected to the American Academy of Arts and Sciences
1989	With Bishop, awarded the Nobel Prize in Physiology or Medicine
1988-1989	Works in the laboratory of Bob Weinberg and David Baltimore at the Whitehead Institute
1993	Appointed director of the NIH by President Bill Clinton

Early Life

Harold Eliot Varmus was born to well-educated parents on Long Island just before World War II. His father was a physician, and his mother was a social worker. He attended public schools that, he later wrote, were "dominated by athletics and rarely inspiring intellectually." Originally planning to follow in his father's footsteps, he eventually turned to experimental science "dangerously late in a prolonged adolescence."

Entering Amherst College with the intention of fulfilling premedical requirements, Varmus became "devoted to Dickensian novels and anti-Establishment journalism." He earned his B.A. in literature from Amherst and then indulged himself with "a year of Anglo-Saxon and metaphysical poetry at Harvard graduate school" before returning to his original goal. He earned a medical degree from Columbia and spent two years as a resident physician at Columbia-Presbyterian Hospital in New York City.

(The Nobel Foundation)

His ambitions turned toward a career in academic medicine, and he applied for research training at the National Institutes of Health (NIH). "Perhaps because his wife was a poet," Varmus later remarked, "Ira Pastan agreed to take me into his laboratory, despite my lack of scientific credentials."

His time at NIH led him to an interest in the viruses that cause cancer in animals. During the summer of 1969, Varmus "combined a backpacking vacation in California with a search for a suitable place to study tumor viruses." The search led him to join J. Michael Bishop's research team at the University of California, San Francisco (UCSF), the following summer. He remained at UCSF, reaching the rank of professor by 1979.

The Genetic Basis of Cancer

In 1970, two explanations for the genetic basis of cancer were being offered, and Varmus was determined to explore them. One was the "provirus" hypothesis of Howard Temin, which proposed that tumor viruses insert a copy of their genetic code into the deoxyribonucleic acid (DNA) of each cell that they invade. Before Varmus could make a start, however, the hypothesis was confirmed by Temin and David Baltimore.

The other hypothesis, which did not actually contradict the provirus theory, was the "virogene-oncogene" hypothesis. After five years of work, Bishop and Varmus confirmed part of this conjecture, but they also discovered a surprising and important difference. Further work by the UCSF team and others proved the importance of their work, and, fourteen years later, they were awarded the Nobel Prize in Physiology or Medicine for their discoveries.

From Scientist to Administrator

By the late 1990's, Varmus had coauthored more than three hundred scientific papers and served on several scientific advisory groups. He was chair of the committee that, in 1986, chose the name "human immunodeficiency virus" (HIV) for the virus that causes acquired immunodeficiency syndrome (AIDS).

In a significant departure from his scientific career, Varmus was selected by President Bill Clinton in 1993 to direct the NIH. Thus, Var-

Oncogenes and Cancer

Cells contain proto-oncogenes, which normally control cell growth and development but which can cause cancer when they go awry.

In 1911, Peyton Rous discovered a virus that causes sarcoma, a type of cancer, in chickens. The Rous sarcoma virus (RSV) causes the cell that it infects and all of its descendants to reproduce uncontrollably—a phenomenon that reveals information about the origins of cancer.

The virogene-oncogene hypothesis explored by Varmus and J. Michael Bishop suggests that normal animal cells contain genes called oncogenes that, when activated, cause cells to become cancerous. These oncogenes are normally turned off, but they may be activated by chemicals or radiation. It is supposed that these oncogenes found their way into an animal's genome in ancient times from infection of an ancestor's egg by a virus carrying the corresponding virogene. New infection by a virus carrying an active virogene would also cause cancer.

Varmus and Bishop isolated the virogene in a small piece of the RSV genome and showed that a copy of it was present in uninfected chicken cells—partially confirming the virogene-oncogene hypothesis. Further clever experiments indicated that the gene, instead of originating in the virus, was actually a normal cellular gene that had been captured by an ancestor of the virus.

They collected more evidence showing this oncogene to be an important cellular gene that controls cell replication and development in most animals. By the late 1990's, more than seventy such proto- oncogenes were known to have roles in normal cell development.

Bibliography
Genes and the Biology of Cancer. Harold Varmus and Robert A. Weinberg. New York: Scientific American Library, 1993.
"The Genetic Basis of Cancer." W. K. Cavenee and R. L. White. *Scientific American* 272 (March, 1995).
The Molecular Basis of Cancer. John Mendelsohn et al. Philadelphia: W. B. Saunders, 1995.

mus returned to Bethesda, Maryland, to manage the institute where he began his research. Scientists often make poor managers, as his critics were quick to point out, but Varmus proved to be the exception—perhaps because of his broad interests in literature and outdoor recreation as well as in laboratory science.

Bibliography
By Varmus
"Integration of Deoxyribonucleic Acid Specific for Rous Sarcoma Virus After Infection of Permissive and Nonpermissive Hosts," *Proceedings of the National Academy of Sciences, U.S.A.*, 1973 (with P. K. Vogt and J. Michael Bishop)
"DNA Related to the Transforming Gene(s) of Avian Sarcoma Viruses Is Present in Normal Avian DNA," *Nature*, 1976 (with D. Stehelin, Bishop, and Vogt)
"Form and Function of Retroviral Proviruses," *Science*, 1982
"Oncogenes and Transcriptional Control," *Science*, 1987
"Reverse Transcription," *Scientific American*, 1987
"Polymerase Gene Products of Hepatitis B Viruses Are Required for Genomic RNA Packaging as Well as for Reverse Transcription," *Nature*, 1990 (with R. C. Hirsch, J. E. Lavine, L. J. Chang, and D. Ganem)
Genes and the Biology of Cancer, 1993 (with Robert A. Weinberg)

About Varmus
"Harold E. Varmus." In *The Nobel Prize Winners: Physiology or Medicine*, edited by Frank N. Magill. Pasadena, Calif.: Salem Press, 1991.
Nobel Laureates in Medicine or Physiology: A Biographical Dictionary. Daniel M. Fox, Marcia Meldrum, and Ira Rezak, eds. New York: Garland, 1990.
Nobel Prize Winners: Supplement. Tyler Wasson, ed. New York: H. W. Wilson, 1992.

(Randy Hudson)

Nikolai Ivanovich Vavilov

Areas of Achievement: Botany and genetics
Contribution: Vavilov, the foremost Russian geneticist of the twentieth century, studied the origins, distribution, and genetics of crop plants. He was the principal defender of Mendelian genetics against the attacks of Trofim Lysenko.

Nov. 26, 1887	Born in Moscow, Russia
1906-1910	Studies at the Petrovsko Agricultural Institute in Moscow
1913-1914	Studies genetics in England with William Bateson
1914	Completes a dissertation on plant immunity to infectious disease
1916	Travels to Central Asia to collect cultivated plants
1917	Appointed professor of genetics and plant breeding at the University of Saratov
1920	Named chair of the department of plant breeding at the Agricultural Institute of Petrograd
1924	Appointed head of the institute
1924-1933	Travels to Asia, Afghanistan, the Mediterranean, Italy, Ethiopia, China, Japan, Mexico, Central America, and South America
1929	Elected a member of the Soviet Academy of Sciences
1936	Fired from his position as head of the institute
1940	Arrested as an enemy of the people and imprisoned
Jan. 26, 1943	Dies in Saratov, Soviet Union

Early Life

Nikolai Ivanovich Vavilov (pronounced "vuhv-YEE-luhf") was born in Moscow, Russia, in 1887 as the eldest of three children of Ivan Vavilov, a prominent Moscow merchant. All three were encouraged to pursue scientific careers; his brother, Sergei, became a well-known physicist, and his sister, Lidia, was a physician.

Nikolai Vavilov pursued a degree in agriculture at the Petrovsko Agricultural Institute in Moscow, being graduated in 1910. After a brief period as an assistant at the Poltava agricultural experiment station, he moved to St. Petersburg to do graduate work. In 1913-1914, he studied in England with pioneer geneticist William Bateson and cereal breeder Rowland Biffen.

Vavilov's master of science dissertation, completed in 1914, was on the immunity of plants to infectious diseases. Following his graduation, he taught at the Petrovsko Agricultural Institute.

Professional Career

In 1917, Vavilov was appointed a professor of genetics, plant breeding, and agronomy at the Agricultural Institute of Voronezh and the University of Saratov. At a congress of plant breeders that he organized in Saratov in 1920, he presented his classic paper on the law of homologous series in variation, which was also given at the International Agricultural Congress in the United States the following year.

This law states that if a variation occurs in one species of plants, it is likely to occur in related species. Vavilov cited an impressive amount of data from both wild and cultivated plants in order to support his statement. This principle is useful to the plant breeder because it suggests that if a desirable characteristic is found in one species (a high protein level in a variety of wheat, for example), then a survey of many populations of similar species (other cereal grains, in this case) would uncover strains that exhibited the same characteristic.

In 1920, Vavilov was appointed chair of the Department of Economic Botany and Plant Breeding at the Agricultural Institute of Petrograd. He became director of the institute itself in 1924. With the full support of the Communist government, he was able to direct the rapid expansion of agricultural research in the

Centers of Diversity of Cultivated Plants

Vavilov traveled the globe seeking out cultivated and wild strains of plants in order to create a comprehensive collection for breeding.

Most of the species of crop plants cultivated today were domesticated thousands of years ago by people living in a few well-defined, widely separated areas of the world. As these crops were carried around the world through commerce and migration, much of their original genetic variability was lost. In the 1920's, since natural genetic variability formed the backbone of plant breeding programs—induced mutation and genetic engineering were not then a part of the plant breeder's arsenal—it was an advantage to have at one's disposal as many different strains of cultivated plants and their wild ancestors as possible.

Vavilov recognized that variability of plants under cultivation was greatest in the areas where they had originally been domesticated, especially when indigenous agriculture preserved its ancient forms. He conducted expeditions to the farms of Central Asia, the Mideast, the Mediterranean (including North Africa), Ethiopia, China, Japan, Mexico, Central America, and Peru in order to collect living plant material.

The varieties thus recovered were established on an experimental farm outside St. Petersburg, where a collection of more than two hundred thousand separate strains of plants important to Russian agriculture was amassed.

A particular concern was disease resistance. In its native habitat, alongside its wild relatives, a crop is continually exposed to pathogens and evolves mechanisms of resistance. Transplanted to an area where the pathogen is absent, the crop is more productive since it is disease-free, but the resistance is no longer selected for and tends to be eliminated from the gene pool. If the pathogen is subsequently introduced, the results can be disastrous; the utility of maintaining disease-resistant strains is obvious.

Another major effort, which brought Vavilov into direct conflict with Trofim Lysenko, was the attempt to breed a strain of wheat that could be planted in the spring and would mature in the short growing season of northern Russia. Despite Russia's vast area, the country has less acreage of prime agricultural land than the United States, and developing varieties of staple crops that will perform reliably under subarctic conditions is an important consideration. Existing varieties of spring-planted wheat did not have time to mature, and fall-planted wheat was often damaged by severe winters. Vavilov collected thousands of samples of seed from all the wheat-growing areas of Russia, as well as from North America, and began the tedious process of conducting controlled crosses and testing the progeny for early maturation.

Meanwhile, Lysenko's approach to the same problem was vernalization: cold treatment of winter wheat seed, which was then planted in the spring—a technique that did not originate with him and had not proved successful on a consistent enough basis to be widely adopted. Lysenko not only claimed a suspiciously high success rate but also maintained that the seeds produced by his vernalized wheat had inherited the characteristic of spring germination and maturation in a single season. The conclusions were based on a very small sample size and are most plausibly explained by assuming that some spring wheat seed was included in the initial planting and was inadvertently selected.

In favoring Lysenko over Vavilov, the Soviet government turned its back on research that might have been significant for Russian agriculture. By the mid-1990's, plant breeders had yet to produce an early-maturing, spring-planted wheat.

Bibliography

Crop Genetic Resources for Today and Tomorrow. O. H. Frankel and J. G. Hawkes. Cambridge, England: Cambridge University Press, 1975.

Dictionary of Cultivated Plants and Their Centres of Diversity, Excluding Ornamentals, Forest Trees, and Lower Plants. A. C. Zeven and P. M. Zhukovsky. Wageningen, the Netherlands: Centre for Agricultural Publishing and Documentation, 1975.

The Diversity of Crop Plants. J. G. Hawkes. Cambridge, Mass.: Harvard University Press, 1983.

Soviet Union, helping to establish a network of agricultural research stations and overseeing plant breeding programs that, in terms of their scope and scientific validity, were unequaled, even in the United States.

Vavilov and his colleagues personally traveled throughout the Soviet Union and to the far corners of the globe to collect seeds, tubers, and other living material from cultivated plants and their wild relatives. These were then grown in experimental plots to serve as the raw material from which improved varieties of crop plants could be bred.

Vavilov visited the United States on a number of occasions, the last time in 1932, when he read papers at the International Genetics Conference in Ithaca, New York.

(Library of Congress)

Conflict with Lysenko

In 1935, a threat to Vavilov's scientific career emerged in the person of Trofim Lysenko, a plant breeder of mediocre ability with a talent for exploiting the worsening political climate in Stalinist Russia to his own advantage. Lysenko believed that he had demonstrated the inheritance of acquired characteristics in crop plants.

This position was attractive to the Soviet government for several reasons. It promised quicker results than conventional breeding programs, and it was less tied to Western research. Soviet agricultural output had declined disastrously during forced collectivization, and the agricultural experiment stations made a convenient scapegoat.

Vavilov responded courageously to Lysenko's attacks, condemning him as a charlatan. As a result, he found his position increasingly untenable. He was fired from his job as head of the Agricultural Institute in 1936 and denied permission to travel abroad or collaborate with foreign colleagues. Finally, on August 6, 1940, he was arrested and accused of sabotage and espionage at agricultural institutes and of being a fascist sympathizer.

The charge of sabotage was entirely fabricated. The charge of fascism rested on the tenuous assumption that since the Nazis used the classical Mendelian model of heredity to support their racial theories, anyone who advocated Mendelian genetics was a fascist.

Vavilov was interrogated in Moscow, then transferred to a prison in Saratov, where he died (according to the official death certificate) of edema and dystrophy, probably the result of extreme malnutrition, on January 26, 1943.

In the years following his arrest, much of the genetic material that he had so laboriously collected was lost through neglect. His manuscripts on the centers of origin of cultivated plants remained unpublished until the 1960's, when one of his students, P. M. Zhukovskii, edited them for publication.

Vavilov was married to a fellow agronomist; the couple had two sons, both of whom became physicists. He was an energetic, forceful person who inspired loyalty and admiration in his students, colleagues, and those who worked for him.

Bibliography

By Vavilov

The Origin, Variation, Immunity, and Breeding of Cultivated Plants: Selected Writings of N. I. Vavilov, 1951

Mirovye resursy sortov khlebnykh zlakov, zernovvkh bobovykh, l'na i ikh ispol'zovanie v selektsii, 1957 (*World Resources of Cereals, Leguminous Seed Crops, and Flax, and Their Utilization in Plant Breeding*, 1957)

Piat' Kontinentov, 1962 (five continents)

Proizkhodenie I geografiia kulturnykh rastenii (*Origin and Geography of Cultivated Plants*, 1992)

About Vavilov

Manipulated Science: The Crisis of Science and Scientists in the Soviet Union Today. Mark Popovskii. Garden City, N.Y.: Doubleday, 1959.

Soviet Science. Zhores Medvedev. New York: W. W. Norton, 1978.

The Vavilov Affair. Mark Popovskii. Ann Arbor, Mich.: Archon Books, 1984.

(Martha A. Sherwood)

Rudolf Virchow

Areas of Achievement: Bacteriology, biology, cell biology, immunology, medicine, and physiology

Contribution: Virchow's work in pathology and cell histology established the field of cellular pathology, provided a deeper understanding of several diseases, and influenced public health and sanitation standards.

Oct. 13, 1821	Born in Schivelbein, Pomerania, Prussia (now Germany)
1843	Earns a medical degree from the University of Berlin
1846	Joins the staff at Charite Hospital
1847	Becomes a lecturer at Berlin
1847	Helps establish the journal *Archiv für pathologische Anatomie und Physiologie und klinische Medizin*
1848	Conducts a government study of a typhus epidemic in Silesia
1849	Appointed a professor at the University of Würzburg
1854	Publishes the first volume of *Handbuch der spezellen Pathologie und Therapie*
1856	Becomes a professor at the University of Berlin and head of its Institute of Pathology
1858	Publishes a classic work on cellular pathology
1861	Elected to the Prussian house and forms the liberal party
1870	Begins work on anthropology, ethnology, and Darwinism
1901	His eightieth birthday is honored with a global festival
Sept. 5, 1902	Dies in Berlin, Germany

Early Life

From an early age, Rudolf Ludwig Karl Virchow (pronounced "FIHR-khoh") developed a sense of skepticism: He questioned unbridled hypothesis formation and inexact reasoning cloaked as science. He would maintain this analytic acuity and critical vigor over a fifty-year career.

A military fellowship began Virchow's exposure to medicine at the Friedrich-Wilhelms Institute. In 1843, after earning a medical degree at the University of Berlin, he gave a prestigious presentation on phlebitis that corrected common misconceptions. A series of lectures on pathology followed. His fame grew rapidly. In 1847, he cofounded the journal *Archiv für pathologische Anatomie und Physiologie und klinische Medizin.*

Virchow believed that medicine should influence culture and political processes. In an 1848 report, he criticized the Prussian government as the cause of a typhus epidemic in Silesia; his recommendation was political autonomy. Although Virchow excelled at statesmanship, notably public health issues, his liberalism, scientific insight, and public health reform efforts created many enemies. His position at Charite Hospital in Berlin was suspended in 1849, and his progressive journal, *Medizinische Reform*, ended that same year.

Concentrating on Pathology

When his position at Charite Hospital was jeopardized, Virchow accepted a professorship at the University of Würzburg. The university was located in Bavaria, which freed him of Prussian persecution. He devoted his efforts toward cellular pathology and began publishing *Handbuch der speziellen Pathologie und Therapie*, a six-volume foundational masterpiece on scientific pathology.

Returning to Berlin in 1856, he continued research as a professor at the University of Berlin, directing its Institute of Pathology. Virchow presented a series of twenty lectures, with demonstrations of cellular pathology, that influenced the discipline significantly. In 1858, he published these lectures, with numerous engravings, in the first edition of *Die Cellularpathologie* (*Cellular Pathology*, 1860), a fundamental text that would be translated into many languages. Virchow worked on a second revised edition while preparing, *Die krankhaften Geschwülste* (1863-1867), a treatise covering tumors.

A Return to Politics

With his renown came a revitalized interest in political reform. Virchow's efforts in municipal politics led to the establishment of sewage and water improvement projects in Berlin. He avidly served as a founder of the liberal party and a top representative, coming close to a personal duel with statesman Otto von Bismarck.

While debating against Germanic militarism and consolidation, Virchow helped mobilize and establish medical support for the casualties of the Franco-Prussian War. He wanted medicine to have a key and benevolent role in the political destiny of nations.

Other Studies

In the field of anthropology, Virchow created a German professional society. He conducted re-

(Library of Congress)

Cellular Foundations of Pathology

Virchow's greatest contribution to science was the principle that cells arise from other cells, which complements and extends Louis Pasteur's organic continuity principle.

Virchow carefully formulated the cellular-based and organ-based models of pathology. Disease and inflammation were given a reasoned and localized causality, overturning popular pseudoscientific misconceptions. He opposed the humoral view, which based health completely on the state of a fundamental living fluid—called "lymph," "cytoblastema," "plasma," and other names—carried by the bloodstream. Many of these terms have valid but different meanings in modern biology. He likewise opposed the neural pathologist school, which made the nervous system the primary determining factor. Virchow refined Theodor Schwann's cell theory and its variants, most notably removing the concept of cell generation from noncellular forms.

He identified, named, and studied leukemia, thrombosis, and embolism. Among the structures that he discovered were fibrinogen, amyloid (and its degeneration), hematoidin, and myelin. His extensive research included inflammation and tumor development, focusing on their physiological mechanisms.

Bibliography
Growth of Medical Thought. Lester S. King. Chicago: University of Chicago Press, 1974.

Pathology. Emanuel Rubin and John L. Farber. 2d ed. Philadelphia: J. B. Lippincott, 1994.

Robbins Pathologic Basis of Disease. Ramzi S. Cotran, Vinay Kumar, and Stanley L. Robbins. 5th ed. Philadelphia: W. B. Saunders, 1994.

search with Heinrich Schliemann at the site of ancient Troy and wrote a monograph on artifacts in Trojan graves.

In ethnology, he directed surveys of German schoolchildren and found significant diversity. He worked against unscientific ethnological presuppositions and debated against the misapplication of evolution theory to metaphysics by E. H. Haeckel, his former student.

His work in public health and epidemiology is also recognized. Virchow knew that lack of sanitation, governmental neglect, and political conditions cause diseases such as trichinosis and typhus, and he saw the need for public health care.

In 1901, Virchow's eightieth birthday was celebrated with a global festival. He died in Berlin almost a year later.

Bibliography
By Virchow
Handbuch der speziellen Pathologie und Therapie, 1854-1876 (6 vols.)

Die Cellularpathologie, in ihrer Begründung auf physiologische und pathologische Gewebelehre, 1858 (*Cellular Pathology, as Based upon Physiological and Pathological Histology,* 1860)

Die krankhaften Geschwülste, 1863-1867 (3 vols.)

Gesammelte Abhandlungen aus dem Gebiete der öffentlichen Medicin und der Seuchenlehre, 1879 (*Collected Essays on Public Health and Epidemiology,* 1985)

Virchow Bibliographie, 1843-1901, 1901

Disease, Life, and Man: Selected Essays by Rudolf Virchow, 1958

About Virchow
A Commentary on the Medical Writings of Rudolf Virchow. L. J. Rather. San Francisco: Norman, 1991.

"Rudolf Virchow and Social Medicine in Historical Perspective." D. Pridan. *Medical History* 8 (1964).

Rudolf Virchow: Doctor, Statesman, Anthropologist. Erwin H. Ackerknecht. Madison: University of Wisconsin Press, 1953.

(John Panos Najarian)

Carl von Voit

Areas of Achievement: Biology and physiology

Contribution: Voit's experimental methodology and equipment made it possible to study the metabolism of different types of food and to explain how the body derives energy from proteins, carbohydrates, and fats.

Oct. 31, 1831	Born in Amberg, Bavaria (now Germany)
1848-1854	Studies medicine at the University of Munich
1855	Studies chemistry at the University of Göttingen
1856	Becomes an assistant at the Physiological Institute in Munich
1857	Becomes an instructor at Munich
1860	Coauthors *Die Gesetze der Ernährung des Fleischfressers* (the laws of carnivore nutrition) and becomes an adjunct professor
1863	Promoted to full professor and head of the Physiological Institute
1865	Elected to the Royal Bavarian Academy of Sciences
1865	Cofounds the *Zeitschrift für Biologie*, a biology journal in which most of his and his students' articles would appear
1884	Elected secretary of the mathematical-physical section of the Bavarian Academy
1898	Elected to the Berlin Academy of Sciences
Jan. 31, 1908	Dies in Munich, Germany

(Library of Congress)

Early Life

Carl von Voit (pronounced "foyt") was born in Amberg, in the kingdom of Bavaria, southern Germany, in 1831. He was the son of August von Voit, an architect.

Carl began his career by studying medicine in Munich. After that, he was inspired by Justus von Liebig, who was then a professor at the University of Munich, to take up the study of nutrition and chemistry. On Liebig's advice, he went to the University of Göttingen in 1855 to study chemistry with Friedrich Wöhler for a year, then he took a job as an assistant to Theodor Bischoff at the Physiological Institute in Munich.

Voit remained in Munich for the rest of his career, rising through the academic ranks from assistant, to lecturer in 1857, and finally to full professor and head of the institute in 1863.

Collaboration with Bischoff

Voit made his reputation with experiments on protein metabolism in dogs, carried out in cooperation with Bischoff. They monitored the dogs' intake of nitrogen in dietary protein and were able to account for all the nitrogen excreted, egested (excreted undigested), or retained in the body.

Their results were published as *Die Gesetze*

der Ernährung des Fleischfressers (1860; the laws of carnivore nutrition). This work set a new standard for precise measurement in the study of nutrition.

Treadmill Experiments

Voit was also interested in the effects of exercise on protein metabolism, since Liebig had taught that protein, and only protein, provided the fuel for muscular work.

To test this theory, Voit trained a dog to run on a treadmill. He found little relation between how much the dog ran and the amount of protein that it metabolized. The result cast doubt on Liebig's theory and eventually led Voit to the realization that fats and carbohydrates could also provide energy to the muscles.

The Respiration Chamber

In 1861, Voit began to work with Max Pettenkofer, who had built a chamber big enough to hold a human being, that could collect and measure the gaseous products of respiration. This device enabled them to perform the first complete measurements of all bodily inputs and outputs.

Later Experiments

Voit continued his experiments with dogs, refining his measuring techniques and trying to deduce the specific sequences of biochemical changes involved in metabolism. It was known that foods react in the body with oxygen and release carbon dioxide and water, but Voit began the search for the intermediate stages in the process. This investigation was to grow into a major field of biochemical research.

Voit trained a large number of students who continued his research on nutrition and biochemistry. Their articles appeared in the *Zeitschrift für Biologie*, a journal of biology that Voit, Pettenkofer, and others had founded for that purpose. Voit was quite devoted to his work, and he continued to lecture at the university until the last year of his life. He died in 1908.

Bibliography
By Voit
Physiologisch-chemische Untersuchungen, 1857
Untersuchungen über den Einfluss des Kochsalzes, des Kaffee's, und der Muskelbewegungen auf den Stoffwechsel, 1860

Energy Metabolism

Voit recognized that fats, carbohydrates, and proteins can all serve as sources of energy in the animal body.

The oldest theories of nutrition, dating back to Hippocrates, assumed that foods were interchangeable: Some might be more nourishing than others, but they were all nourishing in the same way. In the early nineteenth century, some thought that protein might be the fundamental nutrient and that the value of foods depended on their content of, or convertibility to, protein.

Consequently, when doctors in nineteenth century Germany advised eating "light" fare in order to lose weight, they had their patients avoid meats and protein-rich foods and restrict themselves to potatoes, beer, bread, and lard. Voit was able to explain why such diets did not work.

Other physiologists realized that protein was not the only nutrient. Justus von Liebig's theory narrowed the role of protein to fueling muscular activity.

Voit proved that not only proteins but also fats and carbohydrates could provide energy to the muscles and that excess energy, from whatever source, could be stored as fat. He warned, however, that even though foods were interchangeable as energy sources, they had individual functions as well and must be eaten in proper proportions.

For weight loss, he advised people to eat less fat and carbohydrates and to exercise more. He also had practical advice for farmers on fattening livestock and creating optimal mixtures of fodder.

Bibliography
Biology in the Nineteenth Century. William Coleman. Cambridge, England: Cambridge University Press, 1977.
History of Physiology. Karl E. Rothschuh. Translated by Gunter B. Risse. Melbourne, Fla.: Robert E. Krieger, 1973.

Die Gesetze der Ernährung des Fleischfressers, durch neue Untersuchungen festgestellt, 1860 (with Theodor L. W. Bischoff)

"Untersuchungen über die Respiration," *Annalen der Chemie und Pharmacie*, 1863 (with Max Pettenkofer)

"Über die Quelle der Muskelkraft," *Zeitschrift für Biologie*, 1870

About Voit

Asimov's Biographical Encyclopedia of Science and Technology. Isaac Asimov. Garden City, N.Y.: Doubleday, 1982.

Dictionary of Scientific Biography. Charles Coulston Gillispie, ed. New York: Charles Scribner's Sons, 1976.

(Sander J. Gliboff)

Count Alessandro Volta

Areas of Achievement: Chemistry, invention, and physics

Contribution: Volta invented the electric battery, which was the first artificial source of continuous electrical current. He also advanced the scientific understanding of naturally occurring electric current and discovered methane gas.

Feb. 18, 1745	Born in Como, Duchy of Milan (now Italy)
1769-1771	Publishes papers describing his invention of an improved electrometer
1775	Appointed a professor of physics at the Royal School of Como
1777	Invents a device to generate static electricity
1778	Discovers and isolates methane gas
1779	Appointed a professor of natural philosophy at the University of Pavia
1791	Invents the eudiometer, an electric pistol, and a lamp using inflammable air as fuel
1800	Invents the voltaic pile, the first electric battery
1801	Demonstrates his battery at the court of Napoleon Bonaparte and awarded a royal medal and six thousand francs
1806	Granted the title of count and appointed senator of the district of Lombardy
1815	Appointed by the emperor of Austria as director of the philosophical faculty at the University of Padua
Mar. 5, 1827	Dies in Como, Duchy of Milan

Early Life

Alessandro Giuseppe Antonio Anastasio Volta's father, Filippo, was a minor nobleman of Lombardy, a district in north Italy. He married Maddena dei Conti Inzaghi, who came from another established family of the region.

Alessandro seemed dull-witted as a child, not speaking until the age of four. He developed rapidly into a model student, however, and continued classical studies until he was sixteen. He had the command of several languages by then, but he was most strongly attracted to the study of the natural sciences, especially physics, chemistry, and electricity.

Early Research

Volta began publishing scientific papers at the age of twenty-four. While fishing one day on a lake near his home, he noticed bubbles rising to the surface, especially in the shallows and marshes. He began collecting samples of the vapors rising above the bubbles and learned that they comprised a flammable gas. These marsh vapors are now known as methane gas, which is produced when organic material decays. Volta published his findings in what became a widely read scientific paper.

Volta was almost fifty when he married Signorina Teresa Peregrini, the youngest daughter of a local nobleman. The couple had three sons: Zanino, Flaminio, and Luigi. Zanino was elected mayor of Como, while Flaminio and Luigi became publishers of a periodical devoted to applied science and industry. Volta's scientific productivity declined significantly, however, once he became a father.

The Creation of the Electric Battery

While examining the conclusions of Luigi Galvani, who had postulated the existence of "animal electricity," Volta found instead that the natural current seen in this experiment resulted from contact between two dissimilar metals.

Volta also observed that current flowed when metal touched some fluids. He learned that the effect could be strengthened when dissimilar metals, such as zinc and silver, were interleaved with moist paper pads. He built a column of eight to ten units of zinc, silver, and

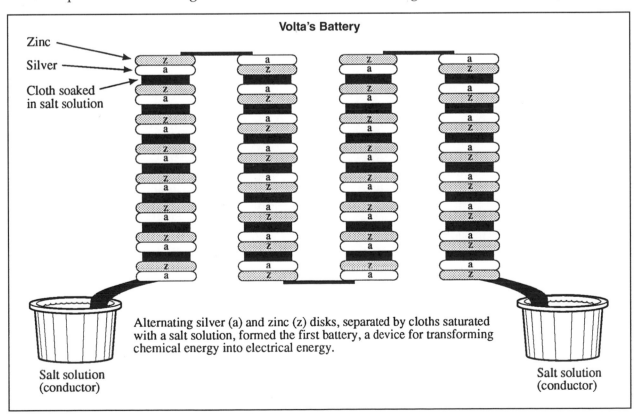

Volta's Battery

Zinc

Silver

Cloth soaked in salt solution

Alternating silver (a) and zinc (z) disks, separated by cloths saturated with a salt solution, formed the first battery, a device for transforming chemical energy into electrical energy.

Salt solution (conductor)

Salt solution (conductor)

wet paper, which produced a weak but steady flow of electrical current. Volta reported his findings to a friend, who caused them to be published in a journal of the Royal Society of London.

The so-called voltaic pile was significant because all previous electrical devices produced only a single spark or discharge. Furthermore, Volta's invention required no external source of electrical charge to produce its current. Volta's battery was a self-contained electrical engine.

The current was increased, Volta demonstrated, when more units were added, as long as the paper pads were kept moist. Current also was strengthened when it was applied to a larger area, and concentrating contact points in a limited area impeded the flow of current. Volta found that he could stimulate a response in human sensory organs and create muscle contractions in animals when he applied electric current.

Volta was called to the court of Napoleon Bonaparte to demonstrate his devices. The emperor not only attended his lectures but also took an active role in the experiments that Volta conducted. Napoleon made Volta a member of the Institute of France and awarded him a gold medal. Later, he conferred the title of count on Volta and inducted him into the French Legion of Honor. Count Volta died in 1827 at the age of eighty-two.

A Natural Source of Continuous Electric Current

Volta built the first chemical-electrical battery.

In 1780, Luigi Galvani was engaged in the study of the nervous system of a frog. He observed that when he pushed a brass wire into a frog's spine, then let the other end of the wire and the frog's leg touch an iron plate at the same time, the frog's leg jumped. This experiment caused Galvani to propose the existence of electrical current in the animal, or animal electricity, even though it was dead. Volta disagreed with Galvani's theory, and he conducted his own experiments. He found that electric current flows when two metals of different types touch, especially when the two metals are immersed in a salt brine.

Volta failed to understand, however, the underlying electrical principles behind his electric battery. In his device, the zinc interacts with the brine, leaving a negative charge on the zinc. Current flows from the negatively charged zinc to the copper element. The chemical reaction consumes the metal elements until they are depleted, when the cell no longer produces current (a dead cell).

At the atomic level, scientists found that the electrons in a nonconducting substance are bound tightly to the nuclei, while free electrons in the outer atomic shell of other substances enable current to be transmitted. The tightly bound substances are called insulators, while substances with free electrons are called conductors.

While experimenting with Volta's battery, also called a voltaic pile, later scientists learned that water is composed of two gases, hydrogen and oxygen. William Cruikshank built an improved battery, delivering a more powerful current, which he used to extract metals and to decompose chemical compounds.

Sir Humphry Davy built a large electric battery and used it to decompose other chemical compounds, leading to the discovery of new substances such as potassium and sodium. Davy further refined battery construction and used his improved devices to discover new metals: calcium, magnesium, barium, and strontium. Building ever-bigger devices, Davy discovered chlorine and produced the first electric light.

Volta's work greatly advanced work on the basic principles of the nature of electricity, creating the foundations of electrochemical science and producing electromagnets, electrical power, electric illumination, and electrically based communication systems.

Bibliography

The Atlas of Scientific Discovery. Colin Ronan. London: Quill, 1983.

Atoms, Electrons, and Change. P. W. Atkins. New York: Scientific American Library, 1991.

"Luigi Galvani and the Electrical Frog Legs." D. S. Halacy, Jr. Chapter 4 in *Science and Serendipity*. Philadelphia: Macrae Smith, 1967.

(AIP Niels Bohr Library, Lande Collection)

Bibliography

By Volta

De vi attractiva ignis electrici, 1769

Lettere [al p. Campi] sull'aria infiammabile nativa delle paludi, 1777

"On the Electricity Excited by the Mere Contact of Conducting Substances of Different Kinds," *Philosophical Transactions of the Royal Society*, 1800

About Volta

Alessandro Volta and the Electric Battery. Bern Dibner. New York: Franklin Watts, 1964.

The Ambiguous Frog: The Galvani-Volta Controversy on Animal Electricity. Marcello Pera. Princeton, N.J.: Princeton University Press, 1992.

Inventors and Discoveries: Changing Our World. Elizabeth Newhouse, ed. Washington, D.C.: National Geographic Society, 1980.

(Russell Williams)

John von Neumann

Areas of Achievement: Mathematics, physics, and technology

Contribution: Von Neumann contributed to quantum mechanics, established a new axiomatic foundation for set theory, took part in the development of the atomic and hydrogen bombs, designed computers, and developed game theory, which has been a major influence on economics, biology, and psychology.

Dec. 28, 1903	Born in Budapest, Hungary
1921-1925	Studies at the Universities of Budapest and Berlin and at the Swiss Federal Institute of Technology
1926	Earns a doctorate in mathematics from Budapest
1927-1930	Serves as a privatdozent at Berlin
1930-1933	Teaches at Princeton University
1933-1957	Serves as a professor of mathematics at the Institute for Advanced Study at Princeton
1937	Becomes a U.S. citizen
1943	Joins the Manhattan Project in Los Alamos, New Mexico
1947	Given the Medal for Merit and the Distinguished Civilian Service Award
1954	Becomes a member of the Atomic Energy Commission
1955	Diagnosed with cancer
1956	Given the Medal of Freedom, the Albert Einstein Commemorative Award, and the Enrico Fermi Award
Feb. 8, 1957	Dies in Washington, D.C.

Early Life

Born Johann von Neumann to a prosperous Jewish banking family that nurtured his intellectual development, John von Neumann was a child prodigy with a remarkable memory. In 1911, his formal public education began at the Lutheran Gymnasium for boys in Budapest. He had a personal tutor in addition to his studies at the Gymnasium.

In 1919, the government collapsed, and Bela Kun, a utopian socialist, seized power. The social structure was in upheaval and the economy halted. Neumann's father fled with his family to Austria, where they lived in exile. Kun's government was replaced by one that persecuted Jews and intellectuals. After several months, the scare about Jews subsided, and the von Neumanns returned to Budapest.

In 1921, John von Neumann enrolled in the University of Budapest. His first love was mathematics, but to please his father he majored in chemistry. He attended only to take the examinations. Von Neumann was simultaneously enrolled at the University of Berlin, which he attended until 1923. Changing universities again, he received a degree in chemical engineering from the Swiss Federal Institute of Technology in Zurich in 1925. In 1926, only five years after beginning college, he received his Ph.D. in mathematics, with minors in physics and chemistry, from Budapest.

Von Neumann was named a privatdozent (lecturer) at Berlin and, while there, received a Rockerfeller grant for postdoctoral work at the University of Göttingen. At Göttingen, he studied mathematics under David Hilbert from 1926 to 1927. In 1928, he read a paper on game theory to a scientific meeting in Göttingen. He remained on the staff at Berlin until 1930.

Computers and Consulting

Von Neumann was invited to lecture at Princeton University in 1930, when Adolf Hitler's rise to power in Germany was beginning. Von Neumann accepted the position and brought his wife, Mariette Koevesi, whom he had married in January, 1930. When Princeton opened the Institute for Advanced Study, he was named one of six professors of mathematics; he would be affiliated with the institute for the rest of his life. In 1936, von Neumann and

Alan Mathison Turing met when Turing was completing his graduate studies at Princeton. Von Neumann was interested in his work on computable numbers and "Turing machines." Turing declined his offer of a position as his assistant in order to return to Cambridge University.

In 1937, von Neumann became a U.S. citizen. In 1943, he was brought onto the Manhattan Project at Los Alamos, where he performed crucial calculations needed for the implosion design of the first atomic bombs. Such tedious and complex calculations led von Neumann to take further interest in computers in the belief that he could improve on their design. His interest led him to the Moore School near the end of the work on the Electronic Numerical Integrator and Computer (ENIAC) and the publication of a draft report that outlined the concept of a stored-program computer.

Von Neumann persuaded the directors of the Institute for Advanced Study to support his project, and he secured funding from RCA, the Navy, and several other institutions. He filled

(Library of Congress)

many positions with people with whom he had worked at the Moore School. Building the computer took six years. The computer, the first to use a flexible stored program, became a prototype for subsequent machines. It was faster and more powerful than any other at the time.

Von Neumann also worked as a consultant for the government and the military and for such organizations as IBM, RAND, Lawrence Livermore Laboratory, Bell Laboratories, the Naval Ordnance Laboratory, and the Central Intelligence Agency (CIA). In 1954, he became

Computers

Von Neumann left a lasting impression in the field of computer science. Although he was not the originator of the concept of a stored-program computer, he is credited with the formalization of the idea.

He published this idea in *First Draft of a Report on the EDVAC* (1945). The draft report, intended as a collection of the ideas from the Moore School team working on computer design, was later viewed as solely von Neumann's ideas and became the formal document on which later computers were based.

The report described and organized the elements of the computer: a central arithmetic unit, memory in which to store information, a central control unit able to organize transfers between the various "registers" in memory in accordance with a program also stored in memory, and input and output. This design became known as the von Neumann architecture. The crediting of von Neumann with the concept of the stored-program computer (and hence, the programmed computers now used) was a source of tension with some of the engineers at the Moore School, particularly John Presper Eckert and John W. Mauchly.

Von Neumann's Electronic Computer Project, begun at the Institute for Advanced Study in 1945, was an attempt to develop a high-speed scientific computer that would be useful to the research community. The machine was officially dedicated in 1952 but was available for use after the spring of 1951. It used magnetic tape as the storage device, and its main input/output device was a Teletype printer. It required 31 microseconds to perform an addition, could store 1,024 words of 40 digits, occupied 36 cubic feet of space, and needed many people to operate it.

What von Neumann achieved in the theoretical aspects of computing is significant: He described the computer in biological terms, rather than mechanical terms. He speculated that com-

puters were analogous to the human central nervous system, in that they were both control systems. In 1948, he made a presentation on "The Logic of Analogue Nets and Automata," which called for a theory of natural and artificial automata based on mathematical logic. Automata here means any system that processes information as part of a self-regulating mechanism.

His logical theory of automata was based on the work of Warren McCulloch and Walter Pitts in the area of neural networks and Alan Mathison Turing's work on computability. Von Neumann was able to extend the theory further to a probabilistic theory of automata because of the work of Claude Shannon on communication theory and some of the work that had been done on the mechanics of cybernetics. This work investigated how biological and technical systems could process information, and how such complex systems could function reliably with unreliable parts.

Von Neumann also studied how organisms could self-replicate. His theories are used today in the study of neural networks, artificial intelligence, and several other areas of theoretical computer science.

Bibliography
The Computer and the Brain. John von Neumann. New Haven, Conn.: Yale University Press, 1958.
First Draft of a Report on the EDVAC. John von Neumann. Philadelphia: Moore School of Electrical Engineering, University of Pennsylvania, 1945.
John von Neumann and the Origins of Modern Computing. William Aspray. Cambridge, Mass.: MIT Press, 1990.
Theory of Self-Reproducing Automata. John von Neumann and Arthur W. Burks. Urbana: University of Illinois Press, 1966.

a member of the Atomic Energy Commission. He worked on the development of the intercontinental ballistic missile (ICBM) during the early 1950's and was a major figure in Cold War politics.

In 1955, von Neumann was diagnosed with pancreatic cancer. Before he died, he turned to the Catholic faith that his family had adopted after 1929. He died on February 8, 1957.

Bibliography
By von Neumann
Mathematische Grundlagen der Quantenmechanik, 1932 (*Mathematical Foundations of Quantum Mechanics*, 1955)
Theory of Games and Economic Behavior, 1944 (with Oskar Morgenstern)
First Draft of a Report on the EDVAC, 1945
The Computer and the Brain, 1958
Collected Works, 1961-1963 (6 vols.; A. H. Taub, ed.)
Theory of Self-Reproducing Automata, 1966 (with Arthur W. Burks)

About von Neumann
John von Neumann. Norman Macrae. New York: Pantheon Books, 1992.
The Legacy of John von Neumann. James Glimm, John Impagliazzo, and Isadore Singer, eds. Providence, R.I.: American Mathematical Society, 1990.

(Maureen H. O'Rafferty)

Hugo de Vries

Areas of Achievement: Botany and genetics
Contribution: De Vries rediscovered Gregor Johann Mendel's laws of heredity. He advanced the idea that mutations are the chief source of genetic variation and the major method by which new species formed.

Feb. 16, 1848	Born at Haarlem, the Netherlands
1866-1870	Studies at the University of Leiden
1870	Studies with Wilhelm Hofmeister in Heidelberg, Germany
1871	Works in Julius von Sachs' laboratory in Würzburg, Germany
1877	Earns a Ph.D. in plant physiology and appointed privatdozent in the physiology of cultivated plants at the University of Halle
1878-1918	Serves as a professor of botany at the University of Amsterdam
1889	Publishes *Intracellulare Pangenesis* (*Intracellular Pangenesis*, 1910), marking the beginning of his work in heredity and variation
1901-1903	Publishes *Die Mutationstheorie* (*The Mutation Theory*, 1909-1910), which describes Mendel's laws of heredity and his discovery of mutation
1905	Publishes *Species and Varieties*
1906	Awarded the Darwin Medal for his work in genetics and evolution
1907	Publishes *Plant Breeding*, dealing with his work in plant heredity
1918	Retires from Amsterdam and settles in Lunteren
1928-1929	Awarded a gold medal by the Linnean Society for his contributions to botany
May 21, 1935	Dies in Lunteren, the Netherlands

De Vries' Discovery of Mutation and Evolution Theory

De Vries' concept that the discrete factors responsible for genetic traits could undergo sudden and radical change remains an important part of genetic theory.

De Vries discovered mutations by studying the different varieties of *Oenothera lamarckiana* (evening primrose). He reasoned that variation was the result of abrupt changes in the genetic factors (pangenes). He took the name "pangene" from Charles Darwin's theory of pangenesis, and it was later shortened to "gene." De Vries called the radical changes "mutations."

He postulated that plants formed by mutations were different enough from their parents to be considered a new species. The short period of time that plants could produce mutants was referred to as the mutation period. De Vries called useful mutations "progressive" and those that were useless or harmful "retrogressive." He believed that only progressive mutations could lead to the formation of new species.

Mutations account for some of the variation in nature, but not to the extent that de Vries suggested. Later experiments performed with evening primrose by other scientists showed that the "mutations" observed by de Vries were mainly the result of other causes; actual mutation was responsible for only a few radical changes.

Bibliography

The Growth of Biological Thought: Diversity, Evolution, and Inheritance. Ernst Mayr. Cambridge, Mass.: The Belknap Press of Harvard University Press, 1987.

"Mendel and the Rediscovery of His Work." E. O. Dodson. *Scientific Monthly* 58 (1955).

A Short History of Genetics. L. C. Dunn. New York: McGraw-Hill, 1965.

Early Life

Hugo Marie de Vries (pronounced "duh vrees"), the son of a government official, grew up in Haarlem, the Netherlands, an area marked by beautiful vegetation. He developed his love for plants from these surroundings. When his family moved to The Hague in 1862, Hugo attended the Gymnasium (high school) there.

When de Vries began his studies at the University of Leiden, he was already quite knowledgeable in botany because of his early interest in plants. After completing his undergraduate work, he went to the University of Heidelberg to study plant physiology with Professor Wilhelm Hofmeister. Later, he worked in the laboratory of Julius von Sachs in Würzburg, Germany. He received his doctorate in 1877 with a dissertation on the "stretching" of cells as a result of osmosis.

(Library of Congress)

Teaching and Research

De Vries began teaching as a lecturer at the newly formed University of Amsterdam and then became instructor and eventually professor of plant physiology. He continued his studies on the passage of water into and out of the cell (osmosis) and the laws governing this process.

He discovered that when cells are placed in solutions that have the same amount of dissolved substances (solutes), there is no net loss or gain of water. In other words, its isotonic point is reached.

Work in Heredity and Evolution

After working on the physiology of plants, de Vries turned to experiments on plant heredity inspired by Charles Darwin's evolutionary theory. De Vries' book *Intracellulare Pangenesis* (1889; *Intracellular Pangenesis*, 1910) further developed Darwin's theory of heredity, pangenesis, but did not include the notion that environmentally induced traits could be inherited. He proposed that discrete (separate) particles carried hereditary information.

De Vries repeated Gregor Johann Mendel's classic experiments, leading to the rediscovery of Mendel's principles of heredity—segregation and dominance. This work reinforced the idea that the hereditary units are discrete units, and other European geneticists rediscovered Mendelism at the same time.

De Vries continued his work in plant genetics and used his findings to advance his own model of evolution. He claimed that variation in nature was caused primarily by mutation of the genetic characters. He defined mutations as sudden, large, and discrete changes in hereditary factors. He reasoned that evolution consists of rare but drastic changes, while Darwin and his successors contended that evolution resulted from gradual shifts of species over generations.

De Vries devoted the rest of his life to research in evolution, publishing more than seven hundred books and papers. After he retired, he lived in Lunteren, the Netherlands, where he continued his experiments with plants in his extensive garden until his death in 1935. After de Vries' death, his theory of evolution was supported by only a few geneticists, but his concept of gene mutation became an important part of genetic theory.

Bibliography

By de Vries

Intracellulare Pangenesis, 1889 (*Intracellular Pangenesis*, 1910)

Die Mutationstheorie: Versuche und Beobachtungen über die Entstehung von Arten im Pflanzenreich, 1901-1903 (2 vols.; *The Mutation Theory: Experiments and Observations on the Origin of Species in the Vegetable Kingdom*, 1909-1910, 2 vols.)

Species and Varieties: Their Origin by Mutation, 1905

Plant Breeding: Comments on the Experiments of Nilsson and Burbank, 1907

About de Vries

"Hugo de Vries." R. Cleland. *Proceedings of The American Philosophical Society* 76 (1936).

"Hugo de Vries and the Reception of the 'Mutation Theory'." Garland E. Allen. *Journal of the History of Biology* 2 (1969).

"The Work of Hugo de Vries." Alfred F. Blakeslee. *Scientific Monthly* 36 (1933).

(Joel S. Schwartz)

Johannes Diderik van der Waals

Area of Achievement: Physics
Contribution: Van der Waals received the Nobel Prize in Physics in 1910 for his studies on the states of matter and the intermolecular forces affecting their behavior.

Nov. 23, 1837	Born in Leiden, the Netherlands
1862	Takes a job as a secondary school physics teacher and begins to attend the University of Leiden
1866	Appointed headmaster of the secondary school in The Hague
1873	Receives a Ph.D. from Leiden with a dissertation on the continuity of the gaseous and liquid states of matter
1875	Elected to the Royal Netherlands Academy of Sciences and Letters
1877	Appointed head of the physics department at the University of Amsterdam
1896	Appointed secretary of the Royal Academy of Sciences at Amsterdam
1907	Retires from his Amsterdam teaching post
1908	Begins to publish his textbook on thermodynamics, *Lehrbuch der Thermodynamik in iher Anwendung auf das Gleichgewicht von Systemen mit gasförmigflüssigen Phasen*
1910	Awarded the Nobel Prize in Physics
Mar. 8, 1923	Dies in Amsterdam, the Netherlands

Early Life
Johannes Diderik van der Waals (pronounced "vahn dur vals") was born the son of a carpenter in the university town of Leiden in the Netherlands. From an early age he wished to be a teacher, and his first work was as an instructor in elementary schools. In 1862, after taking a job as a secondary school physics teacher, he decided to take a few classes in physics at the local university.

In 1866, van der Waals was appointed headmaster of a school in a nearby town, The Hague. With his professors' encouragement, however, he continued to be enrolled as a graduate student in physics at the University of Leiden. His pursuit of an advanced degree while maintaining a full-time job was unusual, but so were van der Waals' conceptual and communicative abilities.

Correcting a Two Hundred-Year-Old "Law"
His 1873 doctoral thesis was a shockingly simple explanation for the deviations in the behav-

(The Nobel Foundation)

ior of actual gases from the idealized patterns of Boyle's law, first generalized two centuries earlier by Robert Boyle. Van der Waals' identification of one of the causes of this deviation—attractive forces between molecules, now known as van der Waals forces—is an indirect legacy of this work.

The thesis was immediately translated into other languages, and its principles formed the basis for much of van der Waals' later theoretical work. In 1875, he was elected to the Royal Netherlands Academy of Sciences and Letters.

A Lifelong Teacher

At his core, however, van der Waals remained a teacher. In 1877, he was appointed professor of physics at the University of Amsterdam. He was a nurturer of new ideas in others, being one of the first professors to recognize and teach the importance of the phase rule of Willard Gibbs. Knowing firsthand the value of transmitting the work of Dutch researchers to foreigners unfamiliar with the Dutch language, van der Waals was instrumental in getting the proceedings of the Dutch Academy of Science published in both Dutch and English after 1896.

Van der Waals retired from teaching in 1907, succeeded in that post by his own son. In 1908, Leiden physicist Heike Kamerlingh Onnes used van der Waals' advice to succeed in at last liquefying the "permanent" gas helium at a temperature of –267 degrees Celsius. In honor of the wide influence of his work on the study of thermodynamics, as well as in practical applications such as the liquefaction of gases, van

Real Gases Are Not Always Perfect

The attractions between molecules and the space occupied by the molecules themselves affect the behavior of gases at differing temperatures and pressures.

At ordinary temperatures and pressures, many gases behave like the "perfect" or "ideal" gases described by Robert Boyle and others. The pressure (p) and volume (V) of a gas are related to its temperature (T) by a constant number (R), such that $pV = RT$.

During the nineteenth century, researchers learned that gases deviate from the ideal gas laws at high pressures and low temperatures. Under these conditions, all but a few "permanent" gases are liquefied and thus lose the properties of gases. An ideal gas expanding into a vacuum should not change in temperature, since it meets no resistance. Yet, real gases do decrease in temperature.

Van der Waals determined that internal work—work being done to overcome attractions between molecules—must cause the loss of heat in a vacuum and that such attractions contribute to the differing critical temperature points above which gases will not liquefy. This suggested to van der Waals that the so-called permanent gases—hydrogen, oxygen, nitrogen, and carbon monoxide—are not really permanent. They simply had never been cooled below their critical temperatures.

Van der Waals modified Boyle's $pV = RT$ relationship to $(p + a/v^2)(V - b) = RT$. This equation took into consideration the reduced pressure caused by the attraction (a/v^2) exerted by molecules for one another and the excluded volume (b) of the container because of the size of the molecules themselves. The constants a and b vary with different-sized molecules of gases, yet the formula enabled van der Waals to calculate the critical points for gases under a variety of physical conditions.

His equation preserved a molecular and kinetic explanation for what had been a thermodynamic aberration. Yet, neither he nor his contemporaries comprehended enough about molecular bonding to describe van der Waals forces as they are now understood: as a specific function of the radius of the molecule (r^{-6}).

Bibliography

Energy, Force, and Matter: The Conceptual Development of Nineteenth-Century Physics. P. M. Harman. Cambridge, England: Cambridge University, 1982.

General Chemistry. Linus Pauling. New York: Dover, 1970.

The Rise of the New Physics. A. d'Abro. New York, Dover, 1951.

der Waals was awarded the Nobel Prize in Physics in 1910. After a long period of declining health, he died in Amsterdam in 1923.

Bibliography

By van der Waals
Over de continuiteit van den gas- en vloeistoftoestand, 1873 (*The Continuity of the Gaseous and Liquid States of Matter*, 1890)
Lehrbuch der Thermodynamik in iher Anwendung auf das Gleichgewicht von Systemen mit gasförmigflüssigen Phasen, 1908-1912 (with P. A. Kohnstamm)
"The Equation of State for Gases and Liquids" in *Nobel Lectures in Physics, 1901-1921*, 1967

About van der Waals
The Development of Modern Chemistry. Aaron J. Ihde. New York: Dover, 1984.
Great Chemists. Eduard Farber, ed. New York: Interscience, 1961.
"Johann Diderik van der Waals." In *The Nobel Prize Winners: Physics*, edited by Frank N. Magill. Pasadena, Calif.: Salem Press, 1989.

(*J. Eric Elliott*)

Selman Abraham Waksman

Areas of Achievement: Bacteriology and biology
Contribution: Waksman was awarded the Nobel Prize in Physiology or Medicine for his discovery of streptomycin, the first antibiotic effective against tuberculosis.

July 22, 1888	Born in Novaya Priluka, Russian Empire (now Priluki, Ukraine)
1910	Emigrates to the United States
1918	Earns a Ph.D. in biochemistry at the University of California, Berkeley
1927	Publishes a seminal text entitled *Principles of Soil Microbiology*
1929	Becomes a professor of soil microbiology at Rutgers University
1930-1942	Serves as the director of the marine microbiology division of the Woods Hole Marine Biological Laboratory
1939	Elected to the National Academy of Sciences
1944	Isolates and characterizes streptomycin
1948	Receives the Albert and Mary Lasker Award from the American Public Health Association
1950	Named a Commandeur of the French Legion of Honor
1952	Awarded the Nobel Prize in Physiology or Medicine for his discovery of streptomycin
Aug. 16, 1973	Dies in Hyannis, Massachusetts

Early Life
Selman Abraham Waksman was born and spent his early youth in Novaya Priluka, a

Streptomycin

Streptomycin, an antibiotic isolated from the soil microbe Streptomyces griseus, *was the first drug used successfully to fight tuberculosis and numerous other bacterial diseases.*

Waksman spent his career studying soil microbes. As an undergraduate, he used a microscope to examine colonies of fungi and bacteria in soil samples. He found minute colonies of microbes that were neither fungi nor bacteria; he later learned that these microbes belonged to a relatively obscure group known as actinomycetes.

Waksman was amazed at the large number of microorganisms in the soil and became convinced that they did not live in distinct groups but rather that they comprised a complex group of interrelationships. He derived two principles from his early soil studies: that soil is made up of a large number of different groups of microorganisms, each possessing different functions and activities, and that these microorganisms influence one another in a variety of ways.

Waksman's desire to learn more about the role of actinomycetes in soil processes led him to pursue a doctorate in biochemistry. By 1936, he was able to demonstrate that actinomycetes exert considerable influence over the activities of fungi and bacteria in the soil. His decision to seek disease-fighting substances from actinomycetes began in 1939, when his former student René Dubos isolated tyrocidine, a product of soil bacilli that had a destructive effect on disease-producing bacteria. He was also inspired by the need to develop new drugs to treat casualties from World War II.

With financial support from Merck and Company in Rahway, New Jersey, Waksman developed and applied screening techniques for isolating antibiotics in soil and other samples. Over the next ten years, he and his coworkers isolated ten antibiotics from actinomycetes, including three with significant clinical applications: actinomycin, streptomycin, and neomycin.

Streptomycin is second only to penicillin in its effectiveness as a broad-spectrum antibiotic. The antibiotic acts by interfering with a microorganism's ability to synthesize certain vital proteins. Streptomycin was the first antibiotic effective against gram-negative bacteria. Susceptible microbes included those responsible for tuberculosis, plague, influenza, spinal meningitis, typhoid fever, and urinary tract infections. Clinical effectiveness against tuberculosis was demonstrated in 1944, and the drug was mass produced and distributed worldwide by the late 1940's.

Because treatment of bacteria with streptomycin increases the chance of changes in the hereditary material of cells, however, many bacteria are now resistant to streptomycin. As a result, physicians are encountering increasing cases of antibiotic-resistant bacteria. For example, by the 1990's, tuberculosis was experiencing a resurgence among homeless people in the United States.

Bibliography

Actinomycetes and Their Antibiotics, Selman A. Waksman and H. A. Lechevalier. Baltimore: Williams & Wilkins, 1953.

The Antibiotic Era: A History of the Antibiotics and of Their Role in the Conquest of Infectious Diseases and in Other Fields of Human Endeavor. Selman A. Waksman. Tokyo: Waksman Foundation of Japan, 1975.

small Jewish town in the Kiev region of the Ukraine. He grew up in a household run by his grandmother, mother, and seven aunts. Waksman attended a government Latin school in nearby Zhitomir and later in Odessa.

In 1910, after finishing his schooling, Waksman emigrated to the United States. He lived with relatives in New Jersey and attended Rutgers University. At Rutgers, Waksman studied under Jacob G. Lipman, a bacteriologist and dean of the college of agriculture, who was also an immigrant from the Ukraine. Waksman was particularly interested in the biochemistry and microbiology of soil and completed an M.A. in 1916. He returned to Rutgers in 1919 after earning his Ph.D. in biochemistry at the University of California, Berkeley. Waksman remained at Rutgers for his entire career, distinguishing himself as one of the nation's foremost soil biologists.

(The Nobel Foundation)

Streptomycin and the "White Plague"

In 1944, Waksman and his colleagues isolated streptomycin, a new antibiotic taken from actinomycetes found growing in the throats of chickens. In 1945, clinical trials of streptomycin in the treatment of human tuberculosis were an enormous success. The ability of the drug to attack the gram-negative tubercle bacillus meant that humankind finally had an effective cure for the disease that had been called "consumption" and "the white plague."

Waksman's achievement was followed by numerous awards, culminating with the 1952 Nobel Prize in Physiology or Medicine. In his 1954 autobiography, he noted that, since 1940, when the term "antibiotics" did not even exist, the new "wonder drugs" had brought about a medical revolution. He believed that antibiotics could control all infectious diseases of humans and animals. By 1965, more than twenty-five thousand different antibiotic products were saving the lives of millions of patients who would otherwise have fallen prey to diseases caused by bacteria. Waksman died in 1973 at the age of eighty-five.

Bibliography
By Waksman
Enzymes, 1926 (with Wilburt Davidson)
Principles of Soil Microbiology, 1927
The Soil and the Microbe, 1931 (with Robert Starkey)
Humus, 1936
Microbial Antagonisms and Antibiotic Substances, 1945
The Literature on Streptomycin, 1948-1952
Streptomycin, Its Nature, and Practical Application, 1949
The Actinomycetes, 1950-1966
Soil Microbiology, 1952
Actinomycetes and Their Antibiotics, 1953 (with Hubert Lechevalier)
Sergei N. Winogradsky, 1953
My Life with the Microbes, 1954
Perspectives and Horizons in Microbiology: A Symposium, 1955
The Conquest of Tuberculosis, 1964
Jacob O. Lipman, 1966
Actinomycin, 1968
The Antibiotic Era: A History of the Antibiotics and of Their Role in the Conquest of Infectious Diseases and in Other Fields of Human Endeavor, 1975

About Waksman
Scientific Contributions of Selman A. Waksman: Selected Articles Published in Honor of His Eightieth Birthday, July 22, 1968. H. Boyd Woodruff, ed. New Brunswick, N.J.: Rutgers University Press, 1968.
"Selman Abraham Waksman." In *The Nobel Prize Winners: Physiology or Medicine*, edited by Frank N. Magill. Pasadena, Calif.: Salem Press, 1991.

(Peter Neushul)

Felix Wankel

Areas of Achievement: Invention and technology

Contribution: Wankel developed a rotary combustion engine, a variation of which bears his name. In particular, he designed a system of seals that made the engine possible.

Aug. 13, 1902	Born in Lahr, Germany
1921-1926	Works for a bookseller
1924	Opens a machine shop in Heidelberg
1924	Begins thinking about rotary engine design
1934	Hired by BMW to work on rotary valves
1934	Obtains his first patent for a rotary engine
1935	Jailed for several months for his part in exposing a Nazi embezzlement scheme
1935	Established as head of his own research institute, Wankel Versuchswerkstatten (WVW)
1935-1945	WVW designs aircraft engines for the Luftwaffe
1945-1946	Imprisoned by the French government for his wartime work
1951	Starts a new technical center, Technische Entwicklungsstelle, for rotary research
1951	Develops a rotary engine for a motorcycle manufacturer
1959	Introduces the Wankel rotary engine to the public
1969	Given an honorary doctorate by the Munich Technical Institute
Oct. 9, 1988	Dies in Lindau, West Germany

Early Life

Felix Wankel (pronounced "VAHN-kehl") was born in Lahr, in the Black Forest region of Germany. His father was killed in the first month of World War I. Felix and his mother were left a considerable amount of money, but the phenomenal inflation after the war made it worthless.

Wankel attended a general, rather than a technical, high school. He found school boring and was terrible at mathematics. He excelled, however, at creating technical drawings and making models from those drawings. After his graduation in 1921, Wankel immediately began working to support himself and his mother. He found a job with a university bookseller in Heidelberg, first in the printshop and later in the storeroom.

A Self-Taught Engineer

Wankel began taking night classes and correspondence courses. In 1924, he purchased some machine tools and opened his own shop in Heidelberg, where he experimented with engines. Grinding brake drums and cylinders, Wankel gained experience with precision metalwork that would serve him well in later years.

He realized that other rotary engines had failed because of inadequate piston seals and began to conduct experiments with different sealing methods and materials. He also made rotary valves for piston engines. In 1926, Wankel either quit his job at the bookseller's or was fired. Fortunately, he could make money with his rotary valves.

"Germany's Sealer"

Wankel had been a member of the Nazi Party but left it in 1932. Later, he uncovered proof that a local Nazi official was embezzling funds. In 1935, Adolf Hitler, the leader of the Nazi Party, became state chancellor and had all enemies of his party jailed, including Wankel.

In 1936, a friend in the Nazi Party succeeded in getting Wankel out of jail and persuaded the German Air Ministry to give Wankel his own research institute in Lindau. The Wankel Versuchswerkstatten (WVW) contributed to the development of rotary valve engines used by the Luftwaffe, the German air force, in several airplanes. Wankel also made many advances in engine sealing. He was the first to seal a rectangular space successfully, an achievement necessary for his rotary engine. His innovations earned for him the nickname "Germany's Sealer."

The Rotary Engine

After World War II, Wankel spent a year in a French jail for his wartime work. In 1951, the same friend responsible for the first research institute helped him establish another one.

Wankel's Technische Entwicklungsstelle immediately signed a contract to develop rotary valve engines for NSU, a German motorcycle manufacturer. Initially, the company was not interested in Wankel's rotary engine, but he convinced its chief engineer that a practical rotary engine was possible.

In 1957, NSU built the first working rotary engine. Called the DKM (from *Drehkolben Motor*, meaning "rotary piston engine"), it proved that Wankel's design would work. The DKM was not practical, however, and the chief engi-

The Wankel Rotary Engine

Wankel developed a four-stroke internal combustion engine in which all parts move in a circular motion.

A rotary engine is more compact than a reciprocating engine of the same power, yet it has fewer parts, produces less vibration and smoother power, and can operate at higher speeds. As shown in the accompanying sketch, each side of the rotor goes through the four operations of intake, compression, power, and exhaust in one rotation. Thus, each rotor is the equivalent of three pistons in a reciprocating engine.

In Wankel's original design, the rotor spun on one axis, while the entire housing spun in the same direction, at a slightly slower rate, on an axis slightly offset from the rotor. Thus, the rotor could move out of the way, letting the apexes slide past the waist. Wankel called his design the

rotary piston engine. Unfortunately, while it did work, the rotating housing made it impractical.

Walter Froede, who helped Wankel build his first engine, devised an eccentric shaft for the rotor that gives it the same sort of motion while allowing the housing to remain stationary. Froede called it the circuitous piston engine, but it is now known as the Wankel engine. Although it has many advantages over a reciprocating engine, the Wankel rotary engine still faces some engineering problems and has seen limited use.

Bibliography

Principles of the Wankel Engine. Ted Pipe. Indianapolis: H. W. Sams, 1974.

The Wankel Engine. Jan P. Norbye. Radnor, Pa.: Chilton, 1971.

What About the Wankel Engine? Scott Corbett. New York: Four Winds Press, 1974.

The Four Operations of the Wankel Engine

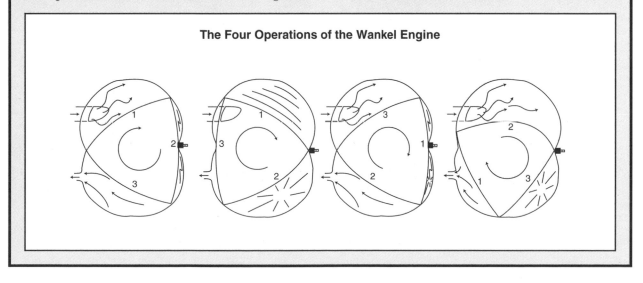

Wankel displays one of his rotary engines at a meeting of German engineers in 1960. (AP/Wide World Photos)

neer designed a variation called the KKM (from *Krieskolben Motor*, meaning "circuitous piston engine"). Wankel thought the KKM less elegant than his DKM, but it is the KKM that is now known as the Wankel rotary engine.

Wankel continued to work on other projects at his research facility until his death in 1988.

Bibliography
By Wankel
Enteilung der Rotations-Kolbenmaschinen: Rotations-Kolbenmaschinen mit parallelen Drehachsen und Arbeitsraumumwandungen, 1963 (*Rotary Piston Machines: Classification of Design Principles for Engines, Pumps, and Compressors*, 1965)
"Rotary Piston Engine Performance Criteria," *Automotive Engineer*, 1964

About Wankel
Notable Twentieth-Century Scientists. Emily J. McMurray, ed. Washington, D.C.: Gale Research, 1995.
The Wankel Rotary Engine. Harris Edward Dark. Bloomington: Indiana University Press, 1974.
Wankel: The Curious Story Behind the Revolutionary Rotary Engine. Nicholas Faith. New York: Stein & Day, 1975.

(*Laurence M. Burke II*)

Otto Heinrich Warburg

Areas of Achievement: Cell biology, chemistry, and physiology
Contribution: A pioneer in biochemistry, Warburg identified the enzymes that enable living cells to obtain energy from food. He also measured photosynthesis and studied the causes of cancer.

Oct. 8, 1883	Born in Freiburg, Germany
1906	Earns a Ph.D. in chemistry from the University of Berlin
1908	Publishes a paper on oxygen consumption in sea urchins
1911	Receives an M.D. from the University of Heidelberg
1913	Appointed head of research at the Kaiser Wilhelm Gesellschaft
1914	Serves in the Prussian Horse Guards during World War I
1918-1931	Heads a laboratory at the Kaiser Wilhelm Institut für Biologie
1920-1924	Discovers the quantum requirements of photosynthesis
1931	Awarded the Nobel Prize in Physiology or Medicine, but not allowed to accept it
1931	Becomes head of the Kaiser Wilhelm Institut für Zellphysiologie
1934	Elected a foreign member of the Royal Society of London
1954-1968	Discovers enzymes for fermentation and photosynthesis
1965	Receives an honorary doctorate from Oxford University
1969	Proves Albert Einstein's photochemical law in photosynthesis
Aug. 1, 1970	Dies in West Berlin, West Germany

(The Nobel Foundation)

Early Life

Otto Heinrich Warburg (pronounced "VAHR-burk") was the son of Emil Warburg, a leading physicist who was then a professor at the University in Freiburg. Otto's mother, Elisabeth Gärtner, was from a South German family. He had three sisters, but no brothers. The family moved to Berlin in 1986 when his father was invited to take the chair of physics at the University of Berlin. Otto, then eleven years old, attended the Friedrichs-Werder Gymnasium (high school) in Berlin.

Through his father, Warburg met leading physicists and chemists of his day, including Albert Einstein and Max Planck. He learned laboratory techniques to measure light and rates of physical processes in his father's laboratory. Warburg's professor in Berlin, Emil Fischer, set two important examples that Warburg followed throughout his career: He worked side by side with his students, and he insisted on repeating experiments until there was no doubt as to the results.

Warburg's Ph.D. thesis concerned extracellular digestive enzymes, but he shortly changed to studying intracellular enzymes. In 1913, he reported that enzymes were attached to "grana" in cells (now known as mitochondria). He developed methods of separating the mitochondria from cells and suspending them in water, allowing the measurement of reaction rates. In experiments on the effects of poisons, he found that narcotics interfere with the attachment of enzymes to grana, while cyanide removes iron.

Scientific Career

Warburg early developed an ambition to find a cure for cancer, which prompted him to study medicine at the University of Heidelberg after earning his Ph.D. While at Heidelberg, he worked in the laboratory of the department of internal medicine. In his work there, he discovered that the oxygen consumption of sea urchin eggs rose sixfold as they multiplied rapidly.

This result led him later, in 1923, to measure the oxygen consumption of cancer cells, which also multiply rapidly. First, however, he needed to learn all the aspects of normal cell respiration, the chemical reactions involved in oxygen consumption in cells. It was with these experiments that he made his mark in science.

Warburg's concern about cancer led him not only to conduct research on cancerous cells but also, by 1954, to speak out against cigarette smoking and pollution from automobile exhaust. He continued his campaign against smoking for the rest of his life and advised people to take extra vitamins as a cancer preventive.

Except for his service in the Prussian Horse Guards during World War I, Warburg dedicated his entire life to science, deciding not to marry and even continuing his research during World War II by moving his laboratory to an estate outside Berlin during wartime bombing. While his laboratory was closed during the Soviet occupation from 1945 to 1950, Warburg wrote books about his research and visited laboratories in the United States, where he carried out experiments on photosynthesis.

His life was not all work. He was very fond of horses and rode for an hour every morning before going to the laboratory. He often went for walks with Jakob Heiss, a retired soldier, who was Warburg's servant-companion for many years. Beginning in 1952, Warburg took up sailing on weekends and during vacations.

Warburg was very interested in everything English; he spoke and read English with ease and always read the London papers. He was thrilled to be awarded foreign membership in the Royal Society of London in 1934 and to

Cell Respiration and Its Applications

Warburg engaged in experiments in cell respiration that led to studies of photosynthesis and cancer.

In what has been called a series of brilliant experiments, Warburg discovered an enzyme needed by cells for using oxygen. He invented the Warburg apparatus to measure oxygen or carbon dioxide uptake and release, which was used by scientists until 1970. It consisted of a shaking water bath with controllable temperature in which test tubes and a manometer were placed. Shaking kept the contents of the tubes mixed.

In 1927, Warburg discovered that carbon monoxide prevents the use of oxygen by yeast cells, just as it prevents hemoglobin in red blood cells from combining with oxygen. He knew that iron compounds catalyze many oxidation reactions and that hemoglobin contains iron. Hemoglobin or yeast cells placed under a light were able to use oxygen even in the presence of carbon monoxide. He then tried light of different wavelengths and found that the respiratory enzyme in yeast absorbed light at the same wavelength as hemoglobin and other iron-containing compounds. Therefore, he concluded, iron must exist in the yeast enzyme.

Warburg was awarded the Nobel Prize in Medicine and Physiology in 1931 for this discovery. (Adolf Hitler forbade the acceptance of Nobel Prizes by German citizens, however, so Warburg was unable to accept the honor.) In 1944, Warburg was selected again for another prize, for his identification of flavins and nicotinamide (both B vitamins) as "hydrogen carriers" in cell respiration. These compounds transport hydrogen ions from food molecules to oxygen, forming water and making energy available for cellular work.

He also applied the techniques that he had used to measure the rate of cell respiration to the study of photosynthesis in plants. He used a suspension of algae cells. The suspension could be treated like a solution and allowed quantitative measurements that could not be done with whole plant leaves, as others had attempted.

Warburg measured the amounts of carbon dioxide and light used and of oxygen produced, but the interpretation of his results—that a very high 65 percent of the light energy was transformed into chemical energy (sugar)—was controversial. Nevertheless, he confirmed his result in 1950. In 1969, he confirmed that Albert Einstein's law of photochemical equivalence, concerning the amount of chemical energy that could be obtained from light, also applies to photosynthesis.

When he measured oxygen use by cancer cells, Warburg found that cancer cells ferment sugar rather than oxidize it, even in the presence of oxygen. Cancer cells, he reasoned, have been damaged somehow and have lost their ability to use oxygen. He decided that this fact was the primary cause of cancer, induced by one of many possible secondary causes (such as smoke). Others contended that fermentation was a symptom of cancer rather than its cause, but no one disputed his experimental results. Warburg's experiments on the effects of the B vitamins on normal cells and cancer cells led him to take vitamin B supplements and to recommend them to others.

Bibliography
Biochemistry. Lubert Stryer. 4th ed. New York: W. H. Freeman, 1995.
The Chemistry of Living Systems. Robert F. Steiner and Seymour Pomerantz. New York: D. Van Nostrand, 1981.
"How Living Things Obtain Energy: A Simpler Explanation." Donald E. Igelsrud. *The American Biology Teacher* 51 (February, 1989).
"How Plants Make Oxygen." Govindjee and W. J. Coleman. *Scientific American* (February, 1990).

receive an honorary doctorate from Oxford University in 1965. He died in 1970.

Bibliography

By Warburg

Über den Stoffwechsel der Tumoren, 1926 (*The Metabolism of Tumours*, 1930)

Schwemetalle als Wirkungsgruppen von Fermenten, 1946 (*Heavy Metal Prosthetic Groups and Enzyme Action*, 1949)

Weiterentwicklung der zellphysiologischen Methoden, angewandt auf Krebs, Photosynthese, und Wirkungsweise der Röntgenstrahlen, 1962 (new methods of cell physiology, applied to cancer, photosynthesis, and mechanism of X-ray action)

The Prime Cause and Prevention of Cancer, 1969

About Warburg

"Otto Warburg." In *The Nobel Prize Winners: Physiology or Medicine*, edited by Frank N. Magill. Pasadena, Calif.: Salem Press, 1991.

Otto Warburg: Cell Physiologist, Biochemist, and Eccentric. Hans Krebs. Oxford, England: Clarendon Press, 1981.

(*Janet Bell Garber*)

James D. Watson

Areas of Achievement: Biology, cell biology, and genetics

Contribution: Watson was the codiscoverer of the structure of deoxyribonucleic acid (DNA), the genetic material. For this work, he was awarded the Nobel Prize in Physiology or Medicine in 1962.

Apr. 6, 1928	Born in Chicago, Illinois
1950	Awarded a Ph.D. in zoology from Indiana University
1950-1951	Conducts research as a National Research Council Fellow at the University of Copenhagen
1951	Joins the Cavendish Laboratory at Cambridge University
1953	Publishes "Molecular Structure of Nucleic Acids" with Francis Crick
1953	Appointed senior research fellow in biology at the California Institute of Technology
1955	Returns to Cavendish Laboratory to collaborate with Crick
1956	Joins the faculty of Harvard University
1962	Awarded the Nobel Prize in Physiology or Medicine
1962	Elected to the National Academy of Sciences
1965	Publishes *Molecular Biology of the Gene*
1968	Takes over as director of Cold Spring Harbor Laboratories
1977	Awarded the Presidential Medal of Freedom
1988-1992	Serves as associate director and then director of the National Center for Human Genome Research

The Three-Dimensional Structure of DNA

Deoxyribonucleic acid (DNA) is a double helical molecule with alternating sugars and phosphates on the outside and paired bases on the inside.

For years, many scientists worked intensely to discover the structure of DNA, the chemical molecule that controls heredity. Several pieces of the puzzle existed, but it was not until Watson began collaborative research with Francis Crick that the puzzle was put together and the structure of DNA was described.

It was known that DNA consists of sugar molecules, phosphate molecules, and four different organic bases called adenine, thymine, guanine, and uracil. Erwin Chargaff had determined that DNA molecules always contain equal amounts of adenine and thymine and equal amounts of guanine and cytosine.

The biochemist Maurice H. F. Wilkins had isolated pure DNA fibers that chemist Rosalind E. Franklin used to take excellent X-ray diffraction photographs. These photographs gave a suggestion as to the three-dimensional shape of the DNA molecule. Wilkins showed Franklin's X-ray diffraction photographs to Watson and Crick, without asking her permission. The photographs suggested to Watson and Crick a way that all the DNA components would fit together.

They built huge molecular models until one fit the X-ray pattern shown by the photograph. The DNA molecule is a double helix, like a twisted ladder, with the sugars and phosphates alternating to form the sides of the ladder and the bases paired in the center forming the rungs of the ladder. Adenine always pairs with thymine, and guanine with cytosine, which accounts for the equal amount of the chemicals as determined by Chargaff.

It was known that DNA replicates itself every time that a cell divides. Since the DNA bases are held together in the center by weak hydrogen bonds, Watson and Crick hypothesized that the molecule could easily unzip into two pieces. Each half could then serve as a template for free nucleotides (the base, sugar, and phosphate subunits of DNA) to make a complementary strand. Other scientists later proved this hypothesis to be correct through extensive experimentation.

Elucidation of the double helical structure of DNA set the stage for future scientists to determine the nature of how this molecule self-replicates, how the sequence of bases encodes hereditary information, and how the information in genes is converted into proteins. Since all living organisms possess DNA, this information served to unlock the genetic secrets of all organisms on Earth and paved the way for the revolution in recombinant DNA technology that has had, and will continue to have, massive scientific, medical, social, and ethical implications for all of humankind.

Bibliography
The Double Helix. James D. Watson. New York: Atheneum, 1968.
The Eighth Day of Creation: Makers of the Revolution in Biology. H. F. Judson. New York: Simon & Schuster, 1979.
How Did We Find Out About DNA? Isaac Asimov. New York: Walker, 1985.
Signs of Life: The Language and Meanings of DNA. Robert Pollack. Boston: Houghton Mifflin, 1994.

Early Life
James Dewey Watson was born in Chicago in 1928, where he attended public schools. He enrolled at the University of Chicago when he was only fifteen years old and received a bachelor of science degree in zoology in 1947 at the age of nineteen.

Watson pursued graduate studies at Indiana University, where he studied the effects of radiation of bacterial virus multiplication. He was awarded a doctoral degree for this work in 1950. During his graduate studies, he was deeply influenced by the geneticists Hermann Joseph Muller and T. M. Sonneborn and the microbiologist Salvador Edward Luria, who directed his thesis work.

An Interest in DNA
After completion of his doctoral research, Watson continued his studies of bacterial viruses as a National Research Council Fellow at the University of Copenhagen. During a trip to

Naples in 1951, he met Maurice H. F. Wilkins and saw the X-ray diffraction pattern of crystalline deoxyribonucleic acid (DNA). This encounter was a significant force in turning Watson's research interests to the chemical structure of DNA and proteins.

In 1951, Watson received an appointment to the Cavendish Laboratory in Cambridge, where he met Francis Crick. Crick was also interested in deciphering the structure of DNA, and they became close collaborators. Many scientists around the world were trying to unlock the secrets of DNA's structure. This piece of information was regarded as the holy grail of biochemical research, and the competition to be the first to describe the structure of DNA was intense.

Elucidating the Structure

By studying the X-ray diffraction patterns of DNA, Wilkins was able to determine that DNA has a double helical structure. Rosalind E. Franklin added another important piece of information: The phosphate groups are situated on the outside of the helix.

Using this information and that of other researchers, Watson and Crick postulated that DNA is a double helix, consisting of two parallel chains of alternating sugar and phosphate groups on the outside of the helix and patterns of four different organic bases bound together in the center of the molecule, like the rungs of a ladder.

They constructed a variety of molecular models of DNA until one provided an identical pattern to the X-ray diffraction patterns seen by Wilkins and Franklin. Their results were published in the scientific journal *Nature* in March, 1953. They had won the race for the structure.

Beyond the Structure of DNA

Watson continued to pursue research in the genetic code at the California Institute of Technology (Caltech) from 1953 to 1955 and again with Crick at the Cavendish Laboratory from 1955 to 1956. Watson accepted a faculty position at Harvard in 1956. During this time, his research interests focused on the role of ribonucleic acid (RNA) in protein synthesis.

The significance of the discovery of DNA

(The Nobel Foundation)

was recognized by the world, and, in 1962, Watson, Crick, and Wilkins were awarded the Nobel Prize in Physiology or Medicine for their pioneering DNA research. Elucidating the structure of DNA was one of the seminal discoveries of the twentieth century. It opened the doors to advances in recombinant DNA technology, human genetics research, and a fundamental understanding of the molecular mechanisms of heredity.

Cold Spring Harbor Laboratory

Watson became the director of Cold Spring Harbor Laboratory in 1968. His research focus expanded to meld his passion for the nucleic acids with his earlier love of virology. Much of his research in later years focused on the induction of cancer by viruses.

The Human Genome Project

In the late 1980's, the U.S. government began to finance the Human Genome Project, a major effort involving hundreds of laboratories, the goal of which was to determine the entire DNA sequence found in human beings. Through this information, it was believed that, among other possibilities, human genes could be mapped and disease-causing genes could be localized, tested for, and possibly corrected.

The National Center for Human Genome Research, a division of the National Institutes of Health, was created to oversee the Human Genome Project. Watson was appointed associated director of the center from 1988 to 1989, then director from 1989 to 1992. In addition to supporting the scientific research involved with the project, he was a strong proponent of examining the ethical issues surrounding the ability to map and sequence the human genome.

Bibliography

By Watson
"Molecular Structure of Nucleic Acids: A Structure for Deoxyribose Nucleic Acid" in *Nature*, 1953 (with Francis Crick)

"Physical Studies on Ribonucleic Acid," *Nature*, 1954

Molecular Biology of the Gene, 1965

The Double Helix: A Personal Account of the Discovery of DNA, 1968

The DNA Story: A Documentary History of Gene Cloning, 1981 (with John Tooze)

Molecular Biology of the Cell, 1983 (with Bruce Alberts, Dennis Bray, Julian Lewis, Martin Raff, and Keith Roberts)

Recombinant DNA: A Short Course, 1983 (with Tooze and David Kurtz)

Molecular Biology of the Gene, rev. ed, 1987 (with Nancy H. Hopkins, Jeffrey W. Roberts, Joan Argetsinger Steitz, and Alan M. Weiner)

The Human Genome Project: Past, Present, and Future, 1990

Houses for Science: A Pictorial History of Cold Spring Harbor Laboratory, with Landmarks of Twentieth Century Genetics: A Series of Essays, 1991 (with Elizabeth L. Watson)

About Watson
DNA Pioneer: James Watson and the Double Helix. Joyce Baldwin. New York: Walker, 1994.

James Watson and Francis Crick: Discovery of the Double Helix and Beyond. David E. Newton. New York: Facts on File, 1992.

The Path to the Double Helix. Robert C. Olby. Seattle: University of Washington Press, 1974.

(Karen E. Kalumuck)

James Watt

Areas of Achievement: Chemistry, invention, physics, and technology

Contribution: Watt invented the first practical steam engine. He also contributed to chemistry, practical physics, and engineering.

Jan. 19, 1736	Born in Greenock, Renfrewshire, Scotland
1754	Goes to Glasgow to learn mathematical instrument making
1757	Becomes a mathematical instrument maker for the University of Glasgow
1764	Marries Margaret Miller
1769	Receives his first steam engine patent
1772	Becomes a partner of Birmingham manufacturer Matthew Boulton
1773	Margaret Miller Watt dies
1776	Marries Anne McGregor
1780	Retires from scientific and technological endeavors
1781	Receives a second steam engine patent
1783	The Watt engine is recognized as the best steam engine available
1784	Elected to Royal Society of Edinburgh
1785	Elected to the Royal Society of London
1814	Becomes one of eight foreign members of French Academie des Sciences
Aug. 25, 1819	Dies in Heathwood Hall, near Birmingham, Warwick, England

Early Life

James Watt was born in Greenock, Scotland. His father was a merchant who did carpentry, building, and contracting. James was a sickly child whose poor health persisted throughout his life. Initially a weak student at Greenock's M'Adam School, Watt preferred carpentry work in his father's shop to attending school. At thirteen, however, he began to study mathematics at Wee-Kirk Street Grammar School and became noted for ability in this subject.

In June, 1754, at the age of eighteen, Watt moved to Glasgow in the hope of learning the trade of mathematical instrument making, which is equivalent to modern mechanical engineering. He next moved to London, in 1755, to perfect this trade in a year's effort. Having done so, Watt returned to Scotland and became a mathematical instrument maker for the University of Glasgow. In addition to this job, Watt engaged in other aspects of his trade in order to make ends meet. On July 16, 1764, Watt married Margaret Miller, his cousin.

Steam Engines

Although Watt is usually credited with inventing the steam engine, other steam engines existed prior to his work. One example was Thomas Newcomen's engine, used only to pump water out of coal mines. Newcomen engines and other "pre-Watt" steam engines were very inefficient, however, because they used huge amounts of steam to produce relatively little power.

Watt's great accomplishment began when the university asked him to repair a small working model of the Newcomen steam engine. Watt became fascinated with the device and became obsessed with making a practical steam engine. His efforts were based on the well-known scientific precepts that steam rushes into an evacuated cylinder and then condenses. Watt's utilization of this basic information, backed financially by the manufacturer John Roebuck, led him to develop his steam engine, to show that it was both new and practical, and to patent it in 1769.

Fame, Fortune, and Later Achievements

About four years after patenting his engine, Watt became a partner of manufacturer Matthew Boulton in Birmingham, England. During this time, Watt's wife Margaret died, which caused him great heartache. Despite personal troubles, by May 22, 1775, Watt and Boulton had persuaded Parliament to renew their steam engine patent and empower it for twenty-five years. This legislation was followed by the organization of a company to produce the engine.

The quick success of the Watt-Boulton company rapidly made Watt wealthy and famous. It also gave him needed resources to improve his engine and make it practical for purposes from removing water from mines, via large models, to powering factory machines, with small engines. He patented these discoveries in 1781.

Watt devised many other inventions, including steam-related throttle valves and governors to control engine speeds. He also made discoveries in other areas, such as machines to reproduce sculpture, copying presses, and scientific proof that water is a chemical compound, not an element.

Watt was aided hugely by his second wife, Anne McGregor, the daughter of a Glasgow dyer, whom he married in 1776 and with whom he would spend the rest of his life. In addition, throughout his life, Watt was a friend and colleague to many great scientists, including Erasmus Darwin and Joseph Priestley.

Watt retired from commercial endeavors in 1800, when his son, James Watt, Jr., became a partner in the engine company. During the

Watt's Steam Engine

Watt did not discover the steam engine, but he made it practical for widespread use with his improvements.

When Watt began his efforts, Thomas Newcomen's steam engines were most used, usually to pump water out of coal mines. These engines are based, like all steam engines, on the ability of cooled steam in a full container to condense into water that no longer fills it. Hence, in an airtight cylinder, a vacuum forms and a well-fitted piston can be sucked up into the space that the steam originally occupied.

Newcomen's engine connected its steam cylinder to a beam hung like a seesaw and having at its other (pump) end, a container of water to be removed from the mine. In each engine stroke, 10 to 20 gallons of water moved upward when the beam end connected to the steam cylinder moved downward. Steam was pumped into the steam cylinder, below its piston, to start each stroke. This steam was cooled by adding to the steam piston cylinder some of the water pumped out. Hence, the entire steam cylinder was cooled during each stroke.

Watt's first innovation was separating the steam cylinder and steam condenser. This allowed the cylinder to be kept hot at all times and cut the cost of pump operation (the fuel used) by

about 70 percent. In addition, his improved cylinder-piston design diminished steam escape from the cylinder and cut fuel costs further. These improvements were major parts of the 1769 steam engine patent granted to Watt.

Watt's first invention was soon followed by the "sun-and-planet" gear system which turned the steam engine's reciprocating (up-and-down) motion to rotary motion in a way that was novel in his day. This modification enabled the use of Watt steam engines of varying sizes to be effective for jobs ranging from pumping mine water to running mills to powering small machines in factories.

Watt's innovations in steam engines were many, including the recognition that the expansive power of steam made it unnecessary to put steam into an engine cylinder through its entire stroke, devising how to connect piston rods to their pump beams without causing damaging rod wobble; and inventing both throttle valves and governors that control steam engine speed.

Bibliography

James Watt and the History of Steam Power. Ivor B. Hart. New York: Henry Schuman, 1949.
James Watt and the Steam Revolution. Eric Robinson and A. E. Musson. New York: Augustus M. Kelley, 1969.

(Library of Congress)

It is no wonder that Watt was admired by great contemporary scientists and elected a member of many prestigious scientific societies. It is also not surprising that a statue raised in his honor and placed in Westminster Abbey bears this inscription:

JAMES WATT

Who, directing the forces of an original genius, early exercised in philosophic research to the improvement of THE STEAM ENGINE, enlarged the resources of his country, increased the power of men, and arose to an eminent place among the most illustrious followers of science and the real benefactors of the world.

Bibliography
By Watt
"Thoughts on Constituent Parts of Water and of Dephlogisticated Air: With an Account of Some Experiments on That Subject," *Philosophical Transactions of the Royal Society*, 1784
"On a New Method of Preparing a Test Liquor to Shew the Presence of Acids and Alkalies in Chemical Mixtures," *Philosophical Transactions of the Royal Society*, 1784
Much of Watt's work is contained in the three-volume work *The Origin and Progress of the Mechanical Inventions of James Watt* (1854), by Patrick Muirhead.

About Watt
James Watt. Andrew Carnagie. New York: Doubleday, Page, 1905.
James Watt. L. T. C. Rolt. New York: Arco, 1962.
James Watt and the History of Steam Power. Ivor B. Hart. New York: Henry Schuman, 1949.
James Watt and the Steam Revolution. Eric Robinson and A. E. Musson. New York: Augustus M. Kelley, 1969.

(Sanford S. Singer)

years of his retirement, Watt puttered in his workshop, often acted as a consulting engineer, and continued to invent useful machines. Unhappily, all of Watt's children except for James Watt, Jr., died at early ages.

Watt's honors included election as a member of the royal societies of Edinburgh in 1784 and of London in 1785, as well as one of the eight foreign associates of the French Académie des Sciences in 1814. After enjoying a long, relatively healthy old age, Watt died in November, 1819, of a sudden illness. He was famous and well liked, and he was viewed as an essential contributor to the Industrial Revolution.

Alfred Lothar Wegener

Area of Achievement: Earth science
Contribution: Wegener is best known for his theory of continental drift, which forms the underlying idea for the theory of plate tectonics and produced a revolution in the geosciences.

Nov. 1, 1880	Born in Berlin, Germany
1905	Receives a Ph.D. in astronomy from the University of Berlin
1906-1908	Serves as a meteorologist for a Danish expedition to Greenland
1908	Begins work as a lecturer in meteorology at the Physical Institute in Marburg
1910	First conceives of the idea of continental drift while looking at a world map
1912	Presents his ideas on continental drift at a meeting of geologists in Frankfurt
1912-1913	Leads his second expedition to Greenland
1914-1919	Serves as a junior military officer during World War I
1915	Publishes an extended account of his theory of continental drift
1924	Assumes a special professorship in meteorology created for him at the University of Graz, Austria
1929-1930	Leads his third expedition to Greenland
1930	Leads his fourth and final expedition to Greenland
Nov., 1930	Dies in Greenland

Early Life

Alfred Lothar Wegener (pronounced "VAY-geh-nehr") was born in Berlin, Germany, on November 1, 1880, to Richard Wegener, a minister and the director of an orphanage, and his wife, Anna.

From his early days, Alfred dreamed of exploring Greenland, and he worked to build up his physical endurance. He attended school at the Kollnisches Gymnasium in Berlin and also studied at the universities in Heidelberg, Innsbruck, and Berlin. He received his doctorate in astronomy from the University of Berlin in 1905.

Meteorological Studies and to Greenland

Wegener's interests soon turned to meteorology, and he began experiments using kites and balloons for making weather observations. In 1906, Wegener and his brother, Kurt, set a world record in an international balloon contest, staying aloft for fifty-two hours.

Wegener was invited to join a 1906 Danish expedition to the unmapped coast of northeastern Greenland as its official meteorologist. In Greenland, he used kites and balloons to study the polar atmosphere.

On returning to Germany, Wegener accepted a position at the Physical Institute of the University of Marburg, where he lectured on meteorology and astronomy from 1908 to 1912. In 1911, he published a book on the thermodynamics of the atmosphere, which included the beginnings of the modern theory of the origin of precipitation.

Wegener returned to Greenland from 1912 to 1913 with Captain J. P. Koch of Denmark on a four-person expedition to study glaciology and climatology. The team members became the first to spend the winter on the ice cap, and they made the longest crossing of the ice on foot, traveling 750 miles.

In 1913, Wegener married Else Köppen, the daughter of meteorologist Wladimir Köppen. Wegener served as a junior military officer during World War I, from 1914 to 1919, and was wounded twice. After the war, he assumed his father-in-law's position as director of the meteorological research department of the Marine Observatory at Hamburg. There, his research demonstrated the probable impact origin of moon craters.

In 1924, a special professorship in meteorology and geophysics was created for Wegener at the University of Graz, Austria, in recognition for his wide-ranging contributions to science. He revisited Greenland from 1929 to 1930, and again in the spring of 1930. That year, he was a member of an expedition that ran into trouble from the start as a result of unusually bad weather.

On his fiftieth birthday, November 1, 1930, Wegener left camp in central Greenland, headed for the west coast, and was never seen alive again. His body was found in May of the following year, and an ice mausoleum was erected over it, marked with an iron cross. All traces of the site have since vanished, buried beneath the snow.

Continental Drift

Wegener is best known today for his ideas on continental drift. He first began to think about this concept in 1910 while looking at a world map and noticing the similarity in shape of the coasts of Africa and South America. At first, he rejected continental drift as improbable, but his interest was rekindled the following year when he learned that similar fossils were present on both sides of the Atlantic.

The prevailing theory of the time suggested that a land bridge once connected the two continents, but Wegener became fascinated with the possibility that Africa and South America had once been joined and then drifted apart and searched for evidence to support his theory.

On January 6, 1912, he presented his ideas on continental drift at a meeting of the Geological Association in Frankfurt, and he published his theories later that year. His ideas were expanded into a controversial book, *Die*

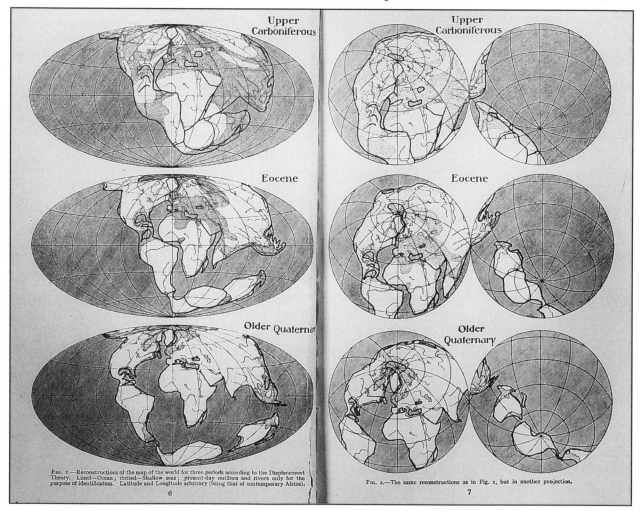

Fig. 1.—Reconstructions of the map of the world for three periods according to the Displacement Theory. Lined—Ocean; dotted—Shallow seas; present-day outlines and rivers only for the purpose of identification. Latitude and Longitude arbitrary (being that of contemporary Africa).

6

Fig. 2.—The same reconstructions as in Fig. 1, but in another projection.

7

Wegener's own drawings depicting the stages of continental drift over Earth's history. (Library of Congress)

The Theory of Continental Drift

Wegener argued that all land was once a part of a supercontinent that he called Pangaea (meaning "all lands") which broke up about 200 million years ago into fragments or continents and drifted apart to their present positions.

Wegener based his theory of continental drift on observations of the jigsaw fit of the continents clearly seen on world maps, particularly for the coastlines of Africa and South America, and on evidence from the fossil record showing similarities between extinct plants and animals of Africa and South America. These fossil similarities were explained at the time by hypothetical land bridges that had connected the two continents.

Wegener theorized that the continents themselves had moved and suggested a mechanism for this action. He proposed that the less-dense continents composed of granite plowed through the basalt of the ocean floor, driven by forces related to the rotation of the earth. As this occurred, the leading edges of the continents were compressed and folded into mountain ranges.

Wegener's ideas were met with widespread resistance and outright hostility. Geologists and geophysicists of the day charged that the forces Wegener proposed were far too small to cause drifting. Furthermore, a test of Wegener's hypothesis by timing radio signals across the Atlantic Ocean between 1922 and 1948 did not reveal progressive widening, as was predicted. The majority of geologists and geophysicists held that the evidence for continental drift was insufficient and that a workable mechanism was lacking.

Following World War II, advances in technology—and, in particular, the new field of paleomagnetism—gave support to Wegener's ideas. Oceanographic studies, culminating in the multinational research effort known as the International Geophysical Year (July, 1957, to December, 1958), resulted in many unexpected findings about the nature of the seafloor and details about the Mid-Atlantic Ridge.

A relationship was demonstrated between the Mid-Atlantic Ridge and earthquake activity. The ridge was found to have a valley formed by tensional forces (rifting) along its crest. Furthermore, the ridge was found to extend continuously through the world's oceans like the seam on a baseball, more than 64,000 kilometers long. Others discovered that the ridge is volcanically active and has high heat flow compared with the surrounding ocean basins. The ridge has little or no sediment covering it, but, more compelling, the age of the seafloor sediments increases from the mid-ocean ridge toward the continents. One of the most critical findings for the theory of continental drift was the discovery of magnetic stripes on the seafloor that are symmetrical on either side of the mid-ocean ridge.

The new seafloor data led Harry Hammond Hess in 1960 and Robert S. Dietz in 1961 to develop the theory of seafloor spreading, which fit well with Wegener's ideas of continental drift. Hess provided an acceptable mechanism for seafloor spreading: the activity of convection currents in the earth's mantle. This mechanism brought the diverse seafloor data and the ideas of continental drift together into a coherent theory. The theory was tested by Drummond Mathews and Fred Vine in 1963, leading to a revolution in earth science that came to be called plate tectonics.

The validation of Wegener's ideas about continental drift took nearly fifty years and the efforts of numerous researchers. Continental drift was an idea ahead of its time.

Bibliography

Earth. Edward J. Tarbuck and Frederick K. Lutgens. 5th ed. Upper Saddle River, N.J.: Prentice Hall, 1996.

Great Geological Controversies. A. Hallam. 2d ed. New York: Oxford University Press, 1989.

"Wegener Proposes the Theory of Continental Drift." Robert G. Font. In *Great Events from History II: Science and Technology*, edited by Frank N. Magill. Pasadena, Calif.: Salem Press, 1991.

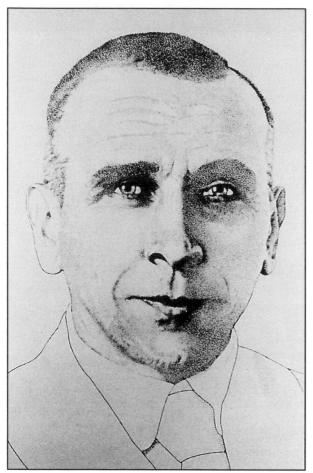

(Science Photo Library)

Entstehung der Kontinente und Ozeane, which was published in 1915, with several later revisions, and first translated as *The Origin of Continents and Oceans* in 1924.

Wegener's theories about the history of the earth departed dramatically from the accepted view in his day. His ideas were met with ridicule and hostility, and they were denounced as, "Utter, damned rot!" by W. B. Scott, a former president of the American Philosophical Society.

The theory of continental drift did not originate with Wegener, although he was the first to publish a logical theory supported by concrete evidence. The jigsaw fit of the continents had been noticed in the early seventeenth century, and the English philosopher Francis Bacon commented on it in 1620. Wegener assembled numerous lines of supporting evidence and proposed a mechanism for the drifting, but he was unable to convince most of his contemporaries.

Despite the rejection of his views at the time, Wegener's compelling ideas attracted interest over the years, and, in the 1950's and 1960's, discoveries in oceanography and geophysics confirmed the drifting of continents and the spreading of seafloors. Today, geologists call this process plate tectonics, and it is a unifying theory that led to a revolution in the geosciences.

Bibliography

By Wegener

Thermodynamik der Atmosphäre, 1911

"Die Entstehung der Kontinente," *Petermanns Geographische Mitteilungen*, 1912

Die Entstehung der Kontinente und Ozeane, 1915; rev. eds.; 1920, 1922, 1929, 1936 [*The Origin of Continents and Oceans*, 1924 (from 3d ed.), 1966 (from 4th ed.)]

Die Klimate der geologischen Vorzeit, 1924 (with W. Köppen)

"Denkschrift über Inlandeis-Expedition nach Grönland," *Deutsche Forschung*, 1928

About Wegener

Great Geological Controversies. A. Hallam. 2d ed. New York: Oxford University Press, 1989.

"Memories of Alfred Wegener." J. Georgi. In *Continental Drift*, edited by S. K. Runcorn. London: Academic Press, 1962.

"The Meteorologist Who Started a Revolution." Patrick Hughes. *Weatherwise* 47 (1994).

(Pamela J. W. Gore)

Steven Weinberg

Areas of Achievement: Cosmology, mathematics, and physics

Contribution: Weinberg, along with Sheldon Glashow and Abdus Salam, tried to construct a mathematical model that would unify all the known forces and particles of matter.

May 3, 1933	Born in New York, New York
1954	Earns a B.A. at Cornell University
1954	Marries Louise Goldwasser
1957	Earns a doctorate at Princeton University
1957-1959	Serves as an instructor of physics at Columbia University
1959-1969	Research associate at the Lawrence Laboratory of the University of California
1969-1973	Serves as a professor of physics at the Massachusetts Institute of Technology (MIT)
1973	Presented with the J. R. Oppenheimer Prize
1973-1983	Named Higgins Professor of Physics at Harvard University
1973	Made a senior scientist at the Smithsonian Astrophysical Observatory
1979	With Salam and Glashow, receives the Nobel Prize in Physics
1983	Named Josey Regental Professor of Science at the University of Texas
1991	Receives the National Medal of Science

Early Life

Steven Weinberg was born in New York City in 1933, where his mother, Eva, and father, Frederick, lived and where Frederick was a court stenographer.

Weinberg was a quiet, almost shy boy, a quality that remained in his adult life. At an early age, he was particularly strong in science and mathematics. One of the best high schools for science was nearby, the Bronx High School of Science, and Weinberg attended school there before enrolling at Cornell University. He was graduated in physics from Cornell at the age of twenty-one and enrolled for graduate work at Princeton University. There, he earned the doctorate in physics in only three years.

Most science at that time was directed toward practical issues—providing for the needs of society or searching for explanations of actions and objects in the everyday world. There had long been a theoretical part of science, however, that attempted to define a set of rules that would govern every action and object from the beginning of the universe. Weinberg chose to join the search for the basic rules of the universe and to carry on his search through mathematics.

Mathematics and physics were only two of Weinberg's many interests. He also expressed interest in cosmology, the study of the nature of the universe, and developed an early fascination with medieval history. He continued the latter interest into his adult life as a member of the American Medieval Academy.

A Communicator in Science

Most often, the contributions of scientists are calculated by their encouragement of other scientists. For Weinberg, part of the work of the scientist was to carry on a great discussion, sharing discoveries both with other scientists and with nonscientists.

As Weinberg began to shape new theories of everything, he began writing—about the particles of which all things are made and about cosmology, the study of the origin and composition of the universe. In the 1960's and 1970's, he wrote more than one hundred thirty articles for scientific journals. By the mid-1990's, that number had grown to more than three hundred articles about his mathematical models to explain the nature of the universe. Other scientists built on his work and writings. Between 1961 and 1978, Weinberg's writings were referred to by other scientists more than those of any other physicist in the world.

At the same time, he wrote textbooks in physics and a number of books to explain modern ideas of the universe to nonscientists. For example, in 1977 Weinberg wrote a book for both nonscientists and scientists that explained the origin of the universe in terms of new discoveries of the particles of which atoms are made. This book, *The First Three Minutes*, was translated into fifteen languages.

Obtaining Scientific Tools

A large part of science work in the last half of the twentieth century involved finding the necessary finances to build complicated and expensive tools. A major tool for the scientists who studied elementary particles was an accel-

Toward a Unified Theory of the Universe

Weinberg proposed that two of the four forces thought to act in particles in the universe—electromagnetism and the weak nuclear force—were different views of the same force.

By the time that Weinberg began his work at Harvard University, scientists and nonscientists alike had been looking for a theory that would explain all the actions and all the materials in the universe for hundreds of years. Along the way, there were steps forward and slides backward.

In the seventeenth century, Sir Isaac Newton thought that all the actions in the universe could be explained by gravity, electricity, and magnetism. James Clerk Maxwell demonstrated in the nineteenth century that electricity and magnetism were different views of the same force. At the beginning of the twentieth century, Albert Einstein proposed that matter and energy were exchangeable.

Experiments to speed up particles from atoms produced an increasing number of subatomic particles whose actions could not be explained simply by electromagnetism or gravity. Then two more forces were discovered, a weak force that was involved in radioactivity and a strong force that held each nucleus of atoms together.

Scientists tried to make sense of the large number of subatomic particles revealed in atom "smashing" experiments. The particles were grouped into two groups: first, electrons and their relatives, and, second, particles that could be described using four or more building blocks called quarks. The first three were called "up," "down," and "strange"; the fourth is "charm." Scientists were beginning to think that they had found all the kinds of particles possible.

In 1967, Weinberg presented a theory in the form of a set of mathematical equations suggesting that the weak force and electromagnetism were alike. Once more, it seemed as if they were different aspects of the same force. The two forces were alike except that one worked on large objects visible in the universe and worked in the very tiny universe of particles that make up atoms.

The next year, Abdus Salam, a professor in England, developed much the same set of equations. Weinberg and Salam were awarded the Nobel Prize in Physics in 1979 for their discovery of this Weinberg-Salam theory that brought together ideas about the forces acting in the universe. The number of forces to consider in a theory of everything was cut to three—gravity, electromagnetism, and the strong force.

As Weinberg filled in his equations, he found that three still unknown particles were needed to complete them. He called these the W^-, W^+, and Z^0 (later W^0) particles. In 1983, a team of scientists led by Carlo Rubbia would discover proof of the existence of these particles using the massive superconductor in Geneva, Switzerland. These particles and the union of electromagnetism and the weak force brought scientists closer to the long-searched-for "theory of everything." In 1992, Weinberg celebrated his achievements with a book called *Dreams of a Final Theory*.

Bibliography

Adventures in Experimental Physics. Bogdan Maglich. Princeton, N.J.: University of Princeton Press, 1976.

Atom: Journey Across the Subatomic Cosmos. Isaac Asimov. New York: E. P. Dutton, 1991.

A Brief History of Time: From the Big Bang to Black Holes. Stephen W. Hawking. New York: Bantam, 1988.

(The Nobel Foundation)

ducting supercollider." The more powerful the supercollider, the closer scientists could approach the energy levels imagined to be present at the start of the universe and identify the basic units of which everything in the universe was built. Some politicians wondered, however, if the work of the supercollider could not be done by computers at a much lower cost than the $4.5 billion needed for the supercollider.

Weinberg explained that not enough was yet known to make useful computer models. As scientists were beginning to identify the pieces of the puzzle of the universe, mathematical equations could help, but they needed to be tested using the huge machines.

In this part of the great conversation about science, Weinberg and his colleagues lost. In 1993, the U.S. Congress stopped funding the supercolliders. Fortunately, the mathematical theories of Weinberg and his coworkers Abdus Salam and Sheldon L. Glashow would soon be tested in a gigantic new accelerator in Europe that was designed and built by a team led by Carlo Rubbia.

Bibliography

By Weinberg
Gravitation and Cosmology: Principles and Applications of the General Theory of Relativity, 1972
The First Three Minutes: A Modern View of the Origin of the Universe, 1977
The Discovery of Subatomic Particles, 1983
Dreams of a Final Theory, 1992

About Weinberg
The Key to the Universe: A Report on the New Physics. Nigel Calder. New York: Viking Press, 1977.
Profiles in Science: Nobel Prize Winners in Physics. Robert L. Weber. London: Techno House, 1980.
"Steven Weinberg." In *The Nobel Prize Winners: Physics*, edited by Frank N. Magill, Pasadena, Calif.: Salem Press, 1989.

(George Wilson)

erator—a gigantic collection of electromagnets and other gadgets designed to make particles gather energy and move faster and faster before colliding with other particles and breaking into smaller units.

A problem for such elementary particle scientists was that the tools required were extremely expensive but did not have any immediately visible practical value. In the United States, the most powerful tools were at the Fermi Laboratory in Chicago, but the collider there was becoming obsolete.

Weinberg became an adviser to the U.S. government and championed government financing of a much more powerful "supercon-

John Archibald Wheeler

Areas of Achievement: Astronomy and physics

Contribution: Wheeler performed seminal research on nuclear fission and helped to develop the hydrogen bomb. He also conducted pioneering investigations into black holes, a term that he coined.

July 9, 1911	Born in Jacksonville, Florida
1933	Receives a Ph.D. from The Johns Hopkins University
1934-1935	Studies with Niels Bohr in Copenhagen, Denmark
1935	Marries Janette Latourette Zabriskie-Hegner
1935	Takes a teaching position at the University of North Carolina but soon moves to Princeton University
1939	Coauthors a paper on nuclear fission with Bohr during his visit to Princeton
1942	Joins the Manhattan Project
1944	Diagnoses the first case of reactor "poisoning" by the by-products of fission
1950	Begins work on developing a hydrogen bomb
1957	Uses the MANIAC computer to determine the result of the collapse of a star
1967	Coins the term "black hole"
1976	Retires from Princeton University and joins the faculty of the University of Texas
1986	Returns to Princeton
1996	Awarded the Wolf Prize for Physics

Early Life

John Archibald Wheeler was born on July 9, 1911, in Jacksonville, Florida. His parents, who were both librarians, frequently moved around the country from one job site to another. John grew up in California, Ohio, Vermont, and Maryland.

A precocious youth, Wheeler began asking his mother about the world of nature when he was three. A dynamite explosion that severely injured his hand at the age of ten, while he was performing an experiment, failed to diminish his interest in science. Wheeler eventually won a scholarship to The Johns Hopkins University in Baltimore, where he earned a Ph.D. degree in physics in 1933.

Early Academic Career

While he was a student, Wheeler developed an interest in the work of Niels Bohr, the Nobel Prize-winning Danish physicist. Beginning in 1934, he spent a year in Copenhagen on a post-doctoral scholarship, where he worked with Bohr as a theoretical physicist.

In 1935, Wheeler returned to the United States to take a teaching position at the University of North Carolina. Immediately after his return, he married Janette Latourette Zabriskie-Hegner; the couple had a son and two daughters. Wheeler stayed at North Carolina only a short time before taking a position at Princeton.

Wheeler and Bohr

In early 1939, Bohr came to Princeton for a short stay. During Bohr's four-month stay, Wheeler sat in on discussions that Bohr had with some of the world's foremost physicists.

Bohr and Wheeler prepared a paper in which they predicted that uranium 235 nuclei would be most successful in sustaining chain reactions. Wheeler continued to work on nuclear fission after Bohr returned to Denmark.

The Manhattan Project

In 1942, Wheeler took a leave of absence from Princeton to work on the Manhattan Project, the U.S. government's secret program to build an atomic bomb during World War II. Wheeler's duties included teaching engineers about fission and researching "poisons"—by-products of fission that absorb neutrons and eventually interrupt chain reactions.

Wheeler insisted that reactors be designed so that countermeasures could be taken should such poisoning occur. In 1944, he diagnosed the first case of reactor poisoning.

The Hydrogen Bomb

After World War II, Wheeler returned to Princeton but would soon return to nuclear weapons research. In 1949, the Soviet Union exploded a nuclear device. To counter the growing Soviet nuclear threat, Wheeler joined physicist Edward Teller in calling for a crash program to develop a thermonuclear or hydrogen bomb—a bomb based on the fusion of hydrogen atoms to form helium and much more powerful than a fission bomb.

President Harry S Truman authorized the hydrogen bomb project in 1950, and Wheeler headed one of two teams set up to develop the device. In conducting its research, Wheeler's team used much of the computer capacity then available in the United States and developed the room-sized MANIAC computer. On October 31, 1952, their efforts paid off when the first thermonuclear device was successfully tested.

Black Holes

When large stars burn out, they collapse into small, compact objects in which the gravitational field is so strong that not even light can escape. Such objects are known as black holes.

The heat and light generated by a burning star balances the force of its gravity. Once a star burns out, its gravity causes it to collapse. What happens next is determined by the star's mass.

When stars burn out that have about the same mass as the sun, they become white dwarfs and continue to glow with leftover energy. Stars with up to three times the mass of the sun become neutron stars. Those with a mass greater than three times that of the sun become black holes.

A black hole is formed when all the material that makes up the star shrinks to a single point called a singularity, which is smaller than a microbe. Here, even time no longer flows. Within a certain distance of the singularity, the gravitational field is so strong that not even light can escape. The outer boundary of this area is called the event horizon.

Although all matter has collapsed to a single point, a black hole's mass remains unchanged. Heavenly bodies such as planets and asteroids orbit the black hole as though it were a burning star.

Compared to burning stars, black holes are extremely compact. Although the sun lacks enough mass to do so, should it become a black hole, its event horizon would measure only about 3.5 miles across and the earth would continue to follow the same orbit as it does now.

One cannot look for black holes because they do not give off light. A number of methods exist, however, for detecting the presence of black holes. When stars are observed to be orbiting something that cannot be identified, it is assumed that the unidentified object is a black hole or a neutron star, which also does not give off light. As dust particles being sucked into a black hole gain heat, they emit X rays that can be detected by satellites.

Black holes can also be detected by a technique known as gravity lensing. When a black hole passes between a star and the earth, its gravity causes the star's light rays to bend, making the star appear brighter.

Scientists, including Wheeler, once believed that a black hole would continue to grow until it sucked in the entire universe. Recent research by Stephen Hawking, a disciple of Wheeler, indicates that matter sucked into a black hole's singularity contributes negative energy, which causes the singularity to decrease. Eventually, the black hole disappears.

Bibliography

Black Holes and Time Warp: Einstein's Outrageous Legacy. Kip S. Thorne. New York: W. W. Norton, 1994.

Invisible Matter and the Fate of the Universe. Barry Parker. New York: Plenum Press, 1989.

Lonely Hearts of the Cosmos: The Scientific Quest for the Secret of the Universe. Dennis Overbye. New York: HarperCollins, 1991.

Black Holes

After leaving the hydrogen bomb project in the mid-1950's, Wheeler returned to teaching. He became increasingly interested in how the universe functions and, in particular, what would happen to a star once it burned out and collapsed as a result of gravitational force.

During the 1930's, researchers proposed that when stars burned out, they became either white dwarfs (small stars that burn residual fuel) or neutron stars (dark objects consisting of neutrons). In a paper published in 1939, J. Robert Oppenheimer proposed that a burned-out star could collapse into a very small mass with such a strong gravitational field that not even light could escape the immediate vicinity of the mass. These objects would come to be known as black holes.

Most scientists, however, including Oppenheimer himself, lost interest in black holes after World War II. Wheeler dug up papers by Oppenheimer and others about collapsing stars. In 1957, he used the MANIAC computer to determine the result of the collapse of star masses.

Wheeler was at first skeptical about the existence of black holes, but, after extensive research, he became convinced that Oppenheimer was right. In 1967, Wheeler coined the term "black hole" for the phenomenon that Oppenheimer had described.

Later Years

Wheeler continued his research into black holes and various aspects of quantum physics while maintaining his teaching duties. In 1976, he retired from Princeton and took a position at the University of Texas, but he returned ten years later. He held the title of professor emeritus at both universities.

In December, 1996, Wheeler was awarded the 1997 Wolf Prize for Physics by the Israeli-based Wolf Foundation for his seminal contributions to physics, including black hole research.

Bibliography

By Wheeler

"On the Nature of Quantum Geometrodynamics," *Annals of Physics*, 1957

Geometrodynamics, 1962

"The Superdense Star and the Critical Nucleon Number" in *Gravitation and Relativity*, 1964 (Hong-Yee Chiu and William F. Hoffman, eds.)

"Geometrodynamics and the Issue of the Final State" in *Relativity, Groups, and Topography: Lectures Delivered at Los Houches During the 1963 Session of the Summer School of Theoretical Physics*, 1964 (C. DeWitt and B. DeWitt, eds.)

Gravitation Theory and Gravitational Collapse, 1965 (with B. K. Harrison, K. S. Thorne, and Masami Wakano)

Spacetime Physics, 1966 (with Edwin F. Taylor)

"Our Universe: The Known and the Unknown," *American Scientist*, 1968

Black Holes, Gravitational Waves, and Cosmology: An Introduction to Current Research, 1974 (with Martin Rees and Remo Ruffini)

"Some Men and Moments in the History of Nuclear Physics: The Interplay of Col-

(Library of Congress)

leagues and Motivations" in *Nuclear Physics in Retrospect: Proceedings of a Symposium on the 1930's*, 1979 (Roger H. Stuewer, ed.)
A Journey into Gravity and Spacetime, 1990
Gravitation and Inertia, 1995 (with Ignazio Ciufolini)

About Wheeler

"Inside the Mind of John Wheeler." John Boslough. *Readers Digest* 9 (September, 1986).
The Manhattan Project. Stephane Groueff. New York: Bantam Books, 1967.
Notable Twentieth-Century Scientists. Emily J. McMurray, ed. Vol. 4. Detroit: Gale Research, 1995.

(Lawrence K. Orr)

Eli Whitney

Areas of Achievement: Invention and technology

Contribution: Best known as the inventor of the cotton gin, Whitney also developed the techniques of mass production through the use of interchangeable parts.

Dec. 8, 1765	Born in Westboro, Massachusetts
1777	Develops machinist skills working in his father's workshop
1788	Enrolls at Yale College
1792	Graduated from Yale and travels to Savannah, Georgia
1793	Invents the cotton gin
1794	Receives a patent for his cotton gin
1798	Secures a federal contract to mass produce ten thousand muskets
1812	Awarded another contract to produce fifteen thousand muskets using the "American system" of prefabricated interchangeable parts
1817	Marries Henrietta Edwards
Jan. 8, 1825	Dies in New Haven, Connecticut

Early Life

Eli Whitney was the first child of Eli and Elizabeth Whitney, frugal New England farmers. When young Eli was five years old, his mother died after giving birth to her fourth child. As the eldest child, he accepted the responsibility of caring for his younger siblings. A hardworking youth, Whitney also assisted his father on the farm and in the workshop, where he produced furniture and farm gear on a lathe.

During the Revolutionary War, Whitney used his mechanical skills to produce nails. After the war, when the price of nails fell, he shifted products, producing higher demand articles such as hat pins and walking sticks. While other, more experienced nailmakers across New England went bankrupt, Whitney survived by learning how to adapt to market conditions.

Education

At the age of nineteen, Whitney expressed a desire to attend college. Although financial hardships and educational deficiencies made this wish seem unrealistic, he plotted to fulfill his dream. Securing employment as a schoolmaster, Whitney earned enough income teaching school during the winter to enable him to attend Leicester Academy during the summer.

For six years, Whitney the schoolmaster and pupil prepared for his college entrance examinations. Upon passing them, he enrolled at Yale College. In 1792, the twenty-seven-year-old Yale graduate left New Haven, Connecticut, for Savannah, Georgia, intending to begin a teaching career.

Inventing the Cotton Gin

Whitney never found employment as a tutor, but he did end up at Mulberry Grove, the plantation of the widow of the Revolutionary War hero Nathanael Greene. His job was to design a machine that would extract seeds from cotton fibers. A mechanical genius, Whitney took less than one year to finish his assignment.

In 1793, he demonstrated a working model for a cotton gin and patented the device the following year. Almost overnight, Whitney's cotton gin made the production of short-stable cotton a highly profitable commodity throughout the American South. Unfortunately, patent infringements robbed him of the profits created by his invention. The disgruntled Whitney never again wasted his time patenting any of his subsequent inventions.

Muskets and Mass Production

In 1798, Whitney received a federal contract to produce ten thousand muskets. The novelty of this contract was its sheer size. Muskets at this time were made one at a time by highly skilled artisans. Whitney, however, promised to design machines that could mass-produce individual musket parts; he then used unskilled labor to assemble them.

When Whitney delivered on this promise, a new age of mass production was born. It was musket making, not the cotton gin, that made Whitney a wealthy man and ushered America into the Industrial Revolution. He died in 1825.

(Library of Congress)

Bringing the Industrial Revolution to America

Whitney's labor-saving inventions altered the social and economic landscape of the early American republic.

Few inventions have had as great an impact on the economic and social history of a region as Whitney's cotton gin on the United States. The original cotton gin (short for "cotton engine") was a relatively simple device housed in a wooden box that contained drums equipped with wire hooks and brushes designed to remove seeds from cotton fibers.

The cotton gin worked successfully on both long-stable cotton, a cotton with easily removable seeds that grew in only a few regions of the American South, and short-stable cotton, a crop that could grow abundantly in almost any warm climate, but that previously was not profitable because of the time required to extract its tiny seeds from the fiber.

Whitney's gin, which could clean as much cotton in a day as fifty workers could clean by hand, opened the southeastern United States to short-stable cotton production. Since the Southern producers of cotton selected slaves for their labor supply, the cotton gin is often associated with the rise of the institution of Southern slavery.

Whitney's other historic labor-saving idea was his application of the uniformity system of production, using interchangeable parts. Whitney designed and built machinery that mass-produced the individual parts of a musket, which could then be assembled by unskilled workers. Future American entrepreneurs such as Isaac Singer, Cyrus Hall McCormick, and Henry Ford adapted Whitney's concept of machine-produced interchangeable parts to revolutionize American business.

Bibliography

Historical Notes on the Cotton Gin. F. L. Lewton. Washington, D.C.: Smithsonian Report, 1937.

The Whitney Firearms. Claud E. Fuller. Huntington, W. Va.: Standard, 1946.

An early drawing of the cotton gin. (The Associated Publishers, Inc.)

Bibliography
By Whitney
An Oration on the Death of Mr. Robert Grant, a Member of the Senior Class, in Yale-College, Connecticut, 1792
Cotton Gin: Patented March 14, 1794, 1959?

About Whitney
Eli Whitney and the Birth of American Technology. Constance M. Green. Boston: Little, Brown, 1956.
The World of Eli Whitney. Jeannette Mirsky and Allan Nevins. New York: Macmillan, 1952.

(*Terry D. Bilhartz*)

Wilhelm Wien

Area of Achievement: Physics
Contribution: Wien won the Nobel Prize in Physics for his discoveries concerning the laws of heat radiation, which made possible the development of quantum theory.

Jan. 13, 1864	Born in Gaffken, near Fischhausen, East Prussia (now Primorsk, Russia)
1882	Studies at the University of Göttingen
1886	Earns a Ph.D. from the University of Berlin with a thesis on the diffraction of light
1890-1896	Assists Hermann von Helmholtz at the Physikalisch-Technische Reichsanstalt, Berlin
1892	Receives *venia legendi* from the University of Berlin
1896-1900	Takes a position as extraordinary professor at the Technische Hochschule, Aachen
1896	Publishes a paper propounding Wien's law
1898	Marries Luise Mehler
1900-1920	Teaches physics at the University of Würzburg
1906-1928	Serves as editor of the *Annalen der Physik*
1911	Awarded the Nobel Prize in Physics
1920-1928	Serves as a professor at the University of Munich
1925-1926	Holds the post of rector at Munich
Aug. 30, 1928	Dies in Munich, Germany

Early Life
Wilhelm Wien (pronounced "veen") was the only son of a landowning farmer. His mother

educated him in history and literature, and a tutor was procured for him so that he could learn French.

When Wien went away to the Gymnasium in Rastenburg in 1875, however, his mathematical training was found to be deficient, and he left in 1880. Private tutoring allowed him to continue his studies.

University Studies and Laboratory Work

Wien enrolled at the University of Göttingen in 1882 to study mathematics. After only a semester, he departed. He resumed study at the University of Berlin in 1883, where he met and began to work for Hermann von Helmholtz. Wien wrote his doctoral dissertation on the diffraction of light and earned a Ph.D. in 1886.

After Wien received his doctorate, Helmholtz suggested that Wien had a duty, as an only son, to help his parents manage their farm. Wien returned home to help his parents reconstruct some farm buildings but came back to Helmholtz's laboratory in 1890 after a drought forced his father to sell his farm.

That year, he became an assistant at the new Physikalisch-Technische Reichsanstalt (PTR). This work gave him a rare background in both theory and experiment. He received the *venia legendi* at the University of Berlin in 1892.

Wien departed from the PTR in 1896 because Friedrich Kohlrausch, the successor to Helmholtz, imposed a plan for research. Wien became an instructor at the Technische Hochschule in Aachen, where he also met and married Luise Mehler. While there, he developed a law that explained the known facts about the distribution of radiation. This law, not the one devised by Max Planck, would be used by Albert Einstein in 1905 as part of his work on the photoelectric effect.

Academia and Experimentation

On the strength of Wien's world-famous work in radiation theory, the German academic establishment extended a position to him as a full professor at the University of Gliessen, where he remained only six months. He then went to the University of Würzburg, where, over the next twenty years, he would do experimental work.

The Wien Radiation Law

By knowing the temperature of an object, the distribution of energy that it will radiate can be known.

A blackbody is an object that completely absorbs all radiation without reflection. There are no perfect blackbodies in nature. Wien's work on blackbody radiation rested on the findings of Ludwig Boltzmann, who had proven in 1884 a law expressing the total energy of re-radiation by such a body.

In 1893, Wien concluded that the wavelength at which the greatest energy is radiated from the body would be inversely proportional to the absolute temperature of the body. This result, as Wien indicated in his 1911 Nobel lecture, would allow an astronomer to determine the temperature of a star.

His study was the last successful treatment of the problem using classical physics, in which the energy at any given wavelength was allowed to take any arbitrary value. The difficulty of the distribution of energy at each frequency, however, could not be solved simply by knowing the frequency at which more energy would be radiated than would be at any other frequency.

In 1896, Wien concluded that the energy near a certain wavelength varied inversely with the fifth power of that wavelength. This equation, however, did not agree with experiments for long wavelengths. Max Planck, by making a quantum assumption for the oscillators allowing them to take only certain values dependent on the frequency of the radiation, would develop the correct distribution law.

Bibliography

Black Body Theory and the Quantum Discontinuity, 1894-1912. Thomas S. Kuhn. Oxford, England: Oxford University Press, 1978.

The Conceptual Development of Quantum Mechanics. Max Jammer. New York: McGraw-Hill, 1966.

The History of Quantum Theory. Friedrich Hund. New York: Barnes & Noble Books, 1967.

In 1897, Wien had found that cathode rays, which would later be used to generate the pictures on a television screen, were in fact particles having a certain mass and a very high velocity that was roughly one-third of the speed of light. This discovery led in 1900 to Wien's doubts about the Newtonian view that mass was constant and not dependent on the relative velocity of a body.

Editorship

In 1906, Planck and Wien were asked to become coeditors of *Annalen der Physik*, then the world's most important physics journal.

Despite his reservations about Planck's quantum theory, which Wien reported in his acceptance address for the 1911 Nobel Prize in Physics, he was a supporter of Einstein's theory of relativity. Wien told Ernest Rutherford that the English scientists had refused to accept relativity because only a German mind could understand it. Wilhelm Wien died in 1928 at the age of sixty-four.

Bibliography
By Wien

"Über die Energievertheilung im Emissionsspectrum eines schwarzen Körpers," *Annalen der Physik*, 1896 ("On the Division of Energy in the Emission-Spectrum of a Black Body," *Philosophical Magazine*, 1897)
Ziele und Methoden der theoretischen Physik, 1914
Aus der Welt der Wissenschaft, 1921

About Wien

Nobel Prize Winners in Physics: 1901-1950. Niels Heathcoate. Freeport, N.Y.: Books for Libraries Press, 1953.
The Tiger and the Shark: Empirical Roots of Wave-Particle Dualism. Bruce R. Wheaton. Cambridge, England: Cambridge University Press, 1983.
"Wilhelm Wien." In *The Nobel Prize Winners: Physics*, edited by Frank N. Magill. Pasadena, Calif.: Salem Press, 1989.

(The Nobel Foundation)

(Drew L. Arrowood)

Eugene P. Wigner

Areas of Achievement: Physics, mathematics, and technology

Contribution: Wigner applied symmetry principles and group theory to atomic, nuclear, and particle physics. He also described neutron absorption and designed the first large nuclear reactors.

Nov. 17, 1902	Born in Budapest, Hungary
1924	Graduated in chemical engineering from the Technische Hochschule, Berlin
1925	Earns a Ph.D. in engineering at the Technische Hochschule
1925-1926	Works as a chemist in a leather factory in Budapest
1926-1927	Assists R. Becker at the Technische Hochschule
1927-1928	Assists David Hilbert at the University of Göttingen
1928-1930	Serves as privatdocent at the Technische Hochschule
1930	Appointed a lecturer at Princeton University
1937-1938	Teaches at the University of Wisconsin
1938-1971	Serves as a professor at Princeton
1942-1945	Works at the Metallurgical Laboratory and at the University of Chicago
1960	Given the Atoms for Peace Award
1963	Awarded the Nobel Prize in Physics
1969	Awarded the National Medal of Science
1971-1994	Serves as a visiting professor at Louisiana State University
Jan. 1, 1995	Dies in Princeton, New Jersey

Early Life

Eugene Paul Wigner was born in Budapest, Hungary, in 1902. His family was Jewish and reasonably well-to-do, as his father was the manager of one of the leading leather tanneries in the country. The city was undergoing a renaissance during the years preceding World War I and had some of the finest Gymnasia (high schools) in Europe.

Wigner was one of the four remarkable scientists—the other three being John von Neumann, Edward Teller, and Leo Szilard—who grew up in Budapest about the same time, emigrated to the United States, and worked on the atomic bomb project; they became known as "the Martians" because of their brilliance.

After high school in Budapest, Wigner moved to the Technische Hochschule in Berlin, where he met Albert Einstein, Max Planck, and Wolfgang Pauli and worked under Michael Polanyi. He took his degree in chemical engineering in 1924 and a doctorate in engineering in 1925.

Wigner initially returned home to Budapest, where his father procured for him a job in the tannery. He tried to follow his father's wishes, but his love for physics drew him back to Berlin and the excitement of the new quantum mechanics.

Wigner wrote papers with several important scientists in Göttingen in the late 1920's and became increasingly interested in applying group theory to quantum mechanics. In 1930, much to his surprise, he was offered a position as lecturer in physics at Princeton University at nearly ten times the salary that he had been receiving in Berlin.

The primary keys to Wigner's character were logic and reasonableness; it was said of him that he was "stubbornly reasonable." He was a true gentleman and was thoughtful and considerate of everyone—students, staff, and peers.

Nuclear Physics in the Manhattan Project

Wigner, like many other immigrant European scientists who had seen fascism and communism up close, hated the Nazis. He was instrumental, together with his friends Szilard and Teller, in fashioning the letter that Einstein sent to President Franklin D. Roosevelt alerting the

U.S. government to the possibility of an atomic bomb.

In early 1942, Wigner took a leave of absence from Princeton and joined the atomic bomb project in Chicago. His job was to design the first large nuclear reactor for the production of plutonium that was to be built in Hanford, Washington, by Dupont. He was present at the startup of the world's first reactor, built by Enrico Fermi in 1942, and then went on to complete the Hanford reactor design successfully. All the plutonium for the Trinity test and the Nagasaki bomb was subsequently produced by the Hanford reactor.

Symmetry Principles

Wigner began his groundbreaking work on symmetry and invariance in the late 1920's when, at the urging of Szilard, he spent two years writing his famous book on group theory and its application to atomic physics. He claimed to have been "teased by the idea" that "if a law of nature works on a system constructed in a certain way, it will also work

Symmetries and Invariance Principles

Wigner clarified the relationship between actions, laws of nature, and invariance principles.

It is an item of faith to a scientist that the laws of nature do not depend on where one stands. They are the same here on Earth as they are in the farthest galaxy, and they were the same in the past as they are today and will be in the future.

This symmetry in nature is defined as an invariance in a pattern that is seen when a system is transformed in space or time. The basis for Albert Einstein's special theory of relativity is that the laws of nature are invariant in transformations relating inertial frames of reference. His general theory of relativity uses the symmetry between inertial and gravitational mass to determine the laws of gravitation.

For every symmetry, there is an associated conservation law. Thus, conservation of energy is associated with symmetry in a transformation in time, while a symmetry in transformation in space is connected to conservation of momentum. These are continuous symmetries because they can be arbitrarily small. There are also inversion symmetries that are discrete—such as parity, which is a mirror reflection, and charge conjugation, which changes all particles to antiparticles. The continuous invariances are believed to be exact and lead to conservation laws that are always obeyed in nature. An inversion may be only an approximate symmetry, however, and can lead to failures in invariance under transformations.

Wigner showed that an action includes both the laws of nature and initial conditions. Thus, the orbits of the planets are all different, even though Sir Isaac Newton's laws are the same for each. Wigner's major contribution was to show that invariance and symmetry principles, when applied to quantum mechanics, lead to far-reaching conclusions not seen in classical science. In quantum mechanics, it is possible to superpose states to produce new allowed states that play fundamental roles in nature.

Symmetries are important in nature, but much of what exists is the result of symmetries that have at one time been broken. This is a quantum mechanical phenomenon, but simple classical analogs can help to explain it.

For example, a spinning roulette wheel is symmetrical, but, when the ball drops into the slot, the symmetry is broken. A liquid has a continuous symmetry since the molecules have a large number of degrees of freedom. When the temperature is lowered and the water freezes, however, the symmetry is broken and the molecules are aligned in a lattice, reducing their degrees of freedom. A similar thing is believed to have taken place in the first trillionths of a second after the big bang. The initial radiation was completely symmetrical, but, as it cooled, a phase change occurred and the symmetry was broken to allow the "freezing out" of particles and antiparticles.

Bibliography
Fearful Symmetry: The Search for Beauty in Modern Physics. A. Zee. New York: Macmillan, 1986.
"Symmetry in Physics: Wigner's Legacy." David J. Gross. *Physics Today* 48, no. 12 (December, 1995).

Oak Ridge National Laboratory, where Wigner conducted research on bomb shelter design. (Martin Marietta)

when the system is rotated or put in motion." Using the ideas of rotational symmetry and group theory, Wigner was able to explain the selection rules of atomic transitions.

Applying symmetry ideas to quantum mechanics, he was able to explain many of the transitions that take place in nuclear reactions. These symmetry principles are now considered the most fundamental part of the description of nature.

Neutron Chain Reactors

Many call Wigner the founder of the discipline of nuclear engineering. His book on the physical theory of neutron chain reactors and the thirty-seven patents that he held in this field strongly influenced the design and construction of present-day power reactors.

He made many important contributions to the theory of neutron diffusion and capture and to the application of the compound nuclear model to nuclear reactions. Also, he was the first to suggest, as early as 1942, that a crystal lattice could be destroyed by radiation, thus weakening the structure of a nuclear reactor.

Civil Defense and Fallout Shelters

Wigner hated and distrusted totalitarian governments, and he feared that nuclear war with the Soviet Union could not be avoided. He advocated a strong civil defense and directed a research effort at Oak Ridge National Laboratory to develop better bomb shelters, arguing that the small cost could save millions of lives if nuclear war were to begin.

Wigner died in Princeton, New Jersey, on New Year's Day, 1995, at the age of ninety-two.

Bibliography
By Wigner

Gruppentheorie und ihre Anwendung auf die Quantenmechanik der Atomspektren, 1931 (*Group Theory and Its Application to the Quantum Mechanics of Atom Spectra*, 1959)

Physical Sciences and Human Values, 1947 (as editor)

Nuclear Structure, 1958 (with Leonard Eisenbud)

The Physical Theory of Neutron Chain Reactors, 1958 (with Alvin M. Weinberg)

Symmetries and Reflections: Scientific Essays of Eugene P. Wigner, 1967

Who Speaks for Civil Defense?, 1968 (as editor)

Survival and the Bomb: Methods of Civil Defense, 1969 (as editor)

Aspects of Quantum Theory, 1972 (as editor, with Abdus Salam)

Reminiscences About a Great Physicist: Paul Adrien Maurice Dirac, 1987

The Recollections of Eugene P. Wigner, as told to Andrew Szanton, 1992 (Andrew Szanton, ed.)

About Wigner

"Eugene Paul Wigner." In *The Nobel Prize Winners: Physics*, edited by Frank N. Magill. Pasadena, Calif.: Salem Press, 1989.

"Eugene Paul Wigner: A Towering Figure of Modern Physics." Erich Vogt. *Physics Today* 48, no. 12 (December, 1995).

(*Raymond D. Cooper*)

(The Nobel Foundation)

Maurice H. F. Wilkins

Areas of Achievement: Biology, genetics, and physics

Contribution: Wilkins' studies of the X-ray diffraction pattern of deoxyribonucleic acid (DNA) helped establish the double helix structure of the molecule.

Dec. 15, 1916	Born in Pongaroa, New Zealand
1922	Moves to England, where he enters the King Edward VI School
1938	Earns a degree in physics from Cambridge University
1938-1939	At the University of Birmingham, conducts graduate research on radar
1940	Earns a Ph.D. from St. John's College in Birmingham
1944	Relocated to the University of California, Berkeley
1945	Becomes a lecturer at St. Andrews University, Scotland
1946	Joins the faculty of King's College in London
1955-1970	Named deputy director of the biophysics unit of the Medical Research Council
1962-1970	Serves as a professor of molecular biology at King's College
1970-1972	Promoted to director of the biophysics unit
1970-1981	Named a professor of biophysics at King's College
1972-1974	Directs the neurobiology unit
1974-1980	Again serves as director of biophysics unit of the Medical Research Council
1981	Named professor emeritus

(The Nobel Foundation)

Early Life

Maurice Hugh Frederick Wilkins was born December 15, 1916, in Pongaroa, New Zealand, as the son of Irish immigrants. At the age of six, Wilkins was brought to England, where he attended the King Edward VI School in Birmingham.

In 1938, Wilkins was graduated from Cambridge University with a degree in physics. He joined the Ministry of Home Security and Aircraft Production and, while at the same time working on his doctorate, conducted research in the newly developing technology of radar. In 1940, he was awarded his Ph.D. from St. John's College.

Great Britain was at war, and Wilkins carried on with his research in the Ministry of Home Security. He was assigned to the group working on the separation of uranium isotopes, a process later used in the development of the atomic bomb. In 1944, Wilkins was relocated to the University of California, Berkeley, where he continued his work on isotope separation.

Research into DNA Structure

Like many physicists after World War II, Wilkins became disheartened with the military applications of his research, and he began looking into other areas. Ultimately, his interest in biology was influenced by a book written by Erwin Schrödinger entitled *What Is Life?* (1944). In the book, Schrödinger suggests that physics could be applied to an understanding of life itself. In essence, he was creating a field called biophysics.

In 1945, Wilkins joined John Randall, his former professor, at St. Andrews University in Scotland. The next year, the two physicists became instrumental in the establishment of the Medical Research Council's biophysics unit at King's College in London, with the idea of merging the fields of physics and biology.

X-Ray Diffraction Studies of DNA

Although James D. Watson and Francis Crick are correctly noted for their achievement in determining the structure of deoxyribonucleic acid (DNA), the diffraction studies of Wilkins and Rosalind E. Franklin were critical in confirming that work.

In 1944, Oswald Avery and his coworkers demonstrated the role of DNA as genetic material in cells. The precise structure of the molecule, however, remained uncertain into the 1950's.

During World War II, Wilkins served as part of the British team assigned to the Manhattan Project, the U.S. development of the atomic bomb. Disillusioned by the ramifications of this work, Wilkins decided to apply his knowledge of physics to biology. In particular, he became interested in the structure of DNA and in 1946 began this research as a member of the faculty at King's College in London.

Although DNA was relatively easy to isolate, what appeared to be a complicated structure made it difficult to study. Initially, Wilkins observed a sample of DNA using a microscope, illuminating the molecule and observing the reflection of light. While manipulating the sample in a small volume of gelatin, he observed the fibrous nature of the DNA molecule.

Correctly assuming that if indeed DNA was a fiber, it should be amenable to X-ray diffraction studies, Wilkins began to analyze the material. In this procedure, X rays were directed through a prepared crystalline sample of the material. Depending on the spacing of individual atoms in the DNA, the X rays would be bent, or diffracted, into a pattern. Through analysis of the pattern, Wilkins hoped to work out a structure.

In 1951, Wilkins was joined at King's College by Franklin, a physical chemist who was prepared to carry out the research begun by Wilkins. Their professional relationship, while often less than smooth, would significantly complement each other's work.

The sharp pattern of the diffraction observed in the crystallography studies suggested certain characteristics for the DNA. The molecule was in the form of a spiral, or helix. Further, the nucleotide bases that made up the DNA were observed in a regular pattern, suggesting a form of steps. Wilkins thought that the molecule was a double helix; because of its width, it was probably composed of two strands.

Watson and Crick correctly deduced the structure first. The diffraction studies carried out by both Wilkins and Franklin, however, quickly confirmed that Watson and Crick were correct in their suggestion of a double helix.

The teams of Watson and Crick and of Wilkins and Franklin published their work in the same issue of the journal *Nature* in 1953. Determination of the structure of the genetic material made possible the burgeoning field of molecular biology and later of biotechnology. Wilkins, Watson, and Crick were awarded the 1962 Nobel Prize in Physiology or Medicine for their work; Franklin had died in 1958.

Bibliography

The Double Helix. James D. Watson. New York: Signet Books, 1968.

The Eighth Day of Creation. Horace Judson. Cold Spring Harbor, N.Y.: Cold Spring Harbor Press, 1996.

The Path to the Double Helix. Robert Olby. Seattle: University of Washington Press, 1974.

Wilkins began his work on the structure of deoxyribonucleic acid (DNA).

By 1951, he had developed the X-ray diffraction techniques that he would use in deducing the structure of DNA. That year, he was also joined by Rosalind E. Franklin. Part colleagues and part competitors, Franklin and Wilkins spent most of the next two years trying to understand the pattern demonstrated by their DNA preparations.

They were beaten in this endeavor by James D. Watson and Francis Crick. Nevertheless, Wilkins and Franklin published their work in papers adjoining that of Watson and Crick.

Awards and Recognition

In 1962, Wilkins, Watson, and Crick were awarded the Nobel Prize in Physiology or Medicine. Wilkins also received the Albert Lasker Award in 1960 and several honorary doctorates. In 1959, he was named a Fellow of the Royal Society of King's College.

Wilkins continued his work with nucleic acids. In the 1960's, he began work on ribonucleic acid (RNA), showing that it too could possess a helical structure. He became director of the Medical Research Council's biophysics unit in 1970 and of its neurobiology unit in 1972. In 1981, he was named professor emeritus at King's College.

Bibliography
By Wilkins
"Physical Studies of Nucleic Acids: Nucleic Acid—An Extensible Molecule?," *Nature*, 1951 (with R. Gosling and W. Seeds)

"Molecular Structure of Deoxypentose Nucleic Acids," *Nature*, 1953 (with A. Stokes and H. Wilson)

"A New Configuration of Deoxyribonucleic Acid," *Nature*, 1958 (with D. Marvin and M. Spencer)

"Molecular Configuration of Nucleic Acids," *Science*, 1963

"X-Ray Diffraction Study of the Structure of Nucleohistone and Nucleoprotamines," *Journal of Molecular Biology*, 1963 (with G. Zubay)

"A Note on Reversible Dissociation of Deoxyribonucleohistone," *Journal of Molecular Biology*, 1964 (with Zubay)

About Wilkins
Nobel Prize Winners: An H. W. Wilson Biographical Dictionary. Tyler Wasson, ed. New York: H. W. Wilson, 1987.

The Nobel Prize Winners: Physiology or Medicine. Frank N. Magill, ed. Pasadena, Calif.: Salem Press, 1991.

Notable Twentieth-Century Scientists. Emily J. McMurray, ed. Detroit: Gale Research, 1995.

(Richard Adler)

Sir Geoffrey Wilkinson

Area of Achievement: Chemistry
Contribution: Wilkinson was a pioneer in analyzing the chemistry of organometallic "sandwich" compounds.

July 14, 1921	Born in Springside, near Todmorden, Yorkshire, England
1941	Earns a B.Sc., first in his class, from the Imperial College of Science and Technology, London University
1943-1946	Serves as a junior scientific officer in the U.K.-U.S.-Canada Atomic Energy Project in Canada
1946	Earns a Ph.D. from Imperial College
1946-1950	Works at the Lawrence Radiation Laboratory
1950-1951	Serves as a research associate at the Massachusetts Institute of Technology (MIT)
1951-1955	Appointed an assistant professor at Harvard University
1955-1978	Named chair of inorganic chemistry, Imperial College
1965	Elected a Fellow of the Royal Society of London
1973	Wins the Nobel Prize in Chemistry
1976	Knighted by Queen Elizabeth II
1978-1988	Appointed Sir Edward Frankland Professor of Inorganic Chemistry, Imperial College
1983-1996	Founds and edits the journal *Polyhedron*
1988-1996	Named professor emeritus
1996	Wins the Davy Medal of the Royal Society of London
Sept. 26, 1996	Dies in London, England

Early Life

Geoffrey Wilkinson, the oldest of three children, was born in Springside in a house that, like most of the village, has been demolished as being unfit for habitation. His father and paternal grandfather were house painters, and his mother worked in the local cotton mill. Wilkinson was introduced to chemistry by his uncle, who owned a small chemical factory and who allowed Geoff (as he preferred to be called by students and colleagues even after he was knighted) to play in the laboratory and accompany him on visits to chemical companies.

Through a Royal Scholarship, Wilkinson attended the Imperial College of Science and Technology in London from 1939 to 1941. After his graduation, he continued to conduct research there under H. V. A. Briscoe before joining a number of young chemists developing nuclear energy in Canada from 1943 to 1946.

For the next four years, he worked with future Nobel chemistry laureate Glenn T. Seaborg in the Lawrence Radiation Laboratory at the University of California, Berkeley, using a cyclotron to study radioisotopes of the lanthanides (the so-called rare earth elements).

(The Nobel Foundation)

Sandwich Compounds

An unusually stable organic iron complex called ferrocene led to the recognition of a hitherto unknown type of chemical bonding and to the discovery of countless completely new organometallic compounds.

In 1951, a new and unusually stable complex between one iron atom and two cyclopentadienide anions was reported by T. J. Kealy and P. L. Pauson. They assigned to the complex the structure of a central iron atom with a single σ bond on either side attached to one of the five carbon atoms of the flat, planar cyclopentadienide ring.

Wilkinson immediately recognized that this structure could not account for the compound's stability. He proposed that all five carbon atoms of each ring contribute equally to the π-bonding to the iron atom, resulting in a "sandwich" in which the iron atom is centered between two "slices" of cyclopentadienide "bread."

Robert B. Woodward had the same idea, and Wilkinson collaborated with him to prove the correctness of this structure through measurements of the compound's infrared and ultraviolet spectra, magnetic susceptibility, and dipole moment. Ernst Otto Fischer and W. Pfab independently confirmed the structure by X-ray diffraction.

Woodward found that the aromatic character of the cyclopentadienide rings was similar enough to that of benzene to permit the compound, subsequently named "ferrocene" in analogy with benzene, to undergo classical electrophilic ("electron-loving") aromatic substitution reactions. Wilkinson prepared ruthenium and cobalt analogues.

The entire class of transition metal and cyclopentadienyl compounds, termed "metallocenes," became known as sandwich compounds.

Bibliography

"Dicyclopentadienyliron." S. A. Miller, J. A. Tebboth, and J. F. Tremaine. *Journal of the Chemical Society* (1952).

"The Discovery of Ferrocene, the First Sandwich Compound." George B. Kauffman. *Journal of Chemical Education* 60 (March, 1983).

"A New Type of Organo-Iron Compound." T. J. Kealy and P. L. Pauson. *Nature* 168 (1951).

According to Seaborg, who presented him with the American Chemical Society's Centennial Foreign Fellowship in 1976, Wilkinson "has made more isotopes of the chemical elements than any other human being." He even accomplished the ancient alchemists' dream of transmuting another element into gold.

Organometallic Chemistry

Because Briscoe advised Wilkinson that he was unlikely to find an academic position in nuclear chemistry in England, in 1950 Wilkinson became a research associate at the Massachusetts Institute of Technology (MIT), where he returned to his first interest as a student—transition metal complexes such as carbonyls (carbon monoxide compounds).

In 1951, Wilkinson became an assistant professor at Harvard University, largely because of his background in nuclear research. Although he carried out some nuclear chemistry there, since he had already begun work on olefin complexes at MIT, he was extremely interested in T. J. Kealy and P. L. Pauson's discovery of an iron and cyclopentadienyl complex in 1951. Together with future Nobel chemistry laureate Robert B. Woodward, he recognized this complex's remarkable molecular structure as a "sandwich compound," work that led to his own Nobel Prize in Chemistry in 1973.

Return to Imperial College

In 1955, Wilkinson succeeded Briscoe in the chair of inorganic chemistry at Imperial College, the only such established chair in the United Kingdom. There, he spent the remaining four decades of his life, working with a relatively small number of students and postdoctoral fellows, almost entirely on the transition metal organometallic complexes.

Wilkinson prepared hundreds of new complexes of ruthenium, rhodium, rhenium, and olefins. His discovery of the so-called Wilkinson's catalyst led to methods for the synthesis of pharmaceuticals. His rhodium catalysts for the industrial hydroformylation of olefins to produce fuels ("syngas") and the resulting patents enabled him to support his research group after his retirement in 1988.

Wilkinson was elected to the Royal Society of London in 1965 and was knighted in 1976. He died suddenly of cardiac arrest in his London home in 1996 at the age of seventy-five.

Bibliography

By Wilkinson

"The Structure of Iron *bis*-Cyclopentadienyl," *Journal of the American Chemical Society*, 1952 (with M. Rosenblum, M. C. Whiting, and Robert B. Woodward)

"Cyclopentadienyl and Arene Metal Compounds" (with F. Albert Cotton) in *Progress in Inorganic Chemistry*, vol. 1, 1959 (Cotton, ed.)

Advanced Inorganic Chemistry: A Comprehensive Text, 1962 (with Cotton)

"The Long Search for Stable Transition Metal Alkyls," *Science*, 1974

"The Iron Sandwich: A Recollection of the First Four Months," *Journal of Organometallic Chemistry*, 1975

Basic Inorganic Chemistry, 1976 (with Cotton)

About Wilkinson

"Geoffrey Wilkinson." Peter V. Bonnesen. In *Nobel Laureates in Chemistry, 1901-1992*, edited by Laylin K. James. Washington, D.C.: American Chemical Society, 1993.

"Geoffrey Wilkinson (1921-96)." John Meurig Thomas and Edward Abel. *Nature* 384 (November 21, 1996).

"Prof. Sir Geoffrey Wilkinson." Malcolm Green and William P. Griffith. *The Independent* (October 1, 1996).

"Sir Geoffrey Wilkinson 1921-96." W. P. Griffith. *Chemistry in Britain* 33 (January, 1997).

(George B. Kauffman)

Daniel Hale Williams

Area of Achievement: Medicine
Contribution: Williams performed the first successful heart surgery, was among the first to suture the spleen successfully, and founded the first interracial hospital in the United States.

Jan. 18, 1856	Born in Hollidaysburg, Pennsylvania
1883	Earns a medical degree from Chicago Medical College
1884	Joins the surgical staff of South Side Dispensary, Chicago
1884	Made attending physician for the Protestant Orphan Asylum
1885	Named demonstrator of anatomy at Chicago Medical College
1889	Appointed to the Illinois State Board of Health
1891	Founds Provident Hospital for African Americans in Chicago
1893	Performs the first successful heart (pericardium) surgery
1894-1898	Serves as surgeon in chief of Freedmen's Hospital in Washington, D.C.
1895	Helps found the National Medical Association
1899	Named visiting professor of clinical surgery at Meharry Medical College in Nashvillee
1902	Performs the second successful spleen operation in the United States
1912	Made associate attending surgeon at St. Luke's Hospital, Chicago
1913	Becomes a founding member of the American College of Surgeons
Aug. 4, 1931	Dies in Idle-wild, Michigan

Early Life

Born in 1856, Daniel Hale Williams grew up in a family that had long fought to establish rights for African Americans. Williams' father, a barber, helped found the Equal Rights League in 1864 to call for better educational opportunities and the right to vote. He died when Daniel was only eleven years old, but Williams always remembered his father's advice, to "get all the education you can."

Education

Williams was graduated from a high school in Janesville, Wisconsin, in 1877. In 1878, he apprenticed himself to a local physician, Henry Palmer, to begin the study of medicine.

After completing his apprenticeship, Williams received his medical degree at Chicago Medical College in 1883. He performed minor operations at the South Side Dispensary in Chicago and practiced surgical techniques in the college's anatomical laboratory as often as he could.

A Gifted Surgeon

Williams began his career when the new principles and methods of antisepsis and asepsis (sterilization against disease-bearing and infectious microorganisms) were being developed. These techniques greatly reduced the risk of infection during operations and made lifesaving surgery on many areas of the body possible.

Williams was a pioneer in developing the surgical techniques needed to operate on these new regions. In 1893, Williams became the first in the world to perform a successful operation on the pericardium, the sac surrounding the heart. In 1902, he became the second in the United States to suture a spleen successfully.

Williams thoroughly researched other surgeons' work on similar cases before each operation and was never afraid to try new techniques. His training with Palmer and his long hours of practice in the anatomy laboratory had also given him the knowledge, skills, and confidence needed to operate rapidly and to make quick decisions, abilities essential to sav-

Heart Surgery

Williams demonstrated that the chest could be opened and successful surgery performed on the heart without risking death from infection.

In July, 1893, Williams watched the condition of a patient with a stab wound to the chest steadily deteriorate. He knew that the knife had probably penetrated the heart. Many surgeons were afraid to open the chest for fear of causing infection, but Williams knew that the techniques of asepsis could prevent infection. He had also read about the recent work of scientists who argued that heart surgery was a theoretical possibility and who had performed successful operations on animals. Most doctors believed, however, that no good surgeon should risk the life of a human patient.

Williams decided to attempt the surgery. After having the operating room thoroughly cleansed, he made an incision between the patient's ribs and cut through the rib cartilage. He tied off a damaged artery and found a wound in the pericardium, through which he could see a very slight wound to the heart that was not bleeding.

Williams decided that the heart wound did not need repair and sewed up the wounded pericardium after irrigating the area with warm saline solution. He then reattached the cartilage and closed the incisions. Three weeks later, he operated on the patient to remove fluids that had drained from the irritated area and accumulated in the pleural sac. No sign of infection was present.

With this surgery, Williams opened the way to ever more complex repairs of not only wounded but also diseased hearts.

Bibliography

The Evolution of Cardiac Surgery. Harris B. Shumacker, Jr. Bloomington: Indiana University Press, 1992.

The History of Cardiac Surgery, 1896-1955. Stephen L. Johnson. Baltimore: The Johns Hopkins University Press, 1970.

The History of Cardiothoracic Surgery from Early Times. Raymond Hurt. New York: Parthenon, 1996.

(The Associated Publishers, Inc.)

ing patients in the days before blood transfusions and X rays.

Dedicated Teacher and Administrator

In 1891, Williams founded Provident Hospital and Training School in Chicago; it was the first interracial hospital and African American nurses' training school in the United States. Williams also helped create professional medical societies for African American doctors to share their expertise.

African Americans had little access to good medical care and few opportunities to study medicine in Williams' time. African American medical students were barred from watching operations in white hospitals. Williams dedicated his life to building an African American medical community to provide better care for his people, beginning with Provident Hospital.

In 1894, he was appointed chief surgeon of Freedman's Hospital in Washington, D.C., which had been established to care for the many impoverished former slaves who had come to the city after the Civil War. Williams reorganized the hospital and added departments of bacteriology and pathology. He again established training programs for African American doctors and nurses. With Williams in charge, the death rate at the hospital dropped dramatically. Of the 533 surgical patients treated there in his first year alone, only eight died.

Travels Across the Country

After leaving Freedman's Hospital, Williams began yearly visits to Meharry Medical College in Nashville, Tennessee, to demonstrate surgical techniques. He also performed operations in people's homes all around the country, saving lives and teaching young African American doctors the art and science of surgery.

Williams retired from surgical practice in 1920 and died in 1931 in Idle-wild, Michigan. His hospital and training school, Provident, provided the model for as many as forty similar institutions in twenty states.

Bibliography

By Williams

"Stab Wound of the Heart and Pericardium. Suture of the Pericardium. Recovery. Patient Alive Three Years Afterward," *New York Medical Record*, 1897

"Penetrating Wounds of the Chest, Perforating the Diaphragm, and Involving the Abdominal Viscera: Case of Successful Spleen Suture for Traumatic Haemorrhage," *Annals of Surgery*, 1904

About Williams

Daniel Hale Williams: Negro Surgeon. Helen Buckler. New York: Pitman, 1954.

"Moses of Negro Medicine." *Ebony* 10, no. 4 (February, 1955).

Sure Hands, Strong Heart: The Life of Daniel Hale Williams. Lillie Patterson. Nashville: Abingdon, 1981.

(Ann Binder)

Thomas Willis

Area of Achievement: Medicine
Contribution: Willis was a skillful anatomist who clarified the circulation in the brain, in a region which is called the circle of Willis in order to commemorate his achievement.

Jan. 27, 1621	Born in Great Bedwyn, Wiltshire, England
1639-1660	Earns B.A., M.A., bachelor of medicine, and doctor of medicine degrees from Christ Church College, Oxford University
1644-1646	Fights for the Royalist cause in the army of Charles I
1650	Resuscitates a young woman after she was hanged in Oxford
1660	Becomes Sedleian Professor of Natural Philosophy at Oxford
1664	Publishes *Cerebri anatomi* (*The Anatomy of the Brain*, 1681)
1667	Publishes *Pathologiae cerebri et nervosi generis specimen* (*An Essay of the Pathology of the Brain and Nervous Stock in Which Convulsive Diseases Are Treated Of*, 1681)
1672	Publishes *De anima brutorum* (*Two Discourses Concerning the Soul of Brutes, Which Is That of the Vital and Sensitive of Man*, 1683)
Nov. 11, 1675	Dies in London, England

Early Life

Thomas Willis was born in 1621 as the son of a yeoman in Wiltshire, England. A large part of his life was spent at Christ Church College, Oxford, where he received a B.A. in 1639, an M.A. in 1642, a B.M. (bachelor of medicine) in 1646, and a D.M. (doctorate in medicine) in 1660. From 1660, Willis had a lucrative practice as a physician in Oxford and London.

Like many of his peers, he took part in the English Civil War (1642-1649) and probably fought in the earl of Dover's auxiliary regiment, which successfully defended the city of Oxford against the Parliamentary forces.

Experiments at Oxford

Willis' first interest as a student at Oxford was in chemistry, and with others he formed a "Clubb" that met weekly at his lodgings to perform experiments. By the 1650's, members of his circle included physicist and chemist Robert Boyle, architect Christopher Wren, and physicist Robert Hooke. Willis' first published work in 1656 was on the chemical topic of fermentation and how it caused all growth and change in plants and animals.

As a follower of William Harvey, the discoverer of the circulation of the blood, Willis also undertook research involving studies in em-

(Library of Congress)

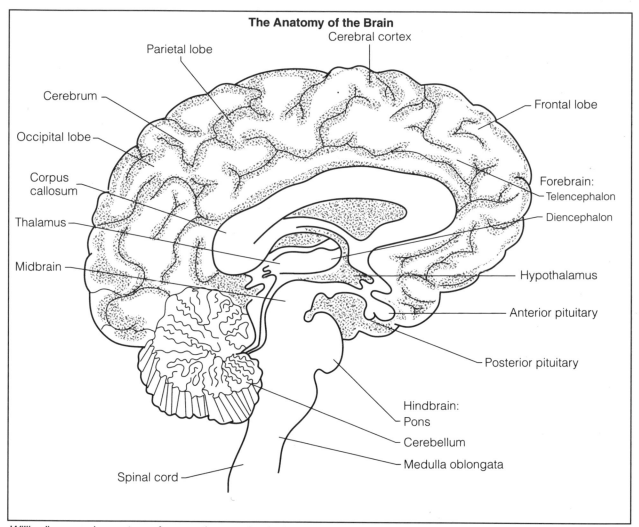

The Anatomy of the Brain

Cerebral cortex

Parietal lobe

Cerebrum

Occipital lobe

Corpus callosum

Thalamus

Midbrain

Frontal lobe

Forebrain: Telencephalon

Diencephalon

Hypothalamus

Anterior pituitary

Posterior pituitary

Hindbrain: Pons

Cerebellum

Medulla oblongata

Spinal cord

Willis discovered a system of connecting arteries in the brain, now known as the circle of Willis. (Hans & Cassady, Inc.)

bryology, morbid anatomy, clinical observations, animal experiments, and comparative anatomy. All these anatomical, physiological, and chemical, and clinical findings were incorporated in Willis' 1664 masterpiece on the structure of the brain—*Cerebri anatomi* (*The Anatomy of the Brain*, 1681). The book was beautifully illustrated by Wren and remained a classic in neurology into the nineteenth century.

In 1650, Willis became famous for helping resuscitate a servant girl after she was hanged for infanticide and brought to a fellow physician's house to be dissected by Willis and others. An account of her resuscitation and later life was published as a broadsheet in 1651 by Richard Watkins as *Newes from the Dead: Or, A True and Exact Narration of the Miraculous Deliverance of Anne Greene.*

In 1660, Willis was made Sedleian Professor of Natural Philosophy (or science) at Oxford, an academic post that he kept until his death from pneumonia in 1675. He was survived by his second wife and two of his eight children.

Bibliography
By Willis

Diatribae duae medico-philosophicae . . . , 1659 (of fevers and urine)

Cerebri anatomi: Cui accessit nervorum descriptio et usus, 1664 (*The Anatomy of the Brain,* 1681)

Pathologiae cerebri et nervosi generis specimen, 1667 (*An Essay of the Pathology of the Brain and Nervous Stock in Which Convulsive Diseases Are Treated Of,* 1681)

The Circle of Willis

Through vivisection and dissection, Willis demonstrated that there was a circle of arteries at the base of the brain by which, if any of the carotid or vertebral arteries became blocked, the remaining ones could maintain blood flow to all the areas of the brain. The circle of arteries was named after him.

As a believer in the mechanical philosophy of the seventeenth century, Willis placed his anatomical findings into a chemical mechanical framework. With Richard Lower, he performed extensive dissections and vivisections of animals in order to come to an understanding of how the brain operates. In demonstrating what became known as the circle of Willis, he tied off both the carotid arteries of a dog, with no adverse results. He injected ink into one artery of a brain and observed it flowing out from the others.

In his book *Anatomi cerebri* (1664; *The Anatomy of the Brain*, 1681), Willis followed the paths of the cranial nerves and classified them according to the functions that they performed. Six of his classifications are still in use. Medieval anatomists had argued that the functions of the brain originated in the ventricles, but Willis located them in the cerebrum and cerebellum , and he drew up a detailed outline of which parts of the brain were responsible for voluntary movements (the cerebrum), involuntary movements (the cerebellum), imagination (the corpus callosum), and memory (the cortex).

Willis also related certain psychiatric problems, such as delirium and insomnia, to differing regions of the brain. This research had a profound influence on the sciences of psychiatry and neurology.

Bibliography
Basic Neuroscience: Anatomy and Physiology. A. C. Guyton. Philadelphia: W. B. Saunders, 1987.
Clinical Anatomy in Action. J. Pegington. 3 vols. London: Churchill Livingstone, 1988.
The Human Brain: A Photographic Guide. N. Gluhbegovic and T. H. Williams. New York: Harper & Row, 1980.

De motu musculari, 1670 (of the motion of the muscles)
De anima brutorum, 1672 (*Two Discourses Concerning the Soul of Brutes, Which Is That of the Vital and Sensitive of Man*, 1683)

About Willis
The Anatomy of the Brain and Nerves. William Feindel, ed. Montreal: McGill University Press, 1965.

Thomas Willis as a Physician. Kenneth Dewhurst. Los Angeles: William Andrew Clark Memorial Library, 1964.
Willis' Oxford Lectures. Kenneth Dewhurst. Oxford, England: Sandford, 1980.

(Lynda Stephenson Payne)

Edward O. Wilson

Areas of Achievement: Biology and zoology

Contribution: Wilson's fundamental work on ants also led him to produce important sociobiology theories about many species, including humans.

June 10, 1929	Born in Birmingham, Alabama
1949	Receives a B.S. at the University of Alabama-Tuscaloosa
1950	Earns an M.S. at the University of Alabama-Tuscaloosa
1954	Participates in an expedition to New Guinea in order to study ants
1955	Receives a Ph.D. from Harvard University
1956	Becomes an assistant professor at Harvard
1958	Promoted to associate professor at Harvard
1964	Becomes a Harvard full professor of zoology
1971	Publishes *Insect Societies*
1975	Publishes *Sociobiology: The New Synthesis*
1979	Wins the Pulitzer Prize for his 1978 book *On Human Nature*
1990	Wins the Gold Medal of the Worldwide Fund for Nature
1990	Awarded Sweden's Crafoord Prize
1993	Given Japan's International Prize for Biology
1994	With Bert Holldobler, publishes *Journey to the Ants*

Early Life

Edward Osborne Wilson was born in Birmingham, Alabama, as son of Edward and Inez Freeman Wilson, who divorced in 1937. Young Edward attended about a dozen primary and secondary schools in an odyssey that began around the time of his parents' divorce. The schools were spread out over many cities because his father, with whom Edward most often lived, was an accountant who led a life of short-term assignments.

Notable among these institutions were spit-and-polish Gulf Coast Military Academy, in Gulfport, Mississippi, and city school Agnes McReynolds Elementary School, in Pensacola, Florida. Their varied operation modes and student populations helped to mold Wilson into an independent thinker. It also appears from Wilson's autobiography *The Naturalist* (1994) that loneliness caused by many moves developed Wilson's love for nature and science.

One important person in his early life was Mrs. Belle Raub, a family friend with whom Edward lived on and off for several years and whom he described, in *The Naturalist*, as a grandmotherly person attentive to all of his needs. Belle was probably a needed anchor in continued movement between mother, father, cities, and schools.

The Wilson odyssey continued with his entry into Murphy High School, in Mobile, Alabama, among others, followed by his attainment of a B.S. and an M.S. in biology at the University of Alabama-Tuscaloosa, in 1949 and 1950, respectively. There, he extensively explored the world of ants. He then went to Harvard University to study for a Ph.D.

From Harvard to New Guinea

At Harvard, Wilson continued to study ants and began to think about their use as models for sociobiology. For example, during his Ph.D. work on an ant genus *Lasius*, Wilson and coauthor William L. Brown identified "character displacement," in which two closely related species rapidly undergo disparate evolution in order to diminish any possible interspecies competition or hybridization into one species. In *The Naturalist*, Wilson generously points out that the phenomenon had already been shown, although not named, by another scientist.

An additional high point of those Harvard years was a ten-month expedition, from 1954 to 1955, in New Guinea, in order to study ants.

Six weeks after his return to the United States in September, 1955, Wilson married Renee Kelly.

Harvard and Ants

Wilson's endeavors showed that he was an outstanding researcher. Therefore, in 1956, a year after receiving a Ph.D. in biology from Harvard, he was made an assistant professor in its biology department. The job first appeared impermanent, as most Harvard junior faculty are weeded out. In 1958, however, Wilson received an offer of a tenured associated professorship in entomology at Stanford University.

Harvard reacted to the threat of his loss with its own offer, and Wilson stayed.

Wilson became a professor of zoology at Harvard in 1964. His other academic positions include a later appointment as Baird Professor of Science and a curatorship in entomology at the Museum of Comparative Zoology. Among his early discoveries was that ants often communicate via chemical substances called pheromones, with distinct tastes/odors. Wilson also formulated a taxon cycle, in which speciation and dispersal of species are linked to varying habitats that creatures encounter as individual populations spread out in the

Ant Pheromones Trigger Behavioral Events

Pheromones are chemical substances made by an organism to alter the behavior of other individuals of the same species. The existence of pheromones enables communication between ants and the formation and survival of ant societies.

Wilson believed that ants communicated with each other in fixed-action behavior patterns, via chemicals that were made by each individual and smelled or tasted by other members of their ant species. He formed this opinion from research which found that ants probably could not hear and were unable to see in their subterranean nests.

In order to study this subject, Wilson first divided ant behavior into a number of individual actions. He did so by carefully watching ants living in glass-sided nests that he designed for such use in the laboratory. Wilson and chemist collaborators then identified the signal substances that triggered these actions.

For example, Wilson noted that when an ant forager found a food item too big to bring back alone, it would touch its abdomen to the ground repeatedly, while quickly returning to the ant nest by a direct route. This behavior seemed to Wilson to resemble the use of a pen to trace an invisible dotted line. Therefore, he surgically removed all the ant's abdominal organs and searched them for signaling substances.

Each organ was crushed and its contents placed on a wooden applicator. Then, the moist applicator was used to lay "trails" from anthills

to food or to places lacking food. The food signal, made in the ant's Dufor glands and identified chemically, caused ants to seek and expect food. All these signal substances (triggers), made by one ant and altering the behavior of other species members, are called pheromones.

Wilson also identified a number of other ant pheromones, such as those used to signal alarm, the recognition of the death of another ant, and the selection of a queen. For example, the signal that an ant is dead and should be removed from an anthill is oleic acid. When daubed on a live ant, a little of this fatty substance causes other ants to remove it bodily from a nest, repeatedly, until the oleic acid either dissipates or is removed by the ant's washing.

The discovery of ant pheromones led other scientists to clarify the basis for many insect biological reactions. It has also become clear that even humans may respond to some pheromones undetectable to other mammal species; for example, humans falling in love is now thought by some to be attributable, in part, to pheromones.

Bibliography

Biology: Life on Earth. Gerald Audesirk and Teresa Audesirk. 2d ed. New York: Macmillan, 1993.
Journey to the Ants: A Story of Scientific Exploration. Bert Holldobler and Edward O. Wilson. Cambridge, Mass.: The Belknap Press of Harvard University Press, 1994.
The Naturalist. Edward O. Wilson. Covelo, Calif.: Island Press, 1994.

Biogeography

Biogeography is the systematic study of the geographical distribution of plant and animal groups, as well as its basis.

A basic biogeography theory is species origin and survival in various world regions as a result of chance starts, such as air dissemination or immigration across land bridges, followed by survival of the fittest.

Major biogeographers at first posed two working hypotheses. One was that surviving organisms arose at the poles and moved toward temperate regions, winning out over organisms already in those regions because they were more adaptable. The other hypothesis involved dissemination from mild environments to harsher ones. Wilson suggested that the spread and dominance of animal groups was related to where they lived, not what they were. He claimed that organisms exist as taxons, which are subspecies, species, or a genus related by common descent. In addition, he envisioned biogeographic dispersion favoring organisms in taxons that lived in marginal regions, such as near rivers or the sunny margins of rain forests, because such organisms were very flexible, had fewer competitors, and could disseminate easily.

Wilson also supposed a taxon cycle in which survival is related to flexibility, size of land mass, and an ever-changing balance of nature that alters a taxon's successes from region to region and across time.

Bibliography
Journey to the Ants: A Story of Scientific Exploration. Bert Holldobler and Edward O. Wilson. Cambridge, Mass.: The Belknap Press of Harvard University Press, 1994.

The Naturalist. Edward O. Wilson. Covelo, Calif.: Island Press, 1994.

Sociobiology and Altruism

Sociobiology explores the biological basis of social behavior of humans and other animals. It may even explain altruism, the phenomenon of unselfishness and self-sacrifice.

Sociobiology attempts to identify the biological basis of social behavior. Wilson produced several valuable propositions which meld biology and social behavior. One generalization often used is that basic biological principles form the foundation for the social behavior of organisms, from ants to humans. Wilson, however, did not sweep the role of the environment out of the picture. He clearly noted that many environmental issues are key sociological determinants.

Another particularly interesting aspect of his sociobiological theories is that anomalous behavior such as altruism may have a genetic basis and have evolved via Darwinian natural selection. This theory provides food for thought, as conventional wisdom argues that natural selection favors only those behavior traits that increase or ensure individual—and therefore species—survival. At first glance, an attribute such as altruism does not fit because it may have the opposite effect, with some organisms perishing for others of their kindred.

Closer inspection, however, points out that altruistic self-sacrifice has survival value for the group of common genes found in closely related organisms within a species. Not only does such behavior conform to natural selection, but a brand-new concept—the preservation of important genes, not simply individuals—becomes a major focus of evolution as well. This concept and others identified by Wilson led to much insightful work by other scientists, as well as beginnings of a synthesis of thought between biologists and social scientists.

Bibliography
The Naturalist. Edward O. Wilson. Covelo, Calif.: Island Press, 1994.

On Human Nature. Edward O. Wilson. Cambridge, Mass.: Harvard University Press, 1978.

Sociobiology: The New Synthesis. Edward O. Wilson. Cambridge, Mass.: The Belknap Press of Harvard University Press, 1974.

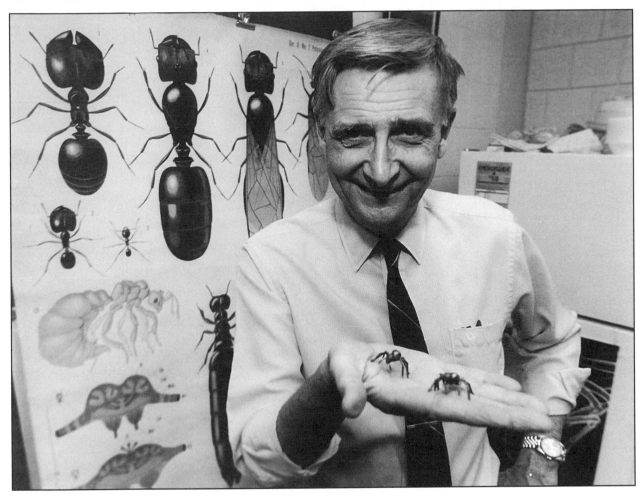

Wilson and his favorite research topic—ants. (AP/Wide World Photos)

world. In 1971, Wilson published *Insect Societies*, a definitive work on ants and other society-forming insects.

Ants and Sociobiology: A Synthesis

Wilson wrote many other important works, including some on sociobiology, a field that explores the biological basis of social behavior. In fact, he became a major figure in the development of this area of science. In the book *Sociobiology: The New Synthesis* (1975), he presented a number of theories on the biology of social behavior in a wide variety of species.

Particularly compelling and provocative was the concept that biological principles of animal society formation apply to human social behavior, described in the book chapter "From Sociobiology to Sociology." Wilson then published the 1979 Pulitzer Prize-winning

book *On Human Nature* (1978). In this work, sociobiology and genes are linked to human traits such as ethics and sexuality.

Works by Wilson also include *Journey to the Ants: A Story of Scientific Exploration* (1994), with Bert Holldobler, a book aimed at the general public. Wilson has thus made a thorough examination of ants and a quantum leap to sociobiology/sociology. It is no wonder that he received many honors, including the Gold Medal of the Worldwide Fund for Nature in 1990, Sweden's Crafoord Prize in 1990, and Japan's International Prize for Biology in 1993.

Bibliography
By Wilson
"Character Displacement," *Systematic Zoology*, 1956 (with W. L. Brown)
Insect Societies, 1971

Sociobiology: The New Synthesis, 1975
On Human Nature, 1978
The Naturalist, 1994
Journey to the Ants: A Story of Scientific Exploration, 1994 (with Bert Holldobler)

About Wilson

Journey to the Ants: A Story of Scientific Exploration. Bert Holldobler and Edward O. Wilson. Cambridge, Mass.: The Belknap Press of Harvard University Press, 1994.

The Naturalist. Edward O. Wilson. Covelo, Calif.: Island Press, 1994.

(Sanford S. Singer)

Georg Wittig

Area of Achievement: Chemistry
Contribution: Wittig, an organic chemist, developed a broad and versatile method for joining carbon units. The Wittig reaction has provided a means of introducing double bonds in specific locations and is extensively used in the synthesis of pharmaceuticals and other complex molecules.

June 16, 1897	Born in Berlin, Germany
1923	Earns a Ph.D. in chemistry from Marburg University
1926	Appointed to the faculty at Marburg as a lecturer
1932-1937	Acts as director of the Technische Hochschule in Braunschweig
1937-1944	Serves as a Special Professor at the University of Freiburg
1944	Accepts an offer to become institute director at the University of Tübingen
1953	Receives the Adolf von Baeyer Medal from the Society of German Chemists
1956-1967	Teaches chemistry at Heidelberg University
1973	Wins the Roger Adams Award of the American Chemical Society
1979	Awarded the Nobel Prize in Chemistry jointly with Herbert C. Brown
1980	Accepts the German Ordens Grosses Verdienstkreuz Award
Aug. 26, 1987	Dies in Heidelberg, West Germany

Early Life

Georg Wittig (pronounced "VIH-tihk") was born in Berlin on June 16, 1897, the son of a

The Wittig Reaction

Organic chemicals are characterized by linked chains of carbon atoms. The Wittig reaction provides a means of adding carbon atoms together to produce carbons joined by double bonds.

In the Wittig reaction, a carbon doubly bonded to an oxygen (an aldehyde or ketone) reacts with a phosphorus ylide to give an olefin or alkene.

Vitamin A acetate can be prepared by reactions shown in the accompanying figure.

Initially, a phosphine (1) reacts with an alkyl halide (2) to form a phosphonium salt (3). This salt is then treated with a strong base to remove a molecule of hydrogen halide and generate the phosphorus ylide (4). Phosphorous ylides are rather stable. The ylide adds to the carbonyl group (5) to give intermediates that eliminate phosphine oxide and generate the new carbon-carbon bonds, as shown in vitamin A acetate (6).

The Wittig reaction is very general and widely applied. A great variety of aldehydes and ketones can be used. The reaction has proven useful in the synthesis of natural compounds such as vitamins A and D and the steroid precursor squalene. Beta carotene, the orange-colored component of carrots, has also been prepared by a Wittig reaction.

Bibliography
Organic Synthesis. Michael B. Smith. New York: McGraw-Hill, 1994.
Ylid Chemistry. William A. Johnson. New York: Academic Press, 1966.

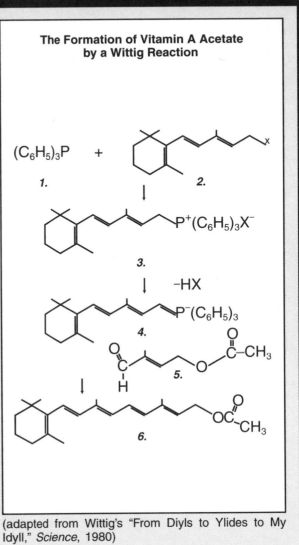

The Formation of Vitamin A Acetate by a Wittig Reaction

(adapted from Wittig's "From Diyls to Ylides to My Idyll," *Science*, 1980)

---

professor of fine arts at the University of Berlin. He was an accomplished pianist and might have pursued a career in the arts rather than the sciences.

Wittig attended school at the Wilhelms Gymnasium in Kassel. In 1916, he began studies at the University of Tübingen, but his undergraduate work was interrupted by service in the military during World War I. For part of this period, he was a prisoner of war in Great Britain.

In 1923, Wittig received his Ph.D. from Marburg University, where he studied chemistry under Karl von Auwers. For the next several years, he taught and conducted research at Marburg, Braunschweig, and Freiburg universities. In his early career, he focused on questions of mechanism and theory rather than on synthesis. He studied diradicals, carbanions, bonding, and molecular structure.

Seminal Discoveries
Wittig became institute director at Tübingen in 1944. It was there that his pioneering work on the preparation of alkenes, carbon compounds with double bonds, was performed using phosphorus ylides.

Wittig did not set out to discover a useful

(The Nobel Foundation)

synthetic method. He was doing fundamental research on the nature of pentavalent group V compounds when an unexpected product formed. Wittig named this unstable nitrogen compound an ylide. He proceeded to repeat the reaction with the element under nitrogen in the periodic chart, phosphorus. The phosphorous ylide was much more stable than the nitrogen one and opened the door to the development of the Wittig reaction.

Practical Applications
In 1956, Wittig moved to Heidelberg University, where he continued to extend the utility of the Wittig reaction. He reacted ylides with numerous carbonyl compounds and demonstrated the wide scope of his method. By the early 1960's, more than a hundred papers on the applications of the Wittig reaction had appeared.

The chemical company BASF engaged Wittig as a consultant for an industrial-scale preparation of vitamin A using an ylide intermediate. Wittig also developed a boron compound that was sold commercially for the determination of sodium ions.

Wittig's continued interest in music was reflected in the name of the review article that he wrote on phosphorous chemistry in 1964: "Variations on the Theme by Staudinger." Hermann Staudinger, a German chemist, had done early work on phosphorous ylides.

Retirement: Idyllic Times
Wittig became professor emeritus at Heidelberg in 1967 and produced fifty papers in the decade after his retirement. He received the Nobel Prize in Chemistry in 1979 at the age of eighty-two, sharing the honor with American Herbert C. Brown. The following year, the German government awarded Wittig the Ordens Grosses Verdienstkreuz its award of highest service. Wittig died on August 26, 1987, in Heidelberg at the age of ninety.

Bibliography
By Wittig
Stereochemie, 1930
"Variations on a Theme by Staudinger," *Pure and Applied Chemistry*, 1964
"From Diyls to Ylides to My Idyll," *Science*, 1980

About Wittig
"George Wittig: Virtuoso of Chemical Synthesis." Robert Shaw. *Nature* 282 (1979).
Notable Twentieth-Century Scientists. Emily J. McMurray, ed. New York: Gale Research, 1995.
"Wittig: Fortune Favors the Prepared Mind." Edwin Vedejs. *Science* 207 (1979).

(Helen M. Burke)

Friedrich Wöhler

Areas of Achievement: Chemistry and medicine

Contribution: Wöhler synthesized urea from ammonium cyanate, thus advancing knowledge of isomerism and striking a blow against the theory of vitalism.

July 31, 1800	Born in Escherheim, near Frankfurt am Main, Germany
1823	Earns an M.D. at the University of Heidelberg
1823-1824	Studies chemical analysis with Jöns Jakob Berzelius in Sweden
1825-1831	Teaches in Berlin
1828	Publishes a description of the synthesis of urea
1831-1836	Teaches in Kassel
1832	With Justus von Liebig, prepares a series of benzoyl derivatives
1836-1882	Serves as a professor of chemistry and pharmacy at the University of Göttingen
1838-1845	Translates Berzelius' textbooks into German
1845	Publishes a method for preparing aluminum
1854	Elected a foreign member of the Royal Society of London
1857	Discovers the first silicon hydrides
1862	Prepares acetylene from calcium carbide
1864	Elected a foreign associate of the Institut de France
1872	Awarded the Copley Medal of the Royal Society of London
Sept. 23, 1882	Dies in Göttingen, Germany

Early Life

Blessed with lively scientific curiosity and supportive parents, Friedrich Wöhler (pronounced "VOY-luhr") received an excellent education in public school and the Gymnasium and took extra instruction in music and languages.

After a year at Marburg University, Wöhler transferred to the University of Heidelberg, where he was awarded a doctorate in medicine in 1823. With the recommendation of his chemistry professor, Leopold Gmelin, Wöhler spent a year in Stockholm studying with Jöns Jakob Berzelius, a master of analytical chemistry.

Wöhler married his cousin Franziska in 1828; they had two children before she died in 1832. In 1834, Wöhler married Julie Pfeiffer, with whom he had four daughters.

Berlin and Kassel

Extending his work on cyanates, Wöhler achieved the synthesis of urea (a component of urine) from ammonium cyanate, gaining considerable fame for this blow against the theory of vitalism.

(Library of Congress)

The Synthesis of Urea

The synthesis of urea (an organic compound) from ammonium cyanate (an inorganic compound) contradicts the theory of vitalism.

The reaction of silver cyanate and ammonium chloride produces a precipitate of silver chloride that can be filtered out, leaving a water solution of ammonium cyanate (a).

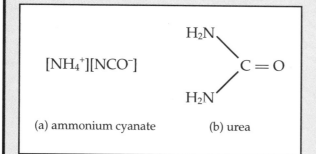

$[NH_4^+][NCO^-]$

(a) ammonium cyanate   (b) urea

N is nitrogen, H is hydrogen, C is carbon, and O is oxygen.

From the water solution of (a), Wöhler obtained crystals that he recognized as urea (b) by certain of its reactions, which were also exhibited by a sample of urea obtained from urine. Ammonium cyanate rapidly forms urea when heated in water solution. Wöhler made only a slight reference to the theoretical significance of the synthesis in his publication on the subject, but he was more effusive in a letter that he wrote to his friend Jöns Jakob Berzelius.

The theory of vitalism, which had existed under a variety of names since at least the time of Aristotle, held that living organisms possessed a "life force" that operated outside the realm of ordinary laboratory experiments. Thus, it was believed that no product of natural origin could ever be prepared in the laboratory.

The theory of vitalism was often contradicted, and it faded in importance over time. History has tended to give Wöhler the credit for ending vitalism and founding modern organic chemistry. Hardly a chemistry text exists that does not refer to Wöhler's achievement in 1828 on the opening page of the organic chemistry chapter.

Bibliography
Philosophy of Nature. Moritz Schlick. Translated by Amethe Von Zeppelin. New York: Greenwood Press, 1949.
"Woehler's Urea and Its Vital Force?—A Verdict from the Chemists." John H. Brook. *Ambix* 15 (1968).
"Wöhler's Preparation of Urea and the Fate of Vitalism." Timothy O. Lipman. *Journal of Chemical Education* 41, no 8 (1964).

Wöhler befriended Justus von Liebig, a professor at the University of Giessen, who was working on compounds called fulminates. Fulminates and cyanates turned out to provide one of the first examples of the phenomenon of isomerism: compounds with the same elemental composition but different properties.

Research on Bitter Almond Oil
In further collaboration with Liebig, Wöhler established the existence of a "benzoyl radical," a group of atoms that remained constant in a series of compounds derived from bitter almond oil.

A substance in almonds called amygdalin yields glucose, hydrogen cyanide, and benzaldehyde when acted on by an enzyme called emulsin, also present in the almonds. Wöhler clarified most of the chemistry of amygdalin, the first example of a common type of natural product called glycosides, and showed that emulsin could be inactivated by boiling.

Research on Metals
Wöhler prepared aluminum from aluminum chloride and potassium, and he also prepared beryllium. He worked out a method for extracting nickel from ore deposits near Kassel, and a refinery was built there. He suggested the use of nickel in coinage. In 1831, the first edition of his textbook *Grundriss der unorganischen Chemie* (fundamentals of inorganic chemistry) was published. It would run through fifteen editions.

Göttingen
A professorship at the University of Göttingen in 1836 brought Wöhler impressive teaching

and administrative duties, and it also made him responsible for inspecting apothecary shops in the province of Hannover. He produced the books *Grundriss der organischen Chemie* (1840; *Wöhler's Outlines of Organic Chemistry*, 1873) and *Practische Übungen in der Chemischen Analyse* (1853; practical exercises in analytical chemistry), as well as a translation of a chemistry textbook by Berzelius. Wöhler's research achievements included syntheses of phosphorus, acetylene, and the first silicon hydrides.

Colleagues

Students flocked to Göttingen from many countries, including the United States. Among those who heard Wöhler's lectures was Ira Remsen, an American chemist who later became president of The Johns Hopkins University and founded the first graduate program in chemistry in the United States.

Loved and respected by students and colleagues and honored by scientific societies in Germany, France, and England, Wöhler maintained an active interest in chemical research until his death in Göttingen in 1882.

Bibliography

By Wöhler

"Über künstliche Bildung des Harnstoffs," *Annalen der Physik und Chemie*, 1828 (On the artificial formation of urea)

Grundriss der unorganischen Chemie, 1831 (fundamentals of inorganic chemistry)

Grundriss der organischen Chemie, 1840 (*Wöhler's Outlines of Organic Chemistry*, 1873)

Beispiele zur Übung in der analytischen Chemie, 1849 (examples for practice in analytical chemistry)

The Analytical Chemist's Assistant, 1852 (Oscar M. Lieber, ed.)

Practische Übungen in der Chemischen Analyse, 1853 (practical exercises in chemical analysis)

Hand-book of Inorganic Analysis, 1854 (A. W. Hofmann, ed.)

Die mineral-analyse in Beispiele, 1861 (*Handbook of Mineral Analysis*, 1871)

Early Recollections of a Chemist, 1875

Aus Justus Liebigs und Friedrich Wöhlers Briefwechsel 1829-1873, 1888 (O. Wallach, ed.; from Justus Liebig's and Friedrich Wöhler's correspondence, 1829-1873)

Briefwechsel zwischen J. Berzelius und F. Wöhler, 1901 (correspondence between J. Berzelius and F. Wöhler)

About Wöhler

"Friedrich Wöhler." A. W. Hofmann. In *Great Chemists*, edited by Eduard Farber. New York: Interscience, 1961.

"Friedrich Wöhler." Robin Keen. In *Dictionary of Scientific Biography*, edited by Charles Coulston Gillispie. Vol. 14. New York: Charles Scribner's Sons, 1980.

"An Unrecognized Renal Physiologist: Friedrich Wöhler." G. Richet. *American Journal of Nephrology* 15, no. 6 (1995).

(*John R. Phillips*)

Granville T. Woods

Areas of Achievement: Invention and technology

Contribution: Woods invented many important electrical devices, including telegraphones to send voice messages, a railway telegraph to send messages between trains and railway stations, and overhead and "third rail" conducting systems used by trolleys and trains.

Apr. 23, 1856	Born in Columbus, Ohio
1872	Moves to Missouri to become a railroad fireman-engineer
1876	Returns to the eastern United States for training in electrical and mechanical engineering
1881	Opens a company in Cincinnati to manufacture telephone, telegraph, and electrical equipment
1885	Patents the telegraphone, which can send messages vocally or using the Morse code
1887	Patents the Synchronous Multiplex Railway Telegraph, which sends messages between moving trains or between moving trains and train stations
1888	Sets up first overhead trolley system for electrically powering trains and the trolley cars named after it
1896	Invents a safe theater dimmer device
1901	Sells a third rail conducting system to the General Electric Company
Jan. 30, 1910	Dies in New York, New York

Early Life

An invention is any useful new device or process developed by study and experimentation.

The art of inventing was the forte of Granville T. Woods, often called "the Black Edison." Woods was born in Columbus, Ohio. At the age of ten, he was taken out of elementary school and began working in a machine shop, where he learned to be a machinist and a blacksmith. During this time, Woods advanced his education by attending night school.

In November, 1872, at age sixteen, Woods moved to Missouri and went to work as a railroad fireman-engineer. In December, 1874, he began working in a rolling mill. During this period of his life, Woods began to study electricity, at first as a hobby. Later, its technology would become his specialty. His great expertise came from reading books that he borrowed from public libraries, friends, and employers.

In early 1876, Woods returned to the eastern United States and received college training in electrical and mechanical engineering over a two-year period. During this time, he also worked in a machine shop. Between 1878 and 1880, Woods was an engineer on the British steamer *Ironsides* and worked for the Danville and Southern Railroad. In 1881, he opened an

(The Associated Publishers, Inc.)

Trolley Systems and Third Rails

These conceptually related systems power trolley cars and subway systems via electrical power overhead and on the ground.

Woods's trolley system is an overhead conducting system that powers trains and trolley cars (the term "trolley car" arose from his invention). It is an electrical power line that runs along the route followed by a chosen vehicle. The vehicle's electric motor is run by the electric current, which passes into it from a pole reaching from vehicle to power line. The system is simple and nonpolluting because fossil fuels are not used by the vehicles. Its disadvantage is that a trolley line prevents vehicle movement outside the track system.

Conceptually akin to trolley systems are the third rail systems which run subway trains in many cities, such as New York City. A third rail is a series of electrical conductors set up along the path of the subway train. Electricity from the conductors enters each car of the train via collectors designed to contact a third rail and runs its electric motor. Availability of electricity along a subway route is turned on and off via electromagnetic switches in the third rail.

This system is more dangerous to passersby than the trolley system because it is on the ground where they might walk. Hence, its use, except in special safeguarded situations, is limited to underground subway tunnels to which pedestrians normally lack access.

Bibliography

Black Pioneers of Science and Invention. Louis Haber. New York: Harcourt Brace Jovanovich, 1970.

Cincinnati's Colored Citizens. Wendell P. Dabney. Cincinnati: Dabney, 1926.

Great Negroes, Past and Present. Russell L. Adams. 3d ed. Chicago: Afro-Am, 1969.

---

electrical company in Cincinnati, Ohio, where he manufactured telephone, telegraph, and electrical equipment.

Some of His Inventions

Over his lifetime, the brilliant Woods obtained many patents. Among the best known were two related to telegraphy. The first, in 1885, was for the telegraphone, which could send messages either vocally or in Morse code. The great advantage of a combined telephone/telegraph apparatus was the ability of telegraphone operators to transmit vocally, especially if they could not read or write. In that case, they flipped a switch that enabled spoken messages to be transmitted to chosen recipients. The invention was purchased almost immediately by the American Bell Telephone Company of Boston, Massachusetts.

The second invention, patented in 1887, was the Synchronous Multiplex Railway Telegraph (SMRT). The SMRT allowed message transmission between several moving trains or between moving trains and railway stations. The device had great value because it prevented many accidents by carrying warnings of dangerous obstacles, such as fallen trees along railway tracks. The SMRT used the telegraph lines that ran alongside railway tracks in an ingenious fashion; that is, it conducted messages to and from telegraph lines via static electricity.

Some of Woods's many other inventions were an improved steam boiler, regulators for electric motors, safe electric light dimmers for theaters, the overhead conducting system used by trains and trolley cars (the term "trolley car" arose from his device), "third rails" used to run the subway systems in large cities, air and electromagnetic brakes, and automatic safety cutoff switches for electrical circuits.

Many of Woods's inventions were purchased by the Bell Telephone Company, the General Electric Company, and the Westinghouse Corporation. Few inventors of any race have produced more electrical inventions than Woods. It was his versatility that led others to compare Woods to Thomas Alva Edison.

A Man to Emulate

Woods moved to New York City in 1890, and it was there that many of his sixty-five patents were taken out between that time and 1910, when he died. His inventions were not only useful but also led to cleaner, safer, and thriftier operation of theaters, public transportation, and cities. For example, the third rail and overhead trolley systems led to legislation requiring all steam railway trains to shift to one of these systems before they entered cities. This law profited the public by leading to cleaner air. Woods's theater light dimmer also made theaters safer by preventing fires, which had previously been very common.

Woods also served as a role model for African American youths by his contributions. He advocated forthright, continuous attempts on the part of young black people to succeed and perseverance in their efforts to find good jobs. Moreover, he advocated that such young people develop skills that would make them more employable, such as a knowledge of mechanics.

Bibliography
By Woods
Other than his patents, Woods published no works.

About Woods
Black Pioneers of Science and Invention. Louis Haber. New York: Harcourt Brace Jovanovich, 1970.
Cincinnati's Colored Citizens. Wendell P. Dabney. Cincinnati: Dabney, 1926.
Great Negroes, Past and Present. Russell L. Adams. 3d ed. Chicago: Afro-Am, 1969.
"The Negro in the Field of Invention." Henry Baker. *Journal of Negro History* 1 (January, 1917).

(Sanford S. Singer)

Chien-Shiung Wu

Area of Achievement: Physics
Contribution: Wu was an experimental physicist who demonstrated that parity (spatial symmetry) is not conserved by the weak nuclear force.

May 31, 1912	Born in Liuho, China
1934	Graduated with a degree in physics from National Central University in Nanjing
1936	Begins doctoral studies in physics at the University of California, Berkeley (UCB)
1940	Receives a Ph.D. from UCB
1944	Begins work at Columbia University for the atomic bomb project
1946	Teaches at Columbia
1952	Named an associate professor at Columbia
1954	With her husband, becomes a U.S. citizen
1957	Demonstrates the nonconservation of parity by the weak nuclear force
1957	Becomes a full professor at Columbia
1958	Elected to the National Academy of Sciences
1964	Becomes the first woman to receive the Comstock Prize from the National Academy of Sciences
1972	Appointed the first Pupin Professor of Physics at Columbia
1975	Becomes the first woman elected president of the American Physical Society
1981	Retires
Feb. 16, 1997	Dies in New York, New York

Early Life

Chien-Shiung Wu was born on May 31, 1912, in Liuho, a town about thirty miles from Shanghai, China. Her father opened the region's first school for girls and was its principal. He encouraged his daughter to read, ask questions, and solve problems.

At nine, Wu was graduated from the fourth elementary grade of her father's school and went as a boarder to Soochow Girls' School, from 1922 until 1930. She was enrolled in the teachers' training program at Soochow but borrowed books from her friends in the academic program so that so could study science until late into the night. She realized that she liked physics best.

Selected to attend China's elite National Central University in Nanjing, Wu studied physics there and continued her involvement as a leader in an underground student movement. Being graduated in 1934, she taught for a year in a provincial university and spent another year doing research in X-ray crystallography at the National Academy of Sciences in Shanghai. China had no graduate instruction in physics, and, as her uncle was willing to pay for her trip to the United States, Wu sailed from Shanghai in 1936.

Shortly after her arrival in San Francisco, Wu was introduced to her future husband, Yuan Chia-liu (Luke Yuan), a Chinese student of physics at the University of California, Berkeley (UCB). As physics at UCB was at its height, Wu chose to study there. Emilio Segrè, who would win the Nobel Prize in Physics, was studying the nucleus during the 1930's, and Wu joined his group.

In July, 1937, when Japan invaded China, Wu was cut off from her family, from news of them, and from returning home until hostilities ended. She heard nothing from her family until 1945. In 1940, she received her Ph.D. and stayed for two further years at UCB. Universities were not hiring women, however, and anti-Asian feeling was high. Wu got a job teaching at Smith College in Massachusetts. Yuan was designing radar devices for RCA in New Jersey, so they met on weekends in New York City.

Research

In the 1940's, universities were desperate to replace physicists doing war work. Wu re-

---

Nonconservation of Parity

Wu helped prove that the law of the conservation of parity—the idea that nature does not differentiate left from right—does not always hold true.

In 1956, Wu was approached by Tsung-Dao Lee. He and Chen Ning Yang were working on a problem created by the K-meson, a newly discovered subatomic particle. The law of parity states that nature has no "handedness," no preference for righthand or lefthand configurations. Lee and Yang thought that the particles in a nucleus might sometimes favor one direction over another, thus violating parity.

No one had ever shown experimentally that parity is always conserved inside the nucleus. Lee and Yang wrote a paper suggesting that parity was not conserved for interactions between subatomic particles involving the so-called weak force. They noted the lack of experimental proof that parity was conserved and suggested that parity conservation be tested experimentally.

Wu, who thought it very unlikely that parity was not conserved, set about the preparation and testing of the equipment required to do the experiment. She worked with scientists at the National Bureau of Standards in Washington, D.C. The results provided experimental confirmation that parity (spatial symmetry) is not conserved by the weak nuclear force. Physicists were amazed.

Lee and Yang shared the 1957 Nobel Prize in Physics for originating the idea and suggesting that conservation of parity should be tested experimentally. Wu did not share the prize.

Bibliography

The Ambidextrous Universe. Martin Gardner. New York: Basic Books, 1964.

"Subtleties and Surprises: The Contribution of Beta Decay to an Understanding of the Weak Interaction." Chien-Shiung Wu. *Annals of the New York Academy of Sciences* (November 8, 1977).

(Library of Congress)

the weak nuclear force—was completed. This result amazed physicists. In 1957, she became a full professor at Columbia and was given an endowed professorship, the first Michael I. Pupin Professorship of Physics, in 1972.

A series of "firsts" for a female scientist followed: an honorary doctorate in science from Princeton in 1958, the Cyrus B. Comstock Award of the National Academy of Sciences in 1964, and election as president of the American Physical Society in 1975. A recipient of the National Medal of Science, the highest award for achievement in science in the United States, Wu received the Wolf Prize in Physics in 1978 "for exploring the weak interaction, helping establish the precise form and the nonconservation of parity for this natural force."

Wu retired in 1981. She died, at the age of eighty-four, on February 16, 1997, in Manhattan as the result of a stroke.

ceived job offers from eight universities and selected Princeton, where, at thirty-one, she was the first female instructor. In 1944, Wu began work at Columbia University on sensitive radiation detectors for the atomic bomb project. After the war, she was asked to remain at Columbia as a research associate, and she became a senior investigator on large grants. After 1946, Wu studied beta decay. In 1947, a son, Vincent, was born to Wu and Yuan. In 1952, Wu finally became a Columbia faculty member, an associate professor with tenure. Wu and Yuan became United States citizens in 1954.

In January, 1957, Wu's most significant work in physics—experimental confirmation that parity (spatial symmetry) is not conserved by

Bibliography
By Wu
Nuclear Physics, 1961-1963 (2 vols.; as editor, with Luke C. Yuan)
Beta Decay, 1966
Elementary Particles, 1971 (as editor, with Yuan)

About Wu
"Chien-Shiung Wu, the First Lady of Physics Research." Gloria Lubkin. *Smithsonian* (January, 1971).
Nobel Prize Women in Science: Their Lives, Struggles, and Momentous Discoveries. Sharon Bertsch McGrayne. Secaucus, N.J.: Carol, 1993.

(Maureen H. O'Rafferty)

Rosalyn S. Yalow

Areas of Achievement: Biology, immunology, and medicine

Contribution: Yalow, the second woman to win a Nobel Prize in Physiology or Medicine, did extensive research on hormones. She developed the analytic immunoassay technique that uses radioactive tags to detect hormones in blood and body tissue.

July 19, 1921	Born in the Bronx, New York
1941	Earns an A.B. at Hunter College, graduating magna cum laude
1942	Receives an M.S. from the University of Illinois, Urbana
1943	Marries Aaron Yalow
1944	Earns a Ph.D. at the University of Illinois
1946-1950	Serves as an assistant professor of physics at Hunter
1950-1970	Works at the Veterans Administration (VA) Hospital in the Bronx
1970-1980	Serves as the chief of nuclear medicine at the VA Hospital
1974-1979	Serves as Distinguished Service Professor at the Mount Sinai School of Medicine
1976	Awarded the Albert Lasker Prize for Basic Medical Research
1977	Wins the Nobel Prize in Physiology or Medicine
1978	The American Diabetes Association establishes the Rosalyn S. Yalow Research and Development Award
1979-1985	Named Distinguished Professor at Large at Albert Einstein College of Medicine, Yeshiva University

Early Life

Rosalyn Sussman Yalow was born on July 19, 1921, to German immigrants Simon and Clara Sussman, who had not received high school educations. She was a stubborn child who by the seventh grade was committed to mathematics. Although her parents wished for her to be an elementary school teacher, one of her high school teachers excited Rosalyn's interest in chemistry.

Sussman entered Hunter College, determined to get a degree in chemistry. After studying with some distinguished physicists, however, she changed her major from chemistry to physics in her senior year.

On the advice of a professor, she worked as a secretary in the laboratory of Rudolf Schoenheimer during her senior year, thus allowing her to enter science through the "back door." In 1943, she married Aaron Yalow, a fellow physics student. Despite the pessimistic attitude of some of her professors, Rosalyn Yalow completed her doctorate in physics in 1944 and set out to find a job.

(The Nobel Foundation)

Radioimmunoassay

Radioimmunoassay involves tagging a substance with radioactive material that will take the same pathway in the human body as the substance to be studied.

In the term radioimmunoassay (RIA), "radio" refers to the radioactive substances used in the test, "immuno" refers to antigen-antibody reactions, and "assay" means to measure. RIA measures hormones that have been tagged with a radioisotope. The procedure requires an antibody called antiserum that will attach to a specific hormone, as well as a sample of the hormone that has been tagged with a radioactive substance.

The medical technologist will incubate a known amount of a "hot" (radioactive) hormone with a known amount of the patient's blood sample or a "cold" hormone. The patient's hormone (the cold hormone) competes with the hot hormone when binding to the antibody. Next, the medical technologist will separate the bound hormone. Finally, a curve is drawn showing the percentage of cold hormone to hot hormone that has attached to the antibody. The total amount of hormone in the patient's blood can then be calculated. This method of measuring can detect amounts of hormone in the picogram (10^{-12}) range.

While Yalow used the technique to measure the amount of insulin in diabetic patients, RIA is now used to measure hundreds of substances in the body. One substance, thyroxine, is measured in newborns. Nurses need only perform a heel prick on the newborn, place a drop of blood on filter paper, and send it off to be tested. What once would have taken a tube of blood now only takes a drop. This technique can be used to screen every newborn and prevent mental retardation.

Bibliography

Clinical Diagnosis by Laboratory Methods. Israel Davidsohn and John Bernard Henry, eds. Philadelphia: W. B. Saunders, 1974.

The Joys of Research. Walter Shropshire, Jr., ed. Washington, D.C.: Smithsonian Institution, 1981.

A Career in Science

The 1930's and 1940's saw a focus on radioactivity and nuclear physics, Yalow's areas of interest. Through introductions by her husband, she was hired by the Veterans Administration (VA) Hospital in the Bronx. Although she had never had a course in biology, she was going to apply physics to physiology.

Radioisotope services were established in seven VA hospitals in 1947. From these pioneer programs, nuclear medicine was developed. Yalow was a part of this movement. She worked closely with Solomon Berson, learning his medicine while teaching him physics.

Radioimmunoassay

Yalow's research involved using radioactive tags to trace the amounts of substances and their movement through the body, a process called radioimmunoassay. A substance is tagged with radioactive material that will take the same pathway in the human body as the substance to be studied. For example, if she wanted to trace the pathway that insulin took, Yalow gave the patient radioactive insulin. The radioactive material can be followed through body scans. Yalow, Berson, and a group of colleagues described the technique in a 1956 article in the *Journal of Clinical Investigation*. The article, which had been rejected by *Science*, described what has become the principle of radioimmunoassay. Yalow and Berson did extensive work tracing the metabolic pathway of insulin, advancing the treatment of diabetics. Radioimmunoassay is now used to measure hundreds of hormones and nonhormone substances such as antibiotics, enzymes, and drugs in the human body.

Honors

Yalow received the Nobel Prize in Physiology or Medicine in 1977. She also won awards almost annually from 1968 to 1988 for her work. She was honored by the American Diabetes Association numerous times for her research into the disease diabetes mellitus. In 1978, the association honored her with the establishment of the Rosalyn S. Yalow Research and Development Award.

Yalow was also elected a member of the

New York Academy of Sciences, the National Academy of Sciences, the American College of Radiology, and the American Association of Physicists in Medicine.

Bibliography
By Yalow
"Demonstration of Insulin Binding Globulin in the Circulation of Insulin-Treated Subjects," *Journal of Clinical Investigation*, 1956 (with S. A. Berson, A. Bauman, M. A. Rothschild, and K. Newerly)
"Assay of Plasma Insulin in Human Subjects by Immunological Methods," *Nature*, 1959 (with Berson)
"Parathyroid Hormone in Plasma in Adenomatous Hyperparathyroid, Uremia, and Bronchogenic Carcinoma," *Science*, 1966 (with Berson)
Peptide Hormones, 1973 (as editor, with Berson)
"Cholecystokinin in the Brains of Obese and Nonobese Mice," *Science*, 1979 (with E. Straus)
Radioimmunoassay, 1983 (as editor)
Radiation and Public Perception: Benefits and Risks, 1995 (as editor, with Jack P. Young)

About Yalow
The Lady Laureates: Women Who Have Won the Nobel Prize. Olga S. Opfell. Metuchen, N.J.: Scarecrow Press, 1982.
The Nobel Duel: Two Scientists' Twenty-one Year Race to Win the World's Most Coveted Research Prize. Nicholas Wade. New York: Anchor Press/Doubleday, 1981.
"Rosalyn S. Yalow." In *The Nobel Prize Winners: Physiology or Medicine*, edited by Frank N. Magill. Pasadena, Calif.: Salem Press, 1991.
The Triumph of Discovery: Women Scientists Who Won the Nobel Prize. Joan Dash. New York: Julian Messner, 1991.

(Linda E. Roach)

Chen Ning Yang

Area of Achievement: Physics
Contribution: Yang was awarded the Nobel Prize in Physics for his hypothesis about the violation of the law of conservation of parity.

Sept. 22, 1922	Born in Hofei, Anhwei, China
1942	Earns a B.S. at National Southwest Associated University, Kunming, China
1945	Travels to the United States to pursue his studies
1948	Earns a Ph.D. in physics from the University of Chicago
1948-1949	Serves as an instructor in physics at Chicago
1950	Marries Chih Li Tu
1954	With R. L. Mills, develops the Yang-Mills theory
1955-1966	Teaches physics at the Institute for Advanced Study
1956	With Tsung-Dao Lee, presents his hypothesis about the conservation of parity
1957	Awarded the Nobel Prize in Physics jointly with Lee
1957	Given the Albert Einstein Commemorative Award
1965	Appointed Albert Einstein Professor of Science and director of the Institute of Theoretical Physics at the State University of New York, Stony Brook
1965	Elected to the National Academy of Sciences
1980	Given the Rumford Medal of the American Academy of Arts and Sciences

Early Life

Chen Ning Yang was the eldest child of Ke Chuan Yang, a professor of mathematics at the Tsinghua University in Peking, China. The Yang family was devoted to cultural and intellectual pursuits. As a youngster, Chen Ning read Benjamin Franklin's autobiography and decided to take "Franklin" as a first name.

After Japanese troops invaded China in 1937, Tsinghua University moved to Kunming and the Yang family followed. There, Frank Yang would earn a B.S. degree in physics in 1942 at the National Southwest Associated University. He subsequently earned an M.S. degree in 1944 at Tsinghua University.

After teaching high school physics for one year, Yang went to the United States to study under Edward Teller and Enrico Fermi at the

Parity Violation

Yang and a colleague solved the theta-tau paradox by describing the conditions under which the law of the conservation of parity does not hold true.

Principles of symmetry and laws of conservation play fundamental roles in the understanding of nature. One example of symmetry is right-left symmetry, according to which the laws of nature will be the same in a system and its mirror image. This means that an observer viewing the evolution of a system in a mirror and an observer viewing the actual process itself could provide equally valid descriptions of that evolution.

One example of conservation is the law of the conservation of parity, according to which the parity of a system must remain the same throughout any process (such as decay) affecting that system. Parity itself is a value, either +1 (even parity), or –1 (odd parity) ascribed to either a particle or a system.

This law of the conservation of parity was developed empirically, as a result of work with atomic spectra, and deduced from the right-left symmetry of electromagnetic forces. The law of conservation of parity was believed to hold in all physics until the early 1950's, when physicists interested in mesons and their weak interactions discovered the theta-tau paradox.

Two particles were observed to disintegrate differently: The theta particle decays into two pi-mesons (or pions), and the tau particle decays into three pi-mesons. Upon measurement, the two particles were discovered to have the same mass, as well as other similarities. It appeared that they were rather the same particle disintegrating in different manners.

A calculation of the parities of the two particles, however, raised questions. The pi-meson has an odd parity. Therefore, the final parity of the decay of the theta particle into two pi-mesons would be even (the product of two odds), while that of the tau particle would be odd. Physicists faced a paradox: Theta and tau particles have different parities and thus cannot be identical without violating the principle of parity.

Yang and his colleague Tsung-Dao Lee wondered if the solution to this puzzle lay in a re-evaluation of right-left symmetry. They discovered that no experimental evidence existed to support the validity of right-left symmetry with respect to weak interactions. The two physicists realized that if right-left symmetry did not hold for weak interactions, then the principle of parity would not be applicable to the decay mechanisms of the theta and tau particles and that they could, in fact, be the same particle.

To prove their conjecture, they suggested that if a beta-decay process and its mirror image were to occur at the same rates, then parity must be conserved. If the process and its image were to occur at different rates, however, parity would not be conserved. Experiments subsequently conducted with cobalt 60 by Chien-Shiung Wu and her collaborators proved theta and tau to be the same meson, called the K-meson.

Bibliography

"Basic Concept in Physics Is Reported Upset in Tests: Conservation of Parity Law in Nuclear Theory Challenged by Scientists at Columbia and Princeton Institute." Harold M. Schmeck, Jr. *The New York Times,* January 16, 1957, p. 1.

Twentieth Century Physics. L. M. Brown, A. Pais, and B. Pippard, eds. Vol. 2. New York: AIP Press, 1995.

University of Chicago, where he completed his Ph.D. in nuclear physics in 1948. It was at Chicago that Yang befriended Tsung-Dao Lee, who had also been a student at National Southwest Associated University. Their friendship and collaboration continued after their days at Chicago, especially while both worked at the Institute for Advanced Study at Princeton University and even after Lee went on to Columbia. It eventually led them to the Nobel Prize in Physics.

The Question of Parity

The intellectual roots of Yang's Nobel Prize reached all the way back to his days as an undergraduate, when he developed his interests in symmetry principles and subsequently in statistical mechanics. His baccalaureate thesis "Group Theory and Molecular Spectra," his master's thesis "Contributions to the Statistical Theory of Order-Disorder Transformations," and his doctoral thesis "On the Angular Distribution in Nuclear Reactions and Coincidence Measurements" all led to subsidiary problems regarding the principle of the conservation of parity. He began to address the issue of parity in earnest while at the Institute for Advanced Study.

Studying elementary particles and weak interactions, Yang proved in one of his first papers that the parity of the pi-meson, or pion, is odd. This finding was essential for the analysis of the theta-tau paradox. It was to solve this paradox that Yang and Lee proposed in 1956 their hypothesis of the violation of the law of conservation of parity, the work that would earn for them the Nobel Prize the following year.

Other Contributions

Yang made other contributions to theoretical physics, among them the Yang-Mills theory, a product of his collaboration with R. L. Mills. This theory, proposed in 1954, posits a mathematical principle to describe fundamental interactions for elementary particles and fields.

In addition to conducting his own research and teaching, Yang furthered scientific pursuits as a member of the boards of Rockefeller University, the American Association for the Advancement of Science, the Salk Institute for

(The Nobel Foundation)

Biological Studies in San Diego, and Ben-Gurion University in Israel.

Bibliography

By Yang

"Question of Parity Conservation in Weak Interactions," *The Physical Review*, 1956 (with Tsung-Dao Lee)

Elementary Particles: A Short History of Some Discoveries in Atomic Physics, 1961

"The Law of Parity Conservation and Other Symmetry Laws of Physics" in *Nobel Lectures: Physics, 1942-1962*, 1964

Selected Papers, 1945-1980, with Commentary, 1983

About Yang

"Chen Ning Yang." In *The Nobel Prize Winners: Physics*, edited by Frank N. Magill.

Pasadena, Calif.: Salem Press, 1989.
"A Question of Parity." Jeremy Bernstein. *The New Yorker*, May 12, 1962.
Rochester Roundabout: The Story of High Energy Physics. John Polkinghorne. Essex, England: Longman Scientific & Technical, 1989.

(Rosa Alvarez Ulloa)

Thomas Young

Areas of Achievement: Invention and physics
Contribution: Young provided the first experimental support for the wave theory of light. Many phenomena associated with light from multiple sources could be understood in terms of his principle of interference.

June 13, 1773	Born in Milverton, Somerset, England
1792	Begins medical studies
1800	Completes his medical degree and opens a practice in London
1801	Appointed a professor of natural philosophy at the Royal Institution
1802	Publishes *Lectures on Natural Philosophy and Mechanical Arts*
1802	Appointed foreign secretary of the Royal Society of London
1802	Presents "The Bakerian Lecture: On the Theory of Light and Colours"
1804-1816	Engages in efforts to decipher Egyptian hieroglyphic writing
1817	Publishes the entry "Chromatics" in the *Supplement* to the *Encyclopaedia Britannica*
May 10, 1829	Dies in London, England

Early Life
Thomas Young was born on June 13, 1773, in Milverton, England. From an early age, Young displayed extraordinary talents. By the age of two, he could read with considerable proficiency, and he read the Bible through twice by his fourth birthday. All through his early years, he voraciously devoured books of all kinds, whether classical, literary, or scientific. More than being merely of academic interest, the things that he read profoundly affected him.

When he was sixteen years old, Young decided to abstain from the use of sugar because of his opposition to slavery and its role in the production of sugar.

Young began studies for a medical career in 1792. His talents took him to the finest medical schools: the University of Edinburgh in Scotland, the University of Göttingen in Germany, and finally Cambridge University in England. Having completed a medical degree in 1800, he set up a practice in London that same year.

In 1801, Young was persuaded to accept an appointment as professor of natural philosophy at the Royal Institution, a school of science founded the preceding year by Benjamin Thompson. In 1802, while at the Royal Institution, Young prepared and delivered a series of insightful lectures on the status of science. The lectures were later published under the title *A Course of Lectures on Natural Philosophy and the Mechanical Arts* (1807).

Because of his outstanding abilities in the sciences and because of his fluency in several languages, Young was appointed foreign secretary of the Royal Society of London in 1802, a position that he held for the remainder of his life.

Experiments with Light

Young's first research in optics dealt with the anatomical and optical characteristics of the eye. Soon, his work turned toward the fundamental properties of light. Several of his experiments with colors produced by thin plates of glass suggested to Young that the wave theory was the most productive model describing the propagation of light. More than a century before, Christiaan Huygens proposed the wave theory to rival Sir Isaac Newton's corpuscular (particle) model, but no experiment had decisively eliminated either of the two theories.

Young's experiments strongly supported the wave theory. The great step taken by Young was his introduction of the principle of interference. His double-slit interference experiment, carried out in 1800, provided strong, unequivocal evidence in favor of the wave theory. Reading his paper before the Royal Society of London in 1801, Young demonstrated how the results of his experiments and his interpretation supported the wave theory. He later invented a device that could measure the diameters of very thin fibers based on the wave behavior of light.

(Library of Congress)

Young's Double-Slit Experiment

Young's principle of interference explained the bright and dark bands seen when light passes through two narrow slits. The observed interference pattern strongly supported the wave theory of light.

The earliest experiment demonstrating that light can produce interference effects was performed in 1800 by Young. The experiment was a crucial one at the time, since it added further evidence to the growing support for the wave nature of light.

Young's experimental arrangement is depicted in figure 1. Light from a source at the left, not shown, is incident onto a narrow slit S_1. Two more narrow slits, S_2 and S_3, are parallel to S_1 and symmetrically placed on either side of it. When a screen is placed to the right of these slits, alternate bright and dark bands are observed on it, parallel to the slits. In Young's experiment, the slits were each about 0.1 millimeters in width, and the double slits were separated by 1 millimeter. The screen, 1 meter away, displayed alternating bright and dark bands about 0.6 millimeter wide.

The explanation of the pattern of bright and dark bands, often called fringes, is based on the

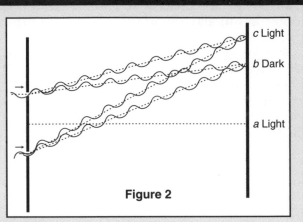

Figure 2

interference of light waves. Light from the source and incident upon the first slit produces waves according to Huygens' principle. Those waves propagate over to the double-slit arrangement. Each thin slit of the double slit produces its own waves, again by Huygens' principle. In the region beyond the double slits, the waves from the two slits interfere.

At point c in figure 2, the light waves from the two slits arrive in phase, that is, crest to crest and trough to trough. The two wave motions add together, producing an increase of the illumination. The same would be true for waves arriving at point a. On the other hand, at point b on the screen, the crest of the wave from the bottom slit meets with the trough of the wave from the top slit. The two waves are out of phase. The two waves cancel each other at this point on the screen; a dark band is observed.

The wave theory as used by Young precisely predicts the locations of each of the bright and dark bands on the screen. The corpuscular (particle) theory of light could not account for the observed phenomena. Thus, Young's experiment was taken to be strong support for the wave theory.

Bibliography

Optical Physics. Max Garbuny. New York: Academic Press, 1965.

Principles of Optics. Max Born and Emil Wolf. London: Pergamon Press, 1980.

Seeing the Light. David Falk, Dieter Brill, and David Stork. New York: Harper & Row, 1986.

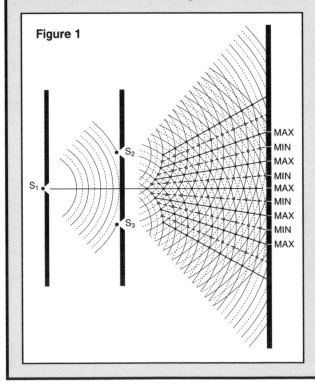

Figure 1

S_2

S_1

S_3

MAX
MIN
MAX
MIN
MAX
MIN
MAX
MIN
MAX

Decryption of Egyptian Hieroglyphics

From about 1804 to 1816, Young devoted himself to the study of languages. In particular, he wished to decipher Egyptian hieroglyphics. When the Rosetta Stone was brought to England in 1801, Young received a copy of the symbols inscribed on it. He was able to show that the markings were not merely pictorial symbols but represented phonetic sounds. His work laid the foundation for the successful decryption of Egyptian writing by Jean-François Champollion in 1822.

Young died in 1829 at the age of fifty-five.

Bibliography

By Young

"The Bakerian Lecture: On the Theory of Light and Colours," *Philosophical Transactions*, 1802

"The Bakerian Lecture: Experiments and Calculations Relative to Physical Optics," *Philosophical Transactions*, 1804

A Course of Lectures on Natural Philosophy and the Mechanical AAS, 1807

Miscellaneous Works of the Late Thomas Young, M.D., F.R.S., . . . , 1855 (3 vols.)

About Young

Light. R. W. Ditchburn, 3d ed. London: Blackie and Son, 1976.

The Rise of the Wave Theory. Jed Z. Buchwald. Chicago: Chicago University Press, 1989.

Theories of Light from Descartes to Newton. A. I. Sabra. New York: American Elsevier, 1967.

(Anthony J. Nicastro)

Hideki Yukawa

Area of Achievement: Physics
Contribution: Yukawa was the first to describe the strong nuclear force. He predicted the existence of the meson particle, and calculated its mass, twelve years before its discovery.

Jan. 23, 1907	Born in Tokyo, Japan
1929	Graduated from Kyoto University
1932	Marries Sumi Yukawa and is adopted by his wife's family
1933	Teaches at Osaka University
1935	Predicts the existence of a fundamental particle with a mass about two hundred times that of the electron
1938	Obtains a D.Sc. from Osaka
1939	Becomes a professor at Kyoto
1940	Awarded the Imperial Prize of the Japan Academy
1948-1949	Invited by J. Robert Oppenheimer to teach at the Institute for Advanced Study in Princeton, New Jersey
1949	Awarded the Nobel Prize in Physics
1949	Elected a foreign associate of the U.S. National Academy of Sciences
1950-1951	Serves as a visiting professor at Columbia University
1953-1970	Directs the Research Institute for Fundamental Physics at Kyoto
1963	Elected a foreign member of the Royal Society of London
1964	Awarded the Lomonosov Gold Medal of the USSR Presidium of the Academy of Sciences
Sept. 8, 1981	Dies in Kyoto, Japan

Early Life

The maiden family name of Hideki Yukawa (pronounced "yew-KAH-wah") was Ogawa. His father, Takuji Ogawa, was a professor of geology at Kyoto University. Hideki was graduated from Kyoto in 1929. In 1932, after he married Sumiko Yukawa, he was adopted by his wife's family—a not-so-unusual custom in Japan—and thereby came to use the name "Hideki Yukawa" for the rest of his life.

Yukawa once reminisced that his entry into the field of theoretical physics was influenced by his mentors: K. Tamaki at Kyoto and Yoshio Nishina at Tokyo. Another contributing factor was his inability to master the art of glassblowing, which derailed his interest in practical science. Shin'ichiro Tomonaga, another future theoretical physicist and Nobel laureate from Japan, was Yukawa's college friend. They studied the then-exploding field of quantum physics together while serving as unpaid assistants for three years at Kyoto University following their graduation.

During this time, Yukawa also expanded his knowledge in quantum physics by attending a series of lectures delivered by Nishina, who returned to Japan in 1928 after studying under Niels Bohr. He also had the opportunity to listen to the lectures of Paul A. M. Dirac and Werner Karl Heisenberg, who visited Nishina's laboratory in Tokyo.

Predicting the Existence of Mesons

Yukawa commenced his teaching career at Osaka University in 1933 while maintaining his research interest in theoretical physics. In his first research publication, he analyzed Heisenberg's 1932 proposal on nuclear structure, a neutron-proton model of the nucleus held together by electron-exchange interactions in which he also noted the absence of an adequate theory of nuclear forces. Enrico Fermi published his neutrino theory of beta decay in 1934.

Yukawa's signal contribution, which originated during a sleepless night following the birth of his second child in October, 1934, significantly extended the ideas of Dirac, Heisenberg, and Fermi. He postulated the existence of a new particle to account for the interaction between nucleons (protons and neutrons) based on his discovery that the range of nuclear force is inversely proportional to the mass of the quanta (packets of energy). From quantum physics calculations, Yukawa also predicted the mass of such a particle to be about two hundred times that of an electron.

Yukawa presented his theory at the meeting of the Japanese Physico-Mathematical Society and proposed the name "heavy quantum" or "U-quantum" for his new particle. His paper describing his finding was published in 1935, in the first volume of the *Proceedings of the Physico-Mathematical Society of Japan*. Initially, Yukawa's prediction of the existence of such a particle did not create much excitement in the Western Hemisphere, partly because of a lack of experimental data.

Cosmon-Mesotron-Yukon-Meson

Yukawa's prediction received experimental support in 1937 when Carl David Anderson and his assistant Seth Neddermeyer reported the presence of particles heavier than electrons but lighter than protons in secondary cosmic rays. This finding elicited a brief scientific note by Yukawa in which he suggested that his "heavy quantum" could be identified with the new cosmic-ray particle, and he proposed the name "cosmon" for this particle.

Anderson and Neddermeyer identified their particle as a "mesotron" ("meso" meaning "intermediate" in Greek, referring to the mass of the particle being between that of a proton and a neutron). J. Robert Oppenheimer proposed the name "yukon" to recognize Yukawa's contribution to the discovery of this particle. In the end, the 1938 proposal of the name "meson" by Homi Bhabha became accepted in the physics literature.

Mu-Meson and Pi-Meson

Subsequent studies revealed that although the particle identified by Anderson and Neddermeyer had the mass required for nuclear quanta, its observed lifetime was 10^{-6} seconds, which is one hundred times longer than the predicted 10^{-8} seconds. Thus, Yukawa's predicted particle remained elusive. Meanwhile, Yukawa and his colleagues in Japan continued to develop the meson theory, despite severe restrictions placed on them because of the

Japanese government's policy of militarism just prior to and during World War II.

To resolve the conflict between Yukawa's prediction and the finding of Neddermeyer and Anderson, Yukawa's colleagues S. Sakata and T. Inoue postulated that the mesons could be of two types. The first type, mu-mesons (muons) did not interact strongly with nucleons; the particles reported by Neddermeyer and Anderson were of this type. The second type, pi-mesons (pions), coupled strongly with nucleons, and their lifetimes should agree with theoretical calculations. It was also proposed that pi-mesons would decay into mu-mesons.

Although the "two-meson" hypothesis was published in Japan in 1942, it came to the attention of scientists in the United States and Europe only in 1946, when an English-language

Mesons: The Particles Binding the Nuclear Glue

Yukawa's theoretical insight into mesons provided a rational explanation of the force responsible for binding together the atomic nucleus.

The atomic nucleus, made up of protons and neutrons, is quite stable. What contributes to this stability? Protons, having the same electric charge, should repel each other, and neutrons, without charge, cannot counteract this repulsion. Yukawa solved the mystery by predicting the existence of a new type of particle, which came to be recognized as a meson.

Yukawa realized that the nuclear force acts only at extremely small distances and that such a force would have to be carried by a heavy particle, heavier than an electron. This is an extension of Werner Karl Heisenberg's proton-neutron model of the nucleus. According to this model, a neutron is a combination of a proton and an electron. Heisenberg also regarded electrons as being fundamental to the nuclear force.

Yukawa's prediction for the existence of an intermediary particle called a meson is based on calculations made from quantum physics, such as Planck's law and de Broglie's law, and using the electromagnetic force as an analogy. At that time, one should remember that only the range of the nuclear forces (that is, the distance at which the force becomes negligible) was experimentally known.

With this limited information, Yukawa postulated that the mass of his new particle should be about two hundred times that of the electron. He arrived at this number by the following steps.

First, Yukawa developed a wave equation for the nuclear force, which is similar to the electromagnetic wave equation. Second, he used Planck's law and de Broglie's law with this equation. According to these laws of quantum physics, a wave frequency f and wavelength λ carry energy (ε) in packets (quanta) of $\varepsilon = hf$, which have a momentum (p) of h/λ.

In these equations, h is Planck's constant (6.63×10^{-34} joules per second). Third, Yukawa calculated that the mass of the quantum (m) in this case is equal to "$m(\text{MeV}) = hc/2\pi r_0$," where c is the speed of light and r_0 is the range of force. MeV is the unit in which the mass of elementary particles is conveniently expressed; it stands for million electronvolts (or mega electronvolt). One electronvolt (eV) equals 1.6×10^{-19} joules, which represents the energy gained by an electron when it is accelerated by a potential difference of 1 volt.

Then, Yukawa derived a figure for m by substituting the known values for c, r_0, and $h/2\pi$, where r_0 is 2×10^{-15} meters; c is 3×10^8 meters per second; and $h/2\pi$ is 10^{-34} joules per second $= 6.55 \times 10^{-22}$ MeV per second. Thus, m has a value of 98.25 MeV, which is almost equal to 100 MeV, which in turn is about two hundred times the mass of an electron, or one-tenth of the mass of a proton.

This force, known as the strong interaction or the strong nuclear force, is identified as one of the four fundamental forces of nature, the other three being gravity, electromagnetism, and the weak interaction.

Bibliography

The Particle Hunters. Yuval Ne'eman and Yoram Kirsh. 2d ed. Cambridge, England: Cambridge University Press, 1996.

The Search for Infinity. Gordon Fraser, Egil Lillestol, and Inge Sellevag. London: Michelin House, 1994.

version of the paper appeared. This delay was partly attributable to the communication block during World War II.

Yukawa's meson hypothesis ultimately received experimental confirmation when Cecil Powell and his colleagues at the University of Bristol found evidence for the existence of pi-mesons in cosmic rays using their newly developed photographic emulsion technique for recording the tracks of fast, charged particles. Yukawa was then awarded the 1949 Nobel Prize in Physics, and Powell received his Nobel recognition in 1950. Anderson, who discovered mu-mesons in 1937, had received the Nobel Prize in Physics in 1936 for his discovery of the positron.

The Doyen of Japanese Physics
In the post war period, Yukawa played the role of doyen (knowledgeable senior member) of theoretical physics in Japan and contributed a share of his $30,000 Nobel cash prize to the establishment of a new Institute of Theoretical Physics at Kyoto. His popular accounts on science, *Creativity and Intuition* and *Tabibito, the Traveler*, appeared in English translation in 1973 and 1982, respectively. He died in 1981.

Bibliography
By Yukawa
"On the Interaction of Elementary Particles: I," *Proceedings of the Physico-Mathematical Society of Japan*, 1935
"On the Theory of Internal Pair Production," *Proceedings of the Physico-Mathematical Society of Japan*, 1935 (with S. Sakata)
"On the Theory of Disintegration and the Allied Phenomenon," *Proceedings of the Physico-Mathematical Society of Japan*, 1935 (with Sakata)

Yukawa explains the formula for a wave equation for a meson with a spin of zero. (AP/Wide World Photos)

"Supplement to 'On the Theory of the β-Disintegration and the Allied Phenomenon'," *Proceedings of the Physico-Mathematical Society of Japan*, 1936 (with Sakata)

"Theory of Disintegration of the Nucleus by Neutron Impact," *Proceedings of the Physico-Mathematical Society of Japan*, 1936 (with Y. Miyagawa)

"Elementary Calculations on the Slowing Down of Neutrons by a Thin Plate," *Proceedings of the Physico-Mathematical Society of Japan*, 1936

"Note on Dirac's Generalized Wave Equations," *Proceedings of the Physico-Mathematical Society of Japan*, 1937 (with Sakata)

"On the Theory of Collision of Neutrons with Deuterons," *Proceedings of the Physico-Mathematical Society of Japan*, 1937 (with Sakata)

"On a Possible Interpretation of the Penetrating Component of the Cosmic Ray," *Proceedings of the Physico-Mathematical Society of Japan*, 1937

"On the Interaction of Elementary Particles: II," *Proceedings of the Physico-Mathematical Society of Japan*, 1937 (with Sakata)

"On the Interaction of Elementary Particles: III," *Proceedings of the Physico-Mathematical Society of Japan*, 1938 (with Sakata and M. Taketani)

"On the Interaction of Elementary Particles: IV," *Proceedings of the Physico-Mathematical Society of Japan*, 1938 (with Sakata, M. Kobayasi, and Taketani)

"Mass and Mean Life-Time of the Meson," *Nature*, 1939 (with Sakata)

"On the Scattering of Mesons by Nuclear Particles," *Proceedings of the Physico-Mathematical Society of Japan*, 1941 (with Y. Tanikawa)

"Attempts at a Unified Theory of Elementary Particles," *Science*, 1955

Creativity and Intuition: A Physicist Looks at East and West, 1973

Tabibito: Aru Butsurigakusha no kaiso, 1958 (*Tabibito, the Traveler*, 1982)

About Yukawa

"Particle Physics in Prewar Japan." Joseph L. Spradley. *American Scientist* 73 (November-December, 1985).

The Second Creation: Makers of the Revolution in Twentieth Century Physics. R. P. Crease and C. C. Mann. New York: Macmillan, 1986.

Thirty Years That Shook Physics: The Story of Quantum Theory. George Gamow. New York: Doubleday, 1966.

(Sachi Sri Kantha)

Pieter Zeeman

Area of Achievement: Physics
Contribution: Zeeman demonstrated that the spectral lines of an atom broaden when it is placed in a magnetic field, for which he shared the Nobel Prize in Physics with Hendrik Antoon Lorentz.

May 25, 1865	Born in Zonnemaire, Isle of Schouwen, Zeeland, the Netherlands
1890	Becomes an assistant to Lorentz at the University of Leiden
1892	Wins the Gold Medal of the Netherlands Scientific Society of Haarlem
1893	Receives his doctorate
1894	Returns to Leiden as privatdocent
1896	Demonstrates the Zeeman effect for sodium
1897	Appointed a lecturer at the University of Amsterdam
1900	Promoted to professor of physics
1902	Wins the Nobel Prize in Physics
1908	Named the director of the Physical Institute at Amsterdam
1921	Elected a foreign member of the Royal Society of London
1922	Receives the Royal Society of London's Rumford Medal
1923	Directs the Laboratorium Physica (renamed the Zeeman Laboratory)
1932	Studies the strong spectral lines of rhenium
1935	Retires from the University of Amsterdam
Oct. 9, 1943	Dies in Amsterdam, the Netherlands

Early Life

Pieter Zeeman (pronounced "ZAY-mahn"), the son of a Lutheran minister, showed aptitude for science at an early age. While at the Gymnasium in Delft preparing for his entrance into a university, he published an account of the aurora borealis from his hometown, Zonnemaire, and impressed the Dutch physicist Heike Kamerlingh Onnes with his experimental capability and grasp of James Clerk Maxwell's theories on heat.

In 1885, he entered the University of Leiden. There, he studied physics under Kamerlingh Onnes, a experimenter with low temperatures, and Hendrik Antoon Lorentz, a theoretician working in magneto-optics.

Magneto-Optics

Under Lorentz's direction, Zeeman experimented with the interaction of magnetism with polarized light. For his careful measurements of the Kerr effect, he was awarded a gold medal by the Netherlands Scientific Society of Haarlem and a doctorate by Leiden.

In 1896, Zeeman studied the effect of magnetism on the spectrum of sodium. His results supported Lorentz's suggestion that a mag-

(The Nobel Foundation)

The Zeeman Effect

The splitting of spectral lines by a magnetic field is known as the Zeeman effect.

Hendrik Antoon Lorentz, who first proposed the Zeeman effect, explained it classically. When an electron in an atom vibrates with a certain frequency, it emits radiation at that frequency. A magnetic field applied perpendicular to the direction of the vibration will exert force on the electron, either increasing or decreasing its speed. Two new frequencies of radiation are produced, one slightly higher and one slightly lower than the original.

Later, the Zeeman effect was explained using quantum theory. When an atom is placed in a magnetic field, its energy state depends on the orientation of its magnetic moment. Since angular momentum is quantized, a limited number of orientations are possible. Radiation is emitted and spectral lines are formed when an electron loses energy by making a transition to a lower energy state. Because a magnetic field causes each energy to split into multiple levels, and be-cause only certain transitions are allowed, the normal Zeeman effect predicts that an atom emits three closely spaced spectral lines when placed in a magnetic field.

Electrons also possess an internal angular momentum that couples to the orbital angular momentum and causes the number of energy states and spectral lines to differ from the number predicted by the normal Zeeman effect. This phenomenon is called the anomalous Zeeman effect.

The Zeeman effect has greatly enhanced the understanding of atomic and molecular structure. It also provides a way of detecting and measuring magnetic fields in space.

Bibliography

Fundamentals of Modern Physics. R. M. Eisberg. New York: John Wiley & Sons, 1964.
Modern Physics. Paul A. Tipler. New York: Worth, 1978.
Spectroscopy and Molecular Structure. Gerald W. King. New York: Holt, Rinehart and Winston, 1964.

netic field could cause a single spectral line to split into three parts and made it clear that the electron is responsible for the production of spectral lines. More precise measurements allowed Zeeman to evaluate the ratio of the charge of the electron to its mass.

For some atoms, the observed number of spectral lines did not agree with the theory. This anomaly set the stage for the discovery of electron spin. In 1902, Zeeman and Lorentz received the Nobel Prize in Physics for their work on the Zeeman effect.

When Zeeman became director of the Physical Institute at the University of Amsterdam in 1897, he tried to continue these investigations, but building vibrations caused by laboratory and city traffic made precise measurements impossible. For this reason, Zeeman often traveled to the University of Groningen to carry out his experiments. Eventually, he abandoned his magneto-optic research until a new laboratory became available.

Later Research

In the meantime, Zeeman ventured into new research areas. He measured the velocity of light in moving, solid, transparent media, such as quartz and glass. His results confirmed Lorentz's predictions that the Fresnel coefficient is related to the wavelength of the light. He also established the equivalency of gravitational and inertial mass for certain crystals and radioactive substances, lending support to Albert Einstein's theory of relativity. Using a technique that he developed for separating isotopes according to their mass, Zeeman helped to discover several isotopes, including argon 38 and nickel 64.

When Zeeman's new laboratory finally opened, he again turned his attention to experiments involving precision measurements of the Zeeman effect. During this period, he and his students investigated the magnetic resolution of some rare gases and the strong spectral lines of rhenium.

Zeeman the Man
Zeeman was dignified but kindly and was loved and respected by his colleagues, staff, and students. He was a meticulous and talented experimentalist, always ready for a challenge. He received many awards and honors for his work, including honorary degrees from at least ten universities and membership in a number of academies. He retired in 1935 and died on October 9, 1943.

Bibliography
By Zeeman
On the Influence of Magnetism on the Nature of the Light Emitted by a Substance, 1900

The Effects of a Magnetic Field on Radiation: Memoirs by Faraday, Kerr, and Zeeman, 1900 (Exum Percival Lewis, ed.)

Zuivere en toegepaste wiskunde, 1902

Strahlung des Lichtes im Magnetischen Felde, 1903

Seismographs and Seismograms, 1908

Researches in Magneto-Optics, with Special Reference to the Magnetic Resolution of Spectrum Lines, 1913

Verhandelingen van Dr. P. Zeeman over magneto-optische Verschijnselen, 1921 (H. A. Lorentz and H. Kamerlingh Onnes et al., eds.; collected works of Dr. P. Zeeman on magneto-optics phenomena)

About Zeeman
Dictionary of Scientific Biography. Charles Coulston Gillispie, ed. Vol. 14. New York: Charles Scribner's Sons, 1976.

Nobel Lectures: Physics, 1901-1921. Amsterdam: Elsevier, 1967.

"Pieter Zeeman." In *The Nobel Prize Winners: Physics*, edited by Frank N. Magill. Pasadena, Calif.: Salem Press, 1989.

"Pieter Zeeman, 1865-1943." Lord Rayleigh. *Obituary Notices of Fellows of the Royal Society of London* 4 (1944).

(Kathleen Duffy)

Fritz Zwicky

Areas of Achievement: Astronomy and physics

Contribution: An original thinker in physics and astronomy, Zwicky helped discover neutron stars. His insights led indirectly to the theory of black holes, extremely dense material from which no light or gravitation can escape.

Feb. 14, 1898	Born in Varna, Bulgaria
1922	Earns a Ph.D in theoretical physics from the Eidgenössiche Technische Hochschule (ETH) in Zurich, Switzerland
1925	Travels to the United States and begins working at the California Institute of Technology (Caltech)
1931-1933	Becomes a colleague of Albert Einstein, a visiting professor at Caltech
1934	Along with astronomer Walter Baade, presents his theory of neutron stars
mid-1930's	Finds the first evidence of dark matter in the universe
1942	Becomes professor of astrophysics at Caltech
1943-1949	Serves as the scientific director of Aerojet General Corporation, one of the first companies to manufacture rocket engines
1945-1946	Travels to Germany and Japan to interview pioneers in jet propulsion research
1949	Receives the Presidential Medal of Freedom from Harry S Truman
1957	Publishes his book *Morphological Astronomy*
Feb. 8, 1974	Dies in Pasadena, California

Early Life

Fritz Zwicky, born in Varna, Bulgaria, just before the turn of the twentieth century, lived in his native land only until he was six. At this young age, his Swiss father, Fridolin, and his Czechoslovakian mother, Franziscka, sent him to Switzerland for schooling. Zwicky excelled in the sciences and mathematics and gravitated toward engineering while still a teenager.

During World War I, Zwicky matriculated in the Eidgenössiche Technische Hochschule (ETH), a well-known technical institute in Zurich whose teachers included physicist Hermann Weyl. He passed his qualifying examinations in 1920 and gained his Ph.D. in theoretical physics two years later, in 1922, writing his thesis on the theory of ionic crystals. Coincidentally, this was seventeen years after Albert Einstein had received his doctorate from the University of Zurich. Zwicky was at one time Einstein's student; he later became the great German physicist's colleague while Einstein was a visiting professor at the California Institute of Technology (Caltech) from 1931 to 1933.

Zwicky remained in Switzerland until 1925, when he became a postgraduate student at Caltech. There, he conducted research alongside the institute's Nobel Prize-winning president, Robert Millikan. Caltech appointed Zwicky assistant professor of theoretical physics in 1927. Two years later, he became associate professor, and finally, in 1942, professor of astrophysics.

Zwicky worked on several different problems within the realm of physics, ranging from

(Library of Congress)

rocket propulsion to the dynamics of colliding galaxies to the philosophy of science. By the late 1930's, he had published several papers on astronomy. These papers gradually uncovered the secrets of supernovas and neutron stars.

Work in Rocketry

Zwicky was among those twentieth century scientists who chose to work in rocketry while it was still new and experimental. In the 1940's, Zwicky helped design and test rocket boosters known as JATO's for the U.S. Army and Navy. The JATO, which stands for "jet-assisted take-off," could be stored under a range of temperature conditions, would not explode upon ignition, and could boost aircraft into the air from short runways at a dramatically steep angle. The JATO was unusual not only because it was a reliable solid fuel rocket but also because its propellant was not a powder but rather a mixture of oxidizer and common asphalt.

Before Zwicky became involved in the JATO project in 1940, he actually failed to understand the potential importance of rocket development. In 1937, when Frank Malina, a young Caltech graduate student, tried to tell Zwicky some of the problems that he was having with his doctoral dissertation on liquid-propellant rockets, Zwicky angrily dismissed him with the opinion that he was wasting his time on an impossible subject. Zwicky insisted that a rocket could not operate in space, as it required the atmosphere to push against in order to provide thrust. By 1940, Zwicky had realized his mistake and worked alongside Malina. Even in the mid-twentieth century, it was difficult for some physicists to conceive of action in a vacuum.

It is ironic that Zwicky was not well known outside the field of astronomy and rocketry. When he died in 1974, his name became a footnote to the history of physics, and he has been remembered only slightly in the literature of physics. He did not gain recognition as one of the giants of astrophysics, as have Subrahmanyan Chandrasekar, Roger Penrose, and

Neutron Stars and Dark Matter

In 1934, Zwicky, working alongside astronomer Walter Baade at the Mount Wilson Observatory, sketched out his vision of neutron stars. Nearly thirty-four years were to elapse before physicists began to accept the theory of neutron stars.

In the 1930's, when Zwicky first began writing about neutron stars, the theory was controversial. At the theory's heart lies the idea that electrons might be forced into the nuclei of stellar atoms and that stars could then become a mass composed only of neutrons. Zwicky and Baade, observing supernova explosions through the Mount Wilson Observatory telescope, believed that supernovas might form neutron stars. If, reasoned the two astronomers, a white dwarf were near the supernova, remnants of material from the exploding star might be absorbed by the white dwarf, which would then contract into an extremely dense core of material. (A white dwarf is a compact star near the end of its existence.)

Zwicky's work on neutron stars led to the possibility that other dense matter might exist in the universe, including black holes. Zwicky also pioneered in the study of the morphology of galaxies. He wondered how galaxies that collide avoid mutual destruction, since their individual stars move by each other so rapidly that it seems the galaxies would tend to fly apart. Yet, many do not. Could some nonluminous form of matter keep these large clustered galaxies together? Zwicky and fellow physicist Sinclair Smith had found the first evidence of dark matter in the universe.

Bibliography

"Black Holes." Roger Penrose. In *The World of Physics: A Small Library of the Literature of Physics from Antiquity to the Present*. Vol 3. New York: Simon and Schuster, 1987.

"Dark Matter in Spiral Galaxies." In *The Universe of Galaxies*, edited by Paul W. Hodge. New York: W. H. Freeman, 1984.

The Shadows of Creation: Dark Matter and the Structure of the Universe. Michael Riordan and David N. Schramm. New York: W. H. Freeman, 1991.

Stephen Hawking. Yet, Zwicky's writings were voluminous (559 publications) and his insights paved the way for the modern conception of the universe's past and its structure. His work formed a cornerstone of twentieth century astrophysical theory.

Bibliography

By Zwicky

"On the Thermodynamic Equilibrium in the Universe," *Proceedings of the National Academy of Sciences*, 1928

"Types of Novae," *Reviews of Modern Physics*, 1940

Catalogue of Selected Compact Galaxies and of Post-Eruptive Galaxies, 1971 (with Margit A. Zwicky)

Morphological Astronomy, 1957

About Zwicky

"A Special Kind of Astronomer." Cecelia Payne-Gaposchkin. *Sky and Telescope* (1974).

"Presidential Addresses on the Society's Awards." Fred Hoyle. *Quarterly Journal of the Royal Astronomical Society* 13 (1972).

(Benjamin Zibit)

Vladimir Zworykin

Areas of Achievement: Physics and technology

Contribution: Zworykin developed electronic tubes that became the foundation of modern television systems. He also engaged in significant work with the electron microscope.

July 30, 1889	Born in Mourom (now Murom), Russia
1912	Graduated from St. Petersburg Institute of Technology
1914-1916	Assigned to the radio corps of the Russian army
1919	Emigrates to the United States
1920	Begins work for Westinghouse Electric Research Laboratories
1926	Given a Ph.D. in physics by the University of Pittsburgh
1928	Receives a patent for an all-cathode-ray television system
1930	Moves from Westinghouse to RCA Laboratories to direct television research
1939	Develops an electron microscope
1940	Publishes *Television*
1943	Elected to the National Academy of Sciences
1947	Promoted to vice president at RCA Laboratories
1951	Receives the Medal of Honor from the Institute of Radio Engineers
1967	Receives the National Medal of Honor from President Lyndon Johnson
July 29, 1982	Dies in Princeton, New Jersey

Early Life

Vladimir Kosma Zworykin (in Russian, pronounced "ZVAHR-kyihn") was born to a comfortably situated merchant family in Murom, Russia, in 1889. He demonstrated an early interest in the natural sciences; while in high school, he often helped his science teacher with class demonstrations and oversaw a small collection of laboratory equipment.

Zworykin honed his interest in physics and engineering during his studies at the St. Petersburg Institute of Technology, where he served as a teaching and research assistant to Professor Boris Rozing (or Rosing). Rozing's interest in a television system based on line-by-line

(Smithsonian Institution)

scanning shaped Zworykin's approach to this new electronic field of research. Study of X rays in Paris at the Collège de France and service in the radio corps of the Russian army during World War I gave Zworykin a deeper grounding in the physics and technology behind the emerging electronic world.

Life as a Research Engineer

The upheaval of the Russian Revolution prompted Zworykin to emigrate to the United States, where, in 1920, he secured a position in television research with Westinghouse Electric Research Laboratories in Pittsburgh, Pennsylvania. Within a decade, he was transferred to the RCA Laboratories in Camden, New Jersey. He spent his career in these research facilities, where he headed a team that developed an iconoscope, an electronic tube for a television camera, and a kinescope, a television picture tube. These successful inventions were the result of Zworykin's persistence in developmental work and the efforts of several other inventors working on television in the 1920's and 1930's.

In much of his work, Zworykin had the personal and financial support of David Sarnoff, the leading proponent of television development at RCA. Zworykin realized that, as a technological system, television required several linked inventions, support from a research institution, several years of developmental work, and a knowledge base gleaned from the work of many scientists and engineers around the globe.

Zworykin's work on television, which resulted in a U.S. patent for an all-cathode-ray system in 1928, coincided with his research centering on electron optics, radiation detection devices, the electron mul-

The Iconoscope and the Kinescope

Zworykin directed the development of the iconoscope, a television transmission tube, and the kinescope, a television receiving tube, which formed the basis of modern electronic television systems.

The iconoscope had a light sensitive surface with more than one million separate photoelectric cells on a camera plate. These cells were created with a coating consisting of cesium oxide, mica, and silver. A signal was sent from a television camera to this screen with a scanning process of electron beams moving rapidly back and forth across the photosensitive surface. The resulting electrical charges corresponding to the intensity of light "seen" by the camera were transmitted to a receiver, which read the light intensity and were sent electronically to the kinescope (picture tube).

The kinescope also had a light-sensitive surface and an electron gun that boosted and transmitted the electrical signals corresponding to the light intensity read by the iconoscope. The electron gun scanned the fluorescent surface of the picture tube and re-created the visual imagery transmitted by the television camera.

Because these two devices were fully electronic in their operation and control, they became the prototype for commercial television in the United States. The iconoscope has been replaced by an improved camera tube, but the modern television picture tube is an improved version of Zworykin's original kinescope.

Bibliography

"The Tube: A Russian Immigrant Pushed Television out of the Rube Goldberg Era." Donald G. Fink. *Science* 84, no. 5 (November, 1984).

Twentieth-Century Inventors. Nathan Aaseng. New York: Facts on File, 1991.

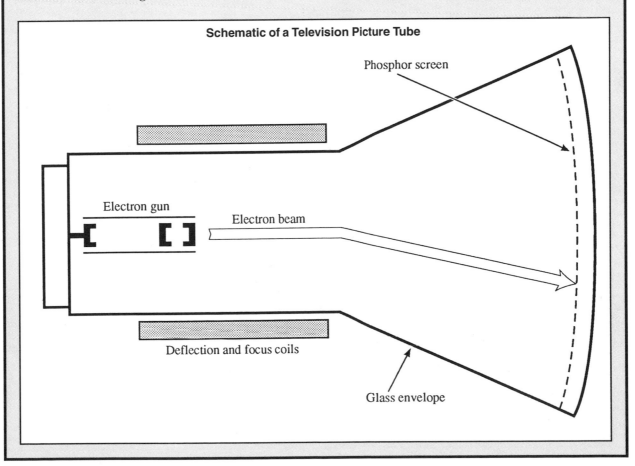

Schematic of a Television Picture Tube

Phosphor screen

Electron gun

Electron beam

Deflection and focus coils

Glass envelope

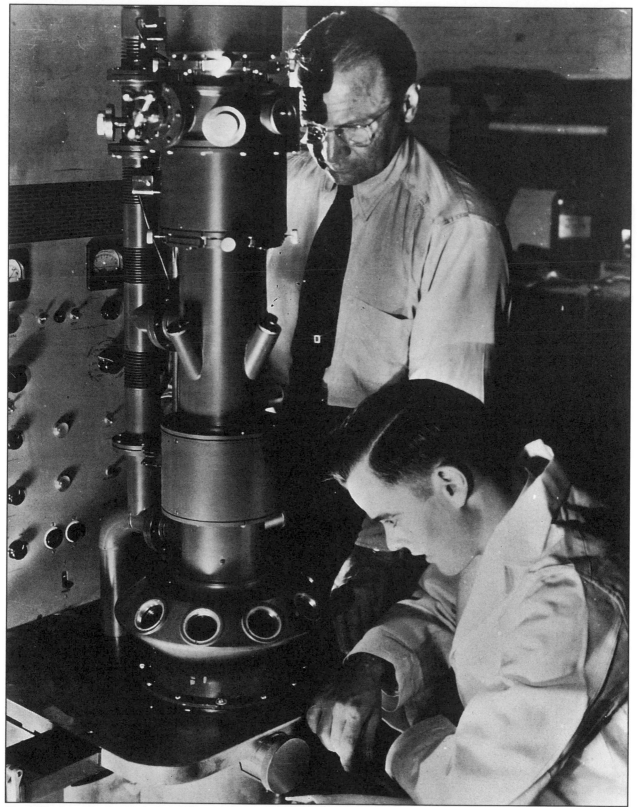

Zworykin (standing) and James Hillier look into the electron microscope that they developed. (Library of Congress)

tiplier, and the electron microscope. After his retirement from RCA in 1954 and until his death in 1982, Zworykin focused his efforts on medical electronics.

Legacy

Zworykin developed an electronic television system with iconoscope and kinescope tubes, the basis for the successful commercial television system marketed in the United States in the 1930's and late 1940's. For this achievement, he holds the title of founder of modern television among the general public, despite some controversy. While others, especially Philo Farnsworth in the United States, also developed working television systems, Zworykin's system became the model for commercial development, in part because of Sarnoff's strong support within the RCA organization.

This achievement is typical of the characteristics of twentieth century technology: dedication to the long-term development of a new technology, a firm grounding in science, and the sustained institutional support of a research laboratory. Zworykin thrived in this setting, and the commercial success of television is his legacy to the world.

Bibliography
By Zworykin
Photocells and Their Application, 1930 (with E. D. Wilson)

"The Iconoscope—A Modern Version of the Electric Eye," *Proceedings of the Institute of Radio Engineers*, 1934

Television: The Electronics of Image Transmission, 1940 (with George A. Morton)

Television in Science and Industry, 1958 (with E. G. Ramberg and L. E. Flory)

About Zworykin
Modern Americans in Science and Invention. Edna Yost. Philadelphia: J. B. Lippincott, 1941.

Zworykin, Pioneer of Television. Albert Abramson. Urbana: University of Illinois Press, 1995.

(H. J. Eisenman)

Glossary

Acetyl: A grouping of atoms, usually designated by the formula CH_3CO, which remains stable through a variety of chemical reactions. Such stable configurations of atoms are usually called radicals. The acetyl radical combines with OH to form acetic acid.

Acid: A chemical that loses a positively charged hydrogen ion in a chemical reaction. *Compare* **Base.**

Adiabatic: Occurring without the gain or loss of heat.

Aerodynamics: The study of the interaction of moving objects with gases, usually the motion of rigid objects through the atmosphere.

Agglutination: The clumping together of parts which keep their original form. Usually used to describe the adhesion of clumps of red blood cells or microorganisms.

Alchemy: The discredited study of techniques to accelerate what were thought to be naturally occurring processes, such as the transmutation of base metals into gold.

Alpha particle: A product of radioactive decay which Ernest Rutherford showed to be identical to a helium atom that has lost two electrons.

Amine: Any molecule in which one of the hydrogen atoms in the molecule NH_3 has been replaced by a radical that contains carbon and hydrogen (a hydrocarbon radical).

Amino acid: Any organic molecule containing both at least one amine and one carboxyl (COOH) group. Amino acids are bound together in chains to form proteins.

Ampere: A unit of electrical current, named for André-Marie Ampère, which is equal to approximately 1 coulomb per second.

Amplitude: The maximum difference in the position of an alternating wave or current from the average.

Anatomy: The structure of an organism or the study of that structure.

Anion: A negatively charged atom or molecule.

Anti-: A prefix meaning "opposite in situation, effect, or activity"; also, "serving to cure, prevent, or alleviate."

Antibiotic: Any substance, such as penicillin, that destroys or inhibits the growth of microorganisms, especially bacteria.

Antibody: A substance, produced by an organism in reaction to the presence of foreign material, which inhibits the toxic effects of that material. Antibodies are specific to particular foreign materials.

Antigen: A molecule capable of stimulating the production of antibodies by an organism.

Antiparticle: A particle that is created or annihilated at the same time that any ordinary subatomic particle is created or annihilated. Antiparticles have an equal but opposite charge, spin, magnetic moment, and parity and an identical mass and average lifetime to their ordinary counterparts. *Compare* **Particle.**

Antiseptic: A substance which can kill disease-producing microorganisms.

Area: The measure of the surface of a two-dimensional figure.

Artery: One of the blood vessels which carry blood away from the heart. *Compare* **Vein.**

Assay: The procedure used to determine the chemical composition of an ore or other unknown substance.

Asteroid: A small celestial body which orbits the sun.

Astral: Having to do with the stars.

Astronomy: The study of the universe beyond the earth.

Asymmetry: A lack of symmetry. Also, for carbon atoms, being bonded to four different atoms or groups.

Atmosphere: The gaseous matter surrounding a celestial body (such as Earth) which is held by that body's gravitational field.

Atom: The smallest unit of an element, once thought to be unchangeable but now known to have a structure which may be changed with the absorption or emission of subatomic particles carrying very large amounts of energy.

Atomic bomb: An explosive device of massive destructive capability whose energy comes from the splitting (fission) of heavy atoms, such as of uranium or plutonium.

Atomic number: The number of protons in the atomic nucleus of a given element, which determines that element's location in the periodic table.

ATP (adenosine triphosphate): A compound used by virtually all organisms for storing energy.

Avogadro's number: A constant, 6.023×10^{23}, representing the number of atoms or molecules in 1 mole of a substance.

Bacillus (*pl.* bacilli): One of a variety of rod-shaped bacteria.

Bacteria (*sing.* bacterium): Single-celled organisms in which chromosomes are not carried in a nucleus. They may act as parasites and cause illness.

Bacteriology: The study of bacteria.

Bacteriophage: One of a number of viruses that infect bacteria, causing their disintegration.

Baryon: A particle, such as a neutron or a proton, which is composed of three quarks.

Base: In chemistry, a chemical that gains a positively charged hydrogen ion in a reaction. *Compare* **Acid.** In genetics, one of four paired groups—adenine, cytosine, guanine, and thymine—that make up DNA.

Beta particle: A high-energy electron released during radioactive decay.

Big bang theory: A theory, based on general relativity, which holds that the universe was produced at a single instant in time and at a single point in space and that it has been rapidly expanding and cooling ever since.

Biochemistry: The study of the chemical processes occurring within living organisms.

Biology: The study of life in all of its forms.

Biometry: The statistical study of biological information.

Black hole: A collapsed star so dense that its gravitational field is strong enough to prevent the escape of any form of radiation, including light.

Blackbody: An ideal body that absorbs all radiation striking it and emits no radiation. Under such conditions, principles of thermodynamics allow the relationship between the temperature of the body and the intensity of radiation at any frequency to be calculated.

Bond: Any of several forces by which atoms or ions are held in a molecule or crystal. Most commonly, chemical bonds involve the sharing of one or more electrons between two atoms.

Botany: The study of plants.

Bubble chamber: An apparatus for detecting the path of particles through the trail of bubbles left by ions created in a superheated liquid.

Calorie: The amount of heat energy needed to raise the temperature of 1 gram of water from 14.5 degrees Celsius to 15.5 degrees Celsius. In nutritional studies, 1 Calorie (or kilocalorie) is equal to 1,000 calories.

Cancer: One of a class of diseases characterized by abnormal cell growth that invades adjacent cell groups.

Capillary: The smallest blood-carrying vessels, which connect arteries and veins. Exchanges between blood and extracellular fluid take place in the capillaries.

Carbon: A naturally occurring chemical element found in all organic molecules. The unique ability of carbon to bond to itself allows the creation of an enormous number of long-chain molecules, which form the basis for life processes.

Carbon dating: Estimation of the age of a once-living object through calculation of its remaining percentage of carbon 14, an isotope of carbon which is naturally radioactive and which has a half-life of 5,700 years. The process of carbon dating assumes that when the carbon was first fixed in the object, the percentage of carbon 14 in the environment was at its current frequency.

Carbon dioxide: A molecule composed of one carbon atom and two oxygen atoms. It is present in small amounts in the atmosphere and is the principal source of carbon for the production of sugar in photosynthesis.

Carcinogen: Any cancer-causing substance.

Carrier: In genetics, an organism with a single recessive gene for a given trait (especially a disease) which does not affect that organism but which can be passed on to offspring that inherit the same recessive gene from the other parent. In many biological phenomena, a molecule to which an active agent is temporarily bound, allowing that agent to be transported across a barrier. In radio, an electromagnetic wave that can be varied in amplitude, phase, or frequency in order to transmit information.

Catalyst: A substance that speeds up or makes possible a chemical reaction without being permanently changed itself. Enzymes are biological catalysts.

Catastrophism: One of several theories which argues that sudden and dramatic geological events have occurred in Earth's history. Various versions emphasize that the earth is extremely old, that the physical forces involved in such events worked in ways that are no longer observable, or that mass extinctions and the creation of a new set of species resulted with each event. *Compare* **Uniformitarianism.**

Celestial: Referring to the sky or the heavens visible from Earth.

Celestial sphere: An imaginary sphere of infinite radius against which celestial objects such as the sun, moon, and stars seem to be projected, as viewed from Earth.

Cell: The smallest structural unit of a living organism capable of independent function.

Cell biology: The study of cell structure and functions.

Celsius scale: The temperature scale, named for Anders Celsius, in which water freezes at 0 degrees and boils at 100 degrees under normal atmospheric pressure at sea level. *Compare* **Fahrenheit scale, Kelvin scale.**

Centigrade scale: Another commonly used name for the temperature scale that officially became the Celsius scale in 1948.

Central Dogma: In molecular genetics, the concept that inherited information is stored in DNA, transferred to RNA, and then read during the formation of protein molecules.

Charge: The positive or negative electricity associated with an object. Ordinarily, ions and subatomic particles have a specific charge associated with them which is an integer multiple of the charge associated with an electron.

Charm: The hypothesized fourth "flavor" of quark. Also, a general term for a quantum number proposed to account for the asymmetry between hadron and lepton behavior and to explain why some particle reactions do not occur.

Chemistry: The study of the structure, properties, and reactions of substances.

Chromosome: The threadlike structures, composed primarily of DNA, which contain most of the genetic information of a cell. Each human cell has forty-six chromosomes arranged in twenty-three pairs, categorized as either sex chromosomes (X and Y chromosomes) or autosomes (the rest).

Circulation: The movement of the blood through the system of arteries, veins, and capillaries as a result of the pumping of the heart.

Classical physics: Physics as understood prior to or without the consideration of the concepts of relativity theory, wave mechanics, and quantum theory.

Cloud chamber: An apparatus for detecting or inferring the path of particles through the trail of drops of liquid formed on ions produced by passing charged particles through a supersaturated vapor.

Color: Referring to one of three basic forms of quarks, each of which can exist in six different kinds, or "flavors."

Combustion: A chemical change (usually an oxidation) accompanied by the production of light and heat.

Comet: A celestial object, visible from Earth only when it is near the sun, which has either an elliptical orbit with high eccentricity or a parabolic path. The gases surrounding a comet form a tail behind it pointing away from the sun.

Compound: In chemistry, a substance composed of two or more elementary substances.

Conductor: A material which allows the passage of electricity. *Compare* **Insulator.**

Congenital: A condition which is not hereditary but which exists from birth.

Conservation: In science, the quality of remaining constant. Many natural laws can be formulated by specifying something which remains constant during a physical process. For example, momentum must be conserved in any collision, and energy must be conserved in any classical process. Quantities such as spin, parity, and the formula $E = mc^2$ must be conserved when subatomic particles decay to produce other particles and energy.

Constant: In a mathematical equation, a quantity which is not allowed to change. *Compare* **Variable.** In physics, one of a number of quantities that seem to be built into the structure of the universe, such as Planck's constant and Avogadro's number.

Continent: One of the major land masses of the earth.

Continental drift: The slow separation of the earth's continents over billions of years from an initial single land mass.

Cosmic: Referring to the cosmos or to the rest of the universe in contrast to Earth.

Cosmic rays: Ionizing radiation which originates outside the earth's atmosphere and which produces secondary radiation within the atmosphere through collisions or decay.

Cosmology: The study of the origin, structure, and processes which shape the universe as an organized whole.

Cosmos: The universe seen as an orderly and harmonious system.

Coulomb: The unit of electrical charge, named for Charles-Augustin Coulomb.

Crossing-over: The separation of linked genetic markers from their original chromosome and their recombination with another chromosome. This process usually involves a reciprocal exchange between two chromosomes.

Crystal: A solid in which the atoms are arranged in a regular spatial pattern.

Culture: In biology, the association of organisms under controlled conditions or the production of such an association (for example, the growth of bacteria for study).

Cyclotron: A device for accelerating charged subatomic particles by using an alternating electric field as they move in a nearly circular path.

Dark matter: Invisible matter in the universe. According to the big bang theory, the rate of expansion of the universe depends on the amount of matter it contains. Estimates based on "visible" matter are far too small for the relatively slow rate of expansion observed, so many cosmologists have suggested the existence of dark, "invisible" matter.

Daughter cell: One of two cells resulting from the division of a single cell, so that the genetic information from the original is contained in each of the new cells. *Compare* **Parent cell.**

Decay: In biology, the decomposition of organic matter resulting from the action of microorganisms. In physics, the spontaneous disintegration of a subatomic particle into a combination of new particles.

Density: The distribution of a quantity, such as energy or mass, per unit of space, such as volume or area.

Di-: A prefix meaning "two."

Diffraction: The modification of a wave by a barrier placed in its path. The amplitude of the wave is increased at some locations and decreased at others, often bending the wave's direction of motion.

Diffusion: The process by which a quantity which is unevenly distributed in space (for example, the intensity of light or the concentration of gas particles or ions) becomes more evenly distributed.

Digestion: The breakdown of food in the body, usually in the presence of enzymes, into relatively small, soluble molecules.

Dipole: A pair of equal but opposite electrical charges or magnetic poles separated by a small distance.

Disease: An abnormal condition of an organism which causes impaired functioning.

Dissection: The procedure by which a deceased organism is cut apart to study its structure. *Compare* **Vivisection.**

DNA (deoxyribonucleic acid): The self-replicating molecule which is the fundamental carrier of hereditary material. Its structure is a double helix, a twisted ladder with sugars and phosphates forming the sides and base pairs in the center forming the rungs.

Dominant: Of a gene, requiring only one copy in order to be expressed as a given trait. *Compare* **Recessive.**

Dys-: A prefix meaning "wrong, painful, or difficult."

$E = mc^2$: Albert Einstein's formula describing the relationship between energy and mass, where E is energy, m is mass, and c is the speed of light.

Earth science: The study of the origin and structure of and geological processes occurring in the earth.

Eccentricity: In astronomy, the degree of an orbit's deviation from a circle.

Eclipse: The partial or total obscuring of one celestial object by another, as viewed from a relative position on Earth. In a solar eclipse, the moon comes between the earth and the sun, blocking the view of the sun from certain locations. In a lunar eclipse, the sun comes between the earth and the moon, blocking the view of the moon from certain locations.

Electricity: A class of phenomena arising from the existence and actions of electrical charges.

Electro-: A prefix meaning "pertaining to electricity" or "pertaining to an electron."

Electrode: An emitter or collector of electrical charges, most often made of a solid material and placed in a liquid, a gas, or an emptied space.

Electromagnetism: The magnetism that arises from electrical charges in motion. Also, the study of the relationship between electrical and magnetic phenomena.

Electron: A very stable elementary particle which carries a negative charge and which is a component of all atoms. Electrons travel in orbits around the atomic nucleus. *Compare* **Neutron, Proton.**

Electronvolt: A unit of energy equal to that absorbed by a single electron falling through a potential difference of 1 volt.

Element: A substance composed of atoms which all have the same number of protons in their nuclei.

Ellipse: An oval-shaped, closed curve defined by a fixed total distance from two points.

Energy: The capacity to do work.

Entropy: A measure of the disorder of a system; the less the order, the higher the entropy. All natural processes involve an increase in the entropy of the closed system within which they occur.

Environment: The totality of external conditions that affect an organism or part of an organism.

Enzyme: A protein with chemical groups on its surface that allow it to be a catalyst for a chemical reaction.

Epidemic: A rapid and extensive spread of a contagious disease among a population.

Equilibrium: The state of any system in which the net result of all acting forces is zero. In chemistry, the state of a reaction in which the forward and reverse reactions occur at equal rates so that there is no change in the concentrations of reactants.

Ether: In chemistry, any compound in which two hydrocarbon groups are linked by an oxygen atom. In medicine, a volatile liquid widely used as an anesthetic. In physics, the all-pervasive, massless medium through which electromagnetic waves were once thought to propagate.

Etiology: The cause or origin of something, such as of a disease.

Evolution: Any change over time, especially the biological phenomenon of change in organisms from generation to generation. According to Charles Darwin, evolution occurs through a gradual process called natural selection, in which random changes take place in organisms and some changes lead to greater reproductive success in a particular environment.

Experiment: A procedure in which certain factors are allowed to vary while others remain constant or are controlled in order to determine the potential influences of the varying factors.

Fahrenheit scale: The temperature scale, named for Gabriel Daniel Fahrenheit, in which water freezes at 32 degrees and boils at 212 degrees at standard atmospheric pressure. *Compare* **Celsius scale, Kelvin scale.**

Fauna: All animals found in a given area. *Compare* **Flora.**

Fermentation: The enzyme-induced breakdown of large molecules (such as sugar) without the presence of oxygen, in order to extract energy. Fermentation reactions produce such substances as beer and wine, in which carbohydrates are broken down to carbon dioxide and alcohol.

Fertilization: The union of a sperm with an egg.

Fission: The breaking apart of a single entity into two pieces. In physics, large atoms break up into smaller fragments, with the creation of energy. *Compare* **Fusion.** In biology, cells divide into pairs to produce the growth of an organism.

Flavor: Referring to one of six basic kinds of quarks—up, down, top, bottom, charm, and strange—each of which can exist in three different forms, or "colors."

Flora: All plants found in a given area. *Compare* **Fauna.**

Fluorescence: The emission of light by a substance after it has absorbed energy.

Fossil: Any remnant or recognizable impression of an organism preserved over geological time.

Frequency: For periodic motions, the number of complete cycles occurring per unit of time. In wave motions, frequency is inversely proportional to wavelength.

Fungus (*pl.* fungi, *adj.* fungal): A plantlike organism that does not produce its own food through photosynthesis, instead absorbing complex carbon compounds from other living or dead organisms. Fungal infections range from minor skin diseases to serious diseases of the lungs and other organs.

Fusion: The joining of two pieces into a single whole. In atomic physics, fusion is the joining of two light nuclei to form a larger one, with the release of great amounts of energy, most of which is carried by high-speed neutrons. *Compare* **Fission.**

Galaxy: One of many large-scale aggregations of stars, dust, and gases in the universe which have some discernible structure.

Gamma rays: High-energy light emitted by decaying atomic nuclei.

Gas: A phase of matter characterized by low density and viscosity, by the capacity to fill any container rapidly, and by high levels of energy relative to liquid or solid states. *Compare* **Liquid, Solid.**

Gene: A portion of a DNA molecule which controls a hereditary characteristic of an organism, either individually or in combination with other genes.

General relativity theory: A theory proposed by Albert Einstein that describes gravitational forces in terms of the curvature of space-time. *See also* **Relativity.**

Genetics: The study of heredity.

Genome: All the genes contained in a single complete set of chromosomes.

Genotype: The genetic constitution of an individual with respect to one or more traits, even if those traits are not expressed. *Compare* **Phenotype.**

Genus: A group of closely related species. *Compare* **Species.**

Geo-: A prefix meaning "pertaining to the earth."

Geocentric: Referring to a former model of the solar system in which the sun and all planets were thought to orbit around the earth. *Compare* **Heliocentric.**

Geology: The study of the origin, history, and structure of the earth.

Geometry: A mathematical system describing spatial properties. Euclidean geometry is said to describe three-dimensional space; modern geometries describe n-dimensional "curved" spaces—that is, spaces which have different properties in different regions.

Giant: Referring to a class of highly luminous, exceptionally massive, relatively old, and relatively cool stars.

Gluon: One of eight kinds of neutral particles thought to bind quarks together.

Grafting: In botany, the joining of part of one plant to the stem or root of another in order to produce a single plant; the root-bearing recipient is called the stock, and the piece grafted on is called the scion. In biology, the transplantation of some part of the body (especially skin) to another part of the body or to another patient.

Gravity: The force exerted by every body on every other body. Between two bodies, it is proportional to the product of their masses and inversely proportional to the distance between them. Gravity is the weakest of the four known physical forces, which also include electromagnetic forces, weak subatomic forces, and strong subatomic forces. The universality of gravitational forces was discovered and described by Isaac Newton in 1687. Albert Einstein's general relativity theory, formulated in 1916, accounts for gravity in terms of the curvature of space-time.

Hadron: Any elementary particle that experiences the strong force.

Half-life: The time needed for half of some initial number of identical radioactive particles to decay. Applied to a single particle, it is the time at which the probability that the particle will have decayed equals 0.5.

Handedness: A property of many objects, including many elementary particles, in which forms can be classified as right-handed or left-handed. These forms differ from the mirror image of the object but not from the rotated object.

Heat: Energy that flows between substances as a consequence of their temperature differences.

Heavy elements: The elements with atomic numbers greater than 150. The energy per neutron or proton required to make a nucleus is relatively constant for nuclei which have between about 50 and 150 nucleons, but it declines for nuclei with a nuclear mass of greater than 150. Heavy elements will undergo fission into smaller fragments if sufficient excitation energy is provided. *Compare* **Light elements.**

Helio-: A prefix meaning "pertaining to the sun."

Heliocentric: Referring to models of the solar system in which all planets orbit around the sun or a point near the sun. *Compare* **Geocentric.**

Helium: The element whose nucleus has two protons and usually two neutrons. It was discovered through analysis of the solar spectrum before it was isolated on the earth.

Heredity: The transmission of characteristics from ancestor to descendant through genes.

High-energy physics. *See* **Particle physics.**

Hormone: A substance produced at one location in a multicellular organism which is carried to another location (the target site), where it has physiological or biochemical effects.

Host: An organism that harbors and provides nourishment to parasites or microorganisms such as bacteria or viruses.

Humors, theory of: The former theory that health is produced by an appropriate balance of four substances, or humors, in the body—blood, phlegm, yellow bile, and black bile. Personality traits were also attributed to these substances.

Hybrid: The offspring of two genetically dissimilar parents.

Hydro-: A prefix meaning "water or fluid."

Hydrogen: The lightest element, whose nucleus contains a single proton.

Hydrogen bomb: A bomb of huge explosive power whose energy source is the joining (fusion) of hydrogen isotopes into helium.

Hyper-: A prefix meaning "high" or "more than normal."

Hypo-: A prefix meaning "low" or "less than normal."

Hypothesis: A conjecture which accounts for a set of facts and that suggests directions for further investigation. To the extent that predictions based on the hypothesis are confirmed, it is said to be supported.

Immune system: An organism's system for responding to foreign materials and microorganisms through the production of antibodies.

Immunity: The resistance of an organism to a disease. Immunity is brought about by previous exposure to the live or dead microorganisms that cause the disease and subsequent antibody production in the body.

Immunology: The medical field which studies the immune system and its functioning.

Inertia: The tendency of a body to remain either at rest or in motion in a straight line unless subjected to a force.

Infrared light: Electromagnetic radiation with a wavelength just longer than the red portion of the visible spectrum.

Inoculation: The process of introducing antigens into an organism, usually for the purpose of producing antibodies and therefore immunity.

Inorganic: Anything not living or the product of organisms. In chemistry, compounds not containing carbon. *Compare* **Organic.**

Insulator: A substance or object which does not conduct electricity; sometimes also used to designate a material that conducts heat very poorly. *Compare* **Conductor.**

Interstellar: Located between or among the stars.

Invention: A new device or process, or the procedure for creating a new device or process.

Ion: An atom or molecule which has attained a net electrical charge by gaining or losing one or more electrons.

Isotope: A variant of an element which has the same number of protons in its atomic nucleus but a different number of neutrons. While some isotopes of an element are stable, others undergo spontaneous radioactive decay.

Joule: A unit of energy, named for James P. Joule, equal to the work done by an electrical current of 1 ampere passed through a resistance of 1 ohm for one second.

K-meson: One of a class of four fundamental particles with masses between 970 and 1,000 electron masses. Neutral K-mesons decay into two or three lighter mesons, while charged K-mesons decay into two leptons (one mu-meson plus one neutrino).

Kelvin scale: The temperature scale, named for Lord Kelvin (Sir William Thomson), in which water freezes at 273.15 Kelvins and boils at 373.15 Kelvins. This assignment makes 0 Kelvin the temperature at which a substance contains no heat energy. One Kelvin is equivalent to 1 degree Celsius. *Compare* **Celsius scale, Fahrenheit scale.**

Kinetic energy: The energy of a body as a result of its motion. Kinetic energy is equal to the mass of a body multiplied by one half of the square of its velocity. *Compare* **Potential energy.**

Latitude: Angular distance north or south of the equator, measured in degrees. *Compare* **Longitude.**

Left-handed. *See* **Handedness**

Lepton: One of six particles having a spin of 1/2—the electron, the mu-meson, the tau particle, and three neutrinos—which do not interact with the strong force.

Light elements: Elements with an atomic number less than about 50. These elements have a relatively low binding energy per nucleon and may undergo fusion to produce heavier elements if sufficient excitation energy is provided. *Compare* **Heavy elements.**

Light-year: The distance traveled by light in a vacuum in one year, which is approximately 10 trillion kilometers.

Liquid: A phase of matter characterized by particle energies intermediate between those of solids and gases and by great resistance to compression. *Compare* **Gas, Solid.**

Longitude: Angular distance east or west of the prime meridian, which passes through Greenwich, England, measured in degrees. *Compare* **Latitude.** Also, in astronomy, the angular distance east from the position of the vernal equinox.

Luminescence: Light emission not accounted for by the temperature of the emitting body, often caused by chemical reactions or electron bombardment.

Lunar: Having to do with the moon.

Lys- or Lyso-: A prefix meaning "pertaining to cells."

Lysis: The bursting of a cell.

Lysosome: An organelle in cells which contains enzymes that attack the cell walls of bacteria; one of the body's nonspecific defense mechanisms against foreign material.

Macro-: A prefix meaning "long" or "large."

Magnet: A body that attracts iron and certain other materials as a result of the alignment of its atoms and the motion of the electrons in them. More generally, any configuration of electrical currents which produces effects similar to those produced by magnetic materials.

Magnetic moment: The torque produced on a magnetic dipole per unit of magnetic field strength. The magnetic moment will increase with the separation of the poles and with the strength of the poles.

Magnitude: In astronomy, a measure of the apparent brightness of a star, from 1 (for the brightest stars) to 6 (for the dimmest visible stars); each unit increase on the brightness scale corresponds to a decrease in apparent brightness by a factor of 2.512. In geology, a measure of the intensity of an earthquake proportional to the logarithm of the total energy released; an increase of one unit on the Richter scale represents a sixtyfold increase in energy released by the earthquake.

Mass: A measure of a body's resistance to acceleration. In classical physics, mass is constant, but, in relativistic physics, mass increases with velocity. In modern physics, in order to avoid confusion, particles are identified by their rest-mass—that is, their mass in a system in which they are not moving.

Mathematics: The study of numerical, spatial, and other formal relationships based on precise definitions and assumptions and through the use of well-defined, logical rules.

Medicine: The science and/or practice which

seeks to diagnose, treat, or prevent disease and other damage to the body.

Mendelism: Commitment to the basic laws of genetic inheritance as articulated by Gregor Johann Mendel.

Meson: A hadron with a full integer spin.

Metabolism: The sum total of chemical reactions which occur in an organism, or a subset of those reactions pertaining to a defined function.

Meteorology: The study of phenomena, especially weather, which occur in the atmosphere.

Micro-: A prefix meaning "small," "one millionth," or "involving microscopy."

Microorganism: Any organism too small to be seen without a microscope.

Microscope: Any device which provides an enlarged visual image of an object. While early microscopes used only visible light, microscopes using X rays and electrons are capable of providing images of much smaller structures.

Milky Way: The galaxy which contains Earth's solar system.

Mold: Any of various wooly fungal growths. Some molds are useful in medicine; Alexander Fleming discovered the antibiotic penicillin in a mold later named *Penicillium notatum.*

Mole: The quantity of a chemical substance that has a weight in grams equal to the molecular weight of the substance.

Molecule: A stable group of atoms held together by chemical forces and entering into characteristic chemical reactions.

Momentum: The directed product of the mass and the velocity of an object or collection of objects. In the case of interactions among objects in a closed system, the total momentum is always conserved.

Mono-: A prefix meaning "single."

Moon: A celestial object which orbits around a planet.

Mu-meson: Also called a muon; one of two leptons with a mass equal to about 200 electron masses and distinguished from one another by the opposite charges that they carry.

Mutagen: An agent which increases the frequency of mutations.

Mutation: An abrupt change in genetic material not resulting from recombination.

Myco-: A prefix meaning "fungus."

Mycology: The branch of biology which studies fungi.

Natural philosophy: Up to the nineteenth century, a term used to designate the scientific study of all nonliving natural phenomena. In the late nineteenth century, synonymous with physics.

Natural selection: The evolutionary process, first described by Charles Darwin in the mid-nineteenth century, by which those organisms whose natural variations make them well suited to survival in the struggle to mature and reproduce are able to increase their frequency in the population; eventually, they crowd out less well suited organisms. Over time, organisms in which many favorable variations accumulate diverge increasingly from their ancestors, creating new species. *Compare* **Punctuated equilibrium.**

Nebula: A cloud of interstellar dust and gas.

Neuro-: A prefix meaning "pertaining to nerves or the nervous system."

Neuron: A nerve cell.

Neurotransmitter: A substance released by a neuron that diffuses across the gaps (synapses) between itself and other neurons, exerting influence on them.

Neutral: Having no charge.

Neutrino: One of three fundamental kinds of uncharged and massless or nearly massless leptons.

Neutro- or Neutr-: A prefix meaning "neutral."

Neutron: An uncharged particle in all atomic nuclei except those of hydrogen. A neutron is composed of three quarks, two down quarks and one up quark. *Compare* **Electron, Proton.**

Neutron star: A star in the final stages of stellar evolution. It consists of an extremely dense mass composed almost entirely of neutrons from which only neutrinos and very-high-energy photons can escape, making the star invisible.

Nitro-: A prefix meaning "containing nitrogen."

Nitrogen: The chemical element with atomic number 7. It makes up about 78 percent of the atmosphere and is a constituent of all proteins.

Nucleic acid: Any of various acids, such as DNA and RNA, which are composed of chains of nucleotides.

Nucleo-: A prefix meaning "pertaining to the nucleus."

Nucleon: The common name for a proton or neutron.

Nucleotide: The structural unit of a nucleic acid, consisting of a sugar, a base, and a phosphate group.

Nucleus: In physics, the dense central portion of an atom containing protons and neutrons. In biology, the dense central portion of a cell containing chromosomes.

Onco-: A prefix meaning "cancer."

Oncogene: A gene which specifies the structure of an enzyme that is a catalyst for cancer-inducing events.

Optics: The study of the generation, transmission, and detection of electromagnetic radiation in or near the visible portion of the spectrum.

Orbit: The path of a body (such as a planet or an electron) about a central body (such as a star or an atomic nucleus).

Organic: Pertaining to any aspect of living matter or to any chemical compound containing carbon. *Compare* **Inorganic.**

Organism: A living thing.

Osmosis: The passage of water through a differentially permeable membrane, usually from a region in which the concentration of dissolved molecules or ions is lower to one in which it is higher.

Ox- or **Oxo-:** A prefix meaning "containing oxygen."

Oxidation: A chemical reaction that increases the amount of oxygen in a compound.

Oxy-: A prefix meaning "containing oxygen or additional oxygen."

Oxygen: The chemical element with atomic number 8. Oxygen comprises about 20 percent of the atmosphere and is essential in all respiration and combustion processes.

Panacea: A remedy for all ailments.

Parabola: A curve formed by a point moving so that its distance from a fixed point remains equal to its distance to a fixed line.

Parent cell: The cell from which any new cell was produced. *Compare* **Daughter cell.**

Parity: In quantum mechanics, a property of a description stipulating what happens when it is simultaneously reflected through all three spatial coordinates. If its sign remains the same, its parity is said to be even; if its sign changes, then its parity is said to be odd. In general, processes are forbidden which would change the parity of their descriptions.

Parthenogenesis: A special type of sexual reproduction in which an egg develops without the introduction of a sperm. Parthenogenesis is most common among insects.

Particle: Any very small piece of matter, such as a molecule, atom, or a hadron, baryon, lepton, or quark. *Compare* **Antiparticle.**

Particle physics: The branch of physics concerned with the properties and behavior of elementary particles. Because much of the experimental work of particle physicists is done using collisions at very high energies, it is often called high-energy physics.

Pathogen: An organism that causes disease.

Pathology: The scientific study of the causes, characteristics, and consequences of diseases.

Periodic table: A table of the elements of increasing atomic number organized into horizontal rows (periods) and vertical columns (groups) in order to illustrate the similarities in chemical properties of members of each group.

Permeable: Having openings, such as pores, through which gas or liquid can pass.

Pharmacology: The scientific study of the composition, uses, and effects of drugs.

Phase: In chemistry, a distinct state of matter, such as a solid, liquid, or gas. In physics, the property of a wave related to a varying point or stage in a period of uniform motion, as compared to a standard position or an assumed starting moment.

Phenotype: The observed characteristics of an organism, as they have developed as a result of the interaction between genetic and environmental factors. *Compare* **Genotype.**

Phlogiston: A hypothetical substance, now discredited, which was thought to combine with metallic ores to form metals and to be released in processes of combustion. In order to account for mass balances, phlogiston was presumed to have negative mass.

Phosphorescence: Luminescence which persists after the removal of the source of excitation.

Photoelectric effect: The emission of electrons resulting from the transfer of energy from photons to electrons. It is notable because the energy of emitted electrons is a function of the frequency of the incident light, rather than its intensity.

Photon: A massless particle which carries the electromagnetic force; the term is often used to describe a packet (quantum) of light. The energy of the photon is proportional to its frequency.

Photosynthesis: A metabolic process carried out in green plants by which carbon dioxide, water, and the energy in light are used to synthesize compounds such as sugar.

Physics: The science which studies matter and energy, and the interactions between them.

Physiology: The science which studies the functioning of living organisms and their constituent parts.

Pi-meson: Also called a pion; one of three mesons with a mass equal to 273 electron masses.

Planck's constant: The ratio between the energy of radiation and its frequency, equal to 6.63×10^{-34} joules per second and represented as h.

Planet: A celestial object which orbits around a star and which is not itself luminous.

Plasma: In physics, a completely ionized gas with nearly zero net charge. In biology, the liquid portion of the blood in which chemically active cells, molecules, and particles are transported.

Plate tectonics: The theory that the outer surface of the earth is composed of large plates whose relative motions produce seismic, volcanic, and other Earth-shaping activities.

Plutonium: A highly reactive heavy metal with atomic number 94. The isotope of plutonium with atomic mass 239 undergoes fission easily and is used as a nuclear fuel, in the production of other radioisotopes, and in fission bombs.

Polarity: A property of a physical system which has two points or regions with different (usually opposite) characteristics, such as different electrical potentials or opposite charges.

Polarization: The process which creates polarity; most often used to describe the process of filtering electromagnetic radiation so that only waves oriented in a specified direction pass through.

Pole: Either of two extremities, such as of the earth's axis or of a magnet.

Polymer: A long chain of identical chemical units which are linked to form a single large molecule.

Positron: An elementary particle having all characteristics identical with an electron except for its positive charge, which is of the opposite sign. The antiparticle of the electron. *Compare* **Electron.**

Potential energy: The capacity of a body to do work as a result of its position relative to other bodies. *Compare* **Kinetic energy.**

Progeny: The offspring or descendants of an organism.

Propagation: In physics, the traveling of light, sound, or radio waves through space or a material.

Protein: One of a class of long chain polymers of amino acids with side chains which are the most fundamental constituents of living organisms.

Proton: A positively charged particle in the atomic nucleus. A proton is made up of three quarks, two up quarks and one down quark. *Compare* **Electron, Neutron.**

Psychiatry: The medical specialty concerned with mental illnesses.

Pulsar: A rapidly spinning neutron star that emits periodic bursts of radio frequency radiation.

Punctuated equilibrium: The theory, championed by Stephen Jay Gould, that evolution occurs through a process of long periods of stability alternating with rapid changes that cause both extinctions and the appearance of new forms of organisms. This theory accounts for perceived gaps in the fossil record; it argues that "missing links" within or between species cannot be found because they existed very briefly or not at all. *Compare* **Natural selection.**

Quanta (*sing.* quantum): Units of any physical quantity whose values are restricted to multiples of a basic unit. More specifically, entities having particle-like characteristics whose properties such as energy, momenta, and charge are quantized.

Quantum chromodynamics (QCD): A theory of the strong interactions among quarks. Its mathematical structure resembles that of quantum electrodynamics, with the quantified characteristic of color replacing charge.

Quantum electrodynamics (QED): The quantum theory of electromagnetic radiation and its interaction with matter. QED incorporates both wave and particle properties of electromagnetic phenomena.

Quantum mechanics: The modern theory of matter and electromagnetic radiation in which many characteristics are quantized; it differs from classical physics primarily at atomic and subatomic levels. Also called quantum theory.

Quark: A theory initiated by Murray Gell-Mann to account for the characteristics of hadrons (mesons) and baryons (such as protons and neutrons). There now seem to be eighteen types of quarks—six basic kinds (flavors), each of which can exist in three different forms (colors). These quarks, held together with eight kinds of gluons, are hypothesized to combine in various ways to form the known varieties of baryons and hadrons. No free quark has been detected.

Quasar: A distant, starlike, and intense object which emits electromagnetic radiation in space.

Radiation: The process of emitting energy in any form. Also, electromagnetic energy in the form of waves with a characteristic frequency, amplitude, and phase.

Radical: An atom or stable group of atoms with at least one unpaired electron, which makes the group chemically reactive.

Radio astronomy: A specialty in astronomy in which data are gathered from the observation of radio frequency emissions from celestial objects.

Radioactivity: The emission of subatomic particles from unstable nuclei. Most radioactivity consists of alpha rays (helium nuclei), beta rays (electrons), gamma rays (high-energy light), and neutrinos.

Reaction: In chemistry, a process in which two or more substances (called reagents or reactants) interact with one another to produce one or more new substances.

Reagent: One of the substances involved in a chemical reaction.

Recessive: Of a gene, requiring two copies in order to be expressed as a given trait. *Compare* **Dominant.**

Recombination: The formation of new combinations of genes in offspring which were not present in the parents. Recombination occurs either through the natural process of crossing-over or through artificial means, as in recombinant DNA technology.

Redshift: The lowering of frequency or increase of wavelength of electromagnetic radiation, indicated by a shift toward the red end of the spectrum. This effect occurs when a celestial source is moving away from the observer.

Reflection: The return of particles or waves from a surface that they strike.

Refraction: The change of direction of a wave as it moves out of one medium and into another medium with a different velocity of propagation. Also, in astronomy, the change in the apparent position of a celestial object as the light coming from that object bends while passing through the atmosphere.

Relativity: In physics, the theory which recognizes the universality of the speed of light and the dependence of measurements of space, time, and mechanical properties such as mass on the motion of the observer relative to the motion of the object being observed; called the special theory of relativity. Also, the physical theory which attributes gravitational forces to fluctuations in the properties of space-time; called the general theory of relativity.

Respiration: A process which includes both the act of breathing and the exchange of oxygen and carbon dioxide between the air and blood.

Retrovirus: A family of RNA viruses which contain an enzyme that catalyses the production of DNA and which integrate themselves into the host's chromosomes.

Right-handed. *See* **Handedness.**

RNA (ribonucleic acid): One of a class of nucleic acids containing the sugar ribose which are involved in the transcription and translation of the genetic material in DNA.

Scattering: The change of direction of a particle produced by a collision with another particle or system of particles. The scattering of particles with known characteristics reveals information about the characteristics of the target particle or system of particles.

Science: A set of human practices which attempt to produce universal knowledge (that is, knowledge independent of time, culture, and observer status) regarding phenomena. Also, the product of such practices.

Seismology: The scientific study of the mechanical properties of the earth and of earthquakes.

Serum: The liquid portion of the blood from which all clotting elements have been removed.

Sidereal: Having to do with the stars.

Solar: Having to do with the sun.

Solar system: The system containing the sun and all of those bodies which orbit around it.

Solid: A phase of matter characterized by relatively low energy and by resistance to changes in both shape and volume. *Compare* Gas, Liquid.

Solid-state physics: The branch of physics concerned with the properties of solids.

Soluble: Capable of dissolving in a liquid, especially water.

Space-time: The system of four coordinates—time and the three dimensions of space—in which a physical object or event can be located.

Special relativity theory. *See* Relativity.

Species: A population of closely related and similar organisms; more narrowly, the set of individuals capable of interbreeding freely with one another to produce fertile progeny. *Compare* Genus.

Spectroscopy: The branch of physics concerned with the production, measurement, and analysis of electromagnetic spectra.

Spectrum (*pl.* spectra): A plot of the intensity of radiation as a function of a given quantity, usually wavelength or frequency. Each molecule and atom has a characteristic set of wavelengths of electromagnetic radiation which it absorbs or emits and which can be modified by such actions as heating and exposure to magnetic fields.

Spin: In classical physics, the rotation of any body about an axis. In quantum mechanics, an intrinsic property of elementary particles at rest which is analogous to classical spin. Leptons, quarks, and baryons (except for the omega particle) have a spin of $1/2$, photons have a spin of 1, and mesons have 0 spin.

Spontaneous generation: The regular spontaneous emergence of life out of inorganic materials, which was long assumed to be possible. Louis Pasteur, among others, showed such a process to be impossible under ordinary conditions.

Standard Model: A theory in physics which incorporates the existence of six types of quarks and six kinds of leptons as fundamental.

Star: Any celestial body which is or has been self-luminous as a consequence of energy generated by nuclear reactions within its interior. Black holes, dark stars, and pulsars are stars which no longer emit light in or near the visible part of the electromagnetic spectrum.

Steady state theory: A cosmological theory, no longer in favor, which incorporates general relativity theory. It proposes the continuous creation of interstellar matter at a rate which allows the universe to expand at the observed pace, at the same time that the mean density of matter in any substantial region remains constant.

Stellar: Having to do with the stars.

Stereochemistry: The scientific study of the spatial arrangement of atoms in molecules and the consequences of that arrangement.

Strangeness: A property of quantum mechanics assigned to baryons and mesons whose conservation in strong interactions but not in weak ones explains why some subatomic interactions occur while others, which might be expected, do not.

Strong force or interaction: The attractive force that acts between nucleons. Quarks feel the strong force, but leptons do not. *Compare* Weak force or interaction.

Subatomic: Pertaining to something smaller

than the atom, usually to elementary particles and their interactions.

Supercollider: A proposed particle accelerator that would direct two beams of fast-moving particles at one another to create collisions in the 40,000 GeV range. (1 GeV, or giga electronvolt, is roughly equal to the amount of energy of the mass of a proton.)

Superconductor: Any material which loses its capacity for electrical resistance and becomes diamagnetic (having a magnetic permeability less than that of a vacuum) at low temperatures.

Supernova: A rare event in which a star suddenly and briefly emits uncharacteristically large amounts of energy.

Symmetry: The quality of having parts which correspond in size, shape, and relative position on opposite sides of a dividing line. In physics, the quality of remaining unaltered with changes in spatial orientation, electrical charge, or parity.

Synchrotron: A particle accelerator which uses repeated electrical field fluctuations to accelerate particles and magnetic fields to restrict their motion to a circle.

Taxonomy: Any system for classifying objects in a hierarchy. The term is most often used to indicate a system for classifying organisms which reflects overall similarities and differences.

Technology: Any system based on the application of knowledge, manifested in physical objects and organizational forms and used to attain specific goals.

Tele-: A prefix meaning "distant."

Telescope: An instrument, such as an optical telescope or a radio telescope, for producing an image of or information about a distant object by the collection and analysis of the electromagnetic radiation which it emits.

Temperature: A measure of the magnitude of the thermal energy contained in a given quantity of matter. Heat always flows from regions of high temperature to regions of low temperature.

Theory: A system of assumptions, accepted principles, and rules of procedure created to predict or otherwise explain some phenomenon or set of phenomena.

Thermo-: A prefix meaning "heat."

Thermodynamics: The branch of physics which studies the change of energy from one form to another, especially the transformations between heat and work.

Thermometer: Any device for measuring the temperature of a body.

Torque: A force which produces rotation; also, the measurement of that force.

Toxin: Any substance which does harm to an organism; also called a poison.

Transfusion: The direct injection of whole blood, plasma, or another solution into the bloodstream.

Transplantation: The removal of an organism or part of an organism from one environment and its introduction into another; often used to describe the removal of an organ or tissue from a donor to replace the defective organ or tissue of a recipient.

Tri-: A prefix meaning "three."

Ultraviolet light: Electromagnetic radiation with wavelengths just below those of the visible spectrum.

Unified theory: Any theory which tries to account for gravitational and electromagnetic phenomena in a single framework which incorporates general relativity theory.

Uniformitarianism: One of several theories about the geological history of the earth and its species. Formerly, the term implied the belief that the earth existed virtually unchanged since the Creation. More recently, it indicates a position taken by many geologists which insists that all geological change can and must be accounted for in terms of the processes currently at work. *Compare* **Catastrophism.**

Universe: The entirety of all existing things.

Uranium: A metallic element with atomic number 92. Its relatively rare isotope with mass number 235 undergoes fission easily, with the release of massive amounts of energy, and is used in fission bombs and as a nuclear fuel.

Vaccination: The injection of a virus, a bacterium, or their proteins (usually in a weakened form) into a body with the purpose of producing immunity.

Vacuum: A portion of space from which all matter has been removed.

Valence: A number which indicates the bonds

that atoms of an element form with other atoms.

Variable: In a mathematical equation, a quantity which is allowed to change, taking on any one of a set of values. *Compare* **Constant.**

Variation: In biology, a group or character trait which is not true to a predetermined type.

Vector: In physics, a quantity which has both magnitude and direction. In biology, an agent which carries an entity to a place where it can act; for example, ticks are vectors for the bacteria which produce Lyme disease in humans.

Vein: One of the blood vessels which carry blood toward the heart. *Compare* **Artery.**

Velocity: A vector quantity which measures both the magnitude and the direction of a body's motion.

Vernal equinox: In astronomy, one of two points where the celestial equator (the circle of the celestial sphere between the two celestial poles, about which the stars seem to rotate) intersects the ecliptic (the plane of the earth's orbit extended to meet the celestial sphere). Also, the time in spring when the sun crosses the earth's equator and when day and night are of equal length everywhere.

Virus: Any of a class of ultramicroscopic organisms containing nucleic acid and at least one protein. Viruses, which can reproduce only in living cells, often cause disease.

Viscosity: The resistance to flow in a fluid or semifluid.

Vitalism: The belief, widely accepted among early nineteenth century biologists and chemists, that living beings contain some special life force which cannot be explained by ordinary physical or chemical forces.

Vitamin: One of a class of organic compounds which an organism needs in small amounts but which it cannot synthesize for itself.

Vivisection: The practice of cutting open a living animal in order to study its physiological characteristics. *Compare* **Dissection.**

Volume: The measure of a three-dimensional object or region of space.

Wave mechanics: The description of atomic and subatomic particles in terms of their wave properties.

Wavelength: The distance between the maximum and minimum lengths of a periodic wave.

Weak force or interaction: The fundamental force which is the only one affecting neutrinos. The weak interaction, which does not conserve parity or strangeness, changes one type of quark into another and is responsible for particle decay in the process of radioactivity. *Compare* **Strong force or interaction.**

White dwarf: A star of low mass which is reaching the end of its life. Typically, it has exhausted its thermonuclear fuel and has contracted to roughly the size of the earth.

X chromosome: The sex chromosome which is always contributed by the female parent and which can be contributed by the male parent. Sex chromosomes determine an offspring's gender; humans normally have two, either XX (female) or XY (male). *Compare* **Y chromosome.**

X rays: Penetrating electromagnetic radiation produced by the collision of high-velocity electrons with a target. Also called Röntgen rays for Wilhelm Conrad Röntgen, who discovered them.

Y chromosome: One of the two sex chromosomes which can be contributed only by the male parent. Sex chromosomes determine an offspring's gender; humans normally have two, either XX (female) or XY (male). *Compare* **X chromosome.**

Zoology: The scientific study of animals.

Country List

Each featured scientist is listed by the primary country or countries where he/she lived and conducted scientific work, which may not be his/her country of birth or death. In addition, scientists who are members of minority groups can be found under **United States** both within the complete listing and grouped by separate headings. The female scientists profiled in the encyclopedia are listed both with their respective countries and under the category **Women**.

African Americans. *See under* **United States.**

American colonies. *See* **United States.**

Argentina
Houssay, Bernardo Alberto
Leloir, Luis F.

Asia Minor. *See* **Greece.**

Asian Americans. *See under* **United States.**

Australia
Bragg, Sir Lawrence
Burnet, Sir Frank Macfarlane
Cornforth, Sir John

Austria
Boltzmann, Ludwig Eduard
Freud, Sigmund
Frisch, Karl von
Gödel, Kurt
Hess, Victor Franz
Landsteiner, Karl
Lorenz, Konrad
Mach, Ernst
Meitner, Lise
Mendel, Gregor Johann
Pauli, Wolfgang
Perutz, Max Ferdinand
Schrödinger, Erwin

Austro-Hungarian Empire. *See* **Austria;**
Hungary.

Basra. *See* **Iraq.**

Bavaria. *See* **Germany.**

Belgium
Bordet, Jules
Duve, Christian de
Helmont, Jan Baptista van
Lemaître, Georges
Prigogine, Ilya

Blacks. *See* **African Americans** *under* **United States.**

Bosnia
Prelog, Vladimir

Brandenburg. *See* **Germany.**

Britain. *See* **Great Britain.**

Canada
Abbott, Maude
Altman, Sidney
Banting, Sir Frederick Grant
Giauque, William Francis
Hubel, David H.
Taube, Henry

China
Lee, Tsung-Dao
Wu, Chien-Shiung
Yang, Chen Ning

Chinese Americans. *See* **Asian Americans**
under **United States.**

Colonial America. *See* **United States.**

Croatia
Mohorovicic, Andrija
Tesla, Nikola

Czech Republic
Cori, Carl F.
Cori, Gerty T.

Czechoslovakia. *See* **Czech Republic.**

Denmark
Bohr, Niels
Brahe, Tycho
Hertzsprung, Ejnar
Jerne, Niels K.
Johannsen, Wilhelm Ludvig
Krogh, August
Ørsted, Hans Christian

England. *See* **Great Britain.**

Egypt
Alhazen
Ptolemy

Florence. *See* **Italy.**

France
Ampère, André-Marie
Arago, François
Arnold of Villanova
Becquerel, Antoine-Henri
Bernard, Claude
Berthollet, Claude Louis
Biot, Jean-Baptiste
Broglie, Louis de
Buffon, Comte de (Georges-Louis Leclerc)
Buridan, Jean
Cassini, Gian Domenico
Châtelet, Marquise du
Coriolis, Gustave-Gaspard de
Coulomb, Charles-Augustin
Curie, Marie
Curie, Pierre
Cuvier, Georges, Baron
Daguerre, Jacques
Dausset, Jean
Descartes, René
Dumas, Jean-Baptiste-André
Fizeau, Hippolyte
Foucault, Léon
Fresnel, Augustin-Jean
Gay-Lussac, Joseph-Louis
Guy de Chauliac
Jacob, François
Joliot, Frédéric
Joliot-Curie, Irène
Lamarck, Jean-Baptiste
Laveran, Alphonse
Lavoisier, Antoine-Laurent
Lehn, Jean-Marie
Lwoff, André
Mariotte, Edme
Monod, Jacques Lucien
Néel, Louis-Eugène-Félix
Pasteur, Louis
Peregrinus de Maricourt, Petrus
Perrin, Jean-Baptiste
Réaumur, René Antoine Ferchault de
Richet, Charles

Rillieux, Norbert
Servetus, Michael

Genoa. *See* **Italy.**

Germany
Agricola, Georgius
Baade, Walter
Behring, Emil Adolf von
Bessel, Friedrich Wilhelm
Bethe, Hans Albrecht
Born, Max
Bothe, Walther
Clausius, Rudolf
Debye, Peter J. W.
Delbrück, Max
Domagk, Gerhard
Ehrlich, Paul
Einstein, Albert
Fahrenheit, Gabriel Daniel
Fischer, Ernst Otto
Gauss, Carl Friedrich
Geiger, Hans
Geitel, Hans Friedrich
Hahn, Otto
Heisenberg, Werner Karl
Helmholtz, Hermann von
Herschel, Caroline Lucretia
Herschel, Sir William
Hertz, Gustav
Hertz, Heinrich
Hildegard of Bingen
Huber, Robert
Humboldt, Alexander von, Baron
Jensen, J. Hans D.
Kepler, Johannes
Kirchhoff, Gustav Robert
Koch, Robert
Kossel, Albrecht
Krebs, Sir Hans Adolf
Laue, Max von
Lipmann, Fritz Albert
Mayer, Maria Goeppert
Merian, Maria Sibylla
Mössbauer, Rudolf Ludwig
Nernst, Walther Hermann
Olbers, Wilhelm
Planck, Max
Prandtl, Ludwig
Röntgen, Wilhelm Conrad
Schleiden, Matthias Jakob
Schwarzschild, Karl

Sommerfeld, Arnold
Stark, Johannes
Stern, Otto
Van't Hoff, Jacobus Henricus
Virchow, Rudolf
Voit, Carl von
Wankel, Felix
Warburg, Otto Heinrich
Wegener, Alfred Lothar
Wien, Wilhelm
Wittig, Georg
Wöhler, Friedrich

Great Britain
Appleton, Sir Edward Victor
Ayrton, Hertha Marks
Bacon, Francis
Bacon, Roger
Barton, Sir Derek H. R.
Bateson, William
Bell, Alexander Graham
Bell Burnell, Jocelyn
Bessemer, Sir Henry
Black, Joseph
Blackett, Patrick M. S.
Blackwell, Elizabeth
Born, Max
Boyle, Robert
Bragg, Sir Lawrence
Brewster, Sir David
Burbidge, Margaret
Cavendish, Henry
Chadwick, Sir James
Crick, Francis
Dale, Sir Henry Hallett
Dalton, John
Darwin, Charles
Davy, Sir Humphry
Dirac, Paul Adrien Maurice
Eddington, Sir Arthur Stanley
Faraday, Michael
Fleming, Sir Alexander
Franklin, Rosalind E.
Gabor, Dennis
Galton, Sir Francis
Gilbert, William
Haldane, J. B. S.
Halley, Edmond
Harvey, William
Hawking, Stephen
Heaviside, Oliver

Herschel, Caroline Lucretia
Herschel, Sir John
Herschel, Sir William
Hewish, Antony
Hinshelwood, Sir Cyril Norman
Hodgkin, Sir Alan Lloyd
Hodgkin, Dorothy Crowfoot
Hooke, Robert
Hopkins, Sir Frederick Gowland
Hoyle, Sir Fred
Huggins, Sir William
Isaacs, Alick
Jeans, Sir James
Jenner, Edward
Jerne, Niels K.
Josephson, Brian D.
Joule, James Prescott
Kapitsa, Pyotr Leonidovich
Kelvin, Lord
Kendrew, John Cowdery
Krebs, Sir Hans Adolf
Lankester, Sir Edwin Ray
Lister, Joseph
Lower, Richard
Lyell, Sir Charles
Macleod, John J. R.
Maxwell, James Clerk
Medawar, Sir Peter
Mitchell, Peter D.
Mott, Sir Nevill
Newton, Sir Isaac
Payne-Gaposchkin, Cecilia
Perutz, Max Ferdinand
Porter, Rodney Robert
Priestley, Joseph
Punnett, Reginald Crundall
Ray, John
Robinson, Sir Robert
Ross, Sir Ronald
Rutherford, Ernest
Salam, Abdus
Sanger, Frederick
Sherrington, Sir Charles Scott
Smith, William
Soddy, Frederick
Starling, Ernest Henry
Sydenham, Thomas
Thomson, Sir Joseph John
Watt, James
Wilkins, Maurice H. F.
Wilkinson, Sir Geoffrey

New Zealand
Rutherford, Ernest

Norway
Bjerknes, Vilhelm
Onsager, Lars

Pakistan
Salam, Abdus

Papal States. *See* **Italy.**

Persian Empire. *See* **Uzbekistan.**

Poland
Copernicus, Nicolaus
Curie, Marie
Hoffmann, Roald
Mandelbrot, Benoit B.
Ulam, Stanislaw

Prussia. *See* **Germany; Poland.**

Russia
Cherenkov, Pavel Alekseyevich
Gamow, George
Kapitsa, Pyotr Leonidovich
Landau, Lev Davidovich
Mendeleyev, Dmitry Ivanovich
Oparin, Aleksandr Ivanovich
Pavlov, Ivan Petrovich
Semenov, Nikolai
Tamm, Igor Yevgenyevich
Vavilov, Nikolai Ivanovich
Zworykin, Vladimir

Rome. *See* **Italy.**

Saxony. *See* **Germany.**

Scotland. *See* **Great Britain.**

Sicily. *See* **Greece.**

South Africa
Barnard, Christiaan

Soviet Union. *See* **Russia; Ukraine;**
Uzbekistan.

Spain
Ramón y Cajal, Santiago
Servetus, Michael

Sweden
Alfvén, Hannes
Arrhenius, Svante A.
Berzelius, Jöns Jakob

Celsius, Anders
Linnaeus, Carolus
Nobel, Alfred
Rossby, Carl-Gustav Arvid
Rydberg, Johannes Robert

Switzerland
Agassiz, Louis
Bloch, Felix
Einstein, Albert
Fischer, Edmond H.
Haller, Albrecht von
Nägeli, Karl Wilhelm von
Paracelsus
Prelog, Vladimir
Saussure, Horace Bénédict de
Servetus, Michael
Zwicky, Fritz

Syracuse. *See* **Greece.**

Thrace. *See* **Greece.**

Turkey. *See* **Greece.**

Ukraine
Waksman, Selman Abraham

United States
Agassiz, Louis
Altman, Sidney
Alvarez, Luis W.
Anderson, Carl David
Anderson, Philip W.
Anfinsen, Christian B.
Apgar, Virginia
Audubon, John James
Axelrod, Julius
Ballard, Robert D.
Baltimore, David
Banneker, Benjamin
Bardeen, John
Barnard, Edward Emerson
Beadle, George Wells
Békésy, Georg von
Bell, Alexander Graham
Berg, Paul
Bethe, Hans Albrecht
Bloch, Felix
Blodgett, Katharine Burr
Bohm, David
Bragg, Robert Henry
Bridgman, Percy Williams
Burbank, Luther

Burbidge, Margaret
Calvin, Melvin
Cannon, Annie Jump
Carruthers, George R.
Carson, Rachel
Carver, George Washington
Chandrasekhar, Subrahmanyan
Cobb, Jewel Plummer
Compton, Arthur Holly
Conant, James B.
Cori, Carl F.
Cori, Gerty T.
Cox, Allan V.
Cram, Donald J.
Cushing, Harvey Williams
Debye, Peter J. W.
Delbrück, Max
Drew, Charles Richard
Dulbecco, Renato
Du Vigneaud, Vincent
Edison, Thomas Alva
Ehrlich, Paul R.
Einstein, Albert
Elion, Gertrude Belle
Faber, Sandra
Fermi, Enrico
Feynman, Richard P.
Fischer, Edmond H.
Fitch, Val L.
Flory, Paul J.
Franklin, Benjamin
Friedman, Herbert
Fulton, Robert
Gajdusek, D. Carleton
Gamow, George
Gell-Mann, Murray
Geller, Margaret
Giauque, William Francis
Gibbs, Josiah Willard
Gilbert, Walter
Glashow, Sheldon L.
Goddard, Robert
Gödel, Kurt
Goodyear, Charles
Gould, Stephen Jay
Gourdine, Meredith C.
Gray, Asa
Guth, Alan H.
Hale, George Ellery
Hall, Lloyd Augustus
Hartline, Haldan Keffer

Hay, Elizabeth Dexter
Heezen, Bruce Charles
Henry, Joseph
Hess, Harry Hammond
Hess, Victor Franz
Hitchings, George Herbert, Jr.
Hoffmann, Roald
Hopper, Grace Murray
Huang, Alice S.
Hubbard, Ruth
Hubble, Edwin Powell
Hubel, David H.
Hyde, Ida H.
Jackson, Shirley Ann
Julian, Percy Lavon
Just, Ernest Everett
Kendall, Edward Calvin
King, Helen Dean
Kornberg, Arthur
Kuiper, Gerard Peter
Kunkel, Louis O.
Land, Edwin Herbert
Landsteiner, Karl
Langley, Samuel Pierpont
Langmuir, Irving
Lawrence, Ernest Orlando
Leavitt, Henrietta Swan
Lederberg, Joshua
Lederman, Leon M.
Lee, Tsung-Dao
Levi-Montalcini, Rita
Lewis, Gilbert N.
Libby, Willard F.
Lipmann, Fritz Albert
Lipscomb, William N.
Luria, Salvador Edward
Luu, Jane X.
McClintock, Barbara
McCormick, Cyrus Hall
McMillan, Edwin Mattison
Mandelbrot, Benoit B.
Massey, Walter E.
Maury, Antonia
Mayer, Maria Goeppert
Mendenhall, Dorothy Reed
Michelson, Albert Abraham
Millikan, Robert Andrews
Mitchell, Maria
Molina, Mario J.
Morgan, Thomas Hunt
Morse, Samuel F. B.

Muller, Hermann Joseph
Mulliken, Robert S.
Nambu, Yoichiro
Nirenberg, Marshall W.
Northrop, John Howard
Olah, George A.
Onsager, Lars
Oppenheimer, J. Robert
Pauli, Wolfgang
Pauling, Linus
Payne-Gaposchkin, Cecilia
Profet, Margie Jean
Rabi, Isidor Isaac
Reed, Walter
Richards, Ellen Swallow
Richter, Burton
Richter, Charles Francis
Rillieux, Norbert
Roberts, Richard
Rous, Peyton
Rowland, F. Sherwood
Rubin, Vera C.
Rush, Benjamin
Russell, Henry Norris
Sabin, Florence Rena
Sagan, Carl
Salk, Jonas
Sandage, Allan Rex
Schawlow, Arthur L.
Schmidt, Maarten
Schwinger, Julian Seymour
Seaborg, Glenn Theodore
Segrè, Emilio Gino
Shapley, Harlow
Sibley, Charles G.
Slipher, Vesto Melvin
Smalley, Richard E.
Snell, George D.
Stanley, Wendell Meredith
Steinberger, Jack
Stern, Otto
Stevens, Nettie Maria
Sturtevant, Alfred H.
Szent-Györgyi, Albert
Tatum, Edward Lawrie
Taube, Henry
Taussig, Helen Brooke
Taylor, Moddie Daniel
Teller, Edward
Tesla, Nikola
Thaxton, Hubert Mach

Thomas, E. Donnall
Ting, Samuel C. C.
Ulam, Stanislaw
Urey, Harold Clayton
Van Allen, James
Van Vleck, John H.
Varmus, Harold E.
Von Neumann, John
Waksman, Selman Abraham
Watson, James D.
Weinberg, Steven
Wheeler, John Archibald
Whitney, Eli
Wigner, Eugene P.
Williams, Daniel Hale
Wilson, Edward O.
Woods, Granville T.
Wu, Chien-Shiung
Yalow, Rosalyn S.
Yang, Chen Ning
Zwicky, Fritz
Zworykin, Vladimir

African Americans
Banneker, Benjamin
Bragg, Robert Henry
Carruthers, George R.
Carver, George Washington
Cobb, Jewel Plummer
Drew, Charles Richard
Gourdine, Meredith C.
Hall, Lloyd Augustus
Jackson, Shirley Ann
Julian, Percy Lavon
Just, Ernest Everett
Massey, Walter E.
Rillieux, Norbert
Taylor, Moddie Daniel
Thaxton, Hubert Mach
Williams, Daniel Hale
Woods, Granville

Asian Americans
Chandrasekhar, Subrahmanyan
Huang, Alice S.
Lee, Tsung-Dao
Luu, Jane X.
Nambu, Yoichiro
Ting, Samuel C. C.
Wu, Chien-Shiung
Yang, Chen Ning

Areas of Scientific Achievement

Astronomy

Alfvén, Hannes
Alhazen
Alvarez, Luis W.
Anaximander
Arago, François
Aristarchus of Samos
Aristotle
Baade, Walter
Banneker, Benjamin
Barnard, Edward Emerson
Bell, Burnell, Jocelyn
Bessel, Friedrich Wilhelm
Bethe, Hans Albrecht
Biruni, al-
Bothe, Walther
Brahe, Tycho
Bruno, Giordano
Burbidge, Margaret
Cannon, Annie Jump
Cassini, Gian Domenico
Celsius, Anders
Châtelet, Marquise du
Copernicus, Nicolaus
Eddington, Sir Arthur Stanley
Faber, Sandra
Fizeau, Hippolyte
Foucault, Léon
Friedman, Herbert
Galileo
Gamow, George
Gauss, Carl Friedrich
Geller, Margaret
Gilbert, William
Hale, George Ellery
Halley, Edmond
Hawking, Stephen
Herschel, Caroline Lucretia
Herschel, Sir William
Hertzsprung, Ejnar
Hewish, Antony
Hooke, Robert
Hoyle, Sir Fred
Hubble, Edwin Powell
Huggins, Sir William
Humboldt, Alexander von, Baron
Huygens, Christiaan
Hypatia
Jeans, Sir James
Kapteyn, Jacobus Cornelius
Kepler, Johannes
Kirchhoff, Gustav Robert
Kuiper, Gerard Peter
Langley, Samuel Pierpont
Leavitt, Henrietta Swan
Lee, Tsung-Dao
Libby, Willard F.
Luu, Jane X.
Maury, Antonia
Maxwell, James Clerk
Michelson, Albert Abraham
Millikan, Robert Andrews
Mitchell, Maria
Nernst, Walther Hermann
Newton, Sir Isaac
Olbers, Wilhelm
Oort, Jan Hendrik
Payne-Gaposchkin, Cecilia
Ptolemy
Rubin, Vera C.
Russell, Henry Norris
Sagan, Carl
Sandage, Allan Rex
Schmidt, Maarten
Schwarzschild, Karl
Shapley, Harlow
Slipher, Vesto Melvin
Urey, Harold Clayton
Wheeler, John Archibald
Zwicky, Fritz

Bacteriology

Behring, Emil Adolf von
Bordet, Jules
Burnet, Sir Frank Macfarlane
Delbrück, Max
Domagk, Gerhard
Ehrlich, Paul
Fleming, Sir Alexander
Hall, Lloyd Augustus
Jacob, François
Kitasato, Shibasaburo
Koch, Robert
Lederberg, Joshua
Leeuwenhoek, Antoni van
Lister, Joseph

Luria, Salvador Edward
Mitchell, Peter D.
Monod, Jacques Lucien
Pasteur, Louis
Reed, Walter
Sabin, Florence Rena
Spallanzani, Lazzaro
Tatum, Edward Lawrie
Virchow, Rudolf
Waksman, Selman Abraham

Biology
Anfinsen, Christian B.
Aristotle
Audubon, John James
Banting, Sir Frederick Grant
Berg, Paul
Bernard, Claude
Carson, Rachel
Crick, Francis
Dalton, John
Darwin, Charles
Dulbecco, Renato
Duve, Christian de
Ehrlich, Paul R.
Franklin, Rosalind E.
Frisch, Karl von
Galen of Pergamum
Gould, Stephen Jay
Haldane, J. B. S.
Hitchings, George Herbert, Jr.
Hooke, Robert
Hubbard, Ruth
Hubel, David H.
Huber, Robert
Isaacs, Alick
Johannsen, Wilhelm Ludvig
Just, Ernest Everett
Kendrew, John Cowdery
Kornberg, Arthur
Lamarck, Jean-Baptiste
Landsteiner, Karl
Leloir, Luis F.
Linnaeus, Carolus
Lipmann, Fritz Albert
Lorenz, Konrad
Lower, Richard
Lwoff, André
Mendel, Gregor Johann
Morgan, Thomas Hunt
Muller, Hermann Joseph

Nirenberg, Marshall W.
Northrop, John Howard
Pauling, Linus
Perutz, Max Ferdinand
Porter, Rodney Robert
Profet, Margie Jean
Punnett, Reginald Crundall
Ramón y Cajal, Santiago
Réaumur, René-Antoine Ferchault de
Rous, Peyton
Sagan, Carl
Schleiden, Matthias Jakob
Sibley, Charles G.
Snell, George D.
Stevens, Nettie Maria
Sturtevant, Alfred H.
Urey, Harold Clayton
Voit, Carl von
Waksman, Selman Abraham
Watson, James D.
Wilkins, Maurice H. F.
Wilson, Edward O.
Yalow, Rosalyn S.

Botany
Burbank, Luther
Calvin, Melvin
Carver, George Washington
Gray, Asa
Haller, Albrecht von
Hildegard of Bingen
Humboldt, Alexander von, Baron
Kunkel, Louis O.
McClintock, Barbara
Mariotte, Edme
Nägeli, Karl Wilhelm von
Ray, John
Saussure, Horace Bénédict de
Theophrastus
Vavilov, Nikolai Ivanovich
Vries, Hugo de

Cell biology
Altman, Sidney
Baltimore, David
Beadle, George Wells
Berg, Paul
Calvin, Melvin
Cobb, Jewel Plummer
Cori, Carl F.
Cori, Gerty T.

Crick, Francis
Duve, Christian de
Ehrlich, Paul
Elion, Gertrude Belle
Fischer, Edmond H.
Gilbert, Walter
Golgi, Camillo
Hay, Elizabeth Dexter
Hodgkin, Sir Alan Lloyd
Hopkins, Sir Frederick Gowland
Huber, Robert
Jacob, François
King, Helen Dean
Krebs, Sir Hans Adolf
Leeuwenhoek, Antoni van
Levi-Montalcini, Rita
Luria, Salvador Edward
McClintock, Barbara
Mendenhall, Dorothy Reed
Muller, Hermann Joseph
Nägeli, Karl Wilhelm von
Nirenberg, Marshall W.
Northrop, John Howard
Oparin, Aleksandr Ivanovich
Ramón y Cajal, Santiago
Roberts, Richard
Sabin, Florence Rena
Schleiden, Matthias Jakob
Stanley, Wendell Meredith
Stevens, Nettie Maria
Szent-Györgyi, Albert
Tatum, Edward Lawrie
Varmus, Harold E.
Virchow, Rudolf
Warburg, Otto Heinrich
Watson, James D.

Chemistry
Altman, Sidney
Ampère, André-Marie
Anfinsen, Christian B.
Arrhenius, Svante A.
Axelrod, Julius
Barton, Sir Derek H. R.
Beadle, George Wells
Becquerel, Antoine-Henri
Bernard, Claude
Berthollet, Claude Louis
Bessemer, Sir Henry
Biot, Jean-Baptiste
Black, Joseph

Blodgett, Katharine Burr
Bohr, Niels
Boyle, Robert
Calvin, Melvin
Carver, George Washington
Cavendish, Henry
Châtelet, Marquise du
Conant, James B.
Cori, Carl F.
Cori, Gerty T.
Cornforth, Sir John
Cram, Donald J.
Curie, Marie
Dalton, John
Davy, Sir Humphry
Debye, Peter J. W.
Domagk, Gerhard
Dumas, Jean-Baptiste-André
Du Vigneaud, Vincent
Ehrlich, Paul
Elion, Gertrude Belle
Faraday, Michael
Fischer, Ernst Otto
Flory, Paul J.
Franklin, Rosalind E.
Fukui, Kenichi
Gay-Lussac, Joseph-Louis
Giauque, William Francis
Gibbs, Josiah Willard
Hahn, Otto
Hall, Lloyd Augustus
Helmont, Jan Baptista van
Herschel, Sir John
Hinshelwood, Sir Cyril Norman
Hitchings, George Herbert, Jr.
Hodgkin, Dorothy Crowfoot
Hoffmann, Roald
Hopkins, Sir Frederick Gowland
Hubbard, Ruth
Hubel, David H.
Huber, Robert
Joliot-Curie, Irène
Julian, Percy Lavon
Kapitsa, Pyotr Leonidovich
Kendall, Edward Calvin
Kendrew, John Cowdery
Kirchhoff, Gustav Robert
Kossel, Albrecht
Krebs, Sir Hans Adolf
Land, Edwin Herbert
Langmuir, Irving

Lavoisier, Antoine-Laurent
Lehn, Jean-Marie
Leloir, Luis F.
Lewis, Gilbert N.
Libby, Willard F.
Lipmann, Fritz Albert
Lipscomb, William N.
Macleod, John J. R.
McMillan, Edwin Mattison
Mayer, Maria Goeppert
Mendeleyev, Dmitry Ivanovich
Millikan, Robert Andrews
Mitchell, Peter D.
Molina, Mario J.
Mössbauer, Rudolf Ludwig
Mulliken, Robert S.
Nernst, Walther Hermann
Nirenberg, Marshall W.
Northrop, John Howard
Olah, George A.
Onsager, Lars
Oparin, Aleksandr Ivanovich
Ørsted, Hans Christian
Paracelsus
Pasteur, Louis
Pauling, Linus
Perrin, Jean-Baptiste
Perutz, Max Ferdinand
Porter, Rodney Robert
Prelog, Vladimir
Prigogine, Ilya
Réaumur, René-Antoine Ferchault de
Richards, Ellen Swallow
Robinson, Sir Robert
Rowland, F. Sherwood
Rush, Benjamin
Rutherford, Ernest
Sanger, Frederick
Seaborg, Glenn Theodore
Segrè, Emilio Gino
Semenov, Nikolai
Smalley, Richard E.
Soddy, Frederick
Stanley, Wendell Meredith
Szent-Györgyi, Albert
Taube, Henry
Taylor, Moddie Daniel
Urey, Harold Clayton
Van't Hoff, Jacobus Henricus
Volta, Alessandro, Count
Warburg, Otto Heinrich

Watt, James
Wilkinson, Sir Geoffrey
Wittig, Georg

Cosmology
Alfvén, Hannes
Alhazen
Bruno, Giordano
Copernicus, Nicolaus
Einstein, Albert
Faber, Sandra
Galileo
Gödel, Kurt
Guth, Alan H.
Hawking, Stephen
Herschel, Sir William
Hoyle, Sir Fred
Lemaître, Georges
Ptolemy
Sagan, Carl
Sandage, Allan Rex
Schmidt, Maarten
Weinberg, Steven

Earth science
Agassiz, Louis
Agricola, Georgius
Alvarez, Luis W.
Anaximenes of Miletus
Appleton, Sir Edward Victor
Ayrton, Hertha Marks
Ballard, Robert D.
Becquerel, Antoine-Henri
Bessel, Friedrich Wilhelm
Bessemer, Sir Henry
Biot, Jean-Baptiste
Bjerknes, Vilhelm
Carson, Rachel
Cassini, Gian Domenico
Cox, Allan V.
Dalton, John
Geitel, Hans Friedrich
Heaviside, Oliver
Heezen, Bruce Charles
Hess, Harry Hammond
Humboldt, Alexander von, Baron
Kelvin, Lord (Sir William Thomson)
Laue, Max von
Libby, Willard F.
Lyell, Sir Charles
Mariotte, Edme
Mohorovicic, Andrija

Néel, Louis-Eugène-Félix
Ptolemy
Ray, John
Réaumur, René-Antoine Ferchault de
Richter, Charles Francis
Rossby, Carl-Gustaf Arvid
Saussure, Horace Bénédict de
Smith, William
Spallanzani, Lazzaro
Wegener, Alfred Lothar

Genetics
Altman, Sidney
Bateson, William
Beadle, George Wells
Berg, Paul
Burbank, Luther
Burnet, Sir Frank Macfarlane
Crick, Francis
Dausset, Jean
Delbrück, Max
Dulbecco, Renato
Ehrlich, Paul R.
Franklin, Rosalind E.
Galton, Sir Francis
Gamow, George
Gilbert, Walter
Haldane, J. B. S.
Huang, Alice S.
Hubbard, Ruth
Jacob, François
Johannsen, Wilhelm Ludvig
King, Helen Dean
Kornberg, Arthur
Landsteiner, Karl
Lederberg, Joshua
Lorenz, Konrad
Luria, Salvador Edward
Lwoff, André
McClintock, Barbara
Mendel, Gregor Johann
Monod, Jacques Lucien
Morgan, Thomas Hunt
Muller, Hermann Joseph
Nirenberg, Marshall W.
Punnett, Reginald Crundall
Réaumur, René-Antoine Ferchault de
Rous, Peyton
Sanger, Frederick
Snell, George D.

Stevens, Nettie Maria
Sturtevant, Alfred H.
Vavilov, Nikolai Ivanovich
Vries, Hugo de
Watson, James D.
Wilkins, Maurice H. F.

Immunology
Anfinsen, Christian B.
Baltimore, David
Behring, Emil Adolf von
Bordet, Jules
Burnet, Sir Frank Macfarlane
Dausset, Jean
Ehrlich, Paul
Jenner, Edward
Jerne, Niels K.
Kitasato, Shibasaburo
Landsteiner, Karl
Medawar, Sir Peter
Pasteur, Louis
Pauling, Linus
Porter, Rodney Robert
Profet, Margie Jean
Richet, Charles
Sabin, Florence Rena
Salk, Jonas
Snell, George D.
Virchow, Rudolf
Yalow, Rosalyn S.

Invention
Archimedes
Ayrton, Hertha Marks
Banneker, Benjamin
Bardeen, John
Bell, Alexander Graham
Bessemer, Sir Henry
Bothe, Walther
Boyle, Robert
Brahe, Tycho
Carver, George Washington
Daguerre, Jacques
Davy, Sir Humphry
Edison, Thomas Alva
Fahrenheit, Gabriel Daniel
Foucault, Léon
Franklin, Benjamin
Fulton, Robert
Gabor, Dennis
Galileo

Geitel, Hans Friedrich
Goddard, Robert
Goodyear, Charles
Gourdine, Meredith C.
Hale, George Ellery
Hall, Lloyd Augustus
Helmholtz, Hermann von
Hooke, Robert
Huygens, Christiaan
Julian, Percy Lavon
Kamerlingh Onnes, Heike
Kapitsa, Pyotr Leonidovich
Kelvin, Lord (Sir William Thomson)
Land, Edwin Herbert
Langley, Samuel Pierpont
McCormick, Cyrus Hall
Marconi, Guglielmo
Morse, Samuel F. B.
Néel, Louis-Eugène-Félix
Nobel, Alfred
Oppenheimer, J. Robert
Réaumur, René-Antoine Ferchault de
Rillieux, Norbert
Roberts, Richard
Tesla, Nikola
Volta, Alessandro, Count
Wankel, Felix
Watt, James
Whitney, Eli
Woods, Granville T.
Young, Thomas

Mathematics
Alhazen
Ampère, André-Marie
Anderson, Philip W.
Archimedes,
Aristarchus of Samos
Avicenna
Bacon, Roger
Banneker, Benjamin
Bessel, Friedrich Wilhelm
Biot, Jean-Baptiste
Biruni, al-
Bjerknes, Vilhelm
Boltzmann, Ludwig Eduard
Celsius, Anders
Chandrasekhar, Subrahmanyan
Châtelet, Marquise du
Coriolis, Gustave-Gaspard de
Dalton, John

Descartes, René
Dirac, Paul Adrien Maurice
Feynman, Richard P.
Galileo
Gauss, Carl Friedrich
Gibbs, Josiah Willard
Gödel, Kurt
Halley, Edmond
Heaviside, Oliver
Helmholtz, Hermann von
Herschel, Sir John
Hopper, Grace Murray
Huygens, Christiaan
Hypatia
Kepler, Johannes
Langley, Samuel Pierpont
Lee, Tsung-Dao
Lemaître, Georges
Mandelbrot, Benoit B.
Maxwell, James Clerk
Mitchell, Maria
Mott, Sir Nevill
Newton, Sir Isaac
Ptolemy
Réaumur, René-Antoine Ferchault de
Rydberg, Johannes Robert
Schwarzschild, Karl
Thaxton, Hubert Mach
Ulam, Stanislaw
Von Neumann, John
Weinberg, Steven
Wigner, Eugene P.

Medicine
Abbott, Maude
Agricola, Georgius
Alhazen
Apgar, Virginia
Aretaeus of Cappadocia
Arnold of Villanova
Avicenna
Banting, Sir Frederick Grant
Barnard, Christiaan
Behring, Emil Adolf von
Békésy, Georg von
Bernard, Claude
Blackwell, Elizabeth
Bordet, Jules
Boyle, Robert
Cushing, Harvey Williams
Domagk, Gerhard

Drew, Charles Richard
Ehrlich, Paul
Fabricius ab Aquapendente, Hieronymus
Freud, Sigmund
Gajdusek, D. Carleton
Galen of Pergamum
Guy de Chauliac
Hartline, Haldan Keffer
Hay, Elizabeth Dexter
Helmont, Jan Baptista van
Herophilus
Hildegard of Bingen
Hippocrates
Hitchings, George Herbert, Jr.
Hopkins, Sir Frederick Gowland
Huang, Alice S.
Hubel, David H.
Hyde, Ida H.
Jenner, Edward
Koch, Robert
Kornberg, Arthur
Landsteiner, Karl
Laveran, Alphonse
Lederberg, Joshua
Leeuwenhoek, Antoni van
Lister, Joseph
Lower, Richard
Macleod, John J. R.
Malpighi, Marcello
Mendenhall, Dorothy Reed
Monod, Jacques Lucien
Olbers, Jr.Wilhelm
Paracelsus
Pasteur, Louis
Pauling, Linus
Pavlov, Ivan Petrovich
Perutz, Max Ferdinand
Profet, Margie Jean
Reed, Walter
Richet, Charles
Ross, Sir Ronald
Rush, Benjamin
Sabin, Florence Rena
Salk, Jonas
Servetus, Michael
Sherrington, Sir Charles Scott
Starling, Ernest Henry
Sydenham, Thomas
Taussig, Helen Brooke
Thomas, E. Donnall
Virchow, Rudolf

Williams, Daniel Hale
Willis, Thomas
Wöhler, Friedrich
Yalow, Rosalyn S.

Pharmacology

Agricola, Georgius
Aretaeus of Cappadocia
Arnold of Villanova
Axelrod, Julius
Dale, Sir Henry Hallett
Domagk, Gerhard
Ehrlich, Paul
Elion, Gertrude Belle
Guy de Chauliac
Hitchings, George Herbert, Jr.
Laveran, Alphonse
Paracelsus
Profet, Margie Jean

Physics

Alfvén, Hannes
Alhazen
Alvarez, Luis W.
Ampère, André-Marie
Anaximander
Anaximenes of Miletus
Anderson, Carl David
Anderson, Philip W.
Appleton, Sir Edward Victor
Arago, François
Archimedes
Aristotle
Arrhenius, Svante A.
Ayrton, Hertha Marks
Baade, Walter
Bardeen, John
Bassi, Laura
Becquerel, Antoine-Henri
Békésy, Georg von
Bell, Alexander Graham
Bethe, Hans Albrecht
Biot, Jean-Baptiste
Biruni, al-
Bjerknes, Vilhelm
Black, Joseph
Blackett, Patrick M. S.
Bloch, Felix
Blodgett, Katharine Burr
Bohm, David
Bohr, Niels
Boltzmann, Ludwig Eduard

Born, Max
Bothe, Walther
Boyle, Robert
Bragg, Sir Lawrence
Bragg, Robert Henry
Brewster, Sir David
Bridgman, Percy Williams
Broglie, Louis de
Burbidge, Margaret
Buridan, Jean
Carruthers, George R.
Cassini, Gian Domenico
Cavendish, Henry
Celsius, Anders
Chadwick, Sir James
Chandrasekhar, Subrahmanyan
Châtelet, Marquise du
Cherenkov, Pavel Alekseyevich
Clausius, Rudolf
Compton, Arthur Holly
Coriolis, Gustave-Gaspard de
Coulomb, Charles-Augustin
Curie, Marie
Curie, Pierre
Dalton, John
Debye, Peter J. W.
Descartes, René
Dirac, Paul Adrien Maurice
Eddington, Sir Arthur Stanley
Einstein, Albert
Fahrenheit, Gabriel Daniel
Faraday, Michael
Fermi, Enrico
Feynman, Richard P.
Fitch, Val L.
Fizeau, Hippolyte
Foucault, Léon
Fresnel, Augustin-Jean
Friedman, Herbert
Fukui, Kenichi
Gabor, Dennis
Galileo
Galvani, Luigi
Gamow, George
Gauss, Carl Friedrich
Gay-Lussac, Joseph-Louis
Geiger, Hans
Geitel, Hans Friedrich
Gell-Mann, Murray
Geller, Margaret
Giauque, William Francis

Gibbs, Josiah Willard
Gilbert, Walter
Gilbert, William
Glashow, Sheldon L.
Goddard, Robert
Gödel, Kurt
Gourdine, Meredith C.
Guth, Alan H.
Hahn, Otto
Hale, George Ellery
Halley, Edmond
Hawking, Stephen
Heaviside, Oliver
Heisenberg, Werner Karl
Helmholtz, Hermann von
Henry, Joseph
Hertz, Gustav
Hertz, Heinrich
Hertzsprung, Ejnar
Hess, Victor Franz
Hodgkin, Dorothy Crowfoot
Hoyle, Sir Fred
Huggins, Sir William
Humboldt, Alexander von, Baron
Huygens, Christiaan
Jackson, Shirley Ann
Jeans, Sir James
Jensen, J. Hans D.
Joliot, Frédéric
Joliot-Curie, Irène
Josephson, Brian D.
Joule, James Prescott
Kamerlingh Onnes, Heike
Kapitsa, Pyotr Leonidovich
Kelvin, Lord (Sir William Thomson)
Kepler, Johannes
Kirchhoff, Gustav Robert
Land, Edwin Herbert
Landau, Lev Davidovich
Langley, Samuel Pierpont
Langmuir, Irving
Laue, Max von
Lawrence, Ernest Orlando
Lederman, Leon M.
Lee, Tsung-Dao
Lorentz, Hendrik Antoon
Luu, Jane X.
Mach, Ernst
McMillan, Edwin Mattison
Mandelbrot, Benoit B.
Mariotte, Edme

Massey, Walter E.
Maury, Antonia
Maxwell, James Clerk
Mayer, Maria Goeppert
Meitner, Lise
Michelson, Albert Abraham
Millikan, Robert Andrews
Mössbauer, Rudolf Ludwig
Mott, Sir Nevill
Mulliken, Robert S.
Nambu, Yoichiro
Néel, Louis-Eugène-Félix
Nernst, Walther Hermann
Newton, Sir Isaac
Onsager, Lars
Oppenheimer, J. Robert
Ørsted, Hans Christian
Pauli, Wolfgang
Pauling, Linus
Peregrinus de Maricourt, Petrus
Perrin, Jean-Baptiste
Planck, Max
Prandtl, Ludwig
Priestley, Joseph
Prigogine, Ilya
Rabi, Isidor Isaac
Raman, Sir Chandrasekhara Venkata
Réaumur, René-Antoine Ferchault de
Richter, Burton
Richter, Charles Francis
Roberts, Richard
Röntgen, Wilhelm Conrad
Rubbia, Carlo
Rubin, Vera C.
Russell, Henry Norris
Rutherford, Ernest
Rydberg, Johannes Robert
Sagan, Carl
Salam, Abdus
Schawlow, Arthur L.
Schrödinger, Erwin
Schwinger, Julian Seymour
Segrè, Emilio Gino
Semenov, Nikolai
Sommerfeld, Arnold
Stark, Johannes
Steinberger, Jack
Stern, Otto
Tamm, Igor Yevgenyevich
Teller, Edward
Tesla, Nikola

Thaxton, Hubert Mach
Thomson, Sir Joseph John
Ting, Samuel C. C.
Tomonaga, Shin'ichiro
Ulam, Stanislaw
Urey, Harold Clayton
Van Allen, James
Van Vleck, John H.
Van't Hoff, Jacobus Henricus
Volta, Alessandro, Count
Von Neumann, John
Waals, Johannes Diderik van der
Watt, James
Weinberg, Steven
Wheeler, John Archibald
Wien, Wilhelm
Wigner, Eugene P.
Wilkins, Maurice H. F.
Wu, Chien-Shiung
Yang, Chen Ning
Young, Thomas
Yukawa, Hideki
Zeeman, Pieter
Zwicky, Fritz
Zworykin, Vladimir

Physiology
Aretaeus of Cappadocia
Aristotle
Banting, Sir Frederick Grant
Békésy, Georg von
Bernard, Claude
Cori, Carl F.
Cori, Gerty T.
Cushing, Harvey Williams
Dale, Sir Henry Hallett
Erasistratus
Fabricius ab Aquapendente, Hieronymus
Fischer, Edmond H.
Galen of Pergamum
Galvani, Luigi
Golgi, Camillo
Guy de Chauliac
Haldane, J. B. S.
Haller, Albrecht von
Hartline, Haldan Keffer
Harvey, William
Helmholtz, Hermann von
Helmont, Jan Baptista van
Herophilus
Hildegard of Bingen

Hodgkin, Sir Alan Lloyd
Hopkins, Sir Frederick Gowland
Houssay, Bernardo Alberto
Hyde, Ida H.
Johannsen, Wilhelm Ludvig
Kendall, Edward Calvin
Kossel, Albrecht
Krebs, Sir Hans Adolf
Krogh, August
Levi-Montalcini, Rita
Lipmann, Fritz Albert
Lorenz, Konrad
Lower, Richard
Macleod, John J. R.
Malpighi, Marcello
Mariotte, Edme
Mitchell, Peter D.
Pavlov, Ivan Petrovich
Profet, Margie Jean
Ramón y Cajal, Santiago
Réaumur, René-Antoine Ferchault de
Richet, Charles
Servetus, Michael
Sherrington, Sir Charles Scott
Spallanzani, Lazzaro
Starling, Ernest Henry
Szent-Györgyi, Albert
Taussig, Helen Brooke
Virchow, Rudolf
Voit, Carl von
Warburg, Otto Heinrich

Psychiatry
Aretaeus of Cappadocia
Freud, Sigmund
Galton, Sir Francis
Pavlov, Ivan Petrovich
Rush, Benjamin

Science (general)
Anaximander
Anaximenes of Miletus
Archimedes
Avicenna
Bacon, Francis
Bacon, Roger
Becquerel, Antoine-Henri
Brewster, Sir David
Bridgman, Percy Williams
Buffon, Comte de (Georges-Louis Leclerc)
Buridan, Jean
Democritus

Empedocles
Franklin, Benjamin
Gould, Stephen Jay
Joule, James Prescott
Lehn, Jean-Marie
Libby, Willard F.
Mach, Ernst
Massey, Walter E.
Medawar, Sir Peter
Millikan, Robert Andrews
Ptolemy
Seaborg, Glenn Theodore
Thales of Miletus

Technology
Ayrton, Hertha Marks
Ballard, Robert D.
Bell, Alexander Graham
Bessel, Friedrich Wilhelm
Bessemer, Sir Henry
Blodgett, Katharine Burr
Bragg, Robert Henry
Curie, Pierre
Daguerre, Jacques
Edison, Thomas Alva
Fahrenheit, Gabriel Daniel
Faraday, Michael
Fermi, Enrico
Foucault, Léon
Fulton, Robert
Gabor, Dennis
Goddard, Robert
Goodyear, Charles
Gourdine, Meredith C.
Hall, Lloyd Augustus
Herschel, Sir John
Hopper, Grace Murray
Huygens, Christiaan
Joule, James Prescott
Kamerlingh Onnes, Heike
Kapitsa, Pyotr Leonidovich
Kelvin, Lord (Sir William Thomson)
Langley, Samuel Pierpont
Langmuir, Irving
Lehn, Jean-Marie
McCormick, Cyrus Hall
McMillan, Edwin Mattison
Marconi, Guglielmo
Morse, Samuel F. B.
Néel, Louis-Eugène-Félix
Nernst, Walther Hermann

Nobel, Alfred
Northrop, John Howard
Oppenheimer, J. Robert
Prandtl, Ludwig
Réaumur, René-Antoine Ferchault de
Rillieux, Norbert
Schawlow, Arthur L.
Teller, Edward
Tesla, Nikola
Thaxton, Hubert Mach
Von Neumann, John
Wankel, Felix
Watt, James
Whitney, Eli
Wigner, Eugene P.
Woods, Granville T.
Zworykin, Vladimir

Virology
Baltimore, David
Berg, Paul
Burnet, Sir Frank Macfarlane
Delbrück, Max
Franklin, Rosalind E.
Gajdusek, D. Carleton
Huang, Alice S.
Isaacs, Alick
Jacob, François
Kunkel, Louis O.
Luria, Salvador Edward
Lwoff, André
Northrop, John Howard

Rous, Peyton
Salk, Jonas
Varmus, Harold E.

Zoology
Agassiz, Louis
Aristotle
Audubon, John James
Bateson, William
Buffon, Comte de (Georges-Louis Leclerc)
Cuvier, Baron Georges
Darwin, Charles
Ehrlich, Paul R.
Frisch, Karl von
Hildegard of Bingen
Humboldt, Alexander von, Baron
Hyde, Ida H.
Krogh, August
Lamarck, Jean-Baptiste
Lankester, Sir Edwin Ray
Laveran, Alphonse
Linnaeus, Carolus
Lorenz, Konrad
Merian, Maria Sibylla
Morgan, Thomas Hunt
Punnett, Reginald Crundall
Ray, John
Réaumur, René-Antoine Ferchault de
Ross, Sir Ronald
Sibley, Charles G.
Sturtevant, Alfred H.
Wilson, Edward O.

Time Line

Born	Name	Country	Area
c. 625 B.C.E.	Thales of Miletus	Greece	Science (general)
c. 610 B.C.E.	Anaximander	Greece	Astronomy, physics, science (general)
c. 585 B.C.E.	Anaximenes of Miletus	Greece	Earth science, physics, science (general)
c. 490 B.C.E.	Empedocles	Greece	Science (general)
c. 460 B.C.E.	Democritus	Greece	Science (general)
c. 460 B.C.E.	Hippocrates	Greece	Medicine
384 B.C.E.	Aristotle	Greece	Astronomy, biology, physics, physiology, zoology
c. 372 B.C.E.	Theophrastus	Greece	Botany
c. 330 B.C.E.	Herophilus	Greece	Medicine, physiology
c. 325 B.C.E.	Erasistratus	Greece	Physiology
c. 310 B.C.E.	Aristarchus of Samos	Greece	Astronomy, mathematics
287 B.C.E.	Archimedes	Greece	Invention, mathematics, physics, science (general)
c. 100	Ptolemy	Greece or Egypt	Astronomy, cosmology, earth science, mathematics, science (general)
129	Galen of Pergamum	Greece/Italy	Biology, medicine, physiology
probably 2d century	Aretaeus of Cappadocia	Greece	Medicine, pharmacology, physiology, psychiatry
c. 370	Hypatia	Greece	Astronomy, mathematics
965	Alhazen	Iraq/Egypt	Astronomy, cosmology, mathematics, medicine, physics
September, 973	al-Biruni	Uzbekistan	Astronomy, mathematics, physics
August or September, 980	Avicenna	Uzbekistan	Mathematics, medicine, science (general)

Born	Name	Country	Area
1098	Hildegard of Bingen	Germany	Botany, medicine, physiology, zoology
c. early 13th century	Petrus Peregrinus de Maricourt	France	Astronomy, physics
c. 1220	Roger Bacon	Great Britain	Mathematics, science (general)
c. 1239	Arnold of Villanova	France	Medicine, pharmacology
c. 1290	Guy de Chauliac	France	Medicine, pharmacology, physiology
c. 1295	Jean Buridan	France	Physics, science (general)
February 19, 1473	Nicolaus Copernicus	Poland	Astronomy, cosmology
November 11 (or December 17), 1493	Paracelsus	Switzerland	Chemistry, medicine, pharmacology
March 24, 1494	Georgius Agricola	Germany	Earth science, medicine, pharmacology
1511?	Michael Servetus	Spain/France/ Switzerland	Medicine, physiology
May 20, 1537	Hieronymus Fabricius ab Aquapendente	Italy	Medicine, physiology
May 24, 1544	William Gilbert	Great Britain	Astronomy, physics
December 14, 1546	Tycho Brahe	Denmark	Astronomy, invention
1548	Giordano Bruno	Italy	Astronomy, cosmology
January 22, 1561	Francis Bacon	Great Britain	Science (general)
February 15, 1564	Galileo	Italy	Astronomy, cosmology, invention, mathematics, physics
December 27, 1571	Johannes Kepler	Germany	Astronomy, mathematics, physics
April 1, 1578	William Harvey	Great Britain	Physiology
January 12, 1580	Jan Baptista van Helmont	Belgium	Chemistry, medicine, physiology
March 31, 1596	René Descartes	France	Mathematics, physics
1620	Edme Mariotte	France	Botany, earth science, physics, physiology
January 27, 1621	Thomas Willis	Great Britain	Medicine

Born	Name	Country	Area
September 10, 1624 (baptized)	Thomas Sydenham	Great Britain	Medicine
June 8, 1625	Gian Domenico Cassini	Italy/France	Astronomy, earth science, physics
January 25, 1627	Robert Boyle	Great Britain	Chemistry, invention, medicine, physics
November 29, 1627	John Ray	Great Britain	Botany, earth science, zoology
March 10, 1628 (baptized)	Marcello Malpighi	Italy	Medicine, physiology
April 14, 1629	Christiaan Huygens	the Netherlands	Astronomy, invention, mathematics, physics, technology
c. 1631	Richard Lower	Great Britain	Biology, medicine, physiology
October 24, 1632	Antoni van Leeuwenhoek	the Netherlands	Bacteriology, biology, cell biology, medicine
July 18, 1635	Robert Hooke	Great Britain	Astronomy, biology, invention
December 25, 1642	Sir Isaac Newton	Great Britain	Astronomy, mathematics, physics
April 2, 1647	Maria Sibylla Merian	Germany/ the Netherlands	Zoology
October 29, 1656	Edmond Halley	Great Britain	Astronomy, mathematics, physics
February 28, 1683	René-Antoine Ferchault de Réaumur	France	Biology, botany, chemistry, earth science, genetics, invention, mathematics, physics, physiology, technology, zoology
May 24, 1686	Gabriel Daniel Fahrenheit	Germany/ the Netherlands	Invention, physics, technology
November 27, 1701	Anders Celsius	Sweden	Astronomy, mathematics, physics
January 17, 1706	Benjamin Franklin	United States	Invention, science (general)
December 17, 1706	Marquise du Châtelet	France	Astronomy, chemistry, mathematics, physics
May 23, 1707	Carolus Linnaeus	Sweden	Biology, botany, zoology

Born	Name	Country	Area
September 7, 1707	Comte de Buffon (Georges-Louis Leclerc)	France	Science (general), zoology
October 16, 1708	Albrecht von Haller	Switzerland	Botany, physiology
October 20, 1711	Laura Bassi	Italy	Physics
April 16, 1728	Joseph Black	Great Britain	Chemistry, physics
January 12, 1729	Lazzaro Spallanzani	Italy	Bacteriology, biology, earth science, physiology
October 10, 1731	Henry Cavendish	Great Britain	Chemistry, physics
November 9, 1731	Benjamin Banneker	United States	Astronomy, invention, mathematics
March 13, 1733	Joseph Priestley	Great Britain	Chemistry, physics
January 19, 1736	James Watt	Great Britain	Chemistry, invention, physics, technology
June 14, 1736	Charles-Augustin Coulomb	France	Physics
September 9, 1737	Luigi Galvani	Italy	Physics, physiology
November 15, 1738	Sir William Herschel	Germany/ Great Britain	Astronomy, cosmology
February 17, 1740	Horace Bénédict de Saussure	Switzerland	Botany, earth science
August 26, 1743	Antoine-Laurent Lavoisier	France	Chemistry
August 1, 1744	Jean-Baptiste Lamarck	France	Biology, botany, zoology
February 18, 1745	Count Alessandro Volta	Italy	Chemistry, invention, physics
January 4, 1746	Benjamin Rush	United States	Chemistry, medicine, psychiatry
December 9, 1748	Claude Louis Berthollet	France	Chemistry
May 17, 1749	Edward Jenner	Great Britain	Immunology, medicine
March 16, 1750	Caroline Lucretia Herschel	Germany/ Great Britain	Astronomy
October 11, 1758	Wilhelm Olbers	Germany	Astronomy, medicine
November 14, 1765	Robert Fulton	United States	Invention, technology
December 8, 1765	Eli Whitney	United States	Invention, technology

Born	Name	Country	Area
c. September 6, 1766	John Dalton	Great Britain	Biology, chemistry, earth science, mathematics, physics
March 23, 1769	William Smith	Great Britain	Earth science
August 23, 1769	Baron Georges Cuvier	France	Zoology
September 14, 1769	Baron Alexander von Humboldt	Germany	Astronomy, botany, earth science, physics, zoology
June 13, 1773	Thomas Young	Great Britain	Invention, physics
April 21, 1774	Jean-Baptiste Biot	France	Chemistry, earth science, mathematics, physics
January 22, 1775	André-Marie Ampère	France	Chemistry, mathematics, physics
April 30, 1777	Carl Friedrich Gauss	Germany	Astronomy, mathematics, physics
August 14, 1777	Hans Christian Ørsted	Denmark	Chemistry, physics
December 6, 1778	Joseph-Louis Gay-Lussac	France	Chemistry, physics
December 17, 1778	Sir Humphry Davy	Great Britain	Chemistry, invention
August 20, 1779	Jöns Jacob Berzelius	Sweden	Chemistry
December 11, 1781	Sir David Brewster	Great Britain	Physics, science (general)
July 22, 1784	Friedrich Wilhelm Bessel	Germany	Astronomy, earth science, mathematics, technology
April 26, 1785	John James Audubon	United States	Biology, zoology
February 26, 1786	François Arago	France	Astronomy, physics
November 18, 1787	Jacques Daguerre	France	Invention, technology
May 10, 1788	Augustin-Jean Fresnel	France	Physics
April 27, 1791	Samuel F. B. Morse	United States	Invention, technology
September 22, 1791	Michael Faraday	Great Britain	Chemistry, physics, technology
March 7, 1792	Sir John Herschel	Great Britain	Astronomy, chemistry, mathematics, technology
May 21, 1792	Gustave-Gaspard de Coriolis	France	Mathematics, physics

Born	Name	Country	Area
November 14, 1797	Sir Charles Lyell	Great Britain	Earth science
December 17, 1797	Joseph Henry	United States	Physics
July 14, 1800	Jean-Baptiste-André Dumas	France	Chemistry
July 31, 1800	Friedrich Wöhler	Germany	Chemistry, medicine
December 29, 1800	Charles Goodyear	United States	Invention, technology
April 5, 1804	Matthias Jakob Schleiden	Germany	Biology, botany, cell biology
March 17, 1806	Norbert Rillieux	United States/ France	Invention, technology
May 28, 1807	Louis Agassiz	Switzerland/ United States	Earth science, zoology
February 12, 1809	Charles Darwin	Great Britain	Biology, botany, zoology
February 15, 1809	Cyrus Hall McCormick	United States	Invention, technology
November 18, 1810	Asa Gray	United States	Botany
January 19, 1813	Sir Henry Bessemer	Great Britain	Chemistry, earth science, invention, technology
July 12, 1813	Claude Bernard	France	Biology, chemistry, medicine, physiology
March 27, 1817	Karl Wilhelm von Nägeli	Switzerland	Botany, cell biology
August 1, 1818	Maria Mitchell	United States	Astronomy, mathematics
December 24, 1818	James Prescott Joule	Great Britain	Physics, science (general), technology
September 18, 1819	Léon Foucault	France	Astronomy, invention, physics, technology
September 23, 1819	Hippolyte Fizeau	France	Astronomy, physics
February 3, 1821	Elizabeth Blackwell	Great Britain	Medicine
August 31, 1821	Hermann von Helmholtz	Germany	Invention, mathematics, physics, physiology
October 13, 1821	Rudolf Virchow	Germany	Bacteriology, biology, cell biology, immunology, medicine, physiology

Born	Name	Country	Area
April 28, 1854	Hertha Marks Ayrton	Great Britain	Earth science, invention, physics, technology
January 2, 1822	Rudolf Clausius	Germany	Physics
February 16, 1822	Sir Francis Galton	Great Britain	Genetics, psychiatry
July 22, 1822	Gregor Johann Mendel	Austria	Biology, genetics
December 27, 1822	Louis Pasteur	France	Bacteriology, chemistry, immunology, medicine
February 7, 1824	Sir William Huggins	Great Britain	Astronomy, physics
March 12, 1824	Gustav Robert Kirchhoff	Germany	Astronomy, chemistry, physics
June 26, 1824	Lord Kelvin (Sir William Thomson)	Great Britain	Earth science, invention, physics, technology
April 5, 1827	Joseph Lister	Great Britain	Bacteriology, medicine
June 13, 1831	James Clerk Maxwell	Great Britain	Astronomy, mathematics, physics
October 31, 1831	Carl von Voit	Germany	Biology, physiology
October 21, 1833	Alfred Nobel	Sweden	Invention, technology
February 8, 1834	Dmitry Ivanovich Mendeleyev	Russia	Chemistry
August 22, 1834	Samuel Pierpont Langley	United States	Astronomy, invention, mathematics, physics, technology
November 23, 1837	Johannes Diderik van der Waals	the Netherlands	Physics
February 18, 1838	Ernst Mach	Austria	Physics, science (general)
February 11, 1839	Josiah Willard Gibbs	United States	Chemistry, mathematics, physics
December 3, 1842	Ellen Swallow Richards	United States	Chemistry
July 7, 1843	Camillo Golgi	Italy	Cell biology, physiology
December 11, 1843	Robert Koch	Germany	Bacteriology, medicine
February 20, 1844	Ludwig Eduard Boltzmann	Austria	Mathematics, physics
March 27, 1845	Wilhelm Conrad Röntgen	Germany	Chemistry, physics

Born	Name	Country	Area
June 18, 1845	Alphonse Laveran	France	Medicine, pharmacology, zoology
February 11, 1847	Thomas Alva Edison	United States	Invention, technology
March 3, 1847	Alexander Graham Bell	Great Britain/ United States	Invention, physics, technology
May 15, 1847	Sir Edwin Ray Lankester	Great Britain	Zoology
February 16, 1848	Hugo de Vries	the Netherlands	Botany, genetics
March 7, 1849	Luther Burbank	United States	Botany, genetics
September 26, 1849	Ivan Petrovich Pavlov	Russia	Medicine, physiology, psychiatry
May 18, 1850	Oliver Heaviside	Great Britain	Earth science, mathematics, physics
August 26, 1850	Charles Richet	France	Immunology, medicine, physiology
January 19, 1851	Jacobus Cornelius Kapteyn	the Netherlands	Astronomy
September 13, 1851	Walter Reed	United States	Bacteriology, medicine
May 1, 1852	Santiago Ramón y Cajal	Spain	Biology, cell biology, physiology
August 30, 1852	Jacobus Henricus van't Hoff	the Netherlands/ Germany	Chemistry, physics
December 15, 1852	Antoine-Henri Becquerel	France	Chemistry, earth science, physics, science (general)
December 19, 1852	Albert Abraham Michelson	United States	Astronomy, physics
December 20, 1852	Shibasaburo Kitasato	Japan	Bacteriology, immunology
July 18, 1853	Hendrik Antoon Lorentz	the Netherlands	Physics
September 16, 1853	Albrecht Kossel	Germany	Chemistry, physiology
September 21, 1853	Heike Kamerlingh Onnes	the Netherlands	Invention, physics, technology
March 14, 1854	Paul Ehrlich	Germany	Bacteriology, cell biology, chemistry, immunology, medicine, pharmacology
March 15, 1854	Emil Adolf von Behring	Germany	Bacteriology, immunology, medicine

Born	Name	Country	Area
April 28, 1854	Hertha Marks Ayrton	Great Britain	Earth science, invention, physics, technology
November 8, 1854	Johannes Robert Rydberg	Sweden	Mathematics, physics
July 16, 1855	Hans Friedrich Geitel	Germany	Earth science, invention, physics
January 18, 1856	Daniel Hale Williams	United States	Medicine
April 23, 1856	Granville T. Woods	United States	Invention, technology
May 6, 1856	Sigmund Freud	Austria	Medicine, psychiatry
July 9, 1856	Nikola Tesla	Croatia/ United States	Invention, physics, technology
December 18, 1856	Sir Joseph John Thomson	Great Britain	Physics
January 23, 1857	Andrija Mohorovicic	Croatia	Earth science
February 3, 1857	Wilhelm Ludvig Johannsen	Denmark	Biology, botany, genetics, physiology
February 22, 1857	Heinrich Hertz	Germany	Physics
May 13, 1857	Sir Ronald Ross	Great Britain	Medicine, zoology
September 8, 1857	Ida H. Hyde	United States	Medicine, physiology, zoology
November 27, 1857	Sir Charles Scott Sherrington	Great Britain	Medicine, physiology
December 16, 1857	Edward Emerson Barnard	United States	Astronomy
April 23, 1858	Max Planck	Germany	Physics
February 19, 1859	Svante A. Arrhenius	Sweden	Chemistry, physics
May 15, 1859	Pierre Curie	France	Physics, technology
1861?	George Washington Carver	United States	Botany, chemistry, invention
June 20, 1861	Sir Frederick Gowland Hopkins	Great Britain	Cell biology, chemistry, medicine, physiology
July 7, 1861	Nettie Maria Stevens	United States	Biology, cell biology, genetics
August 8, 1861	William Bateson	Great Britain	Genetics, zoology
March 14, 1862	Vilhelm Bjerknes	Norway	Earth science, mathematics, physics

Born	Name	Country	Area
December 11, 1863	Annie Jump Cannon	United States	Astronomy
January 13, 1864	Wilhelm Wien	Germany	Physics
June 25, 1864	Walther Hermann Nernst	Germany	Astronomy, chemistry, physics, technology
May 25, 1865	Pieter Zeeman	the Netherlands	Physics
March 21, 1866	Antonia Maury	United States	Astronomy, physics
April 17, 1866	Ernest Henry Starling	Great Britain	Medicine, physiology
September 25, 1866	Thomas Hunt Morgan	United States	Biology, genetics, zoology
November 7, 1867	Marie Curie	Poland/France	Chemistry, physics
March 22, 1868	Robert Andrews Millikan	United States	Astronomy, chemistry, physics, science (general)
June 14, 1868	Karl Landsteiner	Austria/ United States	Biology, genetics, immunology, medicine
June 29, 1868	George Ellery Hale	United States	Astronomy, invention, physics
July 4, 1868	Henrietta Swan Leavitt	United States	Astronomy
December 5, 1868	Arnold Sommerfeld	Germany	Physics
March 18, 1869	Maude Abbott	Canada	Medicine
April 8, 1869	Harvey Williams Cushing	United States	Medicine, physiology
September 27, 1869	Helen Dean King	United States	Cell biology, genetics
June 13, 1870	Jules Bordet	Belgium	Bacteriology, immunology, medicine
September 30, 1870	Jean-Baptiste Perrin	France	Chemistry, physics
August 30, 1871	Ernest Rutherford	New Zealand/ Great Britain	Chemistry, physics
November 9, 1871	Florence Rena Sabin	United States	Bacteriology, cell biology, immunology, medicine
October 8, 1873	Ejnar Hertzsprung	Denmark	Astronomy, physics
October 9, 1873	Karl Schwarzschild	Germany	Astronomy, mathematics
April 15, 1874	Johannes Stark	Germany	Physics
April 25, 1874	Guglielmo Marconi	Italy	Invention, technology

Born	Name	Country	Area
September 22, 1874	Dorothy Reed Mendenhall	United States	Cell biology, medicine
November 15, 1874	August Krogh	Denmark	Physiology, zoology
February 4, 1875	Ludwig Prandtl	Germany	Physics, technology
June 9, 1875	Sir Henry Hallett Dale	Great Britain	Pharmacology, physiology
June 20, 1875	Reginald Crundall Punnett	Great Britain	Biology, genetics, zoology
October 25, 1875	Gilbert N. Lewis	United States	Chemistry
November 11, 1875	Vesto Melvin Slipher	United States	Astronomy
September 16, 1876	John J. R. Macleod	Great Britain	Chemistry, medicine, physiology
September 2, 1877	Frederick Soddy	Great Britain	Chemistry
September 11, 1877	Sir James Jeans	Great Britain	Astronomy, physics
October 25, 1877	Henry Norris Russell	United States	Astronomy, physics
November 7, 1878	Lise Meitner	Austria	Physics
March 8, 1879	Otto Hahn	Germany	Chemistry, physics
March 14, 1879	Albert Einstein	Germany/ Switzerland/ United States	Cosmology, physics
October 5, 1879	Peyton Rous	United States	Biology, genetics, virology
October 9, 1879	Max von Laue	Germany	Earth science, physics
November 1, 1880	Alfred Lothar Wegener	Germany	Earth science
January 31, 1881	Irving Langmuir	United States	Chemistry, physics, technology
August 6, 1881	Sir Alexander Fleming	Great Britain	Bacteriology
April 21, 1882	Percy Williams Bridgman	United States	Physics, science (general)
September 30, 1882	Hans Geiger	Germany	Physics
October 5, 1882	Robert Goddard	United States	Invention, physics, technology
December 11, 1882	Max Born	Germany/ Great Britain	Physics
December 28, 1882	Sir Arthur Stanley Eddington	Great Britain	Astronomy, physics

Born	Name	Country	Area
June 24, 1883	Victor Franz Hess	Austria/ United States	Physics
August 14, 1883	Ernest Everett Just	United States	Biology
October 8, 1883	Otto Heinrich Warburg	Germany	Cell biology, chemistry, physiology
March 24, 1884	Peter J. W. Debye	the Netherlands/ Germany/ United States	Chemistry, physics
May 7, 1884	Louis O. Kunkel	United States	Botany, virology
October 7, 1885	Niels Bohr	Denmark	Chemistry, physics
November 2, 1885	Harlow Shapley	United States	Astronomy
March 8, 1886	Edward Calvin Kendall	United States	Chemistry, physiology
September 13, 1886	Sir Robert Robinson	Great Britain	Chemistry
November 20, 1886	Karl von Frisch	Austria	Biology, zoology
April 10, 1887	Bernardo Alberto Houssay	Argentina	Physiology
July 22, 1887	Gustav Hertz	Germany	Physics
August 12, 1887	Erwin Schrödinger	Austria	Physics
November 26, 1887	Nikolai Ivanovich Vavilov	Russia	Botany, genetics
February 17, 1888	Otto Stern	Germany/ United States	Physics
July 22, 1888	Selman Abraham Waksman	Ukraine/ United States	Bacteriology, biology
November 7, 1888	Sir Chandrasekhara Venkata Raman	India	Physics
July 30, 1889	Vladimir Zworykin	Russia/ United States	Physics, technology
November 20, 1889	Edwin Powell Hubble	United States	Astronomy
March 31, 1890	Sir Lawrence Bragg	Australia/ Great Britain	Physics
December 21, 1890	Hermann Joseph Muller	United States	Biology, cell biology, genetics
January 8, 1891	Walther Bothe	Germany	Astronomy, invention, physics

Born	Name	Country	Area
July 5, 1891	John Howard Northrop	United States	Biology, cell biology, chemistry, technology, virology
October 20, 1891	Sir James Chadwick	Great Britain	Physics
November 14, 1891	Sir Frederick Grant Banting	Canada	Biology, medicine, physiology
November 21, 1891	Alfred H. Sturtevant	United States	Biology, genetics, zoology
August 15, 1892	Louis de Broglie	France	Physics
September 6, 1892	Sir Edward Victor Appleton	Great Britain	Earth science, physics
September 10, 1892	Arthur Holly Compton	United States	Physics
November 5, 1892	J. B. S. Haldane	Great Britain	Biology, genetics, physiology
March 24, 1893	Walter Baade	Germany	Astronomy, physics
March 26, 1893	James B. Conant	United States	Chemistry
April 29, 1893	Harold Clayton Urey	United States	Astronomy, biology, chemistry, physics
September 16, 1893	Albert Szent-Györgyi	Hungary / United States	Cell biology, chemistry, physiology
March 2, 1894	Aleksandr Ivanovich Oparin	Russia	Cell biology, chemistry
June 20, 1894	Lloyd Augustus Hall	United States	Bacteriology, chemistry, invention, technology
July 9, 1894	Pyotr Leonidovich Kapitsa	Great Britain / Russia	Chemistry, invention, physics, technology
July 17, 1894	Georges Lemaître	Belgium	Cosmology, mathematics
May 12, 1895	William Francis Giauque	Canada / United States	Chemistry, physics
July 8, 1895	Igor Yevgenyevich Tamm	Russia	Physics
October 30, 1895	Gerhard Domagk	Germany	Bacteriology, chemistry, medicine, pharmacology
April 15, 1896	Nikolai Semenov	Russia	Chemistry, physics
June 7, 1896	Robert S. Mulliken	United States	Chemistry, physics
August 15, 1896	Gerty T. Cori	Czech Republic / United States	Cell biology, chemistry, physiology

Born	Name	Country	Area
December 5, 1896	Carl F. Cori	Czech Republic/ United States	Cell biology, chemistry, physiology
June 16, 1897	Georg Wittig	Germany	Chemistry
June 19, 1897	Sir Cyril Norman Hinshelwood	Great Britain	Chemistry
September 12, 1897	Irène Joliot-Curie	France	Chemistry, physics
November 18, 1897	Patrick M. S. Blackett	Great Britain	Physics
January 10, 1898	Katharine Burr Blodgett	United States	Chemistry, physics, technology
February 14, 1898	Fritz Zwicky	Switzerland/ United States	Astronomy, physics
May 24, 1898	Helen Brooke Taussig	United States	Medicine, physiology
July 29, 1898	Isidor Isaac Rabi	United States	Physics
December 28, 1898	Carl-Gustaf Arvid Rossby	Sweden	Earth science
March 13, 1899	John H. Van Vleck	United States	Physics
April 11, 1899	Percy Lavon Julian	United States	Chemistry, invention
June 3, 1899	Georg von Békésy	Hungary/ United States	Medicine, physics, physiology
June 12, 1899	Fritz Albert Lipmann	Germany/ United States	Biology, chemistry, physiology
September 3, 1899	Sir Frank Macfarlane Burnet	Australia	Bacteriology, genetics, immunology, virology
March 19, 1900	Frédéric Joliot	France	Physics
April 25, 1900	Wolfgang Pauli	Austria/ United States	Physics
April 26, 1900	Charles Francis Richter	United States	Earth science, physics
April 28, 1900	Jan Hendrik Oort	the Netherlands	Astronomy
May 10, 1900	Cecilia Payne-Gaposchkin	Great Britain/ United States	Astronomy
June 5, 1900	Dennis Gabor	Hungary/ Great Britain	Invention, physics, technology
August 25, 1900	Sir Hans Adolf Krebs	Germany/ Great Britain	Cell biology, chemistry, physiology
February 28, 1901	Linus Pauling	United States	Biology, chemistry, immunology, medicine, physics

Born	Name	Country	Area
May 18, 1901	Vincent du Vigneaud	United States	Chemistry
August 8, 1901	Ernest Orlando Lawrence	United States	Physics
September 29, 1901	Enrico Fermi	Italy/ United States	Physics, technology
December 5, 1901	Werner Karl Heisenberg	Germany	Physics
May 8, 1902	André Lwoff	France	Biology, genetics, virology
June 16, 1902	Barbara McClintock	United States	Botany, cell biology, genetics
August 8, 1902	Paul Adrien Maurice Dirac	Great Britain	Mathematics, physics
August 13, 1902	Felix Wankel	Germany	Invention, technology
November 17, 1902	Eugene P. Wigner	Hungary/ United States	Physics, mathematics, technology
October 22, 1903	George Wells Beadle	United States	Cell biology, chemistry, genetics
November 7, 1903	Konrad Lorenz	Austria	Biology, genetics, physiology, zoology
November 27, 1903	Lars Onsager	Norway/ United States	Chemistry, physics
December 19, 1903	George D. Snell	United States	Biology, genetics, immunology
December 22, 1903	Haldan Keffer Hartline	United States	Medicine, physiology
December 28, 1903	John von Neumann	Hungary/ United States	Mathematics, physics, technology
March 4, 1904	George Gamow	Russia/ United States	Astronomy, genetics, physics
April 22, 1904	J. Robert Oppenheimer	United States	Invention, physics, technology
June 3, 1904	Charles Richard Drew	United States	Medicine
July 28, 1904	Pavel Alekseyevich Cherenkov	Russia	Physics
August 16, 1904	Wendell Meredith Stanley	United States	Cell biology, chemistry
November 22, 1904	Louis-Eugène-Félix Néel	France	Earth science, invention, physics, technology

Born	Name	Country	Area
February 1, 1905	Emilio Gino Segrè	Italy/ United States	Chemistry, physics
April 18, 1905	George Herbert Hitchings, Jr.	United States	Biology, chemistry, medicine, pharmacology
September 3, 1905	Carl David Anderson	United States	Physics
September 30, 1905	Sir Nevill Mott	Great Britain	Mathematics, physics
October 23, 1905	Felix Bloch	Switzerland/ United States	Physics
December 7, 1905	Gerard Peter Kuiper	the Netherlands/ United States	Astronomy
March 31, 1906	Shin'ichiro Tomonaga	Japan	Physics
April 28, 1906	Kurt Gödel	Austria/ United States	Cosmology, mathematics, physics
May 24, 1906	Harry Hammond Hess	United States	Earth science
June 28, 1906	Maria Goeppert Mayer	Germany/ United States	Chemistry, physics
July 2, 1906	Hans Albrecht Bethe	Germany/ United States	Astronomy, physics
July 23, 1906	Vladimir Prelog	Bosnia/ Switzerland	Chemistry
September 4, 1906	Max Delbrück	Germany/ United States	Bacteriology, genetics, virology
December 9, 1906	Grace Murray Hopper	United States	Mathematics, technology
January 23, 1907	Hideki Yukawa	Japan	Physics
May 27, 1907	Rachel Carson	United States	Biology, botany, earth science
June 25, 1907	J. Hans D. Jensen	Germany	Physics
September 18, 1907	Edwin Mattison McMillan	United States	Chemistry, physics, technology
January 15, 1908	Edward Teller	Hungary/ United States	Physics, technology
January 22, 1908	Lev Davidovich Landau	Russia	Physics
May 23, 1908	John Bardeen	United States	Invention, physics
May 30, 1908	Hannes Alfvén	Sweden	Astronomy, cosmology, physics
September 6, 1908	Luis F. Leloir	Argentina	Biology, chemistry

Born	Name	Country	Area
December 17, 1908	Willard F. Libby	United States	Astronomy, chemistry, earth science, science (general)
April 3, 1909	Stanislaw Ulam	Poland/ United States	Mathematics, physics
April 22, 1909	Rita Levi-Montalcini	Italy/ United States	Cell biology, physiology
May 7, 1909	Edwin Herbert Land	United States	Chemistry, invention, physics
June 7, 1909	Virginia Apgar	United States	Medicine
December 14, 1909	Edward Lawrie Tatum	United States	Bacteriology, cell biology
February 9, 1910	Jacques Lucien Monod	France	Bacteriology, biology, genetics, medicine
May 12, 1910	Dorothy Crowfoot Hodgkin	Great Britain	Chemistry, physics
June 19, 1910	Paul J. Flory	United States	Chemistry
October 19, 1910	Subrahmanyan Chandrasekhar	India/ United States	Mathematics, physics
December 7, 1910	Richard Roberts	United States	Cell biology, invention, physics
April 8, 1911	Melvin Calvin	United States	Botany, cell biology, chemistry
June 13, 1911	Luis W. Alvarez	United States	Astronomy, earth science, physics
July 9, 1911	John Archibald Wheeler	United States	Astronomy, physics
December 23, 1911	Niels K. Jerne	Great Britain/ Denmark	Immunology
March 3, 1912	Moddie Daniel Taylor	United States	Chemistry
April 19, 1912	Glenn Theodore Seaborg	United States	Chemistry, science (general)
May 30, 1912	Julius Axelrod	United States	Chemistry, pharmacology
May 31, 1912	Chien-Shiung Wu	China/ United States	Physics
August 13, 1912	Salvador Edward Luria	Italy/ United States	Bacteriology, biology, cell biology, genetics, virology

Born	Name	Country	Area
December 28, 1912	Hubert Mach Thaxton	United States	Mathematics, physics, technology
February 5, 1914	Sir Alan Lloyd Hodgkin	Great Britain	Cell biology, physiology
February 22, 1914	Renato Dulbecco	Italy/ United States	Biology, genetics
May 19, 1914	Max Ferdinand Perutz	Austria/ Great Britain	Biology, chemistry, medicine
September 7, 1914	James Van Allen	United States	Physics
October 28, 1914	Jonas Salk	United States	Immunology, medicine, virology
February 28, 1915	Sir Peter Medawar	Great Britain	Immunology, science (general)
June 24, 1915	Sir Fred Hoyle	Great Britain	Astronomy, cosmology, physics
November 30, 1915	Henry Taube	Canada/ United States	Chemistry
March 26, 1916	Christian B. Anfinsen	United States	Biology, chemistry, immunology
June 8, 1916	Francis Crick	Great Britain	Biology, cell biology, genetics
June 21, 1916	Herbert Friedman	United States	Astronomy, physics
October 19, 1916	Jean Dausset	France	Genetics, immunology
December 15, 1916	Maurice H. F. Wilkins	Great Britain	Biology, genetics, physics
January 25, 1917	Ilya Prigogine	Belgium	Chemistry, physics
March 24, 1917	John Cowdery Kendrew	Great Britain	Biology, chemistry
August 7, 1917	Charles G. Sibley	United States	Biology, zoology
September 7, 1917	Sir John Cornforth	Australia	Chemistry
October 2, 1917	Christian de Duve	Belgium	Biology, cell biology
October 8, 1917	Rodney Robert Porter	Great Britain	Biology, chemistry, immunology
December 20, 1917	David Bohm	United States	Physics
January 23, 1918	Gertrude Belle Elion	United States	Cell biology, chemistry, pharmacology
February 12, 1918	Julian Seymour Schwinger	United States	Physics

Born	Name	Country	Area
March 3, 1918	Arthur Kornberg	United States	Biology, genetics, medicine
May 11, 1918	Richard P. Feynman	United States	Mathematics, physics
August 13, 1918	Frederick Sanger	Great Britain	Chemistry, genetics
September 8, 1918	Sir Derek H. R. Barton	Great Britain	Chemistry
October 4, 1918	Kenichi Fukui	Japan	Chemistry, physics
November 10, 1918	Ernst Otto Fischer	Germany	Chemistry
April 22, 1919	Donald J. Cram	United States	Chemistry
July 16, 1919	William N. Lipscomb	United States	Chemistry
August 11, 1919	Robert Henry Bragg	United States	Physics, technology
August 12, 1919	Margaret Burbidge	Great Britain/ United States	Astronomy, physics
March 15, 1920	E. Donnall Thomas	United States	Biology, medicine
April 6, 1920	Edmond H. Fischer	Switzerland/ United States	Cell biology, physiology
June 17, 1920	François Jacob	France	Bacteriology, cell biology, genetics, virology
July 25, 1920	Rosalind E. Franklin	Great Britain	Biology, chemistry, genetics, virology
September 29, 1920	Peter D. Mitchell	Great Britain	Bacteriology, biology, chemistry, physiology
January 18, 1921	Yoichiro Nambu	Japan/ United States	Physics
May 5, 1921	Arthur L. Schawlow	United States	Physics, technology
May 25, 1921	Jack Steinberger	United States	Physics
July 14, 1921	Sir Geoffrey Wilkinson	Great Britain	Chemistry
July 17, 1921	Alick Isaacs	Great Britain	Biology, virology
July 19, 1921	Rosalyn S. Yalow	United States	Biology, immunology, medicine
July 15, 1922	Leon M. Lederman	United States	Physics
September 22, 1922	Chen Ning Yang	China/ United States	Physics
November 8, 1922	Christiaan Barnard	South Africa	Medicine
March 10, 1923	Val L. Fitch	United States	Physics
September 9, 1923	D. Carleton Gajdusek	United States	Medicine, virology

Born	Name	Country	Area
December 13, 1923	Philip W. Anderson	United States	Mathematics, physics
January 17, 1924	Jewel Plummer Cobb	United States	Cell biology
March 3, 1924	Ruth Hubbard	United States	Biology, chemistry, genetics
April 11, 1924	Bruce Charles Heezen	United States	Earth science
May 11, 1924	Antony Hewish	Great Britain	Astronomy
November 20, 1924	Benoit B. Mandelbrot	Poland/ United States	Mathematics, physics
May 23, 1925	Joshua Lederberg	United States	Bacteriology, genetics, medicine
January 29, 1926	Abdus Salam	Pakistan/ Great Britain	Physics
February 27, 1926	David H. Hubel	Canada/ United States	Biology, chemistry, medicine
June 18, 1926	Allan Rex Sandage	United States	Astronomy, cosmology
June 30, 1926	Paul Berg	United States	Biology, cell biology, genetics, virology
November 25, 1926	Tsung-Dao Lee	China/ United States	Astronomy, mathematics, physics
December 17, 1926	Allan V. Cox	United States	Earth science
April 2, 1927	Elizabeth Dexter Hay	United States	Cell biology, medicine
April 10, 1927	Marshall W. Nirenberg	United States	Biology, cell biology, chemistry, genetics
May 22, 1927	George A. Olah	Hungary/ United States	Chemistry
June 28, 1927	F. Sherwood Rowland	United States	Chemistry
April 6, 1928	James D. Watson	United States	Biology, cell biology, genetics
July 23, 1928	Vera C. Rubin	United States	Astronomy, physics
January 31, 1929	Rudolf Ludwig Mössbauer	Germany	Chemistry, physics
June 10, 1929	Edward O. Wilson	United States	Biology, zoology
September 15, 1929	Murray Gell-Mann	United States	Physics
September 26, 1929	Meredith C. Gourdine	United States	Invention, physics, technology
December 28, 1929	Maarten Schmidt	the Netherlands/ United States	Astronomy, cosmology

Born	Name	Country	Area
March 22, 1931	Burton Richter	United States	Physics
March 21, 1932	Walter Gilbert	United States	Cell biology, genetics, physics
May 29, 1932	Paul R. Ehrlich	United States	Biology, genetics, zoology
December 5, 1932	Sheldon L. Glashow	United States	Physics
May 3, 1933	Steven Weinberg	United States	Cosmology, mathematics, physics
March 31, 1934	Carlo Rubbia	Italy	Physics
November 9, 1934	Carl Sagan	United States	Astronomy, biology, cosmology, physics
January 27, 1936	Samuel C. C. Ting	United States	Physics
February 20, 1937	Robert Huber	Germany	Biology, cell biology, chemistry
July 18, 1937	Roald Hoffmann	Poland/ United States	Chemistry
March 7, 1938	David Baltimore	United States	Cell biology, immunology, virology
April 5, 1938	Walter E. Massey	United States	Physics, science (general)
March 22, 1939	Alice S. Huang	United States	Genetics, medicine, virology
May 7, 1939	Sidney Altman	Canada/ United States	Cell biology, chemistry, genetics
September 30, 1939	Jean-Marie Lehn	France	Chemistry, science (general), technology
October 1, 1939	George R. Carruthers	United States	Astronomy, physics
December 18, 1939	Harold E. Varmus	United States	Cell biology, virology
January 4, 1940	Brian D. Josephson	Great Britain	Physics
September 10, 1941	Stephen Jay Gould	United States	Biology, science (general)
January 8, 1942	Stephen Hawking	Great Britain	Astronomy, cosmology, physics
June 30, 1942	Robert D. Ballard	United States	Earth science, technology
March 19, 1943	Mario J. Molina	Mexico/ United States	Chemistry

Born	Name	Country	Area
June 6, 1943	Richard E. Smalley	United States	Chemistry
July 15, 1943	Jocelyn Bell Burnell	Great Britain	Astronomy
December 28, 1944	Sandra Faber	United States	Astronomy, cosmology
August 5, 1946	Shirley Ann Jackson	United States	Physics
February 27, 1947	Alan H. Guth	United States	Cosmology, physics
December 8, 1947	Margaret Geller	United States	Astronomy, physics
August 7, 1958	Margie Jean Profet	United States	Biology, immunology, medicine, pharmacology, physiology
July 15, 1963	Jane X. Luu	United States	Astronomy, physics

BIOGRAPHICAL ENCYCLOPEDIA of SCIENTISTS

Index

In the following index, volume numbers appear in **bold face** type and page numbers appear in normal type. The names of scientists who are profiled in the encyclopedia are shown in **bold face**.

sexual reproduction in **3:** 806
and viruses **2:** 347; **3:** 857, 863
Bacteriophages **2:** 347-348;
3: 856-857, 863
Ballard, Robert D. 1: 85-88
Baltimore, David 1: 88-90; **3:** 654
Banneker, Benjamin 1: 91-93
Banting, Sir Frederick Grant
1: 93-96
Bardeen, Cooper, and Schrieffer
theory. *See* BCS theory.
Bardeen, John 1: 96-100; **3:** 723
Barium **2:** 543
Barnard, Christiaan 1: 101-104
Barnard, Edward Emerson
1: 104-106
Barton, Sir Derek H. R. 1: 107-109
Baryons **2:** 499
Bases **1:** 62
Bassi, Laura 1: 109-111
Bateson, William 1: 112-115; **3:** 700;
4: 1061
Battery **2:** 341, 481; **5:** 1308
Bayliss, William **5:** 1221
BCS theory **1:** 99; **3:** 723; **4:** 972
Beadle, George Wells 1: 115-117;
3: 806; **5:** 1243-1244
Becquerel, Antoine-Henri 1: 118-121
Bednorz, J. Georg **3:** 723
Bees **2:** 454-455; **4:** 1076
Behring, Emil Adolf von 1: 122-125;
2: 381; **3:** 749-750
Békésy, Georg von 1: 125-128
Bell, Alexander Graham 1: 128-131;
4: 929
Bell Burnell, Jocelyn 1: 132-134;
3: 615
Bénard instability **4:** 1054
Berg, Paul 1: 134-137
Bernard, Claude 1: 138-141
Berson, Solomon **5:** 1380
Berthollet, Claude Louis 1: 141-143
Beryllium **1:** 261; **5:** 1275
Berzelius, Jöns Jakob 1: 144-146
Bessel, Friedrich Wilhelm 1: 147-149
Bessemer, Sir Henry 1: 149-151
Best, Charles **1:** 94; **4:** 879-880
Beta decay **2:** 312; **4:** 1141
Beta particles **1:** 119; **4:** 912
Bethe, Hans Albrecht 1: 152-154;
5: 1174
Big bang theory **2:** 400, 484, 502, 537,
566; **3:** 650; **4:** 1147
Binary stars. *See* Double stars.
Biochemistry **3:** 642; **4:** 1003

Biology **1:** 57. *See also* Biochemistry;
Biophysics; Cell biology;
Sociobiology.
Biophysics **5:** 1354
Biot, Jean-Baptiste 1: 44, 155-157;
3: 670
Biotin **2:** 371
Birds **1:** 65, 67; **3:** 851; **5:** 1192-1193
Birds of America, The (Audubon)
1: 66-67
Birkeland, Kristan **1:** 11
Biruni, al- 1: 158-159
Bischoff, Theodor **5:** 1304
Bishop, J. Michael **5:** 1296-1297
Bjerknes, Vilhelm 1: 160-162
Black, Joseph 1: 162-164
Black holes **2:** 566; **4:** 1162; **5:** 1170,
1342
Blackbody **1:** 177; **3:** 690, 747;
4: 1038-1039; **5:** 1347
Blackett, Patrick M. S. 1: 165-167
Blackwell, Elizabeth 1: 168-170
Blalock, Alfred **5:** 1249
Blalock-Taussig shunt **5:** 1249
Bloch, Felix 1: 170-172
Blodgett, Katharine Burr 1: 173-175
Blood **2:** 360, 402; **3:** 854; **4:** 1110
color of **3:** 854
Blood-brain barrier **1:** 72
Blood flow **3:** 764
Blood transfusion **2:** 337-338, 360
Blood types **3:** 781-782
Blood vessels **3:** 590
Blue baby syndrome **5:** 1248-1249
Bohm, David 1: 175-178
Bohr, Niels 1: 178-182; **2:** 347, 355,
390; **3:** 600, 777; **4:** 1019, 1128,
1131, 1167; **5:** 1211, 1291, 1340
Boltzmann, Ludwig Edward
1: 183-185
Bombastus von Hohenheim,
Philippus Aureolus
Theophrastus. *See* **Paracelsus.**
Bondi, Hermann **3:** 650
Bonds, chemical **4:** 1023
Bone marrow transplantation
5: 1268-1269
Boranes **3:** 841
Bordet, Jules 1: 186-188
Born, Max 1: 189-192
Bosons **4:** 897
Botany **3:** 835; **4:** 1074; **5:** 1265
Bothe, Walther 1: 192-195; **3:** 833
Boundary layer **4:** 1045
Boyle, Robert 1: 196-198; **5:** 1316

Boyle's law **1:** 197-198; **4:** 894; **5:** 1316
Bragg, Sir Lawrence 1: 199-202
Bragg, Robert Henry 1: 203-205
Bragg, William Henry **1:** 199, 201
Brahe, Tycho 1: 206-208; **2:** 557;
3: 741
Brain **3:** 590, 662; **4:** 1071; **5:** 1363
anatomy of the **5:** 1362
Brain surgery **2:** 318
Brattain, Walter **1:** 97
Breeding. *See* Animal breeding;
Crossbreeding; Inbreeding; Plant
breeding.
Breit, Gregory **4:** 1064
Breuer, Josef **2:** 448
Brewster, Sir David 1: 208-211
Bridgman, Percy Williams
1: 211-214
Briscoe, H. V. A. **5:** 1356
Broglie, Louis de 1: 214-216; **4:** 1167
Bruno, Giordano 1: 217-219
Bubble chambers **1:** 20
Bubonic plague **3:** 749
Buckminsterfullerene **5:** 1199
Buffon, Comte de (Georges-Louis
Leclerc) 1: 220-222
Bunsen, Robert **3:** 747
Buoyancy **1:** 48
Burbank, Luther 1: 223-225
Burbidge, Geoffrey **1:** 226; **4:** 1118
Burbidge, Margaret 1: 226-228;
4: 1119
Buridan, Jean 1: 229-231
Buridan's ass **1:** 230
Burnet, Sir Frank Macfarlane
1: 231-234
Butterflies **4:** 926

Calculus **4:** 982
California Institute of Technology
2: 550; **5:** 1400
Caloric theory **3:** 713-714
Calorimetry **1:** 163
Caltech. *See* California Institute of
Technology.
Calvin, John **5:** 1185
Calvin, Melvin 1: 235-238
Calvin cycle **1:** 236-237
Calx **1:** 142; **4:** 1050
Camera obscura **2:** 325
Canals **2:** 459
Cancer **1:** 276; **4:** 1110; **5:** 1297,
1324-1325
and viruses **1:** 90; **2:** 363; **4:** 1110
Cannon, Annie Jump 1: 238-240

Watson, James D. 2: 307, 309;
5: 1326-1329, 1354
Watt, James 5: 1330-1332
Wave mechanics 4: 1167
Wave-particle duality 1: 177, 190,
215, 279
Wave properties
of light 1: 190; 2: 446; 3: 847;
5: 1386
of matter 1: 177, 190, 215
Waves 3: 673; 4: 1167
Weak force 4: 1141; 5: 1224, 1338,
1377
Weak interactions 3: 812
Weather 4: 1107
Wegener, Alfred Lothar 3: 609;
5: 1333-1336
Weinberg, Steven 2: 515-517; 4: 973,
1116, 1141; 5: 1337-1339
Weinberg-Salam theory 2: 516;
4: 1116; 5: 1338
Weldon, Walter 1: 112
Wheat 5: 1299
Wheeler, John Archibald
5: 1340-1343
White blood cells 2: 338
White dwarf 1: 264-265; 2: 375;
5: 1342, 1396
Whitney, Eli 5: 1343-1346

Wien, Wilhelm 3: 690; 4: 1039;
5: 1346-1348
Wien's law 4: 1038
Wigner, Eugene P. 3: 694;
5: 1349-1352
Wilkins, Maurice H. F. 2: 443;
5: 1327-1328, 1353-1355
Wilkinson, Sir Geoffrey 2: 422;
5: 1356-1358
Williams, Daniel Hale 5: 1358-1360
Willis, Thomas 3: 853; 5: 1361-1363
Willughby, Francis 4: 1073-1074
Wilson, Edmund Beecher 5: 1230
Wilson, Edward O. 5: 1364-1368
Wing theory 4: 1045
Wittig, Georg 5: 1368-1370
Wittig reaction 5: 1369-1370
Wöhler, Friedrich 5: 1371-1373
Wollman, Elie 3: 686
Wollman, Eugene, and Elisabeth
Wollman 3: 863-864
Women
education of 4: 937
in medicine 1: 169; 3: 590
Woods, Granville T. 5: 1374-1376
Woodward, Robert B. 3: 636; 5: 1357
World War II 3: 664; 4: 1006
Wu, Chien-Shiung 5: 1376-1378,
1382

X chromosome 4: 952
X-ray crystallography 1: 201; 3: 633,
737; 4: 1036
X-ray diffraction 1: 199, 201, 205;
2: 443; 3: 737, 792; 5: 1327, 1354
X rays 1: 119, 201, 205, 278-279;
2: 453; 3: 633, 792; 4: 1101-1102
and mutation 4: 964

Y chromosome 4: 952; 5: 1230
Yalow, Rosalyn S. 5: 1379-1381
Yang, Chen Ning 3: 811; 4: 1141;
5: 1377, 1381-1384
Yeast 4: 1015
Yellow fever 4: 1078-1079
Yerkes Observatory 2: 549; 3: 659
Yersin, Alexandre 3: 750
Ylem 2: 484
Ylides 5: 1369-1370
Young, Thomas 1: 190; 2: 446; 3: 582;
5: 1384-1387
Yukawa, Hideki 4: 1141; 5: 1278,
1387-1391

Zeeman, Pieter 2: 550; 5: 1392-1394
Zeeman effect 4: 1019; 5: 1212, 1393
Zero population growth 2: 384
Zoology 1: 57
Zwicky, Fritz 1: 79; 5: 1394-1397
Zworykin, Vladimir 5: 1397-1401